✳ Histories of Race and Racism

※ Histories of Race and Racism

The Andes and Mesoamerica

from Colonial Times to the Present

EDITED BY **LAURA GOTKOWITZ**

Duke University Press *Durham and London* 2011

© 2011 Duke University Press

All rights reserved

Printed in the United States of America on acid-free paper ∞

Designed by Amy Ruth Buchanan

Typeset in Minion by Keystone Typesetting, Inc.

Library of Congress Cataloging-in-Publication Data appear

on the last printed page of this book.

CONTENTS

ACKNOWLEDGMENTS

This book first began to take shape at a conference convened at the University of Iowa in October 2002, where historians and anthropologists working in the United States and Latin America presented papers on racial meanings, mestizaje, indigenous social movements, and new nation-building paradigms. Many of the papers included in the book were first presented at the conference. The thinking that went into the book also benefited from the contributions of a number of other scholars who participated in the conference, and I would like to thank them here: Carlos Aguirre, Ana Alonso, Florence Babb, Dan Balderston, Darío Euraque, Michel Gobat, Jeff Gould, Laurie Graham, Charles A. Hale, Zoila Mendoza, Mercedes Niño-Murcia, Patricia Oliart, Jacki Rand, Carol Smith, Chuck Walker, Kay Warren, Mary Weismantel, and Eileen Willingham. I wish to thank Ernesto Silva for providing the expert simultaneous translation that made the discussions at the conference possible. Special thanks are owed to Marisol de la Cadena for coorganizing the conference and for her contributions to it. A different volume in Spanish was published by Marisol in Colombia. I would also like to express my thanks to the institutions that provided funding: the Wenner Gren Foundation, the Latin American Studies Association Special Projects Fund, the University of Iowa Arts and Humanities Initiative, and the University of Iowa International Programs Special Projects. My thanks go to Mercedes Niño-Murcia—director of the Latin American Studies Program at the University of Iowa when the conference was convened—who offered crucial support for this project.

I would like to thank Rossana Barragán, Carla Espósito Guevara, Michel Gobat, and María Lagos for their extensive comments on an early draft of my introduction to the volume, and Martha Hodes and Florencia Mallon for their comments on a penultimate one. My thanks also go to the audience at the 12th Reunión Anual de Etnología at the Museo Nacional de Etnografía y Folklore in La Paz for comments and questions, and to colleagues in the history department at the University of Iowa for feedback at the very end. I am grateful to Pamela Calla, Brooke Larson, and Sinclair Thomson for conversations about various issues raised by the book. My deep thanks go to Valerie Millholland, Miriam Angress, and Gisela Fosado at Duke University Press for their generous assistance and advice, and to Neal McTighe for guiding the manuscript through the production process. Many thanks, as well, to the two anonymous readers for the press for their helpful comments and suggestions, to Jo Butterfield, Dana Quartana, and Sue Stanfield for assistance with various phases of the project, and to Todd Erickson for preparing the maps. I extend my thanks to Jane Walter, Eileen Willingham, and Janet Hendrickson for their translations of the chapters originally written in Spanish. The translations were edited by me, and any errors are mine. Finally, many thanks to Salvador Schavelzon for the photo of Bolivia's 2006–07 Constituent Assembly that appears on the cover of the book.

Introduction

Racisms of the Present and

the Past in Latin America

LAURA GOTKOWITZ

"The wounds are open . . . and it will be a long time before they heal."[1] This somber phrase sums up widespread sentiment about the violence that broke out in Cochabamba, Bolivia, on January 11, 2007. On that day, hundreds of men and women assaulted each other physically and verbally in the streets and squares of Bolivia's third largest city. On one side were city dwellers with baseball bats; on the other were coca growers and other peasants with sticks. Three men died. Hundreds of people were wounded. No consensus has been reached about the causes of the aggression. Many people believe the spark was a call by the prefect to annul the results of a July 2006 referendum on departmental autonomy, which had been rejected in Cochabamba.[2] Others highlight a larger struggle over power between supporters and opponents of Evo Morales Ayma, Bolivia's first indigenous president and leader of the Movimiento al Socialismo (MAS).[3] Still others emphasize outcomes over causes. They call attention to the open expression of racist sentiments long hidden from view.[4] They point to a confrontation between opposing political forces, which became a battle between rich and poor before taking the form of a racial conflict between "q'aras" (non-Indians) and "indios"—a conflict the "mestizo" region of Cochabamba had presumably overcome.[5]

The violence of January 11, 2007, was not an isolated occurrence. Alarming episodes of racialized violence have also been recorded in Santa Cruz, Sucre, and other Bolivian cities. When describing such confrontations, some Bolivians have been reluctant to use the word "racism"—either because they fear it will aggravate the conflict, or because they do not believe racism played a role.[6] But the word has been circulating a great deal in news analysis and scholarly works, more than it ever did in the past. One recent report on the violence of January 11th noted, "It is clear that racist imaginaries persist semi-submerged in history, ready to flourish in times of conflict. . . . Expressions of racism and intolerance toward an other who is different are part of a social imaginary that inhabits the consciousness of the majority of [Bolivian] citizens."[7] Another commentary observed that the tragic events of January 11, 2007, have made "race" an indispensable analytical category.[8]

The scale of racialized violence in Bolivia stands out in the broader Latin American context, but the shifting discourse on race and racism seems to reflect a more general trend. Not long ago, an air of uncertainty surrounded discussions about race in many Latin American countries. Was race a valuable category of analysis? Did use of the word "race" reinscribe racism? Was the term so laden with biologized logic that it could signify nothing except the idea of intrinsic biological inferiority? Today it seems the tide has turned. A significant body of scholarship has emerged, not only from Bolivia but from many other Latin American countries, that aims to understand racism in its multiple forms, from the hidden and everyday, to the open and crushingly violent; from, for example, the Ecuadorian labor market, which channels men of African descent into jobs as security guards, porters, and drivers, to the racialized terror, both verbal and physical, that undergirded Peru's decade of civil war.[9] To understand these diverse forms of racism—hidden and structural, open and violent—more and more scholars and activists are finding it impossible not to use the controversial word "race." What accounts for this shift, from what some consider a long history of denying racism in Latin America to recognition of its multiple forms? And how are we to understand the specific shapes that racism takes? Are we witnessing a new or neoracism? A cultural racism? Or does the term "racial ambivalence" better capture the workings of race and racism in present-day Latin America? What types of antiracist activism and policy have come to the fore at this time of increasingly visible racism? Was there really such a totalizing denial of racism in the past, as is often thought?[10]

With these questions at its center, this volume seeks to understand race and racism in present-day Latin America by looking closely at the history of racemaking in particular empirical contexts. The chapters, by an interdisciplinary group of scholars, focus on the experience and representation of indigenous peoples in parts of the Andes and Mesoamerica: Peru, Bolivia, Ecuador, Mexico, and Guatemala (see maps 1 and 2). Although the essays do not directly address the history of race and racism in Colombia, El Salvador, Honduras, Nicaragua, Costa Rica, or Panama, works on some of these countries are used to illustrate particular points. Rather than provide a systematic comparison of the Andes and Mesoamerica, this volume highlights points of similarity and difference between and within the two areas. The essays were selected not only because they illuminate the uses of race in a particular place but because they shed light on dynamics that transcend national boundaries.

The Andes and Mesoamerica are the two areas of Latin America where the status of "Indians"—or "the people called Indians"—has been a central focus of state policy and of political disputes about assimilation, segregation, citizenship, and nationhood.[11] Indigenous peoples of Peru, Bolivia, Ecuador, Mexico, and Guatemala—comprising approximately 36 million persons— account for 90 percent of the indigenous population in the Americas.[12] In all five countries, indigenous peoples have been important political actors as well as victims of abusive and intrusive government policies. Today, indigenous movements in these Andean and Mesoamerican nations have captured national and international attention. Together these attributes make these countries a focal point for understanding the common and distinct effects of race and racism in indigenous societies of Latin America. In different ways, contemporary indigenous movements across the Andes and Mesoamerica have incited a broad debate about the realities of racism. They have also drawn attention to the connections between discrimination today and a history of colonialism and violence.

Of course, the history of race and racism in the Andes and Mesoamerica cannot be fully understood by looking exclusively at the experience of indigenous peoples, or by focusing on selected places only. But such a focus does permit an in-depth treatment of local contexts in which race is produced, wielded, and transformed. Since this volume centers on race, racism, and indigenous peoples, it considers only briefly how perceived contrasts between indigenous peoples and people of African descent shaped emerging concepts of race; and it does not explore how racial ideas were mapped onto and transformed by the European and Asian migrants who entered Latin American countries at certain historical junctures. That said, some of the studies included here do discuss how the categories "Spanish," "white," "ladino," and a host of words signifying racial mixture were configured and reconfigured in relation to the political actions and everyday practices of Indians, Africans, and their descendants. And although none of the chapters deal directly with immigrants, a couple of them point to the formative role that foreigners

Map 1. Modern Mesoamerica, showing principal places discussed in this volume.

Map 2. The Modern Andes, showing principal places discussed in this volume.

played in the construction of racial imaginaries during the nineteenth and twentieth centuries, and provide signposts for future research.

While this book treats a number of different countries, readers will notice that many of the essays focus on Bolivia. The reason is simple: racism in recent years has become highly visible in Bolivia not only in the intensity of its violence but also as a focus of public debate. This is not to suggest that racism did not exist previously. Nor is it to say that Bolivia is the only Latin American country in which racism has become more visible. Nevertheless, a set of political circumstances has brought race and racism to the surface of public life in Bolivia with particular force. Why? The ascension of Evo Morales to the presidency opened up space for fierce battles over competing visions of political power, ethnic rights, and visions of the nation. And those battles have been fought out in part in the language of race. Progovernment and opposition groups have accused each other of defending racist agendas. On several occasions, conflicts over political or regional power have been transformed into arenas for racialized violence. In response to such episodes, governmental and nongovernmental organizations have launched forums, marches, and research initiatives to protest, study, and explain racism. Present-day Bolivia thus illustrates tendencies with parallels in other Latin American countries.

By focusing closely on Bolivia at salient historical moments, and by contrasting aspects of Bolivia's history and contemporary reality with those of Ecuador, Peru, Guatemala, and Mexico, this book zeros in on the peculiar dynamics of race and racism in specific empirical contexts from the early colonial era to the present. For while the evidence does point to common global and regional forces, an emphasis on local experience and thought is crucial for understanding the effects of race and how race and racism connect with other forms of power and identity, such as class, gender, nationality, and regionalism. An understanding of local dynamics can in turn open up questions about the uses of race in empirical contexts not directly treated here. Rather than contemplate what race means, the essays included here consider, above all, the consequences of race and the work that race does to create and reproduce social hierarchies, domination, and violence.[13]

Biology, Culture, and the Work of Race

Any discussion of race and racism in Latin American history necessarily entails a dialogue with the burgeoning literature on race and racism in North America and Europe. First, because much of the work on race and racism in

Latin America is implicitly or explicitly comparative. Second, because there is a great difference of opinion—in Latin America and beyond—about the historical trajectory of racism and about what race means. In regard to Latin America, some scholars highlight ideologies of race specific to the region; other scholars point to similarities and continuities between North America and South America. On the whole, the essays in this volume question the idea of a peculiarly Latin American concept of race, while clearly rejecting transhistorical meanings. The emphasis here is on local similarities *and* differences.

Four principal tendencies mark the vast and varied body of work on race and racism in diverse global settings, and these tendencies are echoed in recent work in and on Latin America.[14] A first group of studies maintains that racism is necessarily linked with an ideology of intrinsic biological inferiority.[15] This particular notion harkens back to the scientific or classical racism of the late nineteenth century, when "natural" differences were seen more and more as distinctly "biological" differences.[16] While the sense of a tight fit between biology and race hardly prevails in the scholarship on race and racism today, the notion still has its adherents, those who might distinguish an overtly biological form of racism from a presumably more open, cultural one. An extreme manifestation of this view would even say that in the absence of an ideology of biological inferiority there is no racism.[17]

A second line of thought, common among many scholars writing about race today, centers on distinct, historically rooted forms of racism and the emergence of a new racism, neoracism, or cultural racism in the aftermath of the Second World War. Those who follow this logic emphasize the role of culture as the basis of racist practice and thought. For some of these thinkers, the "new" racism is part of a global racial project that emerged from the political right during the 1960s. Accordingly, classical (i.e., scientific or biological) racism, including open expressions of white supremacy, was discredited after the Second World War. To sustain racist positions in a new context, the argument goes, reactionary intellectuals needed to distance themselves from the old racism and invent one that was new. Leaving behind biological perspectives and the idea of natural inequalities, such ideologues began to emphasize "cultural" differences. In a new, presumably antiracist context, it was necessary to express and interpret racial differences in a seemingly nonracial manner. Indeed, these changed circumstances made it possible for racism to be reproduced even in societies and institutions that openly denounced discrimination.[18]

A third, increasingly influential way of thinking about race and racism bypasses this binary approach to biology and culture altogether. Instead, a good many scholars are now suggesting that race and culture are so completely interrelated that it is impossible to differentiate a biological racism from a cultural one.[19] That is to say, racism is neither exclusively biological nor exclusively cultural; instead it represents a combination of the two. In contrast to the above-mentioned studies that chart a new racism or a cultural racism, this third set of works suggests that there was not a clearly defined era of biological racism that gave way to a clearly defined era of cultural racism. Instead, the ostensibly biological racism already had a cultural content.[20] What is often observed about race today, its flexibility, had likely always been an element of the concept of race.[21] Along these same lines, several recent works have emphasized an underlying connection between ideas about biology and concepts of culture, and how difficult it is to fully separate one from the other. On the one hand, understandings of biology are culturally specific; on the other, culture itself is sometimes viewed as a biological force.[22]

For a growing number of scholars, the force of racism resides precisely in this relationship between the cultural and the biological, in the synthesis of the two. The ambiguity of the connection between the cultural and the biological is a prerequisite for the emergence and production of racial thought.[23] In other words, the synthesis of the biological and the cultural gives force to racial discourse. This synthesis also makes racism more versatile and gives it a greater capacity to transform itself and survive. For if racism can be molded and remolded to fit changing historical circumstances, it can also be used to maintain economic and social privileges in distinct contexts. The combination of the rigid and the flexible is the essence of racism; it is fundamental to its elasticity and to its power.[24]

This fusion of the cultural and the biological is not and has not been the same thing everywhere or at all times. Nor is it always perceived and understood in exactly the same terms. Talk about the cultural has been especially prominent in scholarly discussions of race and racism in the Latin American context. Indeed, much scholarly work on Latin America has emphasized what might be called the peculiarly cultural dimensions of race.[25] Recent scholarship qualifies such a conclusion, for it provides ample evidence of the role that culture played, for example, in the racism of nineteenth-century North America. As such, this scholarship calls into question the idea of a distinctly Latin American notion of race. Not only in Latin America but also in North America, not only in the twentieth century but in many other temporal settings, race is and has been conceptualized as a fusion of the cultural and the biological.[26] When we talk about the flexible character of race and racism, its shifting cultural and biological content, we are talking necessarily about something that transcends national and continental boundaries.

A number of recent works on seventeenth-century Spain and Latin America disclose the deep history of this fusion of the cultural and the biological. To be sure, some scholars of colonial Latin America question or even reject the relevance of the word "race," since religion rather than biology served to mark innately hierarchical differences. By the same token, some scholars continue to assume that "modern" notions of race are necessarily rooted in biology or phenotype. But, as Kathryn Burns and Sinclair Thomson discuss in their essays on race in the Andes, and as Laura Lewis and María Elena Martínez show for New Spain, such concepts had specific meanings in colonial Latin America, meanings that changed over the course of the colonial era. So rather than reject the relevance of race for colonial Latin America, we need to study its shifting coordinates, uses, and effects; we need to understand how culture could be innate and how religion could be considered akin to blood—and how blood could represent both biological and cultural heritage.[27]

A fourth way of thinking about race and racism combines the second and third perspectives outlined above. Some scholars would say racism is and always has been a mix of the biological and the cultural. It is and has been very difficult to clearly distinguish between the logics of biology and culture. But these scholars would add that we have witnessed an important historical transformation, that allusions to intrinsically biological differences have much less force in the world today. These allusions exist, but they occupy the margins of racial discourse. In the twenty-first century, culture is racism's dominant figure; it lies at the center of racist rhetoric and practice.[28]

There is, however, another way of thinking about these biological racisms seemingly at the margins of racial discourse. For the most striking thing about them is their persistence in "popular" consciousness and discourse despite the fact that they have been widely discredited. In reality, they are not as marginal as they may seem. Though biology is overshadowed by cultural frameworks and discourses, it remains a powerful element of racial thinking. Indeed, the period after the Second World War, when scientists presumably rejected ideas of biological race, is now more accurately viewed as a time when race was reconstructed, not only as a cultural category but also as a biological category. The notion of biological race was challenged, but the concept did not die.[29]

We have, then, no clear consensus about what race means. That very conclusion offers important signposts for thinking about the endurance of racism. Many recent works indicate that the staying power of racism has to do with its capacity to adapt to new circumstances, whether all at once—in response to major historical turning points—or in a more continuous and ongoing manner. Another fundamental point has to do with the historical specificity of race, with the idea that race and racism are made and remade in distinct historical and political contexts. Put most simply, racism is grounded in specific historical conditions; there is not one form of racism that transcends space and time.[30] Finally, many recent works move beyond a clear-cut divide between the meanings of race in North America and Latin America, beyond a divide between a presumably rigid biological racism in the north, and a more flexible, cultural one in the south. The most compelling studies instead illuminate the peculiar dynamics of racial meanings in specific empirical contexts. In so doing, they show how race and racism articulate with other forms of power, identity, and social relations.[31]

That such distinct conclusions may be drawn about the meanings of race should prompt us to reframe the questions we ask. Rather than contemplate whether race is understood in cultural or biological terms, or through a combination of the two, we should ask, as Thomas Holt does, What *work* does race do? What effects does race have?[32] And how can we explain the apparent intensification of racism in present-day Latin America, the hidden and overt forms that Latin American racisms take?

In thinking about the work race does, we must consider the ways that race may speak for—that is, do work for—other forms of identity and power, such as class, gender, nationality, and regionalism.[33] The essays in this volume by Deborah Poole and Rudi Colloredo-Mansfeld illustrate such connections between race, gender, and regionalism by showing how women were contested signs of regional identity or racially defined regions. Andrés Calla and Khantuta Muruchi in turn consider how racism became increasingly visible—violently visible—in the context of a political struggle over regional power. Rossana Barragán shows how the construction of racial categories in a nineteenth-century census was integrally linked with assumptions about gender and class, while Kathryn Burns notes that sexual violence against native and enslaved women was a defining characteristic of conquest and colonialism. As scholars have shown, the construction and deployment of racial concepts can have differential effects for men and women—and weighty implications for diverse forms of sexual policing, politics, and violence.[34]

History, Racialization, and Racemaking

If the more pertinent questions have to do with the effects of race, rather than with what race means, then it is also necessary to consider the political, economic, and cultural contexts that shape and give life to those uses, practices, and effects. To understand the effects of race, we need to zero in on specific racial moments, on the acts of racialization that take place at particular historical junctures. By "racialization" I mean the construction of racial stereotypes via political discourse, cultural performance, social policy, censuses, physical or verbal violence, and other acts of marking.[35] Racialization is not simply a discursive or cultural process. It goes hand in hand with the exercise of political and economic power. It is often accompanied by the exploitation of labor and the expropriation of land.[36] Four major moments of racialization form the backdrop of the essays in this volume.[37] Each moment is considered in a section of the book. Although these moments do not exhaust the discussion, they serve to illustrate some of the principal effects of race in colonial and modern Latin America.

The Uses of Race in Colonial Latin America

The first moment of racialization is considered in the essays by Kathryn Burns and Sinclair Thomson; taken as a whole, that moment is the long era of Spanish colonialism (c.1500–1820s).[38] The conquest and colonization of Latin America involved competing motivations and objectives. While Spaniards sought riches and social ascendancy, they also aimed to convert indigenous people to Christianity.[39] Their efforts to consolidate power and achieve those goals required collaboration and compromise with native peoples. And the political frameworks that resulted from those collaborations involved ideas about race. Much disagreement persists about the historical conditions that gave rise to modern concepts of race, and about whether race originated in the colonial Americas or was brought there by Europeans, as Sinclair Thomson discusses in his essay.[40] We know with certainty that the Spaniards' approaches to race changed as the colonial order unfolded. Though the colonizers eventually settled on a policy that attempted to segregate Indians from non-Indians—the better, they believed, to control, convert, and exploit—they never gave up on the idea of assimilation, which was applied to the indigenous nobility, as Kathryn Burns notes. As segregation fell apart in practice, and "new peoples" were born or forcibly introduced as slaves, so too did a host of new words come forth, which the Spaniards used to name them.[41]

What kind of labels were these? Who invented them? Were they racial terms? Were they *modern* racial terms? What effects did they have? The essays by Burns and Thomson ask us to reflect on just such questions, and to think critically about the uncritical and unselfconscious use of language from another place and time. Kathryn Burns begins by asking what race meant in early colonial Latin America, and whether or not racial categories were salient in that time and place. To get at these questions, she looks closely at the specific terms that Iberians and their descendants used to mark differences. She shows that categories such as "mestizo" and "mestiza," "mulato" and "mulata," and "criollo" and "criolla" had specific meanings in sixteenth- and seventeenth-century Cuzco, meanings that contrast sharply with those employed today. In colonial Cuzco, race was as much about ancestry as it was about the purity or impurity of blood and the politics of religious conversion.[42] Burns concludes that using the term "race" without reflection, as a transhistorical classification, obscures local forms of differentiation and discrimination that may have had just as much weight. In so doing, she echoes Michelle Brattain's recent call to resist transhistorical uses of the word "race." Brattain writes: "Historians cannot stop studying race or using racial designations, but we should find ways to do so that refuse to fix or obscure their meanings."[43] Burns's chapter on the colonial Andes shows that the refusal to fix race requires attention to two distinct levels of analysis: the everyday processes, encounters, and contests by which race was made and unmade; and the "world-historic horizon of imperial rivalries," rivalries that were at once religious, political, military, and economic.[44]

Sinclair Thomson continues this discussion of the politics of colonial categories, but shifts the terrain to a late colonial moment of widespread social and political rupture. His essay focuses on subaltern uses of race over the course of the great Andean insurgency of 1780–81. Like Burns, Thomson reminds readers to heed local uses, processes, and meanings. He puts special emphasis on the categories that emerged outside of dominant institutions and discourses, often in the heat of political battle—in battles led by subaltern sectors. As Burns does, Thomson reminds us to avoid imposing the present on the past—or the past on the present. But because he focuses on the late colonial era, Thomson is also able to consider continuities, to consider what we might call the presence of the old in the new. One colonial concept of race that still has power today revolves around honor and status. Another links the words "race" and "nation." Thomson pays close attention to this particular usage, to the power of racial identities as tools to claim justice and the rights of a community or a nation. (A vivid example of this use of race is provided in Esteban Ticona's chapter on an Aymara leader of the early twentieth century.) Though the late colonial era was an important moment for the configuration of racial concepts and ideologies, just as the early colonial period had been, Thomson nevertheless concludes that this moment of crisis and transition did not represent an epistemic break. It is precisely because terms like "Indian" sprang from histories of conquest and colonization, from histories of exploitation, expropriation, and coerced conversion, that they remain powerful terms of identification and struggle today.

A focus on these varied levels of colonial reality further reveals that race was construed in relational terms, and that Indians and Africans were incorporated into the colonial order in contrasting ways.[45] As other scholars have shown, the difference turned ultimately on the links between religion and enslavement, on the perceived capacity of Indians, as opposed to Africans, for Christian conversion. In other words, the potential for conversion eventually exempted most Indians from slavery, while the enslavement of Africans and their descendants was instead justified by religion.[46] Furthermore, while black slaves could acquire freedom individually, the colonial state never offered freedom to them as a group.[47] For Africans, the experience of slavery entailed the destruction of a group identity, whereas the colonial state recognized Indians as a collectivity and granted certain rights to them.[48] Of course, at the level of lived experience, as Kathryn Burns mentions, and as a number of other scholars have explored in depth, relations between Indians and Africans could involve both enmity and alliance.[49] If race is the result of accrued layers of historical practice and thought, its making is also shaped by local encounters and conflicts, by the contingent and highly charged situations of rebellion, war, and everyday life.[50]

Racialization and the State in the Long Nineteenth Century

A second central moment of racialization in Latin America is the long arc that spans the late eighteenth century to the early twentieth, a time critical for the making of modern Latin American nations and states. The long nineteenth century, as it is known, is associated with liberal ideology and policy, with free trade, anticlericalism, and the privatization of corporate institutions and landholding. It also witnessed new technologies of regulation, vision, and classification, and a concomitant expansion of state institutions. These expanding powers of the state emerged in routines and institutions such as the census, obligatory military service, schools, courts, asylums, and hospitals.[51] But the long nineteenth century was not just marked by the expansion of bureaucratic power, or by the state's increasing regulation of bodies. It was also characterized by new forms of exploitation and expropriation that drove the region's unprecedented export boom during the second half of the century. Still, the forms of economic abuse that marked this era were not always entirely new, for some of them mirrored those of the colonial era: coercive labor drafts and the widespread seizure of communal land. These two types of exploitation were not implemented in the same way throughout the region. The specific forms that they took are key to understanding the effects of race in particular nations during the long nineteenth century.

The transformation of land and labor systems in nineteenth-century Latin America is closely associated with that package of laws and policies known generically as the liberal reforms. But the substance of the reforms, and their effects, varied significantly both between the Andes and Mesoamerica and within the two regions.[52] Even though liberal elites throughout the continent privileged private property, they did not take action everywhere to deliberately undermine or eliminate Indian corporate communities. And in practice, liberal laws meant enormously diverse things for land tenure and ethnic relations. Consider Bolivia and Guatemala, the two countries addressed in the second part of the book. In both nations, the liberal reforms had particularly violent ramifications, and the state played a major role. Still, the tenor of the laws differed dramatically. In Bolivia, state authorities waged a direct assault against communal landholding that greatly reduced the land base of Indian communities.[53] Guatemalan liberals, in contrast, did not outlaw the Indian community or wage a direct assault against it.[54] Rather than directly expropriating land, the Guatemalan liberal reforms engendered unprecedented systems of forced indigenous labor. As Arturo Taracena discusses in his chapter in this volume, political and economic changes wrought by conservative governments (1839–71) paved the way for the coercive practices of the late nineteenth-century liberal era (post-1871).[55]

A close look at the trajectory of the liberal reforms in Bolivia and Guatemala sheds light on the effects of race in nineteenth-century Latin America. Despite key differences, liberal projects in both countries entailed exceptionally violent policies toward Indian communities, and those policies shaped and were shaped by ideas about race. Scholarship on Latin America typically associates liberalism with assimilation, but recent works on Bolivia and Guatemala have challenged that equation. Rather than effacing Indianness, liberal statemakers in these two countries retained the category "Indian" (e.g., in censuses and secondary laws), and sought in certain instances to establish separate forms of education and justice to perpetuate a hierarchical status quo. What work did race do in this context? The essays by Taracena and Barragán show that race did the work of class. In different ways, ideas about race fixed the status of Indians as agricultural workers.

In his chapter on ethnicity and the state in nineteenth-century Guatemala, Taracena shows that liberal elites remade forms of segregation on the ground—notwithstanding a professed desire to assimilate Indians. He mentions some exceptions to this rule: up to a point, liberal elites did seek to assimilate *alcaldes* and *principales* (indigenous authorities), who were viewed as essential intermediaries between the state and Indian communities. But liberal elites considered the vast majority of Indians unfit for incorporation into the nation. In part, liberals furthered segregation via a series of secondary laws, laws that had forceful effects in the realm of education. But it was the persistence of forced Indian labor that above all undermined the vision of a homogenized nation.[56] As Greg Grandin has shown, the Maya elite grouped in Quetzaltenango's "El Adelanto" society, made up of literate and bilingual landowners and merchants, challenged this equation between race and class by promoting a vision of ethnicity that separated indigenous culture from the figure of the impoverished worker.[57] These municipal leaders were rejecting, precisely, the conflation of Indianness with servile labor. For in postindependent Guatemala, systems of coercive labor affected, above all, the indigenous population, the nation's majority. To be sure, poor ladinos (non-Indians), as Taracena notes, were compelled to provide labor for road construction projects during the nineteenth century and the first half of the twentieth century.[58] But Indians were burdened not only by this particular obligation but also by forced agricultural labor on plantations and haciendas.[59] Indeed, Guatemala's liberal reforms engendered one of the harshest and longest lasting systems of coerced labor in all of Latin America. The only way to escape the drafts was to be bound by debt peonage to a particular landlord.[60] If Guatemala lies at one extreme in this regard, Taracena's chapter reminds us that racemaking, in general, is integrally linked with the organization of labor.

As Taracena shows, the effects of a racialized system of labor were also manifest in Guatemala's dominant ethnic ideology, an ideology rooted, until recently, in a rigid duality between Indians and ladinos.[61] The term "ladino" has a long history. In the early colonial era, it signified a native speaker of

Spanish, but by the late seventeenth century "ladino" had taken on a much wider meaning: it came to mean anyone who was not an Indian, including mestizos, poor Spaniards, ladinized Indians, free blacks, and eventually also foreigners.[62] As Taracena notes, this bifurcated categorization was linked with an ideology of Indian degeneration. It also helps explain why slaves and free people of color have been largely invisible in Guatemala's national history.[63] The ideology of Indian-ladino bipolarity distorted Guatemala's multiethnic and multiracial reality: it was premised on the subordination of Indians and the invisibility of most mulattos and blacks.

In Bolivia, as in Guatemala, political discourse and policy demonstrate a tight fit between prevailing notions about agricultural labor and conceptions of Indianness in the postindependent era. Forced labor drafts never acquired the same status in Bolivia that they held in Guatemala; *colonaje*, not debt peonage, was the prevalent form of rural labor in the Andean country prior to the 1952 revolution. Nevertheless, *colonos* (dependent estate laborers who owed labor and service duties in exchange for a plot of land) were almost invariably considered Indians—in everyday life, in laws, and, as Rossana Barragán shows, in the census, a central means of racialization.

New techniques of classification that racialized particular people by fixing them to specific social, racial, and occupational categories came hand in hand with the expropriation of land and the exploitation of labor in post-independent Bolivia, as they did elsewhere in Latin America. Indeed, as Barragán underscores, the type of marking that characterized the work of the modern census is unique. The ascription of racial identities functioned very differently in this ritual of the state than it did in myriad encounters of everyday life. In both realms, contests, negotiations, and disagreements could characterize efforts by some people to impose a race on others. But there was a difference. The conversations that may have transpired when census takers intruded on their subjects' lives (conversations that, unfortunately, were not recorded) would have been powerfully negated by the state official who decided which racial category to mark on the census.[64] As Martha Hodes has shown in her work on the U.S. census, census-taking in the late nineteenth century was becoming a "tool of science," a science that was at once arbitrary and exacting, that could slip but also fixed. A census taker's decision about the race of an individual or a family was an act of subordination that was sealed by the weight of the state.[65]

In postindependent Bolivia, the census was not used for the purpose of political representation, as it was in the United States, but it did become a tool of science in the late nineteenth century. In fact, it was a science so exacting that Bolivian census takers did not need to ask people what race they were: the meanings of race were already understood. The primary purpose the census served in the late nineteenth century was to represent and then broadcast the social order (for purposes of immigration promotion, for example). In her analysis of an 1881 census of the city of La Paz, Barragán argues that the authors of the census did not need to provide a definition of "race," because race was already embedded in the occupational structure; race and occupation were one and the same. There could be no rural laborers who were not Indians, and there could be no Indians who were not rural laborers. Likewise, none of the people listed under the educated or professional classes were Indians. Nor were there, or could there be, white market vendors. The census racialized by equating race with occupation and occupation with race.[66] And in part because the occupational structure was highly gendered, so too, Barragán shows, were the racial classifications employed in the census. For example, many more women than men occupied the category "mestizo."

Along with labor systems and the census, a third central site of racemaking in postindependent Latin America was educational policy and the school, which government authorities began to extend to rural areas in this era. Brooke Larson's essay demonstrates that modernizing elites in the early twentieth century invested immense symbolic authority in education by imbuing it with the power to remake races and create a unified nation. But there was no consensus about the kind of education that would best achieve the nation's unity or its advance. Larson shows that political elites grappled with distinct approaches to rural education before settling on a segregationist model that privileged manual labor for the countryside and for Indians, and literacy for cities and non-Indians. The outcome of similar disputes was much the same in Guatemala, where plans to assimilate native peoples by teaching them Spanish soon became a project to make Indians good agricultural workers.[67] In Bolivia, the proponents of separate forms of education revived a colonial model of race: they sought to preserve the "pure" Indian in a rural habitat while keeping at bay the social and political dangers presumably posed by hybrid peoples, that is, by people identified as mestizos and mestizas, and as cholos and cholas. The goal of the policymakers was to preserve racial, spatial, and class hierarchies.

If we look further at Indian-state relations in late nineteenth-century and early twentieth-century Bolivia and Guatemala, parallels are also visible in politicians' support for separate structures of justice. In both countries, the republican state revived colonial caste in secondary laws, even as lawmakers embraced the theory of juridical equality.[68] But the minor laws and decrees were more coherent and more fully codified in Guatemala. Furthermore, as Taracena shows, in Guatemala the assignation of racial categories had exceptional force, for there was a tight fit not only between rural labor and Indianness but between *forced* rural labor and Indianness. In Guatemala, acts of marking—in the census, in legislative debates, in the *libretas*—were reinforced by the everyday experience of coercion on the ground, in the nation's economic center, in the coffee plantations.[69]

The essays in part two of the book thus show that racial exclusions were integral to the liberal project. But the form that those exclusions took cannot be understood by looking at ideology alone. Race and racism are shaped by "major shifts in a political economy" as well as by "the cultural systems allied with that political economy."[70] While the uses of race in late nineteenth-century Latin America were influenced by colonial concepts, they were not straightforward legacies of the past. To be sure, the labor drafts imposed on Indians in late nineteenth-century and early twentieth-century Guatemala hark back to colonial institutions. It would be wrong, however, to call them a holdover from that past. In Guatemala, forced indigenous labor was the devastating outcome of the late nineteenth-century coffee export boom.[71] The fact that coercion did not have the same force in Bolivia has a great deal to do with the absence of an agricultural export boom there in the late nineteenth century.

Racialization and Nationalist Mythologies in the Twentieth Century

A third fundamental moment of racialization in Latin America spans the period stretching roughly from the 1920s to the 1960s. These decades were a critical time for nationmaking, a time marked by renewed efforts to expand and strengthen nation states in the face of burgeoning social mobilization, revolutionary movements, and a recent history of imperial incursions. Scholars generally associate this period of nationmaking with the terms "*mestizaje*" and "*indigenismo.*" In works on Latin America, the two concepts are used most frequently to signify an ideology or cultural project that seeks to forge national unity. But the word "mestizaje" also signifies real-life processes of cultural or biological mixture. In "popular" renderings (textbooks, public history, and oral history), "mestizaje" is used almost exclusively in this sense, as Deborah Poole notes in her essay in this volume. Scholarly works on the colonial era have explored these quotidian aspects of mestizaje.[72] With a few exceptions, works on the modern era generally use the term in regard to ideology.[73] The meanings attributed to "mestizaje" and "indigenismo" nevertheless range widely. In Mexico, "indigenismo" and "mestizaje" are generally understood as overlapping concepts. In other settings, the two ideals may be considered distinct or even diametrically opposed. In Bolivia, for example, "indigenismo" usually means "Indian-centered," while "mestizaje," referring to "the cult of the mestizo," is associated with the erasure of Indians.[74] A wealth of studies have mapped out and analyzed ideals of mestizaje in the works of prominent intellectuals, and examined the relationship between mestizaje and social policy, particularly in revolutionary Mexico.[75] The chapters included in part three of this volume, by Seemin Qayum, Deborah Poole, and Claudio Lomnitz, provide distinct perspectives on the roots and political implications of mestizaje and indigenismo, focusing on specific local contexts of Bolivia and Mexico.

In the most general terms, indigenismo constitutes a field of dispute over national identity, regional power, and rights that places "Indians" at the center of politics, jurisprudence, social policy, or study. In its heyday (c. 1910s–40s), indigenismo throughout Latin America was marked by a diversity of political positions and modes of racial thinking.[76] In Mexico, the indigenista project had a decidedly modernizing hue: the state would bring "progress" to Indians via schools, roads, and health clinics. It would liberate them from ignorance and backwardness "while taking their spirit to animate the collective project."[77] In Peru, indigenismo has had a long and varied trajectory; it vacillated in the nineteenth and twentieth centuries between protectionist and revolutionary ends. In the late nineteenth century, Peruvian indigenismo was largely a paternalistic attempt to promote indigenous acculturation. Later, in the eyes of socialist writer José Carlos Mariátegui, it became a revolutionary project to empower Indians. Under Augusto Leguía, the populist and then decidedly authoritarian president, indigenismo was institutionalized in the 1920s in an effort to curb indigenous mobilization and modernize the countryside. With the works of José María Arguedas, a radical novelist and anthropologist, indigenismo in the period after the Second World War once again became a project for indigenous agency and the creation of a culturally pluralistic nation.[78]

In Bolivia, indigenismo influenced legislative debates and state policy, but it was never fully institutionalized. Nor did it become the basis of a specific political movement or party, as it did in Mexico and Peru.[79] Nevertheless, as

Qayum shows in her essay in this volume, indigenismo played an important role in early twentieth-century struggles over regional power, national identity, and the nation's historical origins. It also figured in the educational policy debates of the era, as Larson demonstrates in her essay. And indigenismo influenced the conflicts that raged in Bolivia during the same years over law, rights, and institutions of justice.[80] It was, in short, a key aspect of state building projects during the early decades of the twentieth century. After Bolivia's 1952 revolution, indigenismo would become a more forceful component of revolutionary cultural politics, with manifestations in music, theatre, and film.[81] Throughout Latin America, then, indigenismo resonated powerfully, peaking at distinct moments in different nations and taking on diverse national and regional forms.

While the national trajectories differed significantly, scholarship on indigenismo and mestizaje throughout Latin America has been heavily influenced by the uses of the two tropes in revolutionary and postrevolutionary Mexico. This is true not only because the historiography is so rich but because Mexico was an exporter of mestizaje discourse and of indigenista knowledge and policy. During the first decades of the 1910 revolution, the discourses of mestizaje that emerged from Mexico had revolutionary and anti-imperial overtones, and they came to occupy a central place in the thought of Central America's revolutionary nationalists, such as Nicaragua's Augusto Sandino.[82] After 1940, Mexico's indigenista policies continued to reverberate throughout many Central and South American countries in a more institutionalized guise—via the Inter-American Indigenista Institute with which many Latin American countries established affiliate institutes.

When it comes to Mexico, scholars generally agree on the close connections between indigenismo and mestizaje, with indigenismo, as Claudio Lomnitz recently put it, being that which would make Mexico a mestizo (unified) nation.[83] To be sure, Mexico's leading indigenistas crafted varied visions in revolutionary times: in addition to those who insisted on the assimilation of Indians, there were others who briefly advocated cultural pluralism.[84] But here, perhaps more than anywhere else, indigenismo (the cult of the Indian) emerged in tandem with the dream of assimilation and the affirmation of mixture (the cult of the mestizo). Furthermore, indigenismo in Mexico was closely tied to a rapidly expanding state that put anthropologists at the helm of a host of new institutions.[85] Indeed, in institutional terms, Mexican anthropology became one of the largest and most politically important national anthropologies in the world.[86] There were two sides to this burgeoning indigenista action: the developmentalist and the aesthetic.[87]

In the revolutionary and postrevolutionary context, both anthropologists and artists figured centrally, for they were the ones who helped the state reach the largely illiterate countryside and who could do so visually, with objects and images.[88] Even before the revolution, intellectuals and anthropologists were trying to influence state policy by deploying ideas that linked the nation and its progress with race. But these social scientists gained a much more powerful forum for their work with the development of an institutional framework for anthropology after the revolution triumphed. And while intellectuals of the Porfirian era (1876–1911) sought to mold the image of Mexico abroad, the revolutionary anthropologists intruded directly on rural communities.[89] Through their work in Mexico's extensive indigenista institutions, as Ana Alonso has shown, anthropologists played a key role both as arbiters of indigenous culture and as participants in the "public staging of mestizaje," the creation of spaces that conveyed or performed a national myth. Archeological objects were a fundamental to such enactments or "living" museums. And one key role of the anthropologist was to decide which aspects of indigenous culture merited inclusion in this "national patrimony."[90] While this national project challenged U.S. imperialism, it failed to value the elements of the national mix equally. In aiming to integrate Indians, indigenismo valued the Hispanic far and above the indigenous.[91]

Seemin Qayum's chapter on Bolivia vividly shows this discriminatory underside of indigenismo. In charting the dispute that emerged over which location the centerpiece of the Tiwanaku ruins would occupy when transferred to the city of La Paz, she reveals just how much ambivalence could mark indigenista visions. Would the monument occupy a prominent place, close to spheres of government and commerce? Or would it be consigned (as was ultimately the case) to a residential area on the city's margins? The contrast with Mexico could not be more striking. In Mexico, where the national capital was constructed atop Aztec ruins, the veneration of those ruins became central to the physical and cultural space of the nation. The reason for the difference, Qayum suggests in her chapter, lies in the balance of force, that is, the Bolivian ruins were relegated to the margins in the early twentieth century because of the threat (and fear) of ongoing indigenous mobilization. In Mexico, when the revolutionary state and its teams of anthropologists set out to make indigenous ruins the national patrimony, indigenous political movements and leaders had essentially been defeated and were being incorporated, via a complex political process, into the revolutionary state. The relationship between political force and the force of indigenismo seems to have been different in Peru, for interest in the Inca past at times ran parallel with indigenous mobilization. In the 1910s and 1920s, interest in the Inca past coexisted with indigenous movements that were similar to and perhaps even connected with those in Bolivia.[92]

The distinct trajectories of indigenista anthropology and archeology in Mexico, Peru, and Bolivia remind us of an underlying principle. In all three cases, indigenismo was defined by tensions and contradictions: there was a struggle to herald the glories of the past without igniting the indigenous political movements of the present. In Nicaragua and El Salvador, where indigenous mobilization was effectively suppressed, this dynamic reached an extreme: idealizations of mixture valorized the indigenous past, but they were predicated on the disappearance of living indigenous cultures.[93] In fact, at the level of educational and legal policy, indigenista tendencies sometimes emerged precisely in response to indigenous mobilization, as a tool that government officials used to contain indigenous movements.[94]

Poole's analysis of the Guelaguetza festival in Oaxaca, Mexico, shows the racialized underside of indigenismo and mestizaje today. Although the Guelaguetza is presumably based on indigenous cultural expressions, Indians are unable to participate in it. Indeed, the festival excludes Indians in an age of neoliberal multiculturalism, just as the pluricultural character of Oaxaca and the Mexican nation are being officially recognized. As Poole shows, the exclusions that mark such forms of multiculturalism have a long history. In the nineteenth century, the Oaxacan state tried to articulate a discourse of political unity based on the de facto fragmentation and indigenous control of Oaxaca's many municipalities. By these means, the state staked a claim on the cultural identities of municipalities where state control was weak, where indigenous traditions, authorities, and communal property had weight. The neoliberal cultural politics of the present day build on this tactic of linking cultural diversity with political legitimization and state-building.[95] They also coincide with the persistence of extreme inequalities. Though Oaxaca is Mexico's "cradle of multicultural diversity," it is also one of the country's poorest states. It is known for high numbers of indigenous political prisoners, the militarization of indigenous territories, and elevated rates of indigenous poverty. Such forms of structural racism obviously belie state backing for a festival to affirm indigenous culture. The festival, moreover, fully excludes the cultural expressions of black Oaxacans from its vision of an authentic re-gional identity. In the local lexicon, blacks (unlike Indians) are not an ethnic group but a race that lies beyond the boundaries of the regional culture.

The exclusionary characteristics of multiculturalism that Poole maps out for present-day Oaxaca give insight into the contradictions of mestizaje and indigenismo in a more general sense. Poole argues that mestizaje, the quest for a homogenous nation, is an intrinsically unfinished project.[96] And indi-genismo, for its part, may work to sustain and regulate the diversity that mestizaje only presumably negates. For even as proponents of mestizaje her-alded unity, they asserted differences: they could claim the distinctiveness of the mestizo nation only by continuously invoking the Indian and the nation's indigenous origins.[97] Mestizaje, then, is about both sameness and difference. It is about a future that will never be achieved—precisely because that fu-ture is sacrificed to the maintenance of hierarchical distinctions grounded in race.[98]

This is not to say that indigenismo and mestizaje are simply negative constructs. In Mexico, as numerous scholars have shown, the racism of Por-firian Mexico cast a shadow on, and to some extent became a part of, revolu-tionary indigenismo.[99] Or as Alan Knight put it, although "official indi-genismo may . . . have softened . . . some of the earlier excesses of full-fledged biological racism . . . [indigenismo] contained its own contradictions, which led it to devise racist formulae of its own."[100] In Peru, likewise, indigenista discourse had many racist qualities.[101] Yet it would be wrong to conclude that all manifestations of indigenismo served exclusively or necessarily to re-inscribe racism.[102]

While studies of indigenista politics have long focused on non-Indian intellectuals and institutions, recent works on Mexico, Peru, and Bolivia look instead to the influence of both indigenous and nonindigenous artists, intel-lectuals, actors, and activists.[103] And they journey beyond the realm of ideas to music, theatre, and other forms of lived experience. As Michelle Bigenho demonstrates for the case of revolutionary Bolivia, a consideration of these "embodied" practices reveals that certain aspects of indigenista performance challenged racist views of Indians.[104] Zoila Mendoza shows, likewise, that artistic forms associated with Peruvian indigenismo in the early twentieth century were not the simple product of elite manipulation of popular culture. Instead, indigenista music and art resulted from exchanges among artists and intellectuals of diverse social backgrounds, both urban and rural.[105] While recognizing the contradictions of indigenismo and mestizaje, Mendoza underscores the important fact that some artists and intellectuals gave national value to indigenous culture at a time when dominant elites were scorning it.[106] In Mexico, as Ana Alonso notes, some of the state's indigenista institutes (those that date to the revolutionary era) have local legitimacy to this day, as genuine defenders of indigenous culture. For although the agents of the indigenista institutes were bearers of internal colonialism, to some extent they were also respected advocates for indigenous causes who contributed to the valorization of indigenous culture.[107] Moving beyond ideology to lived forms of indigenismo and mestizaje certainly reveals sites of discrimination, but it may also uncover arenas of struggle, disagreement, and exchange.

It is precisely the lived experience of mestizaje that made it such a powerful state project in revolutionary Mexico, as Claudio Lomnitz argues in his chapter of this collection. Numerous scholars have emphasized the deep resonance of ideologies of mestizaje in Mexican society and politics. As they have shown, positive appraisals of mestizaje emerged early on, in the Porfirian era.[108] But it was the 1910 Revolution that made mestizaje a particularly powerful state project. Works on mestizaje in Mexico often emphasize intellectual production, and thus focus on the works of such thinkers as Manuel Gamio, José Vasconcelos, and Andrés Molina Enríquez. In addition, scholars have explored the links between mestizaje and revolutionary state policies, especially concerning education and agrarian reform. They have also examined cultural sites such as museums, music, and theatre. In his chapter, Lomnitz focuses on a different kind of lived space: routes of transit across the border between Mexico and the United States. He argues that three key factors account for the transformation of the mestizo into Mexico's "national race": state policy and the quest for a national subject; the nature of the economy and its concomitant geography of internal migration; and, above all, lived experience on the two sides of the border with the United States. The border as a space of violence, exploitation, opportunity, and change is crucial to understanding the transformation of the mestizo into Mexico's "national race." There is nothing unusual about a nationality becoming associated with a race, as Lomnitz emphasizes. But he argues that this idea had particularly deep roots in the popular imaginary of early twentieth-century Mexico: the border with the United States gave such ideals special force.

As numerous studies have shown, the transformation of the frontier into the U.S.-Mexico border was a multifaceted historical process marked by territorial conquest, labor exploitation, the displacement of rural peoples, railroad construction, U.S. investment, heightened state regulation, and shifting ideas about gender and race.[109] The early twentieth century marked an important turning point in what was unquestionably an extended process; during these decades, movement across the border, and control of the area by both Mexico and the United States, greatly increased.[110] Mexico's 1910 Revolution figured centrally in this context. As Alexandra Stern has shown, the revolution increased U.S. awareness of the border and its increasingly "dangerous" fluidities, for the revolution entailed the comings and goings of revolutionaries and refugees, as well as laborers.[111] Taking place at a time of heightened nativism in the United States, and with it a full-scale remaking and racialization of immigration law, this increased attention to the border entailed the criminalization of Mexicans and Mexican Americans, who were transformed into "aliens" or carriers of disease. Just as Mexico was equating Mexican nationality with a unified mestizo race and eliminating racial categories and questions from its census, the United States was using ethnic quotas to codify a highly racialized immigration law that turned Mexicans into a race.[112] The U.S. Census Bureau defined the Mexican race in 1930 as being made up of "persons born in Mexico or with parents born in Mexico . . . who are 'not definitely white, Negro, Indian, Chinese or Japanese.'" Ultimately the "Mexican race" became synonymous with "illegal."[113] This codification of a Mexican race exemplifies the ways that the border with Mexico, in a more general sense, has been a "locus for the reinforcement of boundaries marking the body politic, whether expressed in national, racial, or gendered terms."[114]

Lomnitz underscores the reciprocal relationship between racemaking on the two sides of this charged border, and suggests that the experience of discrimination and exploitation in the United States engendered the notion of a unified Mexican race in Mexico. It was in the United States that Mexicans first became a race, and that experience of racialization helped make the idea of a Mexican race, a mestizo race, both possible and necessary on the Mexican side of the border. Lomnitz's chapter thus points to the importance of connections across the boundary with the United States for understanding ideas about mestizaje and the uses of race in Latin America more broadly.[115] His chapter also draws attention to an underlying tension that has marked mythologies of mestizaje: the tension between narrowly nationalist concepts of "raza" versus pan–Latin American notions. In the present age of globalization, Lomnitz asks, has the nationalist strain run its course?

Anti-Racist Politics and Racism Today

The fourth moment treated in this volume has to do with the dynamics of race, racism, and antiracism in present-day Latin America. A number of recent works, many by Latin American authors, expose and reflect on the myriad forms of racism that mark Latin American societies today. These include the discriminatory effects of labor markets, workplaces, and schools; biased treatment by the police and legal systems; de facto exclusion from public space; and the diverse forms of violence, both verbal and physical, that state agents or private citizens perpetrate against racial "others."[116] Some recent works also note a greater willingness by Latin American governments to acknowledge the existence of racism and its destructive force. In the late 1990s, officials in Brazil, Mexico, and Argentina established institutions to deal with charges of racial discrimination.[117] Brazil's recent endorsement of affirmative action policies is the most far-reaching of such measures. This much disputed initiative was designed to address discrimination in government employment, contracts, and university admissions. The outcome of the policies is far from clear, but the proposal did spark a national conversation about race and racism.[118] If nationalist intellectuals downplayed racism in the past, activists and intellectuals in many parts of Latin America have clearly ended the silence today.[119]

A number of factors have contributed to the intensification of racism in Latin America—and to a growing public awareness of its silent, structural, and violent forms. Certainly one fundamental element is the waves of migration that have taken place in Latin America in the past thirty years or so, "on a scale not seen . . . since the Conquest."[120] The recent migrations have a special quality: in the final decades of the twentieth century, human migration *within* Latin America acquired special significance alongside migration from Latin America to other continents. Diverse factors provoked the massive movements, but two issues take center stage: armed conflict (in Central America and the Andes) and economic crisis throughout the region.[121] In many instances, the flows of migrants have caused racial tension and hostility. News reports and scholarly works testify to the backlash against the unprecedented numbers of migrants, who are often scapegoats for rising unemployment (or the perception of rising unemployment) in their new surroundings. Immigrants have also been viewed by members of receiving nations as a threat to cultural homogeneity—even if homogeneity is a myth. In certain situations, as in Argentina at the height of the cholera epidemic of the early 1990s, such backlashes culminated in expulsions.[122] But we should be cautious about assuming a singularly hostile response. In Argentina during the 1990s, official and popular expressions of xenophobia placed responsibility for social and economic troubles on the shoulders of Bolivian, Paraguayan, and Peruvian immigrants.[123] In 2002, however, as the Argentine economy entered into crisis and immigrant workers joined forces with national workers in the *piquetero* movement, the scapegoating of foreigners subsided. This is not to say that immigrant workers no longer experience discrimination, persecution, or violence, for they do. But the official stigmatization that typified Argentina in the 1990s receded—at least for a time.[124]

The brutal civil wars taking place from the 1970s to the 1990s are a second key context for understanding the intensification of racism and the more open discussions of it in present-day Latin America. In Guatemala and Peru, the end of the wars ushered in a climate of historical reflection and opened space for discussion about the rights of indigenous peoples as well as racism. Public expression of the memories of terror that haunt so many lives helped bring this awareness of racism to the fore. In Guatemala, the great majority of the people killed in the course of the counterinsurgency were Indians.[125] In Peru, less than 20 percent of the population speaks Quechua, according to the 1993 census, yet Quechua was the native language of 75 percent of those who died in the armed conflict between the Peruvian military and the insurgent group Sendero Luminoso (Shining Path).[126] Overall, 85 percent of the victims of terror lived in the isolated rural hamlets of Peru's highland departments.[127] The Peruvian Truth and Reconciliation Commission report of 2003 revealed, however, that until the violence began to affect people in urban areas no public memories of the violence were discernible.[128] Until then, those memories remained invisible, hidden in the homes of rural indigenous victims, whose experiences were not considered worthy of national outcry.[129] Although 75 percent of the victims in Peru were men, indigenous women suffered some of the most brutal forms of violence, including rape and forced domestic service (for Sendero Luminoso or the army).[130] In Guatemala as well, anti-Indian racism was intertwined with sexual abuse and domination.[131]

In large part, truth commissions in the two countries helped bring the hidden memories of these racialized conflicts to light.[132] Indeed, the Peruvian commission convened public hearings "to hear and make heard the victims," and a significant portion of that testimony was broadcast on television. Such public inquiries are unique in the history of Latin American truth commissions.[133] In both Peru and Guatemala, the commissions reported that the primary victims of the violence were indigenous.[134] The report of the Guatemalan Comisión para el Esclarecimiento Histórico (known as *Guatemala: Memoria del Silencio*) concluded that acts of genocide had been perpetrated against the country's Maya majority.[135] In Peru, testimony collected from the victims not only exposed abuse and violence but denounced discriminatory treatment by judicial officials, and demanded equal treatment.[136] In both countries, truth commissions underscored the racialized effects of the repression and called for measures to redress the victimization of indigenous peoples.

Equally important, Peru's Comisión de la Verdad y Reconciliación and Guatemala's Comisión para el Esclarecimiento Histórico acknowledge the historical forces and underlying structural factors that militated toward these tragic results of the wars. Though racism was rampant during the years of armed conflict, and manifest in brutal ways, it was already embedded in the social, economic, and political structures of the colonial and neocolonial past. The Guatemalan report linked the brutality of the late twentieth century with a history stretching back to the Spanish conquest.[137] It singled out three structural causes of the violence: economic exclusion, racism, and political authoritarianism.[138] Likewise, the Peruvian report situates the roots of the violence in the colonial and neocolonial history of ethnic and social hierarchy, racism, and political exclusion.[139] But the work of truth commissions can cut many ways. As Elizabeth Oglesby points out, one danger is an overemphasis on pain and suffering, for such an emphasis may deprive the victims of agency, conceal their participation in collective action, and perpetuate stereotypes of Indians as passive or easily manipulated victims.[140] A great deal depends on how such a report will be publicized, and by whom. In Guatemala, allusions to the report tend to focus on the details of the brutality, without giving adequate attention to the report's consideration of the historical and social conditions that produced the brutality.[141] Notwithstanding these limitations, truth commissions in the two countries undoubtedly played a key role in breaking the silence about racism and in helping to spark a debate about indigenous rights.[142]

The recent history of indigenous mobilization is a third factor that helps explain the escalation of racism in Latin America and the more open discussion of its effects. In the countries considered in the final section of this volume, a primary locus of social conflict is the challenge that indigenous movements have posed to exclusionary conceptions of the nation and to non-Indians' hold on political and economic power. The past two decades have witnessed the rise of forceful indigenous movements in Latin America. In Guatemala and Bolivia, indigenous mobilization resulted in far-reaching proposals for constitutional reform, the election of indigenous mayors and congressional deputies, and, in the case of Bolivia, the landslide victory of a president who self-identifies as, and is identified publicly as, indigenous. In specific instances, Latin American legislatures or popular referendums have approved changes to constitutions, thus recognizing the multicultural, pluri-cultural, or plurinational character of nations and conferring specific rights —sometimes including rights to territory and land—on indigenous peoples, as well as on peoples of African descent.[143]

Indigenous movements of today not only claim cultural, social, juridical, and economic rights; they also call attention to centuries of discrimina-tion.[144] They combine demands for cultural rights and profound political transformation with the condemnation of racism.[145] But the rise of indige-nous movements has also been accompanied by racist reactions, including but not limited to acts of violence. On the whole, indigenous demands for auton-omy and self-determination have not implied secession from the nation-state.[146] Nevertheless, indigenous movements have often been viewed by their opponents as a threat to the nation, as a force that promotes division, racism, or reverse racism.[147]

Not surprisingly, the responses to indigenous movements among distinct social sectors in Central and South America have varied—for many different reasons. At specific junctures, indigenous movements have garnered support from sympathetic non-Indian intellectuals and members of the middle class who do not identify as indigenous. In Bolivia, support has certainly been expressed by non-Indians for the demands of indigenous movements—in the press and sometimes also in the streets. But the media and human rights organizations have also recorded episodes of violence, violence that inter-twines the defense of regional interests with the defense of racial and social hierarchies. Much of this conflict has pitted regional elites (from the eastern departments of Santa Cruz, Beni, Pando, and Tarija) who endorse depart-mental autonomy and decentralization, against proponents of the nationalist indigenous project that emanates from the country's western highlands (sup-porters of this project defend a very different form of autonomy, the auton-omy of indigenous communities).[148] The rejection of a neoliberal economic model in Bolivia has opened up space for a fierce battle over these competing visions of the nation. In this context, racism has materialized in many different ways: in the dissemination of racialized historical narratives; in the defense of ethnic hierarchies and city space; and in acts of symbolic and physical violence—in public insults, false rumors, and mass beatings. On several different occasions in Santa Cruz, Cochabamba, and Sucre, struggles over regional power—over departmental autonomy, the constitution, and the location of the nation's full capital—have been transformed into arenas of racialized violence. The crux of the matter is the dispute over who will hold economic and political power.[149]

In Ecuador, the reactions against indigenous movements were initially more muted. Still, as in Bolivia, the crescendo of indigenous mobilization and its expressions of collective power provoked fear and a racist discourse among some members of the Ecuadorian right and the nation's upper classes.[150] At first, in the early 1990s, massive lowland mobilizations garnered impressive support not only from highland indigenous communities but from non-Indian elites in many parts of the country. But other groups voiced their opposition to these movements. In part they objected to demands for land redistribution. They were also angered by indigenous views of the nation, by the idea that the nation comprised diverse nationalities. To opponents of indigenous movements, this notion appeared to threaten national sovereignty and the state. Racist language depicting Indians as lazy and unproductive was deployed at the time to counter indigenous demands for territory.[151] In recent years, the opposition has become more virulent and has reacted with open hostility to indigenous political initiatives in Ecuador.[152] Indeed, the disparagement of indigenous movements has sometimes garnered a wide audience on television and in the press.[153] In both Ecuador and Bolivia, the media have helped disseminate anti-Indian discourses by giving disproportionate voice to the opponents of indigenous movements, allowing the public to express unsubstantiated rumors of antiwhite violence, and covering indigenous protest in a highly selective fashion that amplifies rare moments of indigenous violence.[154]

The trajectory of indigenous movements in Guatemala contrasts sharply with that in Ecuador and especially in Bolivia. In Bolivia, where indigenous peoples are viewed by many to have attained an important place in government with the presidency of Evo Morales, and where broad constitutional reforms have been fiercely contested, a racialized conflict took an explosive course. In Guatemala, the indigenous agenda was apparently tamed, and a kind of racial ambivalence prevailed over open expressions of racial superiority and inferiority, at least in certain locations. When the peace accords were signed in Guatemala in 1996, significant political change seemed likely. Mayas were finally recognized as the nation's majority, and indigenous issues and actors took leading roles in electoral contests.[155] The 1995 agreement on the rights and identity of indigenous peoples, signed by the government and the umbrella rebel organization, the Unidad Revolucionaria Nacional Guatemalteca (URNG), was an important indicator of the changes that were taking place.[156] The agreement called for the officialization of indigenous languages, indigenous representation in all levels of government administration, the acceptance of customary law, the recognition of communal land, the distribution of land to land-deficient communities, and other measures. A number of the points in the agreement were then incorporated into the 1996 peace accords—but they were not automatically implemented.[157] In a May 1999 referendum, a majority of Guatemalans voted against proposed constitutional changes, including a series of indigenous rights and the designation of Guatemala as a "multicultural, ethnically plural, and multilingual state."[158] The tactics used by the "no" campaign were telling: they centered on the revival of a latent threat, on the idea that the proposed reforms would renew ethnic conflict and perhaps even spark a civil war.[159]

Although such racial anxieties persist, the response to expressions of indigenous political and economic power in Guatemala in recent years has been to a large extent more ambivalent; open expressions of hostility have given way, in many cases, to guarded acceptance.[160] In the region of Chimaltenango, as Charles R. Hale has shown, ladinos (non-Indians) generally express respect for indigenous culture, believe that racism should be eradicated, and affirm equality. Yet they are also apprehensive about the prospect of Maya social and political power, and in certain contexts they reject the very ideals of equality they may affirm in other situations. Their racial ambivalence combines the affirmation of equality with an unwillingness to relinquish power. This contradictory position is in part a consequence of the Guatemalan state's support for multiculturalism. With the rise of neoliberal multiculturalism, and partial acceptance in official spheres of the Maya movement's cultural demands, the frequency with which ladinos publicly voice opinions about indigenous inferiority has declined. Economic changes have also contributed to the shift in racial sensibilities; in some local settings, ladino control of the economy has come partly undone, for increasing numbers of middle-class Mayas now occupy positions higher on the economic ladder.[161] The decline of overt racism is most apparent in these more advantaged spheres. At lower levels of the social hierarchy, discrimination remains ubiquitous.

How do discrimination and intolerance operate in these distinct contexts of ethnic mobilization? In his article on Ecuador, Rudi Colloredo-Mansfeld considers the subtle work of race in a changing urban sphere and within the indigenous movement itself. Like Poole, Colloredo-Mansfeld contemplates the question of who participates, and who will decide who participates, in a public performance of ethnic culture. As Qayum does, Colloredo-Mansfeld charts the struggle over a symbol, over the physical location (and relocation) of a statue of an Indian. He shows that the effort to remove this sculpture from the central plaza of the city of Otavalo was a reaction against the growing presence of indígenas and indigenous businesses in the city. He concludes by considering the role that representations of ethnicity have played within the indigenous movement itself. An urban indigenous culture has flourished in parts of Ecuador in recent years, yet it occupies the margins of the national indigenous movement. Without discounting the indigenous movement's accomplishments, Colloredo-Mansfeld looks critically at the way the movement may contribute to reproducing racial stereotypes. Ecuador's indigenous movement, he concludes, reinscribed an old (no longer valid) spatial hierarchy, one that equates "indigenous" with rural and "mestizo" with urban.

In contrast to the sharp divide in Ecuador, the boundary between rural and urban is highly porous in present-day Bolivia, and this porousness shows up clearly in the culture of Bolivian cities and in the nation's indigenous movements. Fifty percent of the adult population of La Paz self-identified as Aymara in the 2001 census and 10 percent as Quechua. In El Alto, a full 74.2 percent of the city's approximately 800,000 inhabitants identified as Aymara and 6.4 percent as Quechua.[162] As several recent studies have shown, El Alto is home to a dynamic urban Aymara culture, especially among its youth (who in many cases do not know the Aymara language). In recent years, this vibrant ethnic culture has dovetailed with a rising political radicalism. Though tensions certainly surface between rural and urban sectors, organic connections between the two spheres have been central to contemporary indigenous movements in Bolivia.[163]

Esteban Ticona's essay sheds light on the roots of this urban effervescence. His essay shows that urban social networks were key to indigenous movements of the early twentieth century, and to their leaders' efforts to decolonize knowledge, authority, and space—to forge spaces of social and racial equality. Ticona takes us back to an especially vibrant time of urban indigenous mobilization, the 1920s in La Paz. His article focuses on the life of the

Aymara educator, writer, and legal expert, Eduardo Leandro Nina Qhispi, whose political activism is a striking example of longstanding engagement in national politics by urban indigenous leaders. Ticona discusses how Nina Qhispi's efforts contributed to the decolonization of Bolivian society by linking the "education of the Indian" (a crusade championed by non-Indian elites, as Larson discusses) with the diffusion of liberatory texts, the affirmation of native cultures, and the struggle against the exploitation of the hacienda. Via written communications and the promotion of schools, Nina Qhispi presented an alternative vision of the nation, an antiracist vision rooted in intercultural respect and coexistence. His view of a decolonized Bolivia not only implied equality and the recognition of indigenous rights but respect for indigenous thought. "Indigenous," for Nina Qhispi, encompassed both the city and the countryside. It could refer to rural laborers or urban educators, to members of Indian communities or urban workers.

Charles Hale's chapter on Guatemala reveals yet another trajectory of the urban and the ethnic. In the aftermath of Guatemala's long civil war, the longstanding sense of Guatemalan society as rigidly divided between Indians and ladinos no longer holds. Drawing on ethnographic fieldwork in poor urban neighborhoods of Chimaltenango, Hale shows that young people in particular have rejected the dichotomous racial view and staked out (implicitly or explicitly) a middle ground as "mestizos"—a category that until recently had little clout in Guatemala, as Taracena makes evident in his chapter. In a study of two high school classes, Hale found that a striking one-third of the students identified as "mestizo" (rather than indigenous or ladino). Before exploring the cultural worlds of these young people, Hale traces the contradictory terms of Guatemala's bipolar ethnic ideology and how it has begun to be questioned and challenged by diverse social actors. He then considers why the new "mestizo" groups have begun to emerge in the years since the civil war, and discusses the political potential of their "mestizaje from below." Will the new mestizos become public critics of the prevailing racial hierarchy? Will they contribute to struggles against racism and help forge a society based on ideals of cultural pluralism? Will they find points of alliance with the Maya movement in its struggle for collective rights? Or will they become supporters of a quasipopulist right?[164]

Focusing on Peru, the chapter by María Elena García and José Antonio Lucero links the question of shifting ethnic identities and ideologies with the geopolitics of scholarship and knowledge. Indigenous movements have contributed in recent years to a broader effort to decolonize diverse forms of knowledge, authority, and space—including, as García and Lucero show, academic space. Such struggles necessarily provoke questions about sources and voices, about who decides who is and who is not indigenous, and about who determines who will speak for an indigenous movement. While their focus is Peru, García and Lucero note that indigenous movements throughout the region elicit these queries and provoke disputes about authenticity and legitimacy.[165] Indigenous identity is dynamic and multifaceted: it may be rural, urban, or transnational; proletarian, peasant, or professional; monolingual, bilingual, or trilingual.[166] By taking seriously disputes about authenticity, and disputes about who will speak, García's and Lucero's chapter also interrogates and challenges the sense of Peru as a place with "failed" indigenous movements. To conclude that Peru has not experienced "strong" indigenous movements like those in other Latin American countries is to presume a great deal not only about what it means to be indigenous but about what constitutes a social movement.[167]

Overall, the articles in the final part of the book show that diverse types of social movements have played a key role in exposing and contending with racism (racism that is in part a reaction against the very strength of those movements). They also point to the role that intellectuals may play in antiracist politics. The final chapters in the volume, an essay by Andrés Calla and Khantuta Muruchi and an epilogue by Pamela Calla and the research team of the Observatorio del Racismo of the University of the Cordillera (La Paz), explore the forms of racism that surfaced in Bolivia when an assembly to rewrite the constitution was convened in 2006–07. The work is part of a joint effort by the University of the Cordillera and Bolivia's Defensor del Pueblo (Ombudspersons' Office) to research, educate, and take action against the diverse forms of racism that mark Bolivia's current political conjuncture and that obstruct efforts to forge a society rooted in equality and intercultural relations and respect. A team of young researchers has been working on this project in diverse locations of Bolivia under the direction of the anthropologist Pamela Calla. Their collective project seeks to understand how and why racism and violence intensified in particular parts of the country, and how racism and violence became so alarmingly intertwined.[168]

The chapter by Calla and Muruchi focuses on the racialized discourses and confrontations that erupted in Sucre from September to November of 2007, as Bolivia's Constituent Assembly entered a phase of profound crisis. The crux of the conflict was a dispute over a demand to return Bolivia's "full capital" to Sucre (Sucre is the site of the judicial branch of government; La

Paz houses the legislative and executive branches). During the course of the Constituent Assembly, opposition groups began to drum up support for the reinstatement of Sucre as full capital.[169] At first this was a quiet affair with little popular support, but it gained momentum between July and November 2007 due to a concerted strategy. The government refused to entertain the demand for full-capital status, and this refusal also made the movement surge. By November, conflict filled the streets of Sucre. Opposition groups occupied the Gran Mariscal Theatre, where plenary sessions of the Assembly had been held. As a result, the final phase of the Constituent Assembly was relocated to a military college on the outskirts of Sucre. In the course of two days of confrontations between government security forces and capitalía supporters (from the 24th to the 25th of November), 200 people were wounded and three men of Sucre were killed: a lawyer, a student, and a carpenter. Their deaths have not been fully investigated. Civic leaders and citizens of Sucre have demanded a complete inquiry into the deaths as well as an apology from the government. The deaths are known as the deaths of La Calancha, the name of the area near the military college where the confrontation peaked.[170]

This context of an escalating conflict over a new constitution frames the discussion of political mobilization and racial discrimination that Calla and Muruchi pursue. Their analysis centers on the months just before the conflict spiraled out of control and culminated in the deaths of La Calancha. Focusing on the marches and demonstrations carried out in Sucre by university students who backed the growing demand to return the full capital to Sucre, the authors identify and discuss ongoing shifts between a structural or silent racism that presumably characterized the past, and one that became brazenly open and physically violent.[171] The aggression recorded in recent years, they argue, is a response to a series of "transgressions" of the social and political order that are in turn rooted in Morales's ascension to the presidency. While underscoring the significance of overt racism and violence, Calla and Muruchi do not chart a linear process. Instead they emphasize ongoing shifts between hidden or structural expressions of racism and more open expressions. Both modes of discrimination, they show, are equally damaging.

An epilogue to Calla and Muruchi's chapter by Pamela Calla and the research group of the Observatorio del Racismo updates the discussion by briefly describing the violence of May 24, 2008, and the antiracist agenda that emerged in its aftermath. On that day, approximately forty people of indigenous and peasant origin were forced to walk shirtless to the central plaza of

Sucre, where they were humiliated and obliged to burn symbols of their own culture and pledge allegiance to the flag of Sucre. The course of events that culminated in this violence is complex, but I attempt to summarize it here in order to provide context for the chapter by Calla and Muruchi and the epilogue on the events of May 24th.

Each May, the people of Sucre commemorate the revolt of May 25, 1809, one of the first revolts in the long process that would culminate in Bolivian independence in 1825. By tradition, the president of the republic and other government officials travel to Sucre on this day to participate in the festivities. As the 199th anniversary of the May uprising approached in 2008, civic leaders and citizens of Sucre reiterated their demand that President Morales apologize for the November 2007 deaths of La Calancha and pay heed to a series of regional demands. In this tense context, and for the first time in Bolivian history, the president planned to hold a separate celebration rather than attend the official one in the main plaza of Sucre. The parallel event was to be held in the Sucre stadium, with members of progovernment delegations from the countryside. In response to remarks that he was not welcome in Sucre unless he apologized for the deaths of November 2007, and due to clashes that took place between the military and opposition groups just outside the stadium early on the morning of May 24th, President Morales ultimately decided not to travel to Sucre at all. This was the first time in Bolivian history that a president was absent from the commemorative events of May 25th. By the time news of the president's decision was available, the rural delegations had already reached Sucre; they had come to greet the president in the Sucre stadium, where they were to receive a donation of ambulances. Because the stadium became a site of confrontation, progovernment supporters gathered in a different neighborhood to plan for a possible meeting in a nearby town. Many were dressed in festive clothing, because they had prepared for a celebration with the president. Later that day, some members of these progovernment delegations, who had taken up lodging in a neighborhood on the fringes of the city, were attacked by members of the opposition. In the course of those attacks, about forty people of indigenous and peasant origin were forced to walk to the plaza, site of the physical and symbolic violence discussed in the epilogue.

The events of May 24th are still under investigation. While we know what happened—much of it was captured on film—questions remain concerning the identities of the perpetrators and their modes of organization. No responsibility has been assigned judicially. Rather than focus on the event itself, the epilogue by the Observatorio del Racismo describes how this racial violence triggered efforts to forge an antiracist legislative agenda in Bolivia and briefly maps out the dilemmas posed by subsequent efforts to create an antiracist law.

In order to understand the work that race does today, we must take seriously the connections between hidden and overt forms of racism discussed in the final chapter and epilogue of this volume. These essays also remind us to think carefully about the relationship between racism and political mobilization, to consider when political brokering or violence is political, and when, how, and why it becomes racialized. The chapters in the final part of the book also highlight connections between racisms of the present and memories of the past. To be sure, the contemporary status of indigenous movements, neoliberal multiculturalism, and racial discourse differs significantly in Ecuador, Peru, Mexico, Guatemala, and Bolivia. But there are also some striking similarities, particularly when we look from a historical perspective at the experience of Guatemala and Bolivia. In both countries, indigenous peoples are today the recognized majority. And when indigenous issues hit the center of the political agenda, the backlash is both formidable and deeply rooted in recollections of the past. Powerful images of insurrectionary Indians have played a key role in the hostile response to indigenous movements in both countries. In Bolivia, the supply of insurrectionary images is especially abundant; these images reach back to earlier insurrectionary times, to anticolonial rebellions of the 1780s and the civil war of 1899.[172] Still it is notable that present-day indigenous mobilization in Bolivia and Guatemala can be a reminder of a relatively recent populist revolutionary past. The era of populist incorporation in both nations was associated with a social revolution in which Indians constituted a powerful political force. In both countries, indigenous mobilization radicalized seemingly moderate reforms.[173] The images of insurrection that haunt those who do not wish to relinquish power, status, or space hark back in certain instances to the revolutionary times of the 1940s and 1950s. In Guatemala, it is the image of the massacre of ladinos by Indians in Patzicía, which took place amid clientelistic struggles over the presidency that accompanied the triumph of the October Revolution of 1944.[174] In Bolivia, it is the image of Indians "invading" the city after the triumph of the 1952 revolution, or the image of peasant militias from the valleys "invading" lowland regions.[175] With this history in mind, our perspective on race and racism in the current conjuncture may shift. The violence that took place in Cochabamba, Sucre, and elsewhere in recent times does not just show that racism was there where people assumed (or wished to believe) it was not. Instead it reveals the enduring power of racism, and people's capacity to reproduce racism in a new context and a new guise.[176]

In her conclusion to the volume, Florencia Mallon reflects on elite and subaltern uses of race over the long sweep of Latin American history and draws attention to successive efforts toward multiethnic egalitarianism. She zeroes in on two crucial contexts of political opening: the early nineteenth-century struggles over nationhood that followed the wars of independence, and the twentieth-century revolutionary and socialist movements inaugurated by the Mexican Revolution. At these junctures, racial hierarchies and racist ideologies were openly contested and potentially altered—only to be reinscribed. Mallon brings to the fore a long history of antiracist politics and practices. She concludes by underscoring a fundamental tension that marks the concept of race. At once a tool of domination and a powerful source of collective and self-identification, race has been both an enduring instrument of statemaking and a contradictory trait of movements for social and political change.

✳

The essays in this book insist on a historical perspective because the memories, categories, images, and "political imaginaries" of the past shape and give life to the racisms of the present, even as they change and take on new meanings in distinct historical situations.[177] This means, too, that expressions of racism are not everywhere the same, for as people react to the political and social changes in their own world—affirming them, violently rejecting them, or ambivalently resigning themselves to them—they also visit (or are visited by) the ghosts of a peculiar collective past. It is not surprising that an emphasis on the past is voiced especially by scholars who work in or on places marked by histories of extreme violence. The depth of the violence in Guatemala compels observers to analyze not only victimization but the historical structures, processes, and imaginaries that could lead to such horrors. When the Guatemalan truth commission set about its work in the late 1990s, it had to consider who did what to whom, and how. But it was also crucial for the commission to understand *why* the repression took place, and why it was racialized.[178]

Analysts of Guatemalan history and politics have placed special emphasis on the role of memory, on the need to remember and confront the past in order to construct a "collective new beginning"—and, conversely, to "create hopeful images that might help people transcend what history has wrought."[179] But such attention to the past has been evident elsewhere, too. The social movements that pushed for Bolivia's Constituent Assembly of 2006–2007 posited a similar relationship between the future and the past, for they viewed the assembly as an act of refoundation, as an act that would confront and undo enduring colonial realities. Ecuador's Constituent Assembly of 1997 was similarly couched as an act of refoundation. And Peru's Truth and Reconciliation Commission rooted the racist violence of the civil war in a history of conquest and colonialism. In different ways, and for different reasons, the constituent assemblies of Bolivia and Ecuador and the truth commissions of Peru and Guatemala became (among other things) forums where histories of race and racism had to be written or revealed. The actors involved in these diverse proceedings pursued distinct objectives, but the results of their work overlap to some degree. Wittingly or unwittingly, these varied forums called attention to the connections between hidden and overt forms of racism—and exposed the violence of both.

❋ THE PHOTOS ON THE FOLLOWING PAGES CAPTURE A BRIEF SLICE OF time that preceded and followed the violence that took place in Sucre, Bolivia, on May 24, 2008. On that day, approximately forty people of indigenous and peasant origin were forced to walk shirtless to the central plaza, where they were humiliated and obliged to burn symbols of their culture and pledge allegiance to the flag of Sucre.

The images capture graffiti that appeared on the walls of Sucre in the days immediately before and after May 24. In accordance with a municipal regulation, the walls of buildings in the Bolivian capital are white. During the months of conflict that enveloped the city in 2008, the pristine façades of its colonial structures became both blackboard and battleground.

The first two images record the racist language used by groups opposed to the MAS government led by Evo Morales. They reveal how the political conflict had become racialized: anti-MAS sentiment is expressed as anti-Indian insult. The first of these two images includes the much-used slur discussed by Andrés Calla and Khantuta Muruchi in their chapter in this volume: the equation of MAS with llamas, a term used to insult a peasant or indigenous person. The second image is a sign of the charges of reverse racism that emerged in the course of the past several years of political transformation and conflict. The MAS government is accused not only of drug trafficking but of racism and of fostering an environment that tolerates lynching, because it presumably privileges the rights of indigenous peoples over those of nonindigenous peoples.

The next four images appeared during the days just following the violence of May 24th. The first denounces the beatings of Indians. The second designates May 25, 2008—the 199th anniversary of Sucre's anticolonial revolt—as marking 199 years of violence and racism. Rather than liberty and equality, the graffiti suggests, the uprising ushered in 199 years of discrimination. The third image evidences the accusations and counteraccusations that circulated in Sucre regarding members of the crowd responsible for the violence. It questions (with the word "*dizque*!!") the rumor that the perpetrators were "Indian students" who beat their "Indian parents."

The final image expresses the sense of indignation associated with what was perceived to be the opposition's monopoly-like hold on the local press. It also evinces a refusal to accept silence. The visible layers of erasure and ink—in all six images—are traces of a long battle waged on the city's white walls.

Figure 1. Anti-MAS graffiti equating MAS supporters with llamas.
Sucre, May 17, 2008. Credit: Laura Gotkowitz.

Figure 2. Anti-MAS graffiti associating MAS with lynching, drug trafficking, and racism.
Sucre, May 18, 2008. Credit: Michel Gobat.

Figure 3. Graffiti denouncing the violence of May 24, 2008: "To Kick Indians is not Christian!!" Sucre, May 28, 2008. Credit: Michel Gobat.

Figure 4. Graffiti denouncing the violence of May 24, 2008, as the manifestation of 199 years of violence and racism. Sucre, May 28, 2008. Credit: Michel Gobat.

Figure 5. Graffiti questioning rumors that Indian students were responsible for the violence of May 24, 2008: "Indian students kick, beat their Indian parents / So they say!!" Sucre, May 28, 2008. Credit: Michel Gobat.

Figure 6. Graffiti denouncing the press in Sucre: "The walls will stop speaking when the press tells the truth." Sucre, May 28, 2008. Credit: Michel Gobat.

Notes

1. Romero 2007, 3.

2. Ibid., 12–13. The prefect, an elected official since the December 2005 elections, is the highest authority of a department. The prefect in power at the time (Manfred Reyes Villa) was a leading member of the opposition to the government of Evo Morales. For an in-depth analysis of the events of January 11th, see Equipo Permanente de Reflexión Interdisciplinaria 2007. For a summation of the political, social, and economic factors at stake, see also Carvajal 2007, 74–75.

3. Zegada 2007, 80. Morales was elected in a landslide victory in December 2005 and re-elected in December 2009. He is the first Bolivian president to self-identify, and to be identified publicly, as indigenous. On the politics of indigenous identity in present-day Bolivia, see Canessa 2006.

4. Tórrez 2007, 40–41.

5. Zegada 2007, 81.

6. Romero 2007, 15.

7. Equipo Permanente de Reflexión Interdisciplinaria 2007, 8–9, 11.

8. Tórrez 2007, 45–46.

9. De la Torre 2005, 62–63. See, for example, Cervone and Rivera 1999; de la Torre 1996, 1999, 2005; Castellanos Guerrero 2001; Comisión de la Verdad y Reconciliación 2003; Ari Chachaki 2007a, 2007b; Manrique 1995, 1996; Observatorio del racismo en Bolivia 2008; *Fe y Pueblo* 2007; Equipo Permanente de Reflexión Interdisciplinaria 2007; Arenas Bianchi et al. 1999; Casaus Arzú 1991; Taracena 2002, 2004.

10. See, for example, Lasso 2007. In her study of the myth of racial equality in early postindependent Colombia, Lasso shows that the silencing of racism was not a done deal: denunciations of racism had to be actively eliminated from the public sphere.

11. The term "Indian" bears the traces of a history of conquest and colonialism. The colonial act of naming the region's diverse ethnic groups "Indians" was a powerful mark of racial domination, one that aimed to homogenize those groups by assigning them to a uniform category. Yet the term Indian has also been reappropriated as a sign of self-identification, especially in recent times, one shaped by struggles against diverse forms of colonialism. The phrase "the people called Indians," from the seventeenth-century Huarochirí Manuscript—in all likelihood the work of Andean authors—beautifully captures the complex history of the word "Indian." See Salomon and Urioste 1991, 41 and 153. See also Sinclair Thomson's chapter in this volume.

12. Warren 1998a, 8. The importance of indigenous peoples to a national polity or economy cannot be reduced to a demographic calculus. In Colombia, just 2 percent of the population identifies as indigenous or lives in a territory set aside for indigenous peoples (*resguardo*), yet the size of the territories and the resources concentrated in them make indigenous lands a site of conflict. Indigenous peoples occupy

an important place in the Colombian national consciousness, due in part to the strength of their political organizations (Rappaport 2005, 1–2).

13. My discussion of the "work" race does, and how it is linked with other forms of power, is inspired by Holt 2000, see especially 27–28 and 119–20. On the connections between "race-thinking" and other types of power, see also Silverblatt 2004, especially 17–18. On the forceful links between regionalism and race in Latin American history, see Appelbaum et al. 2003b; Weinstein 2003. On race, gender, and sexuality, see, for example, Findlay 1999; Stepan 1991; Caulfield 2000; Putnam 2002; de la Cadena 2000; Weismantel 2001; Gotkowitz 2003; Stolcke 1994; Smith 1995; and several of the essays in Appelbaum et al. 2003a.

14. The work on race and racism in Latin America is vast and growing. For some of the recent works published in Latin America, see endnote 9 of this introduction. Recent works published in the United States include Hale 2006; de la Cadena 2000; L. Lewis 2003; Silverblatt 2004; Zulawski 2007; Larson 2004; Wade 1997, 2003; Poole 1997; Putnam 2002; Appelbaum 2003; Appelbaum et al. 2003a; Fischer 2004; Roldán 2002; Ferrer 1999; de la Fuente 2001b, 2008; Helg 1995, 2004; Graham 1990; Gould 1998; Mallon 2005; Grandin 2000; Andrews 2004; Bronfman 2004; Gotkowitz 2007; Clark 1998; Colloredo-Mansfeld 1998, 1999; Dulitzky 2005; Dzidzienyo and Oboler 2005; Gustafson 2006; Htun 2004; Knight 1990; Safford 1991; Lomnitz 2005; Smith 1995, 1997; Stepan 1991; Stolcke 1994; Weinstein 2003; A. Stern 2003; Weismantel 2001; Weismantel and Eisenman 1998; Sanders 2004; Canessa 2005.

15. The following discussion of the tendencies that mark works on race and racism draws on Hale 2006, 30.

16. Wade 1997, 10.

17. Stoler 1997, 197; Hale 2006, 30; Wade 1997, 10–12.

18. Winant 2001, 2, 272, 290–93, 300–308. See also Hale 2006, 28–31. For more on the undoing of scientific racism from within the scientific community, see Wade 1997, 12–14. The declarations made by UNESCO after the Second World War, those concerning the fundamental sameness of all human beings, are often taken to exemplify the view that took hold in this era (Wade 1997, 13).

19. Hale 2006, 30.

20. Stoler 1997, 197–98. See also Silverblatt 2004, 17.

21. Silverblatt 2004, 198, 251; Hodes 2003; Wade 2003; A. Stern 2003.

22. A. Stern 2003, 205, n. 4.

23. Stoler 1997, 187.

24. Ibid., 198; Holt 2000, 7–9, 18–21, 119; Hodes 2003.

25. See, for example, NACLA 2001b, 15. See also Wade 2008 for a recent discussion of such works.

26. Stoler 1997; Winant 2001; Hodes 2003; Holt 2000, 7–9; Gordon 1999; Jacobson 1998; Appelbaum et al. 2003. For a similar approach, concerning the history of race and racism in Germany, see Chin and Fehrenbach 2009, especially 13–14.

27. Martínez 2008, 266. Martínez argues that the colonial concept of purity of

blood was itself based on a specific understanding of race. But she does so cautiously, emphasizing that both categories were linked with religion and lineage (Martínez 2008, 12–13). She also shows how purity of blood had peculiarly gendered connotations, with implications for a kind of sexual policing and politics.

28. Hale 2006, 210; see also 28–31.

29. In 1949, with the Nazi attempt to annihilate European Jews a vivid and harrowing memory, UNESCO set out to create an antiracist public education project and convened a group of scientists and social scientists to refute the scientific racism of the Nazis. But the international team had trouble agreeing on basic principles. In the end, it produced two distinct "statements on race." Only a minority of the scholars concluded that race was a social construct rather than a biological truth; another group held fast to the idea of innate racial differences. To be sure, the second group did not defend biological racism, but nor did that group's statement fully repudiate the concept of race (Brattain 2007).

30. Holt 2000, 20–21, 27.

31. Ibid. See also Poole 1997.

32. See Holt 2000, 27. A related way to approach such reframing is to consider how and when race is "operationalized." See Chin and Fehrenbach 2009, 14–15.

33. Chin and Fehrenbach 2009, 14–15. For a discussion of diverse approaches to explaining racism and the need to link "individual thought, belief, and action" with "societywide phenomenon," see Holt 1998.

34. See, among others, Martínez 2008; Stolcke 1994; Burns 1998.

35. The term "racialization" is generally used to refer to the use of hierarchical discourses, images, and practices to mark differences among human beings (see Appelbaum et al. 2003b, 2). Racialization also refers to the ways that race becomes imbued with meaning and importance, to the ways that the fiction of race comes to be considered something real (see A. Stern 2003, 205, n. 4).

36. Holt 2000, 53.

37. In their introduction to *Race and Nation in Modern Latin America*, Appelbaum et al. (2003b) develop an illuminating historical analysis of race that centers on four key moments in modern Latin American history (the independence struggles of the early nineteenth century, the late nineteenth-century decades of state-building, the populist era of the 1930s and 1940s, and the post–Second World War period). While the editors recognize diverse factors and forces, their analysis centers on nation-building—on the powerful and persistent relationship between nation-building and race. Their primary concern is to trace changing definitions of race in modern Latin America and to understand the ways that those varied meanings have been shaped by processes of nationmaking (Appelbaum et al. 2003b, 2–9). While race is clearly central to nationmaking, my purpose in highlighting four key moments of the colonial and modern eras is to think broadly about the many different types of economic, social, and political work that race may do—including the work

of nation-building but also the effects of labor markets, social policy, state violence, and the hierarchical encounters of everyday life.

38. This is not to reduce the complexities and shifting characteristics of colonial life and rule to a single moment, but instead to highlight the centrality of colonial racemaking and its legacies for postindependent societies.

39. See S. Stern 1992.

40. See also Schwartz and Salomon 1999; Martínez 2008.

41. Schwartz and Salomon 2000.

42. Another important category is "caste." As L. Lewis (2003) discusses, if race was blood—"bad blood"—caste referenced any kind of non-Jewish or non-Muslim ancestry; caste was more than blood, it could include social connections and cultural qualities (L. Lewis 2003, 22–26). On the distinctions between race and caste, and how they overlapped at particular junctures, see also Martínez (2008). On caste in colonial New Spain, see also Cope (1994). On the meanings of caste after independence, see the chapter by Barragán in this volume.

43. Brattain 2007, 1413.

44. Burns, this volume.

45. L. Lewis 2003, 26.

46. Ibid., 29–31.

47. Ibid., 20–22.

48. Ibid., 26; Lomnitz 1992. Some studies suggest that these divergent conceptions of Indianness and blackness hardened over the course of the colonial era. The concept of purity of blood was first deployed in the fifteenth century against *conversos*. At that time purity amounted to the absence of a Jewish or heretical background; it meant immaculate Christian lineage. As the concept journeyed to and acquired new meaning in the colonies, purity came to be associated with Spanishness and eventually with whiteness, while impurity became more closely connected with blackness (Martínez 2008, 1–2, 243–49, 267–68, 271–72). Still, even when purity moved closer to phenotype, religion never dropped out (ibid., 249, 270).

49. Restall 2005, 3–4; L. Lewis 2003, 5.

50. See Martínez 2008, 249, 270.

51. On these forms of power, and their connections with ideas about race, see Holt 2000, 34–35, 53; Appelbaum et al. 2003b; Poole 1997.

52. Gotkowitz 2007, 39–42.

53. If in 1880 Indian communities held approximately half of Bolivia's farmland, by 1930 their holdings had been diminished to less than a third (Klein 1992, 152).

54. McCreery 1989; McCreery 1994, 181–86.

55. See also Reeves 2006.

56. Taracena 2002, 267, 337.

57. Grandin 2000. See especially chapter 6.

58. Taracena, this volume.

59. Ibid. For a more detailed discussion of the segregationist tendencies of agricultural labor, see Taracena 2002, 267–337.

60. In Guatemala, the coercive draft—or *mandamiento*, as it was known—was codified in an 1877 law that made departmental authorities responsible for granting requests from planters for Indian labor. There was one critical exception: workers who already owed debts to employers were exempt. In essence, then, the mandamiento served to enforce debt peonage, which represented the primary form of rural labor in Guatemala (McCreery 1994, 188–193, 220, 222–23). As Taracena shows, although the rules changed over the course of the early twentieth century, in one way or another forced indigenous labor remained the primary form of rural work until the October Revolution of 1944. And even after the revolution triumphed, some voices championed coercion as a means to lift the nation's production and "civilize" Indians. To be sure, the revolutionaries repealed a 1934 vagrancy law, which obliged men who did not have a land title or an "adequate profession" to work 100 or more days on a plantation. They also rescinded the law requiring road work, and placed restrictions on debt labor. Nevertheless, vagrancy continued to be a crime and all Guatemalan men were obliged to hold evidence of employment or ownership of land (Grandin 2004, 38). In short, traces of the old system of coerced labor persisted in the countryside. See also Taracena 2004.

61. For further discussion of the ideology, and how it has begun to come undone, see Charles Hale's chapter in this volume.

62. Lokken 2004. On the incorporation of free blacks and mulattos into the ladino category, see ibid.

63. On this invisibility, see Lokken 2004. Lokken argues that the invisibility was a product of colonial officials' overwhelming dependence on the labor of the indigenous majority (10); as a result, both free and enslaved blacks enjoyed a certain social mobility that allowed them to contest the burdens and racial stigma of tribute and, eventually, to assimilate into the ladino (non-Indian) sector of society (10). See also Komisaruk 2010.

64. Hodes 2006.

65. Ibid., 258.

66. Comparative insight on Latin American censuses can be gained from the following works: Grieshaber 1985; Clark 1998; Nobles 2000; A. Stern 2003, 20; A. Stern 2009; Loveman 2009; Taracena's essay in this volume.

67. Taracena, this volume.

68. On the nineteenth century, see Barragán 1999; on the early twentieth century, see Gotkowitz 2007, 43–45, 62–68.

69. Libretas contained copies of labor contracts and lists of debts, credits, and the number of days worked (McCreery 1994). Segregationist measures were strongest in Guatemala, but some such tendencies (in the draft or in educational policy) were visible at the local level in other Central American countries. See Gould 2005, 67–68.

70. Holt 2000, 21–22. Holt argues that "the meaning of race and the nature of racism articulate with (perhaps even are defined by) the given social formation of a particular historical moment." By social formation, he means "all the interrelated structures of economic, political, and social power, as well as the systems of significa-tion (that is, cultural systems) that give rise to and/or reflect those structures" (22).

71. Gould and Gudmundson 1997.

72. See, for example, Mörner 1967.

73. But see Mallon 1996; Smith 1997; Gould 1998; de la Cadena 2000.

74. Programa de Investigación Estratégica en Bolivia 2007. On the overlapping uses of indigenismo and mestizaje in Mexico, see Knight 1990; Tenorio Trillo 2009.

75. See, among others, Brading 1988; Knight 1990; Vaughan 1997; Vaughan and Lewis 2006b; Dawson 2004; Tenorio Trillo 2009.

76. De la Cadena 2000; Knight 1990; Mallon 1992; Mendoza 2000; Poole 1997; Wade 1997; Poole 1990. On the links between this wave of indigenismo and nineteenth-century ideas about Indians, see Earle 2007.

77. Lomnitz 2006, 343. See also Lomnitz 2001b, 231.

78. García 2005, 66–73.

79. Zulawski 2000.

80. Gotkowitz 2007, 43–45, 62–68.

81. Bigenho 2006; Salmón 1997.

82. Gould 2005, 53.

83. Lomnitz 2001a, 231. See also Knight 1990; A. Stern 2003, 191; de la Peña 1999, 290.

84. See Dawson 2004; de la Peña 1999, 291–92; S. Lewis 2006, 176.

85. The National Institute of Anthropology and History was founded in 1929; the National School of Anthropology and History in 1938; and the Inter-American Indi-genista Institute in 1940.

86. National in the sense of anthropologists who study their own nation (Lomnitz 2001a, 230).

87. Lomnitz 2001b. See also Vaughan and Lewis 2006b, 13; Alonso 2004.

88. Alonso 2004.

89. Lomnitz 2001a, 242, 250–52. Such interventions could have positive implica-tions. In the early twentieth century, they entailed efforts to increase the salaries of government employees in order to pressure landlords to raise the pay of their peons, as well as attempts to distribute land, to promote the building of roads and schools, and to provide medical services (ibid., 252).

90. Alonso 2004.

91. Ibid.

92. Klarén 2000, chapters 8 and 9; de la Cadena 2000, chapter 2.

93. Gould 1998, 2001. On mestizaje in Honduras and Guatemala, see, respectively, Euraque 2004; Taracena 2005. For a comparative perspective on mestizaje in Central America, see Gould 2005. On mestizaje in Central America and the Hispanic Carib-bean, see also Gudmundson and Scarano 1998.

94. Gould 2005, 62; Gotkowitz 2007, 65–67.

95. Poole's article thus forces us to rethink the commonly held notion of a linear switch from an assimilationist mestizaje (of the 1950s and 1960s) to a neoliberal multiculturalism (of the 1990s). It reminds us that multiculturalism has a history: the power of multiculturalism as a tool of governance today owes something to the historical depth of the ideal of multiculturalism as a form of political authority. On the historical roots of official multiculturalism, see also Wade 2003, 276–77.

96. See also A. Stern 2003, 188.

97. Poole, this volume.

98. See Wade 2005, 245.

99. Lomnitz 2001a. See also Poole's article in this volume.

100. Knight 1990, 101. See also A. Stern 2003; Kourí 2010.

101. See de la Cadena 2000.

102. See Mendoza's discussion of this problem (2008, 1–15, 169–81, 184, n. 7).

103. See Dawson 2004; Mendoza 2008; Bigenho 2006; López 2006.

104. Bigenho 2006. On the lived experience of mestizaje, see also Wade 2005.

105. Mendoza 2008, 7.

106. Ibid., 181.

107. Alonso 2004.

108. Hale 1989; Tenorio Trillo 2009; Kourí 2010.

109. See especially Truett and Young 2004; Katz 1981; Alonso 1995; A. Stern 2004.

110. Truett and Young 2004.

111. A. Stern 2004, 303.

112. A. Stern 2004, 299–300; A. Stern 2009.

113. Ngai 1999, 91.

114. Truett and Young 2004, 11. On racemaking, violence, and the making of borders in Latin America, see also Derby 1994; Turits 2002.

115. For other such transborder perspectives on race, involving both shared and unshared boundaries, see, for example, Seigel 2009; Rosemblatt 2009.

116. Castellanos Guerrero 2001, 623; de la Torre Espinosa 2005, 63–64; de la Torre Espinosa 1999; Pallares 2002, 60.

117. Dulitzky 2005, 53.

118. Ibid.; Htun 2004, 72. For a detailed discussion of the measures, the controversy over them, and their history, see Htun 2004. On such policies in Colombia, see Wade 2008, 189.

119. But we should be careful not to assume a complete turnabout. The supposed silence of the past was far from totalizing. Just a few of the examples of the antiracist discourses that emerged in earlier times are the antidiscrimination clauses that were incorporated into some of Latin America's "social constitutions" of the 1940s. These clauses did not emerge from thin air; they were the product of intensive lobbying and grassroots political activism. See Gotkowitz 2007, 101–3, 319, nn. 5–6; Htun 2004, 64–65; Bronfman 2004. On antiracist social movements of the late nineteenth century

and early twentieth century, see Ferrer 1999; de la Fuente 2001b; and Andrews 2004. For distinct perspectives on such movements in the era of the early nineteenth-century wars of independence, see Múnera 1998; Helg 2004; Lasso 2007.

120. *NACLA* 2001a, 13.

121. Ibid.

122. Grimson 2001.

123. Grimson 2005, 25. On the racism of the 1990s, see also *NACLA* 1999, 50–52.

124. Grimson 2005, 28–29. On the persistent discrimination, see, for example, "El costo del 'sueño argentino,' " *Opinión* (March 24, 2008): 10A.

125. Warren 2002, 157.

126. Degregori 2004, 81, and 81 n. 20. On the role of race and racism in the conflict, see also Manrique 1995; Manrique 1996; S. Stern 1998.

127. Milton 2007, 6; García 2005, 36.

128. Comisión de la Verdad y Reconciliación 2003, 102.

129. This contrasts sharply with the situation in Argentina, Chile, and Uruguay, where the primary victims of the violence did become the subjects of public opinion (Comisión de la Verdad y Reconciliación 2003, 102–103).

130. Milton 2007, 22; Degregori 2004, 81.

131. Hale 2006, 160–61.

132. On the forces that made this possible in Peru, and the human rights and memory work that took place before the commission was established, see Degregori 2004.

133. Milton 2007, 7; García 2005, 54.

134. García 2005, 48; Comisión de la verdad y Reconciliación 2003, 130–31.

135. Grandin 2003, 339; Hale 2006, 66–67; Sanford 2003.

136. Degregori 2004, 82.

137. Grandin 2003, 340; Grandin 2005.

138. Grandin 2003, 342. See also Oglesby 2007.

139. Milton 2007, 4, 7.

140. Oglesby 2007, 91–92.

141. Ibid., 78–79, 91–92. On the scope and limits of the Peruvian commission, and alternative forms of truth telling, see Milton 2007.

142. García 2005, 36.

143. *NACLA* 2005, 19; Wade 1997, 1; Andolina 2003; Van Cott 2000; Rappaport 2005.

144. Castellanos Guerrero 2001, 623–24.

145. Zamosc 1994, 56, 63; Pallares 2002, 59.

146. Jackson and Warren 2005, 554.

147. Lagos and Calla 2007, 28. Jackson and Warren 2005, 565.

148. Gustafson 2006. But it is crucial not to reproduce a dichotomous view, as Gustafson points out. There are certainly people in the western regions who oppose the indigenous projects; likewise, proponents of those projects may be found in the

east, which is itself home to many indigenous peoples. The indigenous peoples who inhabit Bolivia's eastern lowlands include those native to the area as well as migrants from the western highlands. For more on political and social dynamics in Bolivia's east, see Gustafson 2006.

149. Gustafson 2006; Calla and Muruchi, this volume; Equipo Permanente de Reflexión Interdisciplinaria 2007; Observatorio del racismo en Bolivia 2008.

150. Walsh 2001, 197.

151. Sawyer 1997, 66, 73–75. On the roots of Ecuador's contemporary indigenous movements in leftist and indigenous politics of the past, see Becker 2008.

152. Walsh 2001, 180; Lucero 2001, 65. See also Whitten 2004, 449.

153. Walsh 2001, 197.

154. Ibid., 198–99; Romero 2007; Equipo Permanente de Reflexión Interdisciplinaria 2007; Espósito Guevara 2008.

155. Warren 2002, 150. On the course of the peace process, see also Warren 1998a, chapter 2.

156. Warren 2002, 157; Sieder 2001, 205–6.

157. Warren 2002, 158.

158. Ibid., 158–59; Hale 2006, 36.

159. Warren 2002, 171–72.

160. This paragraph is based on Hale 2006.

161. Hale 2006, 11, 20, 30–31, 129–32, 215. On these social tensions, see also Warren 1998a, 28, 47–51.

162. Albó 2006, 333.

163. See especially Albó 2006; Lazar 2008.

164. For a vivid view of a contrasting youth culture, that of El Alto, Bolivia, see Albó 2006, 339–42. The indigenous identities and radical politics that characterize El Alto are not representative of all Bolivian cities.

165. García and Lucero, this volume. On indigenous movements and the politics of knowledge, see also Rappaport 2005.

166. Lagos and Calla 2007, 15.

167. For further treatment of these issues, see Lucero 2006; García 2005. For a consideration of similar questions in the Colombian context, see Rappaport 2005.

168. Albarracín and Calla 2008; Calla 2008. On other efforts to contest racism and decolonize public institutions in Bolivia, see Farthing 2007, 6–7.

169. In 1899, a civil war was fought between Sucre-based Conservatives and La Paz–based Liberals. Following the triumph of the Liberals in this war, legislative and executive branches of government were transferred from Sucre to La Paz. Sucre remained the site of the judicial branch, and the capital of Bolivia, but its full-capital status was lost as La Paz became the nation's seat of government.

170. For a chronology and discussion of these events, see Carrasco Alurralde and Albó 2008; de la Fuente Jeria 2008.

171. For a brief discussion of the forms of racism that marked the Assembly, both inside its sessions and as it spilled into the streets, see also de la Fuente Jeria 2008, 99; Carrasco Alurralde and Albó 2008, 121.

172. The first date refers to the anticolonial rebellions of the late eighteenth century led by Túpac Amaru and Tupaj Katari; the second marks the Indian rebellion for self-rule that dovetailed with Bolivia's civil war of 1899. The violence that erupted in Sucre in November 2007 fed on traumatic memories of an episode from the civil war: the massacre of students from Sucre—soldiers in the Conservative army—by pro-Liberal indigenous forces in Ayo-Ayo. As demands to return the nation's political capital to Sucre intensified, an image of "savage" Indians and "noble" students circulated in the local media (Espósito Guevara 2008, 6–7; Torrico Zas 2008).

173. On Guatemala, see Forster 2001; Handy 1994; Grandin 2004. On Bolivia, see Gotkowitz 2007; as I argue in the book, in order to fully perceive these radical effects in Bolivia it is necessary to view the 1952 revolution in conjunction with the powerful rural unrest of the 1940s.

174. In reality, there were two massacres. In the first, Indians killed fourteen ladinos; in the second—reprisal for the first—the army killed 300 Indians. For ladinos, the massacre of ladinos remains a powerful symbol of Indian racism against ladinos and a reminder of a presumably ever-present threat of indigenous violence. It has become ingrained as an "image of collective Indian retribution" (Hale 2006, 122–23). The massacre of Indians, in contrast, is not embedded in the national imaginary and has only recently begun to be discussed in public (Hale 2006, 52–53, 122–23, 146–47; see also Adams 1992; Adams 1990).

175. On the images of peasant power and confrontation associated with the 1952 revolution, see Gordillo 2007.

176. See Holt 2000, 56.

177. Ibid., 20; Hale 2006, especially chapter 5. On the importance of understanding race and racism historically, see also Holt 1998.

178. Grandin 2003, 340. For a discussion of a similar problematic concerning the 1932 massacre of peasants in El Salvador, see Gould and Lauria-Santiago 2008, 209–39.

179. Hale 1997a, 823–24; Arias 1997, 826.

PART I ❋ The Uses of "Race"

in Colonial Latin America

Unfixing Race

KATHRYN BURNS

Race in lineage is understood to be bad, as to have some Moorish or Jewish race.
—Sebastián de Covarrubias Horozco, *Tesoro de la lengua castellana* (1611)

"We order and command that no one, of whatsoever quality and condition, be received into the said Order . . . unless he be a Gentleman . . . born of legitimate matrimony, and not of Jewish, Moorish, Heretic, nor Plebeian race."
—Real Academia Española, *Diccionario de autoridades* (1726–39)

The word "race" has never been stable. Old dictionaries make this clear, while pointing up the persistent racism that avails itself of categories even as they change.[1] Covarrubias, for example, begins his definition of *raza* with "the caste of purebred horses, which are marked with brands to distinguish them," and moves on to cloth, in which race denotes "the coarse thread that is distinct from the other threads in the weave."[2] Only then does he turn to lineage, mentioning Moors and Jews. Jews and Moors also appear in the Real Academia's *Diccionario*, in an embedded snippet of the rules of the prestigious Order of Calatrava, but in significantly augmented company: alongside the races of Heretics and Plebeians. Both definitions emphasize the term's negative associations.[3] And each differs strikingly from modern usages rooted in scientific racism and the many ways it has been used and contested.[4]

Such definitional drift, I'll argue, bespeaks complex histories marked by very local struggles as well as far-flung imperial rivalries. Scholars in many fields increasingly put the term "race" in scare quotes. This is a welcome move to unfix race—to signal that the categories we recognize as racial are not stable or panhistoric—but is only the beginning of a project we can take much further. The point of carefully historicizing racial usages is to better understand both early modern racisms and those of our time.[5]

Consider, for example, that one of the most potent racial insults one could hurl in early seventeenth-century Peru was "*judío*" (Jew). Jews were stigmatized as *la mala casta blanca*, or "bad whites."[6] This is a historically specific frame of reference, one Albert Sicroff calls "religious racism."[7] Its Iberian genealogy is quite involved and links together histories that exist on separate shelves of our libraries: the histories of Spanish Jews, many of whom converted under pressure to Roman Catholicism after the anti-Jewish pogroms of 1391 and were known as *conversos*, and Spanish Muslims who did likewise, known as *moriscos*. By the early fifteenth century, "Old Christians" increasingly regarded "New Christian" populations with deep suspicion.[8] A sincere convert could not, at a glance, be distinguished from a false or backsliding convert, and considerable anxiety centered on those Spaniards who allegedly still practiced in secret a faith they had publicly renounced. Spain's monarchs created the Spanish Inquisition in the late 1470s primarily to discipline suspected "judaizers"—people who were thought to practice Judaism clandestinely. And concerns began to fix on the supposed cleanliness of people's bloodlines. More and more Spanish institutions and municipalities devised and enforced statutes that excluded those not descended from Old Christians.[9]

In short, the Castilian politics of race circa 1492 hinged on the purity of one's Christianity, increasingly defined as a matter not simply of belief and practice but of inheritance, or *limpieza de sangre* (purity of blood)—something that could not be changed at the baptismal font. The intensifying persecution of those believed to be of impure Christian lineage was intimately related to the consolidation of the lineage of the Spanish absolutist state.[10] A militant, intolerant Christianity drove both processes. As the inquisitorial policing of distinctions between correct and heretical Christians got underway, the Spanish monarchs Isabella and Ferdinand were campaigning to defeat the last Iberian stronghold of Islam, the kingdom of Granada. The year they succeeded, 1492, was also the year in which they obliged Spain's remaining Jews to convert to Christianity or emigrate. Ten years later, Muslims were given the same choice.[11] After another century of tensions, Philip III moved to expel all moriscos in 1609.

From 1391 to 1609, the status of New Christians—who were not recognizable at a glance, but were considered by Old Christians to be ineradicably tainted in their blood—became a white-hot political and cultural issue in Spain. And militant Christianity, sharply defined against Spain's internal, demonized Others, was part of the mental baggage that Columbus and the Iberians who followed him brought along as they invaded and subjugated American peoples after 1492. Columbus's famous account of his first voyage begins with the touchstone moment of the fall of Granada: "This present year of 1492 . . . I saw the Royal Standards of Your Highnesses placed by force of arms on the towers of the Alhambra."[12] Columbus's description of the Caribbean peoples he encounters on the other side of the Atlantic has an eerie echo of conflicts of the recent past: according to him, they live in houses that "are all made like Moorish campaign tents."[13] (He refers to his own companions interchangeably as "Spaniards" and "Christians.") Cortés likewise wrote of Yucatecan houses of rooms "small and low in the Moorish fashion."[14] As many historians have noted, the horizon of conquest these men had in mind as they measured their exploits was that of the Spanish *reconquista* and the cleansing of the realm of their sovereigns from the stain of the "sects" of Moses and Mohammed.

Before long, in each American viceroyalty over which Spanish rule was established, those suspected of secretly practicing their Jewish or Muslim faith could be persecuted by an American office of the Spanish Inquisition—and they were persecuted, as Irene Silverblatt shows in the Lima case of Manuel Bautista Pérez.[15] But to expel all non-Christians and suspicious converts was clearly not an option. On the contrary, the Iberian monarchs were obliged by an agreement with the pope to convert the natives of the Americas to Christianity. One way or another, Iberians in the Americas were going to have to coexist with an enormous population of "idolators" and brand new converts—just the kind of people they had learned to despise back home.

Moreover, to stand any chance of success whatsoever, Iberians would need the Americans' help. Assimilation was the initial framework the Spanish Crown advocated during a few brief and experimental years. One royal decree went so far as to recommend that some Spaniards marry Indian women, and some Indian men marry Spanish women, so "that they may communicate with and teach one another . . . and the Indians become men and women of reason."[16] Proximity to Spaniards would give Americans a "good example" of Christian conduct to follow, or so it was thought. When the dramatic news from Las Casas and others showed just how badly things were going, however, royal advisors realized that a new course had to be charted. They gradually assembled the juridical fiction of "two republics," the *república de es-*

pañoles and its corresponding *república de indios*. These were propounded in a series of royal orders strikingly different from those issued not long before. By the 1570s, the crown was betting on a strategy of physical segregation of Indians from non-Indians, and the forced relocation or "reduction" of the former into all-Indian towns.[17] Yet it is crucial to note that the overall goal of assimilation still held for the indigenous nobility, those whom Spaniards indiscriminately termed *caciques*.[18] Special schools were erected to convert the sons of native leaders to Christianity and give them a thoroughly Spanish upbringing. By the late sixteenth century, indigenous nobles were among the Spanish clergy's most enthusiastic new Christians.

However, the "two republics" model failed from its inception to keep Spaniards and indigenous peoples apart. As they settled in and erected towns, cities, and viceroyalties, Iberian immigrants—overwhelmingly male—brought with them numerous African slaves and peninsular slaves of African descent.[19] No one seemed to stay in the place the crown had assigned. And as part of the violence of conquest and occupation, the invading Europeans and their allies took indigenous women as spoils of war, slaves, servants, and sometimes as wives, appropriating native and enslaved women's bodies. Reports from the new viceroyalties mark new categories of people: *mestizo, mulato, zambo,* and so forth. These were not terms of self-identification, but of convenient Spanish labeling. They gave Spanish authorities a linguistic handle on those who fit neither of the two republics—and who seemed, to Spaniards' dismay, to threaten both republics with their disorderly conduct. These were Spaniards' impure New World Others.

Were these new categories racial? They did not imply clear color lines.[20] But they did have to do with race in contemporary Castilian terms, as they referenced and linked the issues of blood (im)purity and fresh conversion to Christianity. These new labels—and that of "Indian" as well—were applied to people who, like the conversos and moriscos of Spain, were new converts (or their descendants). The point was to delineate places for them in a society in which Christianization would, in theory, be assured by Christian masters and priests. Spaniards' designs never worked quite as intended. Still, these designs can be seen as driven by the racial considerations of a particular time and place: the early Castilian mission to impose Christianity and extirpate American beliefs considered false and heretical.[21]

But what exactly did new terms like "mestizo," "mulato," and "zambo" mean to those who were devising them in places like Peru or New Spain?

What kinds of practices, choices, and lifeways are hidden behind them? And can we see in the written record any terms other than those used by Spaniards, perhaps subaltern usages? I'd like to consider these questions by examining the history of the Spanish terms that were being introduced and circulated in sixteenth-century Cuzco. It is hard to trace anything about Cuzco's history before midcentury through archival work, since most of the paper trail has been scattered or lost.[22] But published chronicles are very rich and give us much to go on.

Take part 1, book 9, chapter 31 of the *Comentarios reales* of Garcilaso de la Vega, el Inca, who was born in Cuzco in 1539: "New names for naming new generations." Himself the son of a Spanish father and an Inca mother, Garcilaso focuses this section on mixture, beginning with laudatory comments on Spaniards and their slaves: "There [in America] from these two nations they have made others, mixed in all ways."[23] With this introduction, Garcilaso starts his inventory of categories with Spaniards, noting the distinction between those born in Spain and those born overseas. But what comes across strongly in this passage is the distinctions drawn by Africans:

> The children of Spanish men and women born there [in America] are called *criollo* or *criolla*, to indicate that they are born in the Indies. This name was invented by the blacks. . . . It means, among them, "a black born in the Indies." They invented it to differentiate those who go from here [Spain], and were born in Guinea, from those who were born there. Because they consider themselves more honorable and of better quality, for having been born in the fatherland, than their children who were born in a foreign land. And the parents are offended if they are called criollos.
>
> Spaniards, for like reasons, have begun using this term for those born there, so that Spaniards and Africans born there are called *criollo* or *criolla*.[24]

Here the subjectivity attributed to African men and women is in the foreground; the Spaniards are copycats. And the terms "criollo" and "criolla" refer both to Africans and Spaniards, the better to get across another criterion of difference and hierarchy that mattered: one's natal land or *patria*. Why did birthplace matter? Garcilaso indicates that it had to do with honor and quality, what contemporaries might also have described as *condición*.[25] And Garcilaso means the honor and quality of unfree people. This remarkable passage thoroughly upends our expectations of Garcilaso's contemporaries and imagined readers. He gets us to understand criollos through the subjectivity of African men and women concerned with the defense of their honor.

Garcilaso continues by introducing the terms "mulato" and "mulata," but not as the children of black and white parents, as our histories of colonial Latin America usually define them. By his account, "The child of a black man and an Indian woman—or of an Indian man and a black woman—is called a *mulato* or *mulata*. And their children are called *cholos*. This word is from the Barlovento islands. It means 'dog,' not of pure breed but of the very vicious *gozcones*. And Spaniards use it to defame and insult."[26] Garcilaso moves us further on the terrain of contemporary usage, pointing to active trafficking in words over wide geographic expanses. Here impurity among those of African descent is not just stigmatized but bestialized.

Garcilaso gets to his own background next, and defines "mestizo" with reference to himself: "They call us *mestizos*, to say that we are mixed from both nations," both Spanish and Indian.[27] He approaches this term much more personally. But note that the bounds of his sympathy have limits:

It was imposed by the first Spaniards to have children in the Indies. And because the name [mestizo] was given us by our fathers according to their understanding, I call myself this with pride and am honored by it. In the Indies, however, if one of them is told "you're a mestizo" or "he's a mestizo," they take it as an insult. This is why they have embraced with such enthusiasm the term *montañés* that was but one of the many affronts and insults a powerful man gave them in place of the term *mestizo*. And they fail to consider that although in Spain the name *montañés* is honorable, because of the privileges that were given to the natives of the mountains of Asturias and the Basques, calling anyone who was not born in those provinces by the same name is an abuse.[28]

So are these terms insults? According to Garcilaso, it depends who uses them, to whom they are applied, and where they are used. He ironizes his kin for readily referring to themselves as "mountain people," since according to him this is an insult if used of anyone other than a Basque or an Asturian. The equivalent term is likewise an insult in the Inca language; he adds that "*sacharuna* . . . properly means 'savage.' "[29] He thinks those he broadly defines as his relatives have been the unwitting dupes of a disrespectful "*poderoso*" (a locally powerful man). Garcilaso prefers to (re)claim the term "mestizo," and draws this passage out even further to urge his relations to do the same: "My kinsmen, without understanding the malice of the man who imposed the name on them, take pride in his affront, when they should reject and abominate it and call themselves what our fathers called us and not admit such new, insulting names."[30]

Garcilaso concludes his chapter on "new generations" by introducing terms that I have never seen in any manuscript or, for that matter, any chronicle: "cuatralbo" for someone one part Indian and three parts Spanish, and "tresalbo" for someone three parts Indian and one part Spanish.[31] Perhaps these reflect local usages that did not make it into wider circulation. Such terms—like "*montañés*," which I have come across in the Cuzco archives—may have had a range of reference limited to certain places and to the second half of the sixteenth century.[32]

Because of his efforts to reposition terms in better usage, all the while insisting on their utter novelty and the racism that might inhere in them, Garcilaso unfixes "race" for us while grounding colonial racism in very particular circumstances. He shows us the enormous historical and cultural chasms between his terms and how they operated, his Iberian contemporaries' terms, and ours. This chapter is cited frequently, usually to make a point about Garcilaso's pride in his Spanish-Andean parentage and the losing struggle he was waging to defend himself and his fellow mestizos from disrepute. He was indeed proud. Both his parents were nobles by the standards of their respective cultures, and very important people in Garcilaso's native city.[33] But many of the terms he attempted to fix in part I, book 9, chapter 31 soon drifted away, to catch on other meanings or disappear altogether. "Mestizo" did replace "montañés," as Garcilaso wanted. But it did not lose its powerfully disreputable connotations. And these had nothing to do with the supposed stain of Jewish or Muslim blood.

Or did they? The making of mestizos was a politically charged, historical process, as I have argued elsewhere, and Garcilaso engaged in it after some strenuous fighting had already gone on around the term, both figuratively and literally.[34] It's worth noting that the "Indian mestizo" Garcilaso himself went to war against moriscos for his king during the 1568 revolt in Alpujarras.[35] This is not the place to carry out a complete investigation of the late sixteenth-century history of what the term "mestizo" represented, but I would like to recap some of the investigations done in that direction, and suggest why it is vital to situate them in an imperial context, that of the expanding empire of Philip II. Mestizos might appear to us to have had no possible blood relation to conversos or moriscos. But the point was still debatable in the mid-sixteenth century, when some theorized that Indians were descended from a lost tribe of Israel.[36] Philip II and his advisors must have linked in their minds the imperial dilemma of what to do about all these fresh converts.

Mestizas and mestizos became visible at midcentury because of royal decrees ordering Spaniards to *recogerlos*: to gather them together, to educate and Christianize them, to impart to them "good customs," and, in the case of the boys, to teach them a trade. Acting on these directives, Cuzco's cabildo members decided at midcentury to found a "monastery for mestizas"—a place where the daughters their companions had had with Andean women might be taken in and given a Christian upbringing. Resolving what to do about Cuzco's mestizos seems to have been much more complicated. As Garcilaso's age-set grew up, they were increasingly viewed as a threat. Beginning in the 1560s, in Cuzco, Mexico City, and elsewhere, mestizos were singled out as the protagonists of plots to overturn royal authority. It was then that the term "mestizo" took on an especially sharp edge: Spanish authorities saw mestizos as a group of frustrated, armed, and dangerous aspirants to the legacies of their Spanish fathers.[37]

After this the royal orders came thick and fast. Mestizos were not to live in Indian pueblos, hold certain offices such as that of notary, or bear arms. Nor were they to be ordained as priests, a decision later reversed in law but not in practice.[38] Meanwhile, at precisely this time, Philip II was dealing with another newly converted population he saw as dangerous and restive, the moriscos whose numbers were concentrated in Granada. One rebellion had already occurred in the mountainous Alpujarras region around 1500, in the wake of aggressive Christian efforts to force (and enforce) conversion. Enforcement thereafter had been lax. But by the late 1560s, Philip—concerned that the moriscos constituted a potential Ottoman fifth column capable of assisting his chief enemy, the Turks—determined to launch a fresh effort to wipe out Moorish customs.[39] At the same time Philip was receiving word of the "mestizo mutinies" in New Spain and Peru, he was ordering that moriscos undergo total acculturation, in dress, language, dance, rites, and customs. The result was another major rebellion in southern Spain, beginning December 23, 1568, known as the second revolt of Alpujarras. Philip cracked down even harder, ordering in a 1570 "bando de reducción" that moriscos be deported from Granada and the area be repopulated with Christians.[40]

In Cuzco, in January 1580, Bishop Sebastián de Lartaún wrote to his king with this turbulent imperial horizon in mind. Regarding a royal decree of

1578 ordering him not to ordain mestizos ("whom we here call montañeses"), and to be sure that those already ordained were capable and trained, he responded that he had done his best. Some men had already been ordained by other bishops, wrote Lartaún. As for himself, he wrote, "I have only ordained about five, and to tell the truth that I owe Your Majesty, they are the best priests that I have in my Bishopric, although they do not know much on account of not having had higher education, but as far as evangelizing and living without scandal and knowing the [Quechua] language and living quietly, they do as they should."[41]

He warned his king to consider carefully whether to remove such men from the priesthood, since they might decide to turn their hand to worse endeavors, having discovered that a virtuous life brought them nothing. Moreover, they were relatively free of greed—here Lartaún touches on the commercial activities that he himself then stood accused of—and the native peoples were especially devoted to them. Finally, Lartaún concluded, "They [mestizos] should not be presumed to be like conversos and moriscos, because the latter have a law or sect which is considered rebellious and to which they are stubbornly obedient, some to that of Moses and the rest to that of Mohammad, whereas the natives of this land had none to which they might become so attached and devoted as they [the conversos and moriscos] to theirs, and thus . . . these mestizos should not be held in such suspicion as are conversos and moriscos."[42]

Bishop Lartaún, in short, frames things in terms of the issue that he knows most concerns his monarch: how to defeat those rebelling against Christianity. The second Alpujarras uprising was still fresh in Philip II's mind. Philip's desire to repress the ambitions and thwart the careers of mestizos can thus be seen as part of his wider crackdown on all relatively recent converts. If this is "race" in a period sense, it is also white-hot imperial politics at a moment of maximum tension between the Christian Spanish monarch and his Islamic Ottoman rival. The making of mestizos and other groups was clearly a social process that was at once extremely local and connected to a world-historic horizon of imperial rivalries—religious, political, military, and economic.

Understanding Spanish-American racism in the sixteenth and seventeenth centuries thus means taking into account a local as well as an imperial context, and emphasizing not only Spanish, Amerindian, or African ancestry but the (im)purity of people's blood and the politics of Christian evangelization. We have much more to learn about racism in early colonial Peru and

New Spain—particularly about the dehumanization of those of African or Afro-Peruvian ancestry. Fear of perceived blackness seems increasingly salient in eighteenth-century racism, while earlier paradigmatic fears of Jewish or converso blood seem to become less salient. But fear and loathing of "los negros" clearly existed earlier. The 1654 Cuzco petition of Juan Francisco de Morales provides an example. Morales complained that he had been stripped of his weapons by an overzealous local official and jailed because he had tightly curled, dark hair.[43] This case sounds strikingly similar to the practice of racial profiling in the United States today. The official was enforcing orders from above—"that no mulato or black shall wear a sword nor other arms"— and Morales appeared to him to be of African descent. Yet this 1654 incident also sounds distinctly unlike racial profiling. The witnesses Morales brought to testify on his behalf placed great stress on his legitimacy, and Morales won the case because he was determined to be "the son of Spaniards and legitimate."[44] This incident of racism was embedded in notions of descent, appearance, and (il)legitimacy which we have yet to fully understand.[45]

Historicizing race, as I have tried to do here, is not to deny that long-term continuities can be traced in racist practice; certainly they can. My point is that if we apply our own notions of race to interpret colonial racism, we may miss the very dynamics of difference and discrimination we most want to understand. If we neglect the importance of conversion, for example, then differences show up much more clearly between African slaves and Andean tributaries than between Iberian Jews and Old Christians. Africans and Andeans may have had much more in common in certain historical circumstances than we think.[46] And Spaniards (a term often misleadingly used interchangeably with "white" in the historiography) may have had a lot *less* in common with one another than we think, even viewing each other as incomprehensible savages. Basques, for example, were regarded by other Spaniards as walking stereotypes, while other sixteenth-century Europeans considered Spaniards "the most mingled, most uncertayne and most bastardly."[47]

It is far easier, given the early and midcolonial sources, to see things in relatively elite, Castilian terms than in any others.[48] We can too easily forget that our sources tell us only a certain part of much more complex histories. And obviously I'm telling a very lopsided story here, leaving out the many terms native Americans, Africans, and their descendants must have used in sixteenth-century Cuzco and elsewhere for themselves and those who were attempting to rule them. Occasionally we can see these terms in colonial archives: for example, *pukakunga* (red neck), a term appearing in late eighteenth-century sources around the time of Túpac Amaru's rebellion, seems to have been a common Quechua nickname for Spaniards.[49] Sinclair Thomson takes this term up along with other subaltern terms, using massive political rupture—rather than earlier imperial politics and everyday life—as a way to focus on Andean understandings about collective identity in the late eighteenth century. What did the people whom the Spaniards lumped together as *indios*, *negros*, or *castas* call themselves in earlier centuries, and what kinds of distinctions did they draw? These understandings have barely begun to be investigated.[50] Archival traces of them may be few, but the questions are certainly worth asking.

Notes

A previous version of this essay appeared in *Rereading the Black Legend: The Discourses of Religious and Racial Difference in the Renaissance Empires*, edited by Margaret R. Greer, Walter D. Mignolo, and Maureen Quilligan. Copyright 2007 by The University of Chicago. All rights reserved.

1. See Fields (2003) on why it's not enough to proclaim race a social construction. The move to study race rather than racism, Fields argues, constitutes "the great evasion of American historical literature. . . . Disguised as race, racism becomes something African-Americans are, rather than something racists do." See also Fields 2001, 48–56. As Nelson Manrique points out in *Vinieron los Sarracenos: El universo mental de la conquista de América* (1993, 563), "La 'naturalización' de las desigualdades sociales, atribuyéndolas a la biología es, lo reiteramos una vez más, la esencia del discurso racista."

2. Covarrubias 1989, 896.

3. Compare Covarrubias's definition of "*casta*" (caste) (1989, 316), which is more closely associated with purity.

4. Contemporary U.S. usage, while very much in flux, still focuses on skin color as a mark of race, and especially virulent racism targets those perceived to be of African descent. To be sure, Covarrubias and other far-flung speakers of the Castilian language did mark skin color as a criterion of difference, but in sixteenth-century Castilian racism a person's color and his or her race were not the same thing. See Covarrubias's definition of "negro" in *Tesoro de la lengua* (1989, 826); clearly, other criteria of difference were in play. A large and growing interdisciplinary literature examines the early modern coordinates of race-thinking. See, for example, Floyd-Wilson (2003) on the humors, climate, and geography, or what Floyd-Wilson calls "geohumoralism." Manrique (1993) gives an excellent extended account of the mental horizons of the Europeans who invaded, named, and colonized America.

5. Race is among our most salient "keywords" in the sense that Raymond Wil-

liams explains in *Keywords: A Vocabulary of Culture and Society* (1976, 13). Such terms locate "a problem of *vocabulary*, in two senses: the available and developing meanings of known words . . . and the explicit but as often implicit connections which people were making." Williams recognizes that "of course the issues could not all be understood simply by analysis of the words. . . . But most of them . . . could not really be thought through, and some of them . . . cannot even be focused unless we are conscious of the words as elements of the problems."

6. See Silverblatt 2000, 524–46. An unpublished manuscript by Peter Gose, "Priests, Petty Disputes and Purity of Blood: Unauthorized Threats to Old Christian Status in 17th Century Lima," also addresses the issue. Both Gose and Silverblatt rely on records of the Lima Inquisition, which was charged with rooting out suspected practitioners of Judaism. However, ordinary trial records over matters totally unrelated to Judaism or the inquisition also indicate "Jew" was used in the late sixteenth century and the early seventeenth as an especially potent insult.

7. Sicroff 2000, 589–613.

8. They were especially suspicious of conversos (also known by the derogatory term "*marranos*"), about whom a large scholarly literature exists. See Sicroff 1985, 51–56 on the 1449 Toledo "sublevación anticonversa" and its sequels, including the promulgation in 1449 of the first statute of blood purity in Spain. Further conflict in Toledo in 1467 occasioned "doble conflicto entre conversos y cristianos viejos, y conversos contra judíos" (Sicroff 1985, 88). See also Nirenberg's excellent "Enmity and Assimilation: Jews, Christians, and Converts in Medieval Spain" (2003); he argues that "the conversions of tens of thousands of Jews in the generation between 1391 and 1418 transformed the sacred and social worlds in which they occurred" (139).

9. It would be a mistake to see these historical processes as linear or uniform across Spain; more careful work like Martz's recent study, *A Network of Converso Families in Early Modern Toledo* (2003), is needed. Many conversos were accepted as Christians to the point of being able to marry well among Old Christians. But as Martz points out, the institution of blood purity statutes "raised the stakes" for conversos; "acceptance of Christianity was an attainable goal, but demonstrating a lineage untouched by any Jewish ancestors was not" (401).

10. Perry Anderson does not note the connection in his discussion of Spain in *Lineages of the Absolutist State* (1979, 60–84), but it has been noted many times; see Elliott 1963 and Manrique 1993.

11. According to Richard Fletcher, it was not much of a choice: "Since emigration was permitted only on payment of a fairly substantial sum to the government and on other widely unacceptable conditions—for example, emigrants had to leave their children behind—it proved an unrealistic option for most Muslims" (Fletcher 1992, 167).

12. Las Casas 1989, 17.

13. Ibid., 93, 121. A mountaintop seen along the way reminds Columbus of "a pretty mosque" (ibid., 123). Manrique (1993, 29–35) gives a more extended analysis of the invading Europeans' ready recourse to "*categorías mentales*" (34).

14. Pagden 1986a, 30.

15. Silverblatt 2000, 524–46.

16. Konetzke 1953, 12–13.

17. As Mörner (1970, 27–36) points out, the crown had come to fear the "bad example" Spaniards and other non-Indians would set for an indigenous population considered weak and susceptible.

18. Overemphasis of the "dual republic system" can obscure this important continuity.

19. Before the mid-seventeenth century, large numbers of African slaves were brought to New Spain and Peru. See Bennett 2003 and Bowser 1974.

20. Many unrecognized children born to a Spanish father and Andean mother, for example, "grew up with their mothers as Indians," while others received better treatment from their fathers and grew up more or less as Spaniards. See Lockhart 1968, 166–67.

21. Proof of limpieza de sangre came to mean in Spanish America that one not only had no Jewish or Moorish ancestry but no blood connection to New Christians. See, for example, the documentation Alonso Beltrán Lucero presented to obtain a notarial post (Sevilla, Archivo General de Indias, Lima, 178, n. 12 [1573], expediente 2, f. 1v.).

22. Notarial records, for example, are nonexistent for Cuzco before 1560, and only a few notarial protocolos date to that decade.

23. In the 1966 English edition, Harold Livermore translated this chapter's heading as "New names for various racial groups," and used the term "race" or "racial" where Garcilaso wrote of "generaciones" and "naciones."

24. Garcilaso 1991, 627.

25. Covarrubias 1989, 347.

26. Garcilaso 1991, 627.

27. Ibid.

28. Ibid., 627–28.

29. Ibid., 628.

30. Ibid. However, Schwartz and Salomon (1999, 483) indicate that "in Paraguay, eastern Upper Peru, and Ecuador, *montañés*—which suggests backlander or country-man, and which also may have been associated with an area of Spain that resisted Moorish rule—became the more polite term for people of mixed origin. It won some acceptance among the people it labeled."

31. Garcilaso 1991, 628. This is very different from the much-cited eighteenth-century repertoire of *pinturas de castas* or "casta paintings," in which "castizo" or "castiza" is the standard designation for the former and "coyote" for the latter.

32. See, for example, Archivo Regional del Cusco, Corregimiento, Causas ordinarias, Legajo 2 (1587–1602), expediente 46 (1595), cuaderno 25.

33. His father, Sebastián, was legitimate, related to the noble house of the Duke of Feria, and among the earliest Spanish authorities in the Inca city. His mother,

Chimpu Ocllo, was related to the Inca Huayna Capac. On Garcilaso's Petrarchism in colonial context, see Greene 1992, 1999; on resonances of Quechua orality in Garcilaso's best-known text, see Mazzotti 1996.

34. Burns 1998. In Peru the term was forged in times of war, and as Lockhart (1968, 167) notes, "it is hard to separate Spaniards' feelings about racial mixture, as it affected the mestizos, from their position on legitimacy, for ninety-five per cent of the first generation of mestizos were illegitimate." Yet for Spaniards trying to make it in the opportunistic milieu of mid-sixteenth-century Cuzco, there wasn't necessarily a stigma or problem attached to marrying a mestiza, particularly if she was the daughter of an important Spaniard. Not everyone was trying hard to avoid any taint from new converts.

35. Garcilaso 1951, xxix: Garcilaso "was again in Spain in 1568, for when the Moriscos of Alpujarra were forced into rebellion by the obstinacy of the King, Garcilaso took part in their subjugation."

36. Stolcke 1994, 279. Among those who believed Indians were Jews was the Dominican friar Diego Durán; see Durán 1994. For a refutation of such thinking see the work, originally published in 1590, of José de Acosta (2002, 69–71).

37. Burns 1998. Not much is known about the Cuzco "mestizo mutiny" of 1567, which seems to have involved plotters of various kinds, although it was pinned on the mestizos. Documentation is found in the Archivo General de Indias, 1086; see López Martínez 1964, 367–81. On an alleged mestizo mutiny in Potosí, see AGI, Patronato, ramo 5 (1586).

38. See Mörner 1970, 106.

39. Fletcher 1992, 167–69; Hess 1968, 1–25.

40. According to Fletcher (1992, 168), "A large number of persons, perhaps in the region of 100,000–150,000, were forcibly resettled elsewhere" in Spain. This ended rebellion in Alpujarras, "but only at the cost of spreading the Morisco problem throughout the kingdom of Castile." Expulsion of the moriscos followed from 1609–14, and "it is reckoned that something like 300,000 people were expelled" from Spain.

41. Lissón Chaves 1944, 824. I am very grateful to Alan Durston for bringing this document to my attention.

42. Ibid.

43. ARC, Corregimiento, Causas ordinarias, legajo 14 (1651–54), expediente 283 (1654).

44. Ibid.

45. The rarity of legitimacy in midcolonial Cuzco is striking in the available parish registers in the Archivo Arzobispal del Cuzco, but has yet to be studied. On illegitimacy in midcolonial Lima, see Mannarelli 1993.

46. See O'Toole 2001.

47. Hendricks and Parker 1994, 2, n. 4, citing Jones and Stallybrass 1992, 159–60.

48. Pinturas de castas provide a good example: these used to be treated almost as though they were snapshots. Lately scholars have focused on the paintings' intended

audience, and on who prepared and circulated these artistic statements. Many were made for a Spanish elite. See Katzew 2004; Carrera 2003; Estenssoro Fuchs 2000. As Cope (1994, 4) points out, "We should not assume that subordinate groups are passive recipients of elite ideology."

49. On the complicated definition of "Spaniard" from an indigenous perspective, see Szeminski 1987 and Thomson, in this volume.

50. For excellent work in this direction see O'Toole 2001; Lokken 2001, 175–200. Also Graubart 2004, which begins with the figure of an "Indian servant, mestizo youth" in the 1613 Lima census, and discusses the archival figure of the "mestizo/a en hábitos de indio/a" and dress as a marker of identity.

Was There Race in Colonial Latin America?

Identifying Selves and Others in the Insurgent Andes

SINCLAIR THOMSON

If the enormous, charged literature concerning "race" in twentieth-century social science has shown anything, it is that the category itself is extremely slippery, resisting even the most strenuous efforts to contain its semantic potency. It has proven easier to take apart than to employ in stable and meaningful interpretation, and yet the efforts to dislodge altogether the category of race from scholarly or popular discourse have had only partial success, and sometimes even heightened its currency. One of the ways critics have challenged racist thinking is by seeking to remove the aura of "naturalness" from race. This has been attempted, first, by pointing out that race is a category existing in cultural discourse rather than a natural phenomenon inhering in human identity and verified by science. In this sense, to deconstruct is to denaturalize. Second, historians have sought to demonstrate how ideas of race have come into being and changed over time in connection with major processes in world history (especially stages of colonization, enslavement, and "enlightenment"). To historicize, in other words, is to denaturalize.

In the mainstream historiography of the Americas, colonial historians have often resorted to the language of race unselfconsciously. They assume that the reader will understand what is meant by such language, and find it unobjectionable or at least an adequate means of expression. Thus, for many historians writing in English and Spanish, colonial history could be conveyed in terms of racial identities, racial divisions, and racial mixture, with limited interrogation of the categories of analysis, their historical validity, and, as

Kathryn Burns argues in her essay, the stakes involved for understanding racism past and present.

But where the project to historicize has been pursued, the effort has led to distinct positions, with the discrepancies between them rarely addressed. One position asserts that contemporary or "modern" notions of race do not emerge until the latter part of the eighteenth century, with the breakdown of feudal statuses and theological orthodoxy, the development of Enlightenment scientific classification, or the expansion of Atlantic slavery. Another position holds that modern notions of race emerged in the nineteenth century, with Darwinist theory, the reconsolidation of social hierarchies within nascent nation-states, or in the aftermath of slave emancipation.

In both of these cases, the so-called modern notion is contrasted with earlier notions of collective identity. Frequently, scholars distinguish an earlier (and in some versions more fluid) "cultural" definition of difference from a later (and more rigid) "naturalized" definition. The earlier period may be thus seen as lacking in "racial" discourse altogether, with difference determined by such things as religion, and hierarchy defined by rationality, letters, and other signs of civilization.

Other accounts acknowledge a prehistory of race or elements of protoracial thinking before the era assumed to be modern. In this perspective, for example, the doctrine of "purity of blood" in fifteenth-century Iberia recast religious differences in a way that would set the stage for racialization in colonial Spanish America.[1] Hence the earlier conception is defined genealogically, through metaphysical tropes of blood and birth, and located in collective subjects. The later conception taken to be modern is instead defined through scientific classification framed in terms of physical biology and physiognomy, and located in the bodies of individual subjects.

In noting a distinction of this sort, historians of the so-called early modern period and the so-called modern period can find much on which to agree. The historicizing imperative would be justified since significant differences are discerned between one era and another, and the epochal phase of spreading Enlightenment, capitalist development, imperial expansion, and nation-state formation around the turn of the nineteenth century can bear the weight of historical judgment about "modern" racial hierarchy.

While alternative positions can be taken, they have gained little ground. The argument that the West has always been marked by racist discrimination or that racism long predates the so-called modern period has received limited scholarly acceptance.[2] The view that scientific racism first emerged in the colonial Americas, rather than in Europe, has yet to be absorbed. Cañizares Esguerra insists on the originality of this intellectual invention, yet concedes that the scientific racial discourse of New World Creoles and émigrés was so peripheral as to be overlooked back in Europe. But it would be a mistake to assume that enlightened European thinking about race in general was not informed by Spanish American writings. It may be, again following Cañizares Esguerra, that the medieval and Renaissance philosophical frames of earlier New World intellectuals were repudiated in eighteenth-century northern Europe. Yet as Qayum has shown in the case of Alcides D'Orbigny, a French natural scientist of the nineteenth century, chroniclers and observers (whether treated as savants or informants) of Spain's New World possessions could be important references for leading European scientists of race.[3]

The first wave of European colonialism and the Spanish American context have been overlooked or treated in simplified terms within the broad-scope Western historiography of race. Scholars of Atlantic historiography have often cast the era of first-wave colonialism as premodern, and treated racism as more of a European and North American pathology than a Latin American affliction.[4] The effect is that modern developments are understood to radiate out from the metropole, rather than emerge in the periphery or through some complex dialectic between the two. Yet for nearly three centuries before the advent of a modernity associated with the Enlightenment, the industrial revolution, and liberalism, Iberian writers addressed familiar questions concerning collective identity and otherness in a broad context of Atlantic colonization, state-building, slavery, and scientific thought. They did so in ways that exceeded notions of lineage, stock, or blood in a merely abstract sense. Observations about phenotypical difference were among Columbus's first musings on the nature of New World inhabitants. Writing in seventeenth-century Peru, Fray Bernabé Cobo displayed a keen interest in phenotypical attributes, including color, and their transmission through parentage.[5] The second and third chapters of his *History of the New World* (1653) were entitled "Of the names that were given to the natives of the Indies and of their color" and "Of the physical make-up, body proportions, and facial features of the Indians." Northern Atlantic discussions of the emergence of racial discourse have neglected or downplayed what Pagden, referring to the Spanish American colonial context, called the origins of comparative ethnology.[6]

But these concerns were not limited to intellectual elites. They were evident in mundane aspects of colonial life, including administrative schema and popular discourse. In Mexico, colonial actors fashioned an elaborate language for the multitude of social types produced through the intergenerational sexual unions of people of European, Indian, and African origin. Classification depended, in principle, on biological parentage, and in part was gauged according to personal appearance, including corporal features. According to Cope, this "caste system" developed during the seventeenth century, and was institutionally established in Mexico City by the middle of that century. The early emergence of this system complicates the idea that supposed modern racialist notions were a phenomenon of the eighteenth or nineteenth centuries.[7]

There are then a series of problems with some of the standard assumptions concerning race and modernity in the Atlantic world. First of all, the idea of a temporal division between cultural and biological understandings of race is simplistic. More careful scrutiny discloses a complex discursive field in the earlier period as well as in the presumably modern period. Just as notions of breeding and inherited physical characteristics informed earlier thinking, notions of lineage and blood were employed in later speculation. If significant shifts have taken place from colonial to contemporary times, they occurred through a complicated and gradual process rather than an epistemic break or abrupt transition. Rather than assume that colonial Latin America lay outside the bounds of modern formation and consciousness, we should think further about the ways in which conquest and colonial domination in Spanish America shaped the development of racial identification.

A further problem arises from the fact that common understandings of race do not hinge only on the distinction between lineage and biology emphasized in this scholarly literature. Even if we accept deconstructive critiques leveled against racial science and acknowledge that race has no stable historical meaning, this does not diminish the strong sense of collective identities deriving from the history of conquest, colonization, and slavery in the Americas. These identities—even if perceived as cultural or ethnic rather than racial—continue to resonate with familiar racial identities, since popular racial categories have long overlapped with other imaginaries about extended communities, whether they were "castes" or "clans," "peoples" or "nations." In colonial Latin America, for example, the term "nación" could be applied not only to particular ethnic groups or provincial polities (of which the Inca were but one), but more loosely to the generic category of Indians. Nation and race overlap here because both involve assumptions about the common ancestry and territorial origin of Indians, as generically distinguished from Spaniards and blacks.[8] Although many twentieth-century observers thought that notions of racial identity were more pronounced in North America than in the south, the proximity between racial and other ethnic categories is also important in different regions of Latin America where the collective identities shaped out of colonial history continue to structure ideologies, hierarchies, and conflicts.[9]

The problem with scholars' flat assertions or denials of the historical reality or analytical validity of race is that the term carries multiple connotations. The ongoing debates are derived from actual historical complexities that we cannot dismiss through loose notions of modernity or overly assured assumptions about modernity's distinctiveness. A closer historical examination yields greater ambiguity, and reveals resonances between earlier and later thinking, even if the signified subject has changed (as from Iberian Jews or Muslims to American Indians or blacks). Even if the signifying language changed (to greater emphasis on color, or more sophisticated modes of classification), the change may be one of degree, and may coexist with a stable set of assumptions about whom is signified (as with Indians, mestizos, blacks, or whites in America from the colonial to national periods).

An exploration of the notion of race or racialism in colonial Latin America within the broader frame of perceptions of collective identity and difference is needed. Anything less oversimplifies colonial Latin American history, as well as the history of racial discourse, and hangs on complacent, if not dubious, narratives of northern European metropolitan dynamism and history-making.

Perhaps the most valuable contribution of recent cultural work on race and identity is its attentiveness to discursive form and construction; that is, to problems concerning the categories and language that are used when race is evoked, and the causes and effects of such language. Much of the political energy of such work has also been deconstructive and directed toward (or against) elite discourses and institutions, thinkers and texts from whence domination is seen to flow. While this recent cultural analysis has produced claims about the discursive-institutional construction of subaltern identities, it has been backed up by insufficient empirical investigation of subaltern subjects. To advance our understanding of identity formation historically, we need to complement studies of elite and intellectual spheres with more grounded studies of local and subaltern actors and of the ways in which notions of collective self and other are shaped and refashioned according to cultural, political, economic, and demographic conditions. A study of Andean highlanders, those "people called Indians," in the words of the anonymous seventeenth-century narrator of the Huarochirí Manuscript, provides the necessary local and subaltern focus.[10]

Kathryn Burns's chapter in this volume allows us to reconsider the constitution of a new colonial order in Latin America in the sixteenth century. In the eighteenth century, the colonial order would meet with profound challenges. This era is important to examine, first of all, in terms of the periodization debate discussed above. By the late eighteenth century, to what extent do we find a new or supposedly modern racial discourse bursting upon the scene or at least beginning to circulate? One way to approach this question is through anticolonial insurgency, since the eighteenth-century Andes were rife with conspiracy and popular mobilization that worked to undermine the stability of Spanish colonial rule. The insurgent moment was not representative of all dimensions of late-colonial society, but it was a critical phenomenon that punctuated late-colonial history and exposed major aspects of Andean social relations and popular social consciousness at the time. Insurgency may then be viewed, as Ranajit Guha has shown, as a significant reflection of subaltern consciousness. Insurgency also offers profound insight into social relations in a key conjuncture, as René Zavaleta Mercado's notion of "crisis as method" makes clear.[11] If indeed "racialization"—in the sense of biological or phenotypical discourse—were fully emerging or coalescing in this period, we would expect to find clear evidence of it in acute moments of social and political antagonism.

If we turn now to the moment of rebellion, what can we learn about Indian perceptions of collective self and other? The focus for this discussion is the great anticolonial insurrection of 1780–81, conventionally associated with the Cuzco leader José Gabriel Condorcanqui, who emerged as the Inca redeemer Túpac Amaru. In La Paz, Julián Apaza, who took the name Tupaj Katari, led Aymara-speaking community forces in what became the main military theater of the war in 1781.[12] But not all insurgents were Indian, for mestizo and Creole participation in popular mobilization was an important strategic concern and at times an effective development. Nor did all Indians take part in insurgency. The majority of Indian nobles and caciques sided with the crown and many led communities into royalist battle against insurgents. Nonetheless, over a long period lasting from the 1730s through the independence wars of the 1820s, Indians made up the great majority of participants in the plots, revolts, and wars that spread throughout the Andes, and insurgent political dynamics acquired a powerful significance within indigenous society. Insurgent political discourse and practice can thus help to expose indigenous perceptions of collective identity formation and allow us to appreciate the significance of racialization within that broader field.

Others

Who Are the Spaniards?

The term "Spaniard" evoked a somewhat vague and open-ended social identity and a broad jural category in colonial Latin America. Most immediately, the term expressed the shared identity of Europeans born on the Iberian peninsula and American-born Creoles. In a legal sense, since colonial law posited a formal separation between the "republic" of Indians and that of Spaniards, all subjects (including mestizos and blacks) who were not members of the Indian republic could be deemed Spaniards. In actual practice, the ostensible division between Spaniards and Indians was not so strict. Despite colonial legislation to the contrary, men described as Spaniards increasingly set themselves up in Indian towns as the colonial period unfolded. Yet in the southern Andean highlands these were almost never peninsular Spaniards, and rarely even Creoles. Rather they were mestizos and cholos whose presence could be distinguished from the great majority of peasant community members and the few native nobles who lived within the Indian town jurisdiction. These mestizos and cholos were often people who had only recently left behind their Indian identity, yet continued to be tied to a town, a local land base, or local kin relations. Taking advantage of the relative permeability and malleability of Spanish identity, some Indians intentionally adopted Spanish cultural norms—dress being a primary marker of distinction—in order to gain exemption from the burdens of tribute payment to the state and mita service in the mines and textile mills.[13] As a result, whether someone was identified as Spanish or not depended upon circumstances and perspective.[14]

Indian insurgents would eventually target those perceived as Spaniards as their prime adversary in the insurrection of 1780–81. For example, insurgents in Oruro believed "it was necessary to kill the Spaniards and it seemed it was the right time" and that "all the haciendas of the Spaniards would belong to the Indians."[15] Yet given the ambiguous margins of Spanish identity, whom were they talking about? While the answer could vary, they were not exclusively thinking of Europeans, and at the very least they were thinking of Europeans and Creoles together.

This antagonism between Indians, on the one hand, and peninsular and

Creole Spaniards, on the other, was by no means foreordained. In some cases earlier in the eighteenth century, anticolonial conspiracies and mobilizations had indeed identified the "yoke of oppression" with Spaniards as a whole. This was true of Juan Santos Atawalpa's movement in the central sierra and lowland region of Peru, for example, as well as the uprisings in Ambaná (late 1740s to early 1750s) and Chulumani (1771) in the region of La Paz. In the 1770s, in urban and trading milieus, prophecies did circulate anticipating an end to Spanish rule.

Yet in other cases, the perceived oppressors were *chapetones* (European-born or peninsular Spaniards) and not the Creoles. In Oruro in 1739, Juan Vélez de Córdoba sought to unify Indians and American-born Spaniards to drive out the Europeans. The urban riots in La Paz, Arequipa, and Cuzco in the 1770s and 1780 likewise targeted abusive Europeans.

Túpac Amaru, acting not only strategically but with the aspiration for a new society in which Indians, Creoles, mestizos, and zambos "could live together as brothers, joined in a single body," would have drawn upon an earlier Peruvianist sense of common identity based upon residence in the Andean patria.[16] And while a radical tradition of anti-Spanish sentiment was also present, it was not an automatic racial reflex on the part of peasant community members. The evidence for 1780–81 suggests that peasant community forces made sustained efforts to follow Túpac Amaru's agenda for an alliance with Creoles, yet that alliance ultimately failed in spite of their efforts. With limited exceptions, beyond the initial moment when Amaru appeared an irresistible force, Creoles themselves did not rally to the Inca's cause. The polarization that emerged with insurgents attacking Spaniards was, then, an outcome of the course of the war; that is, it was a result of political and military processes from among an array of different possibilities. While peasant forces prosecuted the war against Spaniards with great energy, their campaigns were also consistent with Tupamaru policy. Amaru had clearly established that Creoles who did not take his side would be considered traitors and that the lives of traitors would not be spared. As one peasant coca grower interrogated in La Paz put it: "Their object was to finish off all the whites because the native [Creole] Spaniards had become incorporated into the Europeans, whom the king wanted expelled." Though the 1780-81 struggle has gone down in history as a race war, it was not initially or inevitably such a thing, and thinking of it in such terms tends to misconstrue the political nature of the conflict.[17]

The polarization also found expression in insurgents' imagination of

Spaniards as demons beyond the pale of Christian community and humanity. Ritualized violence was considered necessary for confronting malignant beings in a war that was not only political and military in nature, but saturated with spiritual significance for insurgents. The spiritual battle was another plane of the war itself, rather than a prepolitical mode of resistance. This did not imply that all Spaniards were intrinsically demonic, but that most had become so as a result of their immoral deeds and opposition to the religious forces that sustained the insurgent movement.[18]

Spanish identity need not be understood as a racial identity per se, yet the equivalence that insurgents established between European and American Spaniards points to a kind of racial antagonism during the war. There is, furthermore, evidence that so-called modern racial language was employed by insurgents at the time of the insurrection.

Pale Faces and Whites

Though blackness was an established feature of Iberian cultural perception prior to the time of the conquest, the language of whiteness was not.[19] The term "white," referring to people of Spanish identity and ancestry, seems to have had little currency for most of the colonial period. Yet in the final decades of the eighteenth century, it began to circulate. A rare use of such language in the early period is the description of an individual as *un hombre blanco* (a white man) or a *sujeto de cara blanca* (a pale face). It is perhaps not surprising to find such language appearing in situations of polarized social conflict. These usages cropped up in local power struggles, in the apocalyptic prophecies of the 1770s, as well as in conspiracies at the turn of the nineteenth century. In 1781, a new variant was heard among insurgent leaders. Both Andrés Túpac Amaru from Cuzco and Tupaj Katari from La Paz came to speak of *blanquillos* or *señores blanquillitos* (mocking terms for "whiteys").

We have here a new language of color that would normally be associated with phenotypical discourse of the nineteenth and twentieth centuries. It is possible that the category of whiteness derives from Enlightenment racial classification, and that it gained currency around the Atlantic world in the late eighteenth century, at a time of expansion in the African slave trade.[20] Did the language of whiteness refer to already familiar referents? Or does it point to new social conditions and perceptions? In the Andes in the late eighteenth century, how and why would actors have used such terminology? Further empirical study in other (especially elite and intellectual) areas is needed to fill out the field of discourse, yet the evidence I have encountered for popular usage of the term "white" appears primarily in conflictual situations, most dramatically in moments of colonial crisis. The neologism "whitey" is found precisely in the later stage of the insurrection of 1781, once Creoles had generally refused alliance with Indian insurgents.

In the end, Indians spoke more commonly of "Spaniards" than "whites" when referring to a colonial other or adversary. If the language of whiteness is such a recognizable feature of today's color-inflected discourse of race, it was present only in a tentative way in the late-colonial Andes. The term "white" was in some ways of limited semantic value. It was partly redundant given the existence of a "Spanish" identity already associating Creoles with Europeans. Yet the category of "Spaniard" could and did contain more than Creole and European connotations. It included, at least in legal principle, all who were not Indians. This slippage between white and Spanish identity raises the issue of mestizos, castas, and blacks, those subjects who were not themselves white or who fit only awkwardly the social profile of a Spaniard.

Mestizos and Mixtures

Mestizo identity, like Spanish identity, was notoriously supple and susceptible to manipulation by those who sought release from the obligations and stigma attached to Indians. Mestizos could not only be found owning modest property in the countryside, but residing illegally in Indian towns with the tacit acceptance of colonial authorities and community members. In some instances, the separation between mestizos and Indian peasants was blurred by marital and kinship ties, or by pacts in which mestizos farmed community lands in exchange for corresponding tributary payments. In other cases, the line between Indian and mestizo was even fainter, marked only by cheaply acquired Spanish clothing and a handful of Castilian phrases. In these marginal cases, Spanish administrators also spoke of "cholos." In principle, such individuals might be described as Spaniards, but in practice most regional authorities would have found this description laughable.

Indians voiced many of the hostile and derogatory views of mestizos that were uttered by Spanish elites. Their nature was considered typical of halfbreeds, inimical to that of Indians, and they were thought to be prone to violence and haughtiness. And yet this discourse emerged in cases of conflict. Under other circumstances, there would have been a more settled coexistence, or even a diminished sense of distinction within a common Andean rural culture.[21] If conditions were right, Indian communities and mestizos could also become allies. Such alliances could facilitate access to urban centers and Spanish cultural media—as, for example, when a community needed to pen a legal protest against a local adversary. There were also mestizo agitators who stirred up community support to challenge unpopular colonial officials.[22]

This ambivalence in Indian-mestizo relations was also evident in moments of insurgency. Both in Cuzco and La Paz, some mestizos joined supporters of Túpac Amaru, especially early on, and some served as scribes and advisors within upper circles of leadership. By official calculation, the numbers of the mestizo cadre were limited, but in practice there was some overlap with leaders described as Indian. Túpac Amaru's family members were themselves of mixed ancestry, fluent in the ways of Spanish colonial society, and intimate with Creole friends and associates. Bonifacio Chuquimamani, who took the name "Manuel Clavijo" during the war and was said to be Tupaj Katari's most radical counselor, was variously described as an Indian, cholo, and mestizo. At the same time, in radical moments, Indian peasant insurgents could associate mestizos with Spaniards and directly target them. During the siege of La Paz, a letter attributed to the communities of four provinces declared that "there be absolutely no more mestizos."[23] In short, the mestizo category could encompass a range of positions on the spectrum of colonial identity perception, but these were politically contingent.[24]

Native Categories

Other categories of collective identity were not readily understandable within Spanish colonial discourse but nevertheless emerged within indigenous discursive frames, categories in some cases scarcely known to Spaniards. The late eighteenth-century moment of crisis and insurgency reveals these less visible layers of subaltern cultural life and uncovers values otherwise intentionally withheld. Furthermore, such a moment discloses the novel ways in which insurgent consciousness shaped notions of social difference.

The Quechua term "viracocha" had been applied to Spaniards since the sixteenth century, and persists today in rural regions of the Andes. In Inca cosmology, *Viracocha* was apparently worshiped as a primal creator deity, and the name was borne by the eighth ancestor of the Inca royal dynasty. The name then connoted honor and respect. According to some colonial writers, the term reveals how Indians attributed a semidivine or superhuman stature to the foreigners who so remarkably succeeded in establishing their preeminence in Peru.[25] Though such awe of Spaniards did exist initially, ongoing use of the term "viracocha" did not necessarily imply wholesale acceptance of

Spanish dominion. In the early 1750s, rebel leaders in Ambaná (Larecaja province) organized Indian communities "to wipe out or dominate the viracochas," holding that "through force they will overcome everyone . . . because it is their turn to rule."[26]

A more obscure Quechua term, "pukakunga," surfaced to describe the opponents of insurgents in 1781. During peace negotiations, Andrés Túpac Amaru brazenly admonished Arequipeño soldiers, presumably a largely mestizo and Creole force: "You sirs are to blame for not finishing off all the pukakungas. One day you will regret it." Literally "red-neck," "pukakunga" refers to a red-throated, wild game-bird of tropical lowland forests, known today as the Spix's guan. Why Europeans would have been described this way is not clear. Was it due to exotic appearance or a tendency to form boisterous flocks? Or was it because the pukakunga was a bird to be hunted, one whose flesh was especially tasty? In any case, the attribution of animality to the enemy contained a scornful tone.

Another category that Indians employed to describe Spaniards in 1781 was "q'ara," meaning naked, bald, or barren. The term may have also carried animal associations, since the variety of llamas who grow no wool around the face are also known as q'ara in Bolivia and Peru. Yet the primary significance was cultural deficiency. Spaniards were bare like the nonwoolly camelid, or like mountains or plains that bear no crops. In turn they maintained a parasitic relationship with those who were fertile and productive, namely Indians who provided the labor and resources off of which Spaniards lived. The term held a strong moral charge; it implied that Spaniards exploited Indians unfairly and failed to participate in proper relations of social and economic reciprocity. According to the testimony of Santos Mamani, an Oruro insurgent, "The time had come for the relief of Indians and the annihilation of Spaniards and creoles whom they call 'q'aras,' which in their language means 'naked,' because without paying taxes or laboring they were the owners of what they [the Indians] worked on, under the yoke and burdened with many obligations. They obtained the benefits, while the Indians spent their lives oppressed, knocked about, and in utter misfortune."[27] Indians also applied the term to mestizos in La Paz in 1781.[28]

To what extent did these native categories line up with more familiar categories of colonial identity? The term "viracocha" clearly made no distinction between European and Creole subjects, and could coincide with "Spaniard," or "white," since it implied a fundamental contrast with natives. "Viracocha" was not inherently oppositional, yet it could acquire this sense, as it did in

Ambaná in the mid-eighteenth century. Andrés Túpac Amaru's usage of "pukakunga" seems to distinguish between Europeans and Creoles. Yet the term could also apply to Creoles if they were identified with the enemy. The term "q'ara" was applicable to any and all who exploited Indian community members, whether they were Europeans and Creoles, mestizos, or even other Indians. More than any other category, it pointed to class exploitation in Andean and colonial society.[29] None of these terms racialized in the sense of emphasizing inherited physical features. Yet they all referred to and reinforced a sense of otherness that was defined by social and political domination.

Self-understandings

When it came to self-conception, Indian insurgents generally assumed a collective identity in contradistinction to adversaries or potential allies. In other words, insurgent solidarity did not necessarily involve the affirmation of a primary identity. However, insurgents did refer in varied ways to collective selfhood. The conventional colonial categories of "Indians" or "*naturales*" (natives) were employed in particular contexts, especially in formal contact with Spaniards. For example, Túpac Amaru used these terms in letters to potential Creole allies, as did rebel detainees under judicial interrogation. Peasants also stressed their membership in a form of local Indian community—whether that community was expressed as being an *ayllu*, an *ayllu grande*, a *comunidad*, a *común*, or a *gran común*.[30]

When it came to communication with Creoles, Indian insurgents did use a language of common identity based on geographical residence. To be American was not a central feature of the discourse of Indian insurgents, though to be Peruvian was a concept significant in Amaru's letters. Likewise, insurgent leaders addressed Creoles as "paisanos" and "compatriotas" in their correspondence. Such categories continued to be invoked by insurgents—both Indians and their Creole allies—until the late stages of the war, though by that point all parties realized there were effectively no grounds for solidarity in practice. The ambiguity that characterized insurgent identity could be heard when Indian leaders asserted that, in accord with prophecy, it was time for the "kingdom to return to its own."[31] Did the kingdom's "own" refer to those who possessed the kingdom before the Spaniards arrived, or all those born in Andean territory? Did it refer to Indians alone or extend to Creole allies?

One new and positive self-reference did, however, emerge from the insurrection. After Quechua and Aymara forces overcame the last resistance in Sorata, a provincial capital north of La Paz, Andrés Túpac Amaru and his court applied the promised justice and punishment. The Inca leader obliged those who were pardoned—including women, children, and the poor—to dress in Indian garb, chew coca, go barefoot, and call themselves *Qollas*. I know of no other reference of its kind, yet this constitutes important evidence that the imagination of a future Andean social order was part of a long-term Inca memory. It is well known that Inca memory could be associated with royal sovereignty and the restoration of a legitimate monarchy in Peru. It also entailed a vision of integrated political space inspired by Tawantin-suyu.[32] Was this the "single body" that José Gabriel Condorcanqui considered the potential product of the brotherhood of Indians, Creoles, mestizos, and blacks?

The new Andean social order would mean not only Indian self-rule under the Inca, but a novel social and political subjectivity. This status was available not only to Indians, but to some Creoles or mestizos. Rather than a static, bounded identity, the new order entailed transgression and transformation. This reconstitution of identity was symbolized in dress and consumption; it was also politically defined and publicly articulated. Yet if Spanish Creoles and mestizos could join the more encompassing nationlike body of Qollas, did this mean they had to cast off their prior identity, as the shedding of their Spanish dress would suggest? If this were the case, it would seem to signal the obliteration of non-Indians, rather than fellowship or fraternity with them.

Other instances of ethnic cross-dressing can help to address this issue. Following Amaru's metaphor of political kinship across ethnic lines, Creole supporters of Túpac Amaru in Oruro wore Inca tunics while saluting Indians and being saluted back as brothers. This conduct, in 1781, reflected previous insurgent experience in the southern highlands. Especially revealing was the uprising of peasant communities in Caquiaviri (Pacajes province) a decade earlier, in 1771. Townspeople there were forced under pain of death to dress as Indians and make a vow of political and residential identification with the community, a commitment of loyalty and obligation to communal authority.[33] While this was an act of cultural incorporation or assimilation, it did not entail outright elimination of Spaniards. The pact was framed by Indians as one of friendship and federation, with the new communal subjects constituting a distinct ayllu of their own within the larger corporate body. Amid political ceremony, they were inducted as a "new community of Spaniards." This unprecedented arrangement may have represented an Andean reading of Hispanic municipal ideology, as well as an ayllu logic for the incorporation of outsiders.[34]

A sense of bold experimentation and creativity, yielding novel institutions and identities, emerges from this evidence of insurgent political practice and consciousness. In Caquiaviri in 1771, the agents were peasant community members working through procedures of democratic assembly and decision-making. Drawing on a communal tradition, they developed a solution for Indian political hegemony that did not require the outright elimination of Spaniards. A decade later, an apparently similar solution emerged, but in a new idiom and on a new scale. This time the agents were part of a powerful insurgent command under Inca leadership. A Qolla identity was formulated on the basis of an Andean noble tradition—not only for Indians but for mestizos and other Spaniards throughout the southern Andean territory.

*

In the late colonial and insurgent Andean context, Indian perceptions— implicit and explicit—found expression in varied terms of collective identity and difference, of selfhood and otherness. Taken together, the contours of expression reflected insurgents' efforts to identify themselves, their potential allies, and their effective adversaries socially and politically. When the language was blurry, fragmentary, and shifting, this only revealed the erratic yet insistent ways in which insurgent subjects defined themselves through dis-cursive, social, and political practice.

Beneath the assorted language, whether of Spanish provenance, native invention, or a more novel Atlantic inflection, insurgents were seeking to define themselves in ways that evoked solidarities past, present, and future. At stake were significant notions of collective political subjectivity and sov-ereignty, whether on a local, communal level or a broader national plane. Such notions contained a sense of belonging to an integrated collectivity or people, with all the historical memory and properly pacted moral obligations belonging entailed. For Túpac Amaru, it meant that Indians, Creoles, mes-tizos, and blacks might live together fraternally in a corporate body under Inca government. In a more radical variant, to be Qolla evidently signaled an indigenous Andean identity, yet one sufficiently fluid to absorb people not previously defined as Indian. Qolla was not, then, a racial identity in either phenotypical or lineage terms. Its capacity to culturally incorporate and politically rearticulate subjects of diverse origin suggests that Qolla identity proposed a new kind of national community in the Andes. The insurgent imaginary was clearly not one that liberal ideologues of the republican nation-state would share in the nineteenth century. The liberal utopia was premised on the idea that the former corporate differences between Indians, Creoles, mestizos, and blacks would give way to a homogenous form of national identity. Nonetheless, in the late colonial era, the more expansive vision implied by the term "Qolla" inspired a wide spectrum of peasant community members, a small band of educated Indian nobles, and Creole and mestizo radicals.[35]

These questions of identity are important to our understanding a period often assumed to be a watershed in Latin American and Atlantic history. A gradual unfolding, rather than an abrupt epochal shift or epistemic break, transpired in the late eighteenth century and early nineteenth. Notable aspects of the allegedly modern racial outlook were already present or at least anticipated in colonial Latin America. Though the Andean insurrection of the early 1780s has been remembered by some as a furious "race war," the evidence of phenotypical or color-coded racial language was relatively scant within the broader field of insurgent discourse. At the same time, the colored trope of whiteness contains evidence of new developments that were perhaps remotely linked to Enlightenment science. This would be consistent with a more gradual change in language.

But to what extent did the new language indicate changes in social relations among Indians and others? The evidence suggests that the language of whiteness was still working to signify colonial social relations and hierarchy that emerged from that initial phase of extraordinarily violent and creative convergence among peoples of European, African, and American territorial provenance. The connotations of status and nationality that being Spanish conveyed in colonial Latin America were not derived strictly from color-coded racialist criteria (even if color coding did take place in 1492). Yet in the eyes of Indian insurgents, being white—a racialized concept—was to a substantial degree consistent with being Spanish, at least in the critical moment of polarizing conflict. The terms did not start out as synonyms, nor did they wind up in perfect alignment. Yet in the defining moments of the war, through charged political processes, "Spaniard" and "white" came to mean much the same thing for anticolonial insurgents.

Just as the colonial experience was more complex than the conventional historical narrative tends to acknowledge, the nineteenth and twentieth centuries also contain more complexity than the label "modernity" suggests. Racial discourse in this later period, as De la Cadena has shown, was not only constituted in terms of biology and science, but also through other forms of cultural and moral distinction. By reconsidering colonial history from the perspective of collective identity, we can see multilayered textures in the past. *Reconquista* and postconquest preoccupations with purity of blood and lineage, for example, were not simply metaphysical notions. As Nirenberg has indicated, they were rooted in naturalistic conceptions of breeding that anticipated later thinking. In the same way, by attending to colonial dynamics we can also discern greater complexity in the present. The concern with honor and status familiar from colonial history or the old connections between concepts of race and nation (both derived from ideas of lineage) did not disappear with the development of biological science, even if they did undergo shifts of emphasis and reconfiguration.[36]

Yet the point is not simply complexity for complexity's sake. If we reduce the present to a narrow patch contrasted with the past, and set up correspondingly simplistic dichotomies (premodern/modern, culture/biology, blood-lineage/phenotype), we risk overlooking crucial historical elements that can help to address the confusion and conflict of our own time.

If the problem of race is still with us in the early twenty-first century, despite the concerted scientific and scholarly attacks leveled against it, it is not simply because of muddled thinking or inappropriate language. When Andean insurgents challenged Europeans, Spaniards, whites, mestizos, pukakungas, or q'aras in 1780–81, or when they implicitly asserted an identity as members of a dispossessed Andean ayllu or explicitly claimed an identity as Qollas, they expressed a sense of justice and political rights due to them as a community or a nation. Though often overshadowed in academic debates over color and genetics, the connotations of "race" involving an extended community, a people, or a nation is one that retains its currency today and subtends debates over identity politics and racism in North America as well as indigenous struggles and African American cultural movements in Latin America. Collective identities such as Indian, mestizo, Creole, black, or white retain ongoing power because of their derivation from histories of conquest, colonization, and slavery in the Atlantic world. Deconstructive and historical analyses remain important intellectual tools for challenging racist thinking. Yet we should not underestimate the complexity of the histories themselves or dismiss the contemporary political importance of the legacies of domination.

Notes

The author wishes to thank Laura Gotkowitz for her scrupulous editorial work and comments, as well as Ada Ferrer, Seemin Qayum, and Marisol de la Cadena for their helpful suggestions.

1. Nirenberg (2000) argues that the concept of race can be relevant for thinking about premodern societies. In medieval Europe, as the "purity of blood" doctrine shows, there were attempts to "naturalize" social hierarchies and to legitimate them through ideas about reproduction.

2. See, for example, Davis 1966; Hannaford 1996; Sweet 1997, as well as the other contributions to issue 54, vol. 1 of the 1997 edition of the *William and Mary Quarterly*.

3. Cañizares Esguerra 1999, 2001; Qayum 2002b.

4. Two important works illustrate the point. According to Hannaford (1996), racial ideas emerged within a West to which Spain and Portugal were intellectually peripheral and in a modern period associated with Enlightenment science. Fredrickson (2002) places greater emphasis on the medieval and early modern Iberian context. However, his overriding argument that modern racism is either colorcoded (white over black) or anti-Semitic does not permit much reflection on the role of colonial conquest and subsequent domination of indigenous peoples in the Americas.

5. See Cobo 1956, 11–12.

6. On protoanthropology in Spanish America, see Pagden 1986b; Schwartz ed. 1994; MacCormack 1999; Cañizares Esguerra 1999, 2001; Mignolo 2003. This classic anthropological dissociation between treatments of race in settings with large African American populations and ethnicity in settings with larger indigenous populations has been critiqued by Wade (1997).

7. Cope 1994, 24.

8. Cobo (1956, 11–12) generally employs the more particular sense of nation. Yet he slips into a more encompassing notion of "different nations of men" when discussing white Spaniards, blacks from Guinea, and the natives of American lands. Cf. Guamán Poma de Ayala 1980, vol. 3, pp. 857–58.

9. On concepts of race and ethnicity in Latin America, as well as their associations with geographic origin, see Wade 1997. On early modern notions of nation and race, see Hudson (1996), who perceives a more clear-cut distinction between these categories than I do. Appelbaum, Macpherson, and Rosemblatt (2003) pursue the issues of race and nation in the aftermath of the colonial context considered here, as do other contributions in this volume.

10. There are good reasons not to employ the term "Indian," given its colonialist origin and stigma. I employ it since there are no unproblematic alternatives and because it was and remains common in Latin American usage. In the colonial period, the term was used by state and church officials, elites, and in some contexts, Indians themselves. It referred to people assumed to be descended from the original inhabitants of the Americas at the time of conquest. Such people were assigned a legal

jurisdiction separate from that of Spaniards, were expected to pay special tributes (in cash, kind, or labor), and belonged to rural communities or resided in towns or parishes specially designated for them. For a report on what one midcolonial observer referred to as the "modern and artificial" terms "indio" and "natural," see Cobo 1983, 8–9. I also employ the term in keeping with contemporary efforts by indigenous intellectuals to reappropriate the colonial language and revalorize the identity associated with it.

11. Building on Guha's (1999) approach, this chapter treats insurgency as not only a manifestation of subaltern consciousness but also as constitutive of it. See Zavaleta 1983.

12. While Amaru and Katari (or their scribes) spelled the name "Thupa" or "Tupa" in the eighteenth century, Spanish writers at the time wrote "Túpac," a usage which has lasted until now, especially in the Peruvian context. In Bolivia, and especially in Bolivian indigenous movements, attempts to approximate indigenous-language pronunciation have led to the alternative orthographic convention of "Tupaj." Though the name is the same, I use the different spellings "Túpac" and "Tupaj" in recognition of different usage conventions in Peru and Bolivia.

13. According to Bertonio's Aymara dictionary: "One is called a Spaniard for his clothing"; a Spanish woman is "described the same way for her clothing and way of dress." Bertonio 1984, 1:226.

14. For more on Spanish and Creole identity, see Pagden 1987; Kuznesof 1995; Schwartz 1995; Barragán 1996.

15. Testimony cited in Cornblit 1995, 186, 190.

16. The phrase comes from the edict for the province of Chichas. See Lewin 1967, 398.

17. This argument is developed more fully in Thomson 2002. See also O'Phelan Godoy (1995, 118–21), who gives the quote from Diego Estaca's testimony. See Robbins (2002) for a recent view of 1781 as race war.

18. See Szeminski (1987) on the antagonism toward Spaniards and the powerful motives behind the perception of them as demonic. Attention to the conjunctural political and military dynamics in the conflict is a necessary complement to his important analysis. Perceptions of Spaniards varied according to changing circumstances of alliance and confrontation.

19. The Portuguese, possibly adopting Arabic usage, began referring to sub-Saharan Africans as "negros" in the fifteenth century. The term appeared in English in the mid-sixteenth century; "mulatto" became an English term a half-century later. In Jamaica, "mulatto," "sambo," "quadroon," and "mestize" were all borrowed from the Spanish. See Russell-Wood 1995; Jordan 1968, 61; Davis 1984, 331; Davis 1966, 279; and Forbes 1988.

20. Linnaeus's influential *Systema Naturae* (1735) contained a four-part color classification of humankind that flagged European whiteness (*Europaeus albus, Americanus rubescus, Asiaticus luridus, Afer niger*). See Hannaford 1996, 203–4. As

Cobo noted, Spanish American natural scientists had already discussed the phenotypical whiteness of Europeans in the early seventeenth century. Nonetheless, "white" did not catch on as a racial code for Spaniards at that time.

21. Barstow 1979.

22. On the perception and social condition of mestizos and cholos, see Barragán 1990, 1992; Bouysse-Cassagne and Saignes 1992; Ares 1997, 2000; Chambers 2003; and Burns, in this volume.

23. De Ballivián y Roxas 1977, 135–36.

24. Blacks and mulattos shared an ambiguous status within colonial society and an unfixed political identification. In relation to Indian insurgents, their limited Spanish identity could make them both more susceptible to attack and more attractive as potential allies.

25. Bertonio 1984, 1:226; Bertonio 1984, 2:276.

26. ANB Minas T. 127 No. 6/Minas Cat. No. 1517, ff. 5v-6, 11v, 35v.

27. The sense of the q'ara's naked and exploitative character is similar to the outraged description of guampos (another eighteenth-century Indian label for the Spanish enemy) given by Vélez de Córdoba while he organized an earlier anticolonial conspiracy in Oruro. See Lewin 1967, 119. The term "guampo" was apparently derived from the word for "canoe," or the tree out of which a small boat was made, and alluded to the Spaniards' arrival by sea at the time of the conquest.

28. De Ballivián y Roxas 1977, 152. See also Bertonio 1984, 1:356–57; Bertonio 1984, 2:47.

29. I use "class" advisedly here (since capitalism was not fully developed in this setting), as a category of analysis for relations of economic exploitation. See Ste Croix 1981.

30. An ayllu is the traditional unit of communal organization in the southern Andes, and of prehispanic origin. As Andean communal organization is segmentary, a number of smaller ayllu units can compose a larger unit, which the term "ayllu grande" refers to. "Comunidad" is the Spanish-language term for community. "Común" also means community, but can carry the connotation of a municipal unit. "Gran común" suggests the broad, encompassing nature of the común.

31. De Ballivián y Roxas 1977, 154.

32. See Flores Galindo (1987) and Burga (1988) on Andean utopia; Rivera Cusicanqui (1984) on multiple conjunctures of political memory; and Abercrombie (1998) on struggles over the colonization of Andean social memory.

33. Archivo General de la Nación, Argentina, IX 5-5-2, "Al señor Diez de Medina en La Paz . . . ," 1774, fs. 19–21v. See Thomson (2002, 149–62) for this case.

34. On the parallels with Spanish political culture, see Penry 1996.

35. My thinking here is stimulated by Walker's 1999 analysis of Túpac Amaru's movement as a protonationalist project.

36. De la Cadena 2000; Nirenberg 2000; Hudson 1996.

PART II ✳ Racialization and the
State in the Long Nineteenth Century

From Assimilation to Segregation:

Guatemala, 1800–1944

ARTURO TARACENA ARRIOLA

After independence in 1821, ideas and practices of assimilation and segregation shaped the formation of a Guatemalan nation. As a national project began to be constructed over the course of the nineteenth century, Indians were
subjected to institutionalized relations of subordination, especially forced
labor, obligatory specialization in food production, and tribute payment. In
addition, they were largely excluded from education and its opportunities.
Even when schooling was available to Indians, the framework was that of a
differentiated education. These institutionalized relations of subordination
were buttressed by two discriminatory notions. First, there was a discriminatory view of history: in the nineteenth century, the idea of the "degeneration
of the Indian race" took hold in historical treatises and political thought—
degeneration not since the conquest (as maintained in most Latin American
nationalist historiographies) but since the collapse of the Mayan civilization
in the eleventh century. The bias in such ideas made it very difficult for
Indians to meet the "civilizing" requirements of the postindependent state.
Second, there was a discriminatory view of political action: whenever Indians' political activities and alliances could not be explained, elites argued
that they were the victims of "political manipulation" by priests, politicians,
bureaucrats, large landowners, military men, and revolutionaries. These racialized ideas and discourses, coupled with the above-mentioned forms of
institutionalized subordination, essentially excluded Indians from participating in constructing an imagined national community in Guatemala.

"Racism," as the term is often used in present-day Guatemala, is an ideological phenomenon constructed to legitimate economically based structural subordination. Racism is not only expressed in large landholding or capitalist interests but also in smaller economic interests. In time the ideology is internalized, and—even when the conditions of economic subordination have been overcome—the stigma of discrimination continues to have an impact by being reproduced and incorporated into the way that the nation is imagined. The Guatemalan state has not been able to appreciate the social and cultural capital characteristic of the indigenous world. Instead it has tended to see that world in terms of cheap and obedient labor, small agricultural landholders, and voters.

After independence, elites constructed "civilizing requirements" for both Indians and *ladinos* (non-Indians), but the colonial experience put ladinos in a better position to fulfill those requirements. The political practice of the republican state thus tended to produce forms of segregation, even though Guatemala's postindependence elites initially espoused a discourse of assimilation for Indians as well as ladinos. As far as Indians were concerned, the discourse of assimilation was only for appearances. The end result of state action was a differentiated form of citizenship, as was evident in the historical development of citizenship rights, local power, education, military service, labor relations, and access to land. In specific locales, indigenous peoples used different forms of resistance to contest oppressive labor systems and their exclusion from a national community theoretically grounded in equality.

"Civilization" as a Requirement for Assimilation

Following independence from Spain in 1821, Guatemala entered the concert of nations as a member of the Federal Republic of Central America (1824–39). At that time, the main intellectuals of the isthmus were animated by the liberal ideas that had emerged with the revolutions in France and North America. They were motivated, above all, by the Spanish monarchy's political experience in the Cortes de Cádiz (1808–12). Their project for the nation was based on the ideas of Creole patriotism held by members of the Guatemalan elite at the end of the eighteenth century. These patriotic ideals grew out of the Sociedad de Amigos del País (Society of Friends of the Country), which was established in 1797, as well as out of the Cortes de Cádiz. The elite model for the nation in this early period was based on the idea that it was necessary to assimilate both *indígenas* (Indians) and ladinos. For this assimilation to be effective, the Criollo elite (Creole descendants of Spaniards born in

America) considered it necessary to "civilize" both sectors of Guatemalan society.

Civilizing, in this context, was understood as the fulfillment of particular social, cultural, and economic requirements. The first civilizing requirement stipulated that both Indians and ladinos should use Spanish- or Western-style clothing and footwear. The second demanded that they be fluent in Spanish, which was the lingua franca of the kingdom and later of the republic. The spread of the Spanish language, it was thought, would make possible the construction of the Central American nation, and later the Guatemalan nation. The third requirement was for Indians and ladinos to acquire the rudiments of literacy—reading, writing, and basic arithmetic. Fourth, Indians and ladinos should become consumers of Spanish or Western products. Fifth, they should strive to be individual landowners. Sixth, they should produce crops such as indigo and cochineal for the world market, since the cultivation of corn, beans, bananas, etc., was considered characteristic of a subsistence economy and thus antithetical to progress.[1] The final requirement was for Indians and ladinos to profess the Catholic religion, which was viewed as the foundation of Western civilization. Above all, it was necessary to combat indigenous forms of religious organization, which were considered backward. In sum, only by acquiring civilization—as it was understood by the Creole elite—could Indians and ladinos attain full citizenship. The ideal citizen was a landowner or free laborer who could speak Spanish, be a consumer, acquire private property (land and buildings), and produce goods for the world market.

Although elites believed that both Indians and ladinos needed to be civilized, the colonial experience allowed ladinos to begin this civilizing process from a more advantageous position than Indians. The vast majority of the ladinos, though essentially illiterate, were fluent in Spanish. This was generally not the case for members of the various indigenous ethnicities. In addition, ladinos held an increasingly firm position as free laborers and landowners in the city and the countryside. One exception was in the area of road construction, as the state forcibly compelled many poor ladinos to perform this work throughout the nineteenth century and during the first half of the twentieth. On plantations and haciendas, however, only Indians continued to be subject to forced labor. This forced labor diverted Indians away from the state's civilizing requirements by preventing them from becoming private landowners, producers for the export market, or consumers. Furthermore, ladinos benefited from their incorporation into the militias—a process that commenced in the middle of the eighteenth century and contrasted sharply with Indians' explicit exclusion from militias. Since colonial times, ladinos had participated in small, internal commercial networks that connected them directly with the world of the Spanish, even though they were prohibited by law from doing so. After independence, these economic ties became a stimulus for ladinos to embrace citizenship.

In sum, ladinos were well poised to meet the civilizing requirements demanded by the architects of the postindependence Creole project. In contrast, colonial-era discrimination against Indians blocked most of them from meeting those very requirements. At the same time, the growing weight of the Indian-ladino duality caused the black and mulatto population, which was the product of the slave trade, to be erased from collective and individual memory. They became invisible in the conceptualization of Guatemala's ethnic reality. This happened even in towns where their presence was historically significant during the colonial period, such as in San Jerónimo, Gualán, Amatitlán, Escuintla, and Cuilco. The only people who were explicitly characterized as black or mulatto were the Garifunas who came at the end of the eighteenth century, and the Jamaicans who were brought to the banana enclave a century later.

From Segregating Reality to Differentiated Citizenship

The formation of Guatemala's republican state was tied to the idea that there were metahistorical principles—to use an expression from Alain Touraine—to which any other constitutional or legal principle should be subordinated.[2] In Guatemala, some of these metahistorical principles have been "civilizing the indigenous race," "order," "progress," "Indian-ladino bipolarity," and "ladinization." To uphold these metaprinciples, the universal norms contained in Guatemala's diverse constitutions had to be "adjusted" to the country's segregationist realities with secondary laws. In other words, the republican state issued a range of regulations, codes, and decrees designed to exclude Indians from the civilizing dynamic required for citizenship.

The principal way Indians were excluded from citizenship was through government decrees concerning work, education, and land ownership. Under the ostensibly pro-Indian conservative governments from 1839 to 1871, the Guatemalan state promoted an ethnically differentiated citizenship that was justified by an assumption about the supposed immaturity of Indians. Under the rubric of tutelage, the state certainly promoted and protected local indigenous power. Yet this practice also deepened the asymmetry between the assimilation of ladinos and the segregation of Indians.

On August 16, 1839, the conservative government decreed the restitution of the colonial-era laws known as the Leyes de Indias. Multilingualism was officially recognized, and the old posts of interpreter and gobernador of indigenous persons were reestablished. The single system of political administration and justice that had been adopted after independence was renounced. On December 14 of the same year, new language was incorporated into the constitution that recognized the need to maintain a social balance between beings who had equal rights but were nevertheless considered different in terms of their abilities and the learning that was required to know and defend those rights on their own. By thus reviving the spirit of colonial legislation, the conservatives sought to limit spaces for contact, especially between Indians and ladinos. As a result, they reinstated the autonomy of indigenous communities, an autonomy that had been diminished by the introduction of the republican system of government after 1825.

Conservatives considered these changes necessary to deal with the ethnic diversity existing in the republic, and to maintain Creole domination. They used two distinct arguments to justify their project for a differentiated citizenship. On the one hand, conservatives believed that the political rise of ladinos had only produced social, political, and economic instability, as had supposedly been demonstrated in Guatemala by the failure of the liberal government (1831–38) led by Mariano Gálvez. On the other hand, the experience of independent Mexico demonstrated to conservatives that the unconditional granting of citizenship to Indians tended to foment the "caste war" phenomenon that affected the states of Yucatán and Chiapas in the neighboring country.

The contrast between republican anarchy and the stability of interethnic relations during the colonial past led conservatives to support not only the restoration of a special status for indigenous communities but political alliances with those communities. From the perspective of the conservative government, the failed ladino uprisings in La Montaña and Los Altos (between 1837 and 1852) demonstrated the validity of such alliances. Both uprisings also showed that it made sense to bolster indigenous power at the local level in order to check the growing power of regional ladino elites.

Yet the alliance between the state and indigenous communities was based on economic factors as well. In particular, it reflected the state's interest in promoting the production of cochineal for export. Although cochineal production required intensive labor, it did not require massive numbers of indigenous workers, since its cultivation was concentrated mainly in the Amatitlán and Panchoy valleys. In both places, and in the sugar cane zone surrounding the Amatitlán valley, mestizo and mulatto laborers were readily available. The indigenous population thus continued to concentrate on the production of grains and vegetables. This situation explains the commercial orientation of a great number of indigenous communities: their activities centered on the production of basic goods that were sold in the country's main markets, especially in Guatemala City. It also explains indigenous communities' open opposition to the creation of the Estado de los Altos in 1838.[3] The Altense government aimed to subject Indians to a new institutional structure and set them against the central government of Guatemala. In order to modernize the network of roads, the government also sought to increase the communities' obligatory work on the construction of roads and bridges. In fact, it sought to do this at the same time Indians in general remained subject to *mandamientos* that obliged them to work for periods of two to four weeks planting corn and cacao on the haciendas of the southern coast, although they were forced to work in lesser numbers than during colonial times.[4]

Beginning in the 1850s, the substitution of coffee for cochineal as Guatemala's single export crop would change the economic context of interethnic relations. With its extensive cultivation and greater volume of commercialization, coffee required a massive amount of labor for its production and for the construction of roads, ports, railroads, and hydroelectric stations needed to transport the coffee overseas. The conservative government dreamed of attracting European immigrants to help make this economic boom possible.[5] Yet the Europeans did not arrive until much later, and then they came as administrators and business owners. Ladino workers thus took the place of European laborers, with the Indians continuing as forced workers. Eventually, many of the ladinos became administrators and owners of farms. We now know that their emergence as a social group in the Republic of Guatemala did not take place from one day to the next but was a long and arduous social, economic, and political process. It was a process filled with tensions deep within the ladino social group, tensions expressed in struggles between local, regional, and national actors.

Although the rise of a ladino coffee elite is often associated with the triumph of the Liberal Revolution of 1871, its rise had already begun under the auspices of previous governments. From 1823 to 1865, the Guatemalan state issued eighteen laws regarding rent (*censos enfitéuticos*) that primarily affected community land and uncultivated land. These laws largely benefited foreign, Creole, and ladino landowners. In addition, beginning in the early 1860s, conservative authorities began to strengthen the practices of debt peonage (*habilitación de mozos*) within indigenous communities. They also distributed communal and uncultivated plots of land to ladinos in order to encourage coffee and sugar-cane production along the Boca Costa and the southern coast.

These plots of land, along with others that had been rented out since the beginning of the nineteenth century, would be granted as property after the Revolution of 1871. This meant that the appropriation of communal and uncultivated lands by a nonindigenous sector of society (made up of Creoles, immigrants, and ladinos) was being legalized. The change increased tensions and disputes over land, not only between individual Creoles, ladinos, and Indians, but also between communities and municipalities.

In sum, well before the Revolution of 1871, a progressively larger group of ladinos was assuming citizenship by working freely; acquiring land as individuals; producing cochineal and coffee; holding more and more municipal, departmental, and even national offices; and developing trade among towns in the interior part of the country. Indians, in contrast, found themselves more and more neglected in their rural lives. They suffered more than other groups from the growing demand for them to serve as forced laborers who would harvest the new coffee crops. These developments would in turn reinforce Indian ethnic and community identity, and keep Indians on the fringes of citizenship and marginal to a Guatemalan national identity.

Despite the liberal ideology that triumphed with the Revolution of 1871, the reality of segregation was deepened by the boost that the liberal state gave to a series of political measures in the areas of work, land acquisition, and education. These measures would preserve the logic of a differentiated citizenship based on ethnic difference. A key manifestation of this was the spread of forced labor in coffee cultivation through mandamientos and *habilitaciones* (compulsory advanced payment of wages).[6] To guarantee the management of indigenous labor and the distribution of communal land, the liberals contradicted and undermined constitutional norms by means of secondary laws regarding work, land, education, citizenship, population, and nationality.

Managing the system of habilitaciones became such a source of wealth and power for most *jefes políticos* (department-level state authorities) and *alcaldes* (heads of town councils) that the executive branch had to intervene in the

1920s to put an end to the abuses committed against members of the so-called *Batallón de Zapadores* (the military unit charged with constructing and repairing roads, bridges, and other infrastructure) who were assigned to satisfy the labor demands of large landowners. During the same decade, public protests by authorities and indigenous leaders became more evident in the press and in national political debates. Meanwhile, the *mozos* (common laborers) on the large properties voiced their discontent in different parts of the country through hostile demonstrations against the authorities and the ladino population.

The liberal state further intensified segregated forms of life by intervening in arenas of local power. For example, it decreed that in the mixed *alcaldías* (town councils), half of the *regidores* and the *síndico* should be ladinos, while the second of two alcaldes and the other half of the regidores should be Indians. In 1886, the stipulation that the secretary for the mixed alcaldía should be ladino was reaffirmed. These stipulations had economic repercussions. For example, the *alcalde auxiliar* was ordered to act as the *habilitador* on large, private landholdings.[7] And, in a mixed alcaldía, the road commission was to be made up of Indians, while ladinos were to serve on the finance, statistics, and school commissions. In addition, the position of jefe político was created. This was a departmental authority delegated directly by the president, who had the right to intervene in municipal affairs and to obtain labor through the habilitaciones, mandamientos, and vagrancy laws. These measures, which implied the superiority of ladinos over Indians, were reinforced in 1934 by the introduction of the *intendente*, who had to be ladino and who replaced the first and second alcaldes. This situation would last until the Revolution of 1944.

Finally, as per the "Regulations for Day Laborers" and the Constitution of 1879, large landowners gained responsibility for the education of agricultural workers. This was a false solution to the problem of promoting assimilation through education; it did not obtain the desired results. Moreover, an educational system solely for Indians was created: the National Indian Institutes. The first such institute, the School for Indian Civilization, was founded in Jocotenango in September 1876. Institutes in Quetzaltenango and Guatemala City followed. This process culminated with the creation in 1894 of the Agricultural Institute for Indians, which sought to improve the performance of agricultural workers.

By the middle of the twentieth century, the failure of the rural school model was evident. Statistics prepared by the Ubico administration for 1936 put the number of children registered in these schools throughout the entire country at just 37,905. This population was just 45.4 percent of the total number of children in the country, even though Guatemala was predominantly agrarian, with over 75 percent of the country's total population living in rural areas. Of the children registered in the rural schools, just 24,927 passed their exams—47 percent of those registered. This meant that one out of every two children had failed.[8]

Signs of segregation could also be seen in the army. The triumph of the liberal revolution in 1871 resulted in a military that was essentially made up of ladino soldiers and officers from the western part of the country. In 1873, the state began to recruit soldiers for the regular army and the militias among the ladinos from eastern and central Guatemala on a mass scale. The Escuela Politécnica (a military institute) was founded that same year; its students were mainly ladinos or the sons of European immigrants.

Until the 1880s, conscription continued to be carried out mainly among the ladino population. The goal was to cover both the quota for the regular army and that for the militias. After that point, the state began to promote indigenous militias, which would coexist with the ladino militias throughout the country. A decade later, the state included Indians in permanent military service through the Batallón de Zapadores. Its members, who were assigned to construct infrastructure and participate in the coffee harvest, experienced segregation within the military institution itself.

In practice, Guatemala's republican state thus approached ethnic diversity in an unequal manner, adopting an asymmetrical system of segregation and assimilation. Stereotypes and prejudices that originated in the colonial period persisted and even deepened in republican times. The policy of assimilation embraced by the national government encompassed only the ladino sector and, perhaps up to a point, the alcaldes and principales. These indigenous figures were considered essential to the functioning of a national economy that was based on a single export crop. They were also viewed as intermediaries between the indigenous world and the state.

Ideology as Impediment: "The Degeneration of the Indian Race"

There was something even more detrimental to the indigenous population, however, which made it very difficult to pass the civilizing requirements of Creole patriotism. This was the construction of a national discourse that posited the social "degeneration" of Indians as a result, first, of the collapse of

Mayan civilization and later of the Spanish Conquest (the latter presumably intensified the effects of the former). This view revived earlier arguments about the degeneration of cultures in the Americas that had been proposed by Guillaume-Thomas Raynal, Comte du Buffon, and Cornelius de Pauw.[9] But there was a difference. Guatemalan historians downplayed the violence of the conquistadors and, in turn, rehabilitated Hispanic ancestry. The intellectuals and politicians connected with both the conservative and the liberal regimes incorporated this defeatist view into the national history. Their narratives left indelible traces on the imagined national community in the making.

The elite historical narrative of Indian degeneration began to emerge in the late colonial period. For example, in his renowned *Compendium of the History of Guatemala City*, published between 1808 and 1810, Domingo Juárros began with such an affirmation. He said that while pre-Hispanic indigenous kingdoms appeared to be very organized and developed societies (though lacking in Mayan grandeur), there was a vast difference between those civilizations and the poor Indian populations of his own time, which Juárros believed were disorganized and abandoned to stupidity, drunkenness, and laziness. From his perspective, the survival of a variety of indigenous languages was associated with the administrative confusion, cultural isolation, and economic backwardness in which Indians lived, notwithstanding the efforts of the religious orders of the colonial period to teach.[10]

This historical paradox influenced intellectual discourse in the second half of the nineteenth century. At that time, the official history ended up recovering the glorious Mayan past as part of a common historical heritage. Contemporary Indians were simultaneously viewed as a hindrance to progress and the unity of the nation, as an impediment due to their "decadence"—and praised as skillful and submissive workers of the land. That is, a dominant ideology from which racism in Guatemala is derived—and which, up until now, appeared to be insurmountable—cast the Indians encountered by the Spanish in 1524 as already being victims of a process of social and cultural degeneration. From this perspective, the process that commenced when Mayan civilization collapsed was exacerbated by the conquest and colonialism.

For those who espoused Creole patriotism in Guatemala, the truth of this dominant ideology was borne out in practice. To be sure, the foundation of the Guatemalan nation was based on a dual logic. On the one hand, the nation laid claim to the Mayan magnificence evident in the first archaeological discoveries (made in Palenque in 1773) and the written testimonies of the Quiché and Cakchiquel Kingdoms. On the other hand, it claimed the Spanish legacy of the Hapsburg and Bourbon Houses as the source of a Creole culture (as was recognized in the allegories of the Jura de Fernando VII from 1808). The poverty-stricken existence of Indians deep within the territory was nevertheless used to confirm a degenerative process—despite the grandeurs of the past.

Under the conservatives, this view was reinforced by successive decrees that favored the state's tutelage of Indians. The argument for these decrees was the humiliation and neglect suffered by Indians: the declaration of equal rights for all citizens at the time of independence presumably plunged Indians into a situation of even greater disadvantage. According to Ignacio Gómez, the principal economic thinker of the conservative regime, because isolation, division, and localism created a "disastrous hereditary trait," it was crucial to keep the "heterogeneous elements" of Guatemalan society together. They should be joined by "a link like that of the Crown of Castile," which "kept in a single body provinces whose climate and products [did] not differ less than their language, their customs, their interests, and their character."[11]

This view of society was developed further in the historical work of Archbishop Francisco de Paula García Peláez in *Memorias para la historia del antiguo Reino de Guatemala* (1851–52). The archbishop's position on the historical assessment of the pre-Hispanic populations was the same as that of Juárros. García Peláez explained that in defense of its liberty a developed society had been compelled to face the conquistadors. But after being conquered, that society had to be subjugated and evangelized to contain its degeneration and laziness. García Paláez also posited an enormous difference between the pre-Hispanic populations—which he referred to as "less stupid"—and contemporary Indians. Nevertheless, García Paláez was convinced that Indians, by changing their customary food and shelter and by receiving education, would be able to recover "the humanity, beauty, and civilization of the first inhabitants."[12]

A fundamental concern for García Paláez was the central role of indigenous labor in Guatemala's economy. Given the importance of Indians to agricultural production and the supply of basic goods, it was necessary to heed the errors of the past and avoid repeating them in the middle of the nineteenth century. García Peláez thus began by noting that disappointment and poverty produced despair, which caused idleness, which in turn led to vice. This dynamic explained why Indians "will never go except by force to work on the haciendas because of the same and even greater reason that they do not want to do it on their own account, which matters much more to them."[13] The prosperity of the country should be sought, García Peláez maintained, by increasing its population and by making use of its resources, so that all inhabitants would have what was needed for their sustenance. According to this economic argument, it was necessary to enlarge and improve the country's agricultural production by encouraging the virtues of the farmer—not only among Indians, but also among ladinos and even whites. García Peláez cautioned, however, that the plundering of community lands should be avoided.[14]

In line with the works of these thinkers, conservative government officials drew attention to the positive implications of the assimilation of ladinos, who not only had their social and cultural capital to draw on but were helped by measures such as the *censos enfitéuticos* that the state issued to benefit perennial crops such as coffee. Conservatives maintained that these measures would end up transforming indigenous life, making it productive and civilized—just as was happening with the ladinos, who were in the process of becoming integrated into the internal market, the citizenry, and the nation.

Consider, for example, the views of a judge from Escuintla. Commenting on Indians in the region, he acknowledged that the acquisition of property had allowed some Indians to create new needs for themselves. They were "dressed like ladinos" and were "becoming civilized." However, most of the Indians acquired only "the means to live in their same condition of drunkenness and laziness, because bananas provide resources so that they do not have to work." The judge thus recommended forcing Indians of this region "to shift away from banana cultivation" and to "dress like ladinos." With both changes they would "really move forward on their regeneration."[15]

The period that began with the Liberal revolution of June 1871 would in fact allow some Indians—especially members of the elite that controlled local power in the communities—to meet all of the civilizing requirements. They became producers of wealth, individual landowners, literate and bilingual, respectable merchants and citizens, as had the municipal leaders of the city of Quetzaltenango and the members of the "El Adelanto" society.[16] Despite these accomplishments, however, Indians would not succeed in being accepted by ladino elites as an integral part of the national imaginary. It was impossible for Indians to overcome the stigma of the supposed degeneration of their race, which was proclaimed in both official discourse and the everyday discourse of the ladino sector. This stigma of the supposed degeneration of Indians still persists, though it is expressed with different words and for different reasons. The rejection or denunciation of that discourse by Indians is seen as a constant threat to the process of constructing the nation, because it supposedly underscores the strength of their community and ethnic sentiments.

The Liberal Revolution of 1871 represented the political triumph of the emergent ladino coffee-growing sector of the west and its hegemony over Indians and the rest of the ladinos. With the social ascent of this class, the term "ladino" came to mean, in the language of the state, the assimilation or coming together of mestizos, blacks, Chinese, "ladinoized" Indians, whites, Arabs, and Creoles. In contrast to the conservative regime, the liberals would not seek to regulate the spaces where Indians came into contact with ladinos and Creoles. This strengthened the nonindigenous sector throughout the country, which little by little grew to include significant groups of European immigrants (Germans, Italians, Spaniards, English, and French). And so although the eugenic projects of the nineteenth century and the early twentieth contemplated the supposed civilization and racial improvement of the indigenous population, their fundamental purpose ended up being the "whitening" of the non-Indian universe, especially ladinos and Creoles. In intellectual discourse—and probably also in daily life—"whiteness" meant different things to whites (Europeans and North Americans), Creoles, ladinos, and Indians.

Drawing on the theory of social Darwinism, liberal governments composed and publicized a national history that aimed to demonstrate scientifically the "degeneration of the indigenous race." This historiography not only deepened colonial stereotypes but gave rise to an official discourse that openly justified the subordination of Indians and all indigenous matters within the national project. It did recognize Guatemala as a multiethnic nation, but ethnic diversity, in this context, was viewed in terms of historical subordination and an ideology of Indian-ladino bipolarity—not in terms of republican equality. Only those in power could reverse that bipolarity: for example, on October 13, 1876, the government of Justo Rufino Barrios issued the "Decree Declaring the Indians of San Pedro Sacatepéquez [San Marcos] to be Ladinos."

Another way in which the liberal state rigidified Guatemala's ethnic bipolarity was by simplifying its system of data collection and dividing the population into ladinos and Indians (plus a category for "foreigners"). Behind this simplification of the data was a policy that essentially sought the homogenization (civic and cultural) of the ladino sector, rather than propose the homogenization of all Guatemalan citizens. As a result, the ladinos went on to represent Guatemalan nationality, while Indians were simply inhabitants of the country and residents of local administrative units.

Liberals further developed their project for a differentiated (unequal) citizenry through education, which they presented from the start as a means for the formation of citizens. Their approach included teaching Spanish to the indigenous population as a mechanism for assimilation. However, as we have seen, the project soon gave way to the training of good agricultural workers among the Indian pupils (a project much like the one Brooke Larson discusses in the case of Bolivia). The creation of special educational centers exclusively for Indians in the cities, the limited nature of scholarships for those attending the national schools, and the policy that gave large landholders the responsibility for educating their mozos and *colonos* (resident workers), gave a renewed boost to separate education (albeit in the interest of a long-term project for progressive assimilation). Although the liberal constitution did not officially recognize ethnic difference from 1879 to 1944, in political discourse and in secondary laws concerning work, education, land, and citizenship the liberal state did indeed accept such difference as a means to support asymmetry and a segregationist reality.

Indigenous Resistance, Protest, and Participation: The Other Side of the National Project

Though state policy and prevailing views of Indian degeneration paved the way for segregationist practices in nineteenth-century Guatemala, it is important to stress that this was not a seamless process or one that went uncontested. Because of the triumph of the Liberal Revolution of 1871 and the intensification of segregationist policies to benefit coffee cultivation and the centralization of power, groups of indigenous families took flight to the most inaccessible mountains. In the process, they extended the agricultural zone. Moreover, many people took refuge in the growing cities, working as artisans and in marginal jobs. Others chose to flee to Mexico or Belize, or toward the Petén Lowland. A number of departmental officials sounded the alarm by denouncing the excesses committed by the jefes políticos, coffee growers, and the coffee growers' squads of habilitadores in their relentless hunt for these runaway laborers. The end of the nineteenth century was marked by events that transpired in San Juan Ixcoy, Huehuetenango. Pressures on communal land there and the demand for labor, along with the joint maneuverings of municipal and departmental authorities, pushed a number of Q'anjob'al Indians to carry out a widespread massacre of ladino residents and external habilitadores (national and foreign) in July 1898. The Soloma and Chiantla militias chased after the Indians, killing several of them in the mountains and capturing more than sixty, who received sentences ranging from twenty years to life in prison.

At the same time, Indian alcaldes and principales lodged multiple written and verbal protests denouncing the abuses committed by large landowners, habilitadores, and municipal and other authorities. Echoing those petitions, some governors warned central state authorities about the injustices committed and their potential danger. Indian authorities also defended the double system of alcaldías (Indian and ladino) because they deemed this system helpful for upholding their traditions. However, in cases where there was a mixed alcaldía, Indian authorities used that system to the best of their ability to confront ladino power. Likewise, the distinction between primary and secondary laws had some importance to indigenous resistance in that the indigenous elites chose to focus their fight on the inefficacy of the universal precepts of the constitution.

The basic problem was the following: even if all of the state's requirements for equal status as citizens were fulfilled, that is, if the demands for civilization were met (such as speaking Spanish, owning property, being productive, and becoming a consumer), equality, in practice, could not be achieved. Above all, the stigma of degeneration was impossible to overcome. The indigenous municipal authorities of Quetzaltenango (Guatemala's second largest city since the early nineteenth century) said as much in 1894 when they noted that they were still looked down upon even though they were landowners and residents of the head town. They observed that their status hadn't changed, despite the fact that they participated in the organization of the local city government, could develop the intelligence of their children, and contributed to the country's social and political revolution. What they yearned for was "the regeneration of the Indian to achieve civil and political equality to the extent possible, since it was the foundation of democracies."[17]

In the 1920s, Guatemala's national project changed significantly as a result of the new political and intellectual climate of the postwar period and the recovery of Guatemalan coffee production after two decades of depression. The "civilizing requirements" for citizenship foisted on Indians once again became a focus of public discussion. Many voices forecast economic catastrophe

for the country if indigenous forced labor disappeared and denounced Indians' presumed lack of interest in producing beyond what was necessary; this
lack of interest was considered a sign of laziness.

But there were also voices of dissent from this traditional view. For example, in 1920 several prominent citizens from San Juan Comalapa, Chimaltenango, signed a protest letter in which they claimed that Indian freedom
was being destroyed. According to that letter, Indian labor was coveted only
in order to guarantee "the abundant wealth of the rich." The idea that the
Indian "does not love progress nor does he wish to progress," signatories
declared, was not consistent with the reality of the western villages, which in
general were inhabited by Indians, and which were places where workshops
and work in the fields demonstrated exactly the opposite.[18] Likewise, on
April 13, 1920, the "Libertad del Indio," a Unionist club of Cobán, sent a letter
signed by fifty prominent Indians to the National Assembly. The club asked
for an end to the government's abuses against Indian communities and demanded full rights to citizenship for its members. The expansion of the
"liberal clubs" by President Estrada Cabrera (whose administration lasted
from 1898 to 1920) at the beginning of the twentieth century allowed local
indigenous leaders to participate in party politics. With this change, the
Liberal party in turn created the mechanisms for electoral clientelism among
the leaders of indigenous communities. It was a clientelism that undermined
the citizenship of indigenous leaders and set them against the ladino opposition politicians according to the stigma of manipulation. Later, General Jorge
Ubico's government (1931–44) ushered in policies that facilitated the liberation of Indians from debt peonage, from obligatory military service, and
from documentation as indígenas. These were all milestones on the road to
obtaining citizenship, but in practice the policies only deepened Ubico's use
of electoral clientelism with indigenous leaders. This clientelism served to
undermine Indian citizenship in the eyes of the opposition to Ubico's dictatorship. The revolutionaries of October 1944 believed Indians were manipulated by the dictatorship and that they opposed progress, democracy,
and the nation itself.

With the triumph of the October Revolution of 1944, a new stage of
statemaking would commence that involved finally trying to get indigenous
communities integrated into civilization. Government policies regarding citizenship would be directed toward local autonomy and literacy in Spanish.
New assimilationist institutions would be established: the Instituto Nacional
Indigenista was the first of several of these. Their purpose was to achieve the

social and historical "regeneration" of Indians within the Guatemalan nation. Faced with this situation, indigenous communities polished their identities and cultures and thought about new forms of alliance with the local and national authorities who came to power as a result of the October Revolution of 1944. Eventually indigenous communities would challenge the exclusionary national project based on Indian-ladino bipolarity.

*

The formation of a nation is something more subtle and, at the same time, much tougher than the romantic idea that is disseminated about it. The process requires convincing a society made up of millions of people divided into different classes and ethnicities to accept an idea of an imagined community that is constructed to a great extent by the state and the elites. In principle, it is a process of developing loyalties, a process that takes place through long-term practices of public education, political discourse, historiography, and legislation—all of which may in turn lead to national integration. However, in the Guatemalan case, where the ethnic diversity and structural heterogeneity of the society were manifest, the European model for the nation championed up until the time of the October Revolution of 1944 was clearly a failure. The principles of modernity had been applied selectively, resulting in the segregation of the majority of the Guatemalan population: indigenous peoples.

Notes

This chapter has been translated by Jane Walter and edited by Laura Gotkowitz. A longer version appeared first in Spanish as the conclusion to Arturo Taracena Arriola, *Etnicidad, estado y nación en Guatemala, 1808–1944*, vol. 1 (con la colaboración de Gisela Gellert, Enrique Gordillo Castillo, Tania Sagastume Paiz, y Knut Walter) Colección ¿Por qué estamos como estamos? Guatemala: CIRMA, 2002. This chapter synthesizes findings that *Etnicidad, estado y nación* treats in depth. For additional primary and secondary source citations, and a fuller treatment of specific issues, readers may wish to consult chapters of the Spanish volume.

1. In succession during the nineteenth century, these products would be indigo, cochineal, coffee, and sugar cane.

2. Touraine 1978, 56 and throughout. For an analysis of the Central American case, see Acuña 1995.

3. The Estado de los Altos existed for two years as an autonomous entity and

sought recognition as the sixth state of the Federation of Central America. It was reincorporated into Guatemala by Rafael Carrera on January 31, 1840, after Carrera defeated the *alteño* army and occupied the capital, Quetzaltenango.

4. Mandamiento was the official mechanism for sending contingents of indigenous workers to places far from their villages.

5. See Rafael Carrera 1858.

6. The habilitación was designed to cause Indians to go into debt so they would be obliged to work on large properties, even to the detriment of their own crops. This system had an *official* version, which was controlled by the jefe político through the alcaldes, and a *direct* version, which was handled by the large landholders and a network of private habilitadores.

7. The alcalde auxiliar was an assistant to town council authorities and usually administered a rural neighborhood or hamlet. On the evolution of the mixed alcaldías, see Taracena Arriola 2002.

8. *Memoria de la Secretaría de Educación Pública del año de 1936* (Guatemala: Tipografía Nacional, 1937), 128.

9. For ideas about "degeneration" in the Americas, see Duchet 1975.

10. Juárros 1981.

11. Ignacio Gómez, *Oración pronunciada en el Palacio Nacional de Guatemala, en el trijésimo aniversario de la Independencia por el Sr. Lic. Ignacio Gómez* (Guatemala: Imprenta de la Paz, 1851), 6.

12. Francisco de Paula García Peláez in *Memorias para la historia del antiguo Reino de Guatemala* (1851–52), 145.

13. García Peláez 1943, 145.

14. Ibid., 148.

15. Archivo General de Centro América, Ministerio de Gobernación, Legajo 28658, Expediente 130, cited by Lowell Gudmundson, "Tierras comunales, públicas y privadas en los orígenes de la caficultura en Guatemala y Costa Rica," *Mesoamérica* 31 (June 1996): 46–47.

16. See Grandin 2000.

17. Archivo Histórico de Quetzaltenango, Caja 1894, cited by Gregory Grandin, "Por la regeneración de la raza y el progreso material de la ciudad: la nacionalización de la etnicidad en Quetzaltenango," in *Entre comunidad y nación: La historia de Guatemala revisitada desde lo local y lo regional*, ed. Jean Piel and Todd Little-Siebold (Antigua Guatemala: CIRMA/PMS/CEMCA, 1999), 75–76.

18. *El Unionista*. Guatemala, July 13 and 14, 1920.

The Census and the Making of a Social "Order"
in Nineteenth-Century Bolivia

ROSSANA BARRAGÁN

Indio, indígena, mestizo, and *blanco* are terms that seem to transcend both history and community in the Andean region. But what do they refer to in specific historical contexts, and how have their meanings changed over time?[1] One much-discussed change has to do with the apparent transition from a caste system to a class system. Our starting point in looking at the language of race is the assumption that race and ethnicity are not two entirely separate systems but are instead interconnected forms of classification and representation.[2] The challenge, from this standpoint, is to understand how ethnicity forms part of a racial system, or, put differently, how a cultural sphere and occupational categories become racialized. Socioeconomic and cultural elements are in fact framed in a racial structure, and the social structure—in this case the Bolivian social structure of the late nineteenth century—is racialized.

A system of classification and representation was used to register the population for fiscal, administrative, and government purposes in nineteenth-century Bolivia, as it was elsewhere. A close analysis of the Bolivian system sheds light on one of the characteristics of racism as behavior or of racialism as ideology: the imposition of race on individuals and groups.[3] Such imposition undoubtedly involves not only a process of categorization but also the "power of naming."[4] In the nineteenth century, Bolivia's system of classification and its categories were conceived almost exclusively in hierarchical biological terms. Yet, as an analysis of the 1881 census of the city of La Paz will make clear, these biological categories were completely intertwined with socioeconomic criteria. The dynamics of continuity and change that marked the transition from Spanish colony to independent Bolivian republic help explain the racialized nature of the Bolivian social order in the nineteenth century.

Systems of Classification

To classify is to establish a social order by representing that order and setting it down in official records. Classification also implies the creation of rights and duties before the state, and the state in turn possesses the power to classify. But there are many different ways to go about categorizing groups and individuals. Registering someone to pay a tax is not the same thing as registering someone for another purpose, such as for the receipt of some kind of service. Likewise, registering someone as a citizen or a noncitizen is an entirely different act of classification, with very different implications for the person being classified. The frequency and force of the government's presence is another essential feature of any act of classification, for the particular nature of the government's involvement in such endeavors clearly contributes to the formation of individuals and collectivities.

During the colonial era, for example, the state did not carry out general censuses of the population as often as it completed *padrones* (censuses of the population living in Indian communities to facilitate the payment of tribute, which was the principal income of the state). As a result, the "marked" population, over the entire era of Spanish colonization, was basically indigenous. The fiscal motive—tribute collection—that lay behind the padrones is of course well known. In the case of Bolivia, tribute—and thus the padrones—persisted until the end of the nineteenth century, due to the failure to establish a universal system of taxation in the early nineteenth century.

Besides the padrones, few general censuses were conducted in Bolivia during the nineteenth century. There were just three such censuses during this period—in 1845, 1854, and 1900.[5] The first one, José María Dalence's 1845–46 statistical report, as it is known, was closely connected with an early effort by the state to create statistical reports and information. Dalence was a well-known Bolivian intellectual as well as director of Bolivia's first governmental board of statistics. There was little follow-up on his pioneering work, and it was not until the 1870s that another effort was made to count the population. In 1872, a law was passed calling for the creation of a committee or commission on national statistics, to be established in the capital of the republic.[6] One of the commission's promoters was Ernesto O. Ruck, who championed data collection by pointing out its usefulness for the government and the people. "Knowledge is power," Ruck declared in a collection of statistical reports.[7] One of the first manifestations of the state's interest in statistics was the creation of that very commission on statistics.[8] Among the areas to be studied by the commission was the physical condition of the national territory and its population. The commission also sought to create a *catastro* (a registry of land ownership for purposes of taxation). Since the national budget contained no items to finance such an ambitious project, however, the commission concluded that the data would be supplied by government officials as part of their ongoing work and by "private distinguished citizens."[9]

Although the commission on statistics pursued many goals, a fundamental motivation behind all late nineteenth-century statistical work was the effort to increase immigration. The creation of the National Office of Immigration, Statistics, and Propaganda in 1896 (directed by Manuel Vicente Ballivián) clearly reveals that the purpose behind this new zeal to collect data—expressed in distinct branches of the government—was neither taxes nor representational distribution for elections.[10] The order of the words in the office's name is telling: "immigration" comes first. In short, all attempts to count people, goods, and activities were now subordinate to and determined by the hope for the kind of immigration that had taken place in Argentina.[11] To be sure, the data to be amassed was considered essential to "good administration." But it was, above all, linked with a propaganda project, with an effort "to make Bolivia known to the outside world."

In this context, the general censuses that republican governments carried out during the nineteenth century had little political or economic significance. These early censuses can be viewed almost exclusively as a means to represent the social order. But to fully grasp the effects of Bolivia's nineteenth-century census, we need to look closely at its inner workings. What general and specific population categories did census takers use during the colonial and republican periods?

General Categories of Classification: Castes, Classes, and Races

In the colonial era, the term "caste" initially denoted mixed groups and was often used as a synonym for "mestizo." It was applied exclusively to the "mixed" population. During the republican era, in contrast, "caste" acquired a more generic meaning as the word began to be used by intellectuals and state functionaries to designate various sectors of the population. It is thus possible that "caste," to some extent, began to convey a sense of lineage or the transmission of blood in the postindependent period, even as it was losing its specific association with "mixtures." For example, Tadeo Haenke, a German traveler and naturalist, referred to "blacks" and Indians in the late nineteenth century in terms of caste, which he also used as a synonym for "family."[12] Later, in 1832, a government report published in Cuzco used the term "caste" to refer both to Indians and "whites," but also as a general fiscal category for the entire nonindigenous population.[13] That is why George Kubler indicated that the terms "caste," "mestizo," and "non-Indian" were interchangeable in the nineteenth century.[14]

In republican Bolivia, "caste" was a general term of classification for the entire population. However, there was no single terminology with which government officials and intellectuals referred to the population and its various components in the newly created republic. "Classes" and "castes" were spoken of without distinction, and there was even a tendency to slip from the overarching language of class and caste into the discourse of "race."[15]

Over the course of the nineteenth century, the word "class" designated a portion or group of the population; it did not have the economic connotation it carries today. Officials and intellectuals used it to refer to different groups of the population, but they also employed it to establish differences within each class. "Citizens of all classes" was another commonly used phrase, and might have been used to describe distinctions within the army or to express the difference between citizens and noncitizens (or citizens without the right to vote) that marked Bolivia's electoral register.[16] The designation of noncitizens stemmed from an 1834 law (promulgated by President Andrés de Santa Cruz) that called for two electoral registry books, the first for citizens and the second for Bolivians who were not citizens. Citizens, in this context, were those who possessed the qualities required to be considered citizens, such as education, property or income, and independence (the status of not being a servant). Noncitizens were all Bolivians older than eighteen years of age who did not possess these qualities; this group did not have the right to vote, but its members did possess civil rights. It is because these two registry books were used that, even today, when social demands are being expressed, it is often possible to hear the claim: "We are not second-class citizens."

These broad-based uses of the terms "class" and "caste" were not the exclusive purview of government officials but also showed up in many nineteenth-century essays and treatises. In 1830, an anonymous intellectual known as *El Aldeano* (The Villager) employed the term "class" in the sense of portions; the sum of the classes would make up the whole of the population.[17] The author also used "caste" as a general aggregative category to refer, for example, to the "indigenous caste" as opposed to "other castes."

Around the middle of the nineteenth century, intellectuals and government officials began to use the terms "caste" and "race"—and "Spanish" and "white"—simultaneously and interchangeably. One of the first to make this move was José María Dalence. In his well-known *Bosquejo Estadístico en Bolivia* (1851), Dalence devoted an entire chapter to "Races and their Relationships with Each Other," in which he distinguished between "the aboriginal," "the African," and "the Spanish races." Dalence's work was not an isolated example of the use of "race," for it was during the second half of the nineteenth century that the vocabulary of "races" began to prevail over that of "castes." With this shift, an ethos of superiority and inferiority also became ever more explicit.

The Categories

Indios and Indígenas

So, what specific categories did republican-era intellectuals and government officials use to classify the nation's "races" or "castes"? From its very emergence in the colonial era, the term "indio" had been a racialized category. It was used to delineate a group whose characteristics were considered up for debate, and even the group's humanity was in question. The historiography has also demonstrated that "indio" was a fiscal category. But two essential elements of the term have not received sufficient attention. First, an upper stratum of nobles and distinguished people stood out among the population that was classified as Indian, while the rest of this group was absorbed into the sector of nonnobles and commoners.[18] Second, being Indian was very much a legal identity. After independence, the principal changes to the meanings of the term "Indian" took place precisely with respect to these two characteristics.

But before discussing these changes, we should look closely at the colonial roots and significance of the term "Indian." After the debates and controversies that immediately followed the Spanish conquest, Indians were declared free vassals who were not to be subjected to servitude.[19] They were vassals of the crown, whose *caciques* (native lords) were recognized as nobles (even as all other Indians were considered nonnobles). From a legal perspective, this particular "quality"—noble or nonnoble—was used to determine who would be exempt from tribute payments and what type of punishment could be imposed in cases of infractions against the law.[20]

Except for these higher authorities—the caciques—most Indians paid tribute to the Spanish crown as a sign of their recognition of the king's authority or of his role as protector and administrator of the Indies.[21] Moreover, although uncompensated personal service was disallowed, Indians were obligated to carry out a series of services in the mines, the haciendas, and public works. Indeed, these forms of labor were defined as their exclusive duty. According to colonial authorities, this situation was not thought to be bad because it was "offset by a greater good." And it did not contradict Indians' freedom, since there was "a just cause," and forced labor was used "to achieve the common good."[22] The Spanish justified this state of affairs by making reference to Indians' "limited capacity" and the "good" that was implied by Spanish intervention in their lives.[23] The similarity of the Indians' situation to that of peasants in Spain also seemed to justify forced labor. The Indians' "nature" was thought more suitable to the provision of such services:

> As any well-organized Republic requires that its citizens work hard and take responsibility for different trades, duties, and occupations, with some knowing how to work the land, others [knowing] merchandise and negotiation, others [being skilled] in the liberal arts . . . So also, and even primarily, it is desirable and necessary that according to their character and nature, some serve, those who are more suitable for work . . . , and others govern and command, the ones who have a greater ability to reason and the capacity for it.[24]

This passage neatly shows that the social divisions that marked colonial society were in fact based not only on reason but also on a naturalization of differences. In other words, the very conception of those who governed and those who were to be governed was associated with ideas about inferiority and superiority that were in turn rooted in nature.

Such ideas about Indians' natural inferiority had, moreover, important legal implications. During the colonial era, Indians had a special legal status as *miserables*, or wretched ones, since they were people, the Spanish claimed, "whom we naturally feel sorry for because of their condition, quality, and work." The special legal status was justified by Indians' "*imbécil*" nature and their poverty; by their recent conversion to the faith; by their reduced capacity to reason; and by their inability to govern for themselves.[25] This status as miserables at the same time implied certain "pleasures" and "privileges" in both the temporal and spiritual spheres.[26] In secular life, the trials of miserables were supposed to be short and quick, and did not need to follow all of the standard legal requirements.[27] Indians were also allowed to demand a review of the legal proceedings they were involved in at any time.[28] They were permitted to negate the validity of contracts (especially those involving their real estate, if the transaction had not been approved by the Protector of Indians), and they were not required to present a bond when lodging a complaint against an authority.[29] In addition, Indians were to be treated with "fatherly love" in criminal cases and sentencing, which implied greater moderation in the sentences than was the case in general for *rústicos* (people from the countryside) and minors.[30] Finally, Indians could not be accused of contempt of court and were exempt from the legal requirement to swear to the truth, since as rústicos it was thought that they could involuntarily commit perjury.[31] This is in fact why, in the sixteenth-century, Viceroy Toledo ordered that in serious cases where it was necessary to examine witnesses no less than six Indian witnesses would count for one non-Indian witness. All of their declarations together were worth "one suitable testimony."[32] Finally, since Indians were considered miserables "in need of assistance and the help of the legal system and charity as is suitable" and "protection, and defense," they were to be represented by *Protectores de Indios* (Protectors of Indians).[33] In short, Spanish colonialism granted Indians certain privileges—or compensation—due to their inferior condition.

In contrast, during the republican period, those *cacicazgos* that had persisted into the late colonial period were eliminated in such a way that the Indian sphere no longer contained any nobles.[34] Still, Indians continued to pay tribute and were required to carry out a series of services and jobs, but now for the republican state. Although they were no longer miserables (a juridical category referring to those without full civil rights), to a great extent they joined the ranks of the *pobres de solemnidad*. This was a colonial-era legal designation that defined peoples' status in economic—not "ethnic"— terms. In fact, the category included all those who did not earn a minimum annual income and who were in turn allowed to pay a much smaller fee for all legal proceedings.[35] But it would be wrong to conclude that ethnicity played no role at all in this designation. A law enacted in 1826 ordered that the "Bolivians previously called Indians" use a specific form of official paper for all legal purposes, the one with the sixth stamp, just as the pobres de solemnidad were required to do.[36] In practice, then, the two terms—"Indian" and "pobre"—may have been closely associated with each other.

Some very significant legal changes did indeed take place after independence. As Indians' special status was withdrawn, the colonial position of Protector de Indios disappeared and was replaced by that of the *Agente Fiscal* or Public Prosecutor. This official's sphere of activity was not limited to Indians. The office was responsible for all affairs involving law and order for the poor, for women, and for Indian communities.[37]

In the end, Indians' juridical status in the republican era was unclear. The state no longer granted Indians a special legal status, and the concomitant privileges that Indians enjoyed in colonial times disappeared. After independence, Indians theoretically joined the category of Bolivians and thus enjoyed civil rights. They were, however, the only "Bolivians" who paid taxes and who were responsible for providing specific services to the state.

Español, Españoles Americanos, Americanos, and *Blancos*

In stark contrast to the colonial category of "indio," the category of "español," or Spanish, became more and more homogeneous (eventually this occurred with "indio" as well). The differences that existed in Spain between gentlemen and nongentlemen vanished in colonial Latin America. As Solórzano put it: "Compared to the Indians, the most base Spaniards are considered to be more deserving of honor and respect than the noblest Indians."[38] And so even though colonial authorities sought, through laws and regulations, to give Spaniards of a "servile" condition duties similar to those of the Indians, the "Spanish" category implied exemption from those services.[39]

At the end of the eighteenth century, moreover, other terms such as "*americanos españoles*" (Spanish Americans) began to gain importance. This group gradually became known simply as the *americanos*, and in the republican period they were called *blancos* (whites). The origins of these terms are somewhat fuzzy. "Americanos" was used by the crown, but we do not know if it originated with the government or instead emerged in the cauldron of the great rebellions of the late eighteenth century. At any rate, a school was opened in Spain in 1792 for *nobles americanos*, the sons of Spanish nobles born in the Indies, and for the sons of cacique, Indian, and mestizo nobles (mestizo nobles possessed both Indian and Spanish noble blood).[40] In this context, "americano español" emerged as a form of distinction from peninsular Spaniards. "Blanco," in turn, was the result of a triple process. It emerged locally, in specific countries and regions, in opposition to terms designating blacks or slaves; as a form of identification and pride in relation to European whites; and because the term "americano" was associated with the entire territory and its inhabitants.[41] Since Indians could also be considered americanos, the americanos—now also blancos—sought to spell out their distinction from them.

In the end, then, the most prevalent term for the top of the social pyramid in Spanish America was the most racially and color-based one: "blanco."[42] In Bolivia, however, just twenty-five years after declaring independence and just twenty years after the fairly frequent proclamations in the early years of independence about breaking with "the chains of Spain," the intellectual elite identified itself as Spanish.[43] Dalence used "the white race" as a synonym for "the Spanish race" (though he also called it "the white caste"). He considered the white race the most beautiful and virile of all, with natural intelligence and superior physical abilities.[44] In any event, the connection between "blanco" and superiority was already well established at the time of independence. For example, a dictionary published in 1824 associated the word "blanco" with "honest and respected" people.[45] At the end of the nineteenth century, such people would be necessarily understood as being of European background.[46]

Although Dalence placed the white race at the top of the social pyramid, he felt that the aborigines—"the inhabitants that the Spanish encountered when they arrived in these regions"—had the same aptitudes and intelligence as other men, as they were also part of the "Caucasian race."[47] Dalence clearly wrote in defense of the intelligence of the Indians, whom he believed should be divided into "varieties," or families, such as Quechuas or Guaranis, Mojos, Chiquitos, Yuracares, Guarayos, and Sirionos.[48]

But Dalence's view was an exception. For most Bolivian intellectuals, the evolutionary ladder, according to which white was superior and Indian and black were inferior (as outlined by such authors as Comte de Buffon and Ernest Renan), was already fully present at the time of independence. Following François Guizot, José Manuel Cortés, one of Bolivia's first historians, suggested that the conquest was an expression of Spain's "superiority" as a "civilized nation" because "intelligent peoples" were always the ones to achieve "victory."[49] Indeed, Cortés insisted on this point even though he believed Spain had contributed nothing to Europe, and even though he deemed its language "inferior to others." Moreover, Cortés used an evolutionary phrase to refer to the rest of the population, that of non-Spanish origin: he described it as belonging to "the primitive races."[50]

Another author, Baldomero Menéndez, who wrote various descriptive works about the populations of Chile, Perú, and Bolivia, recalled in 1860 that humanity was divided into three races: white (or Caucasian), copper (or American), and black (or Ethiopian). He also explicitly recognized the "varieties" produced by "the union or linkage of these three races with each other." The attributes of the white race, which had been introduced to the Americas through the conquest were, according to this author, "their exceptional intelligence and their aptitude for all kinds of enterprises." These characteristics "made them dominant over the other inhabitants."

The Reinvention of the Mestizo Sphere

In the Andean region during the colonial period, the mestizo category was synonymous with "mixed castes," that is to say, with a mixture of Spanish and Indian. After independence, the uses of the term shifted and it gradually began to take on new meanings. For example, "mestizo," in an aggregative sense, was not at the forefront of the remarkable descriptive work prepared by El Aldeano in the 1830s. First and foremost, this author used the term "intermediate class" to describe those who belonged to the broad occupational category of artisans and workers. Only in a secondary sense did he identify this group as mestizos, that is to say, as artisans who lived in urban centers and who were characterized as the republic's poor. It is important to note that although this group was worse off economically than the indigenous population, which at least had control of its means of production, intellectuals and officials generally situated the artisans in the middle of the social hierarchy, between landowners on the one side and Indians on the other.

But more than one standpoint was taken. Dalence, for his part, did indeed refer to the mixed population in his mid-nineteenth-century works, but he did so without using the term "mestizo race." Perhaps this was because Dalence believed that mixed people were "exactly the same as their fathers," even if they were often "olive-skinned" and did indeed inherit some "minor characteristics from their mothers." There is another plausible explanation: if Dalence—with his love of statistics—had set up the list by race, the white race would have been a tiny minority in comparison to the Indian and mestizo races.[51] Perhaps Dalence did not want to publicize this imbalance. In sum, whites and mestizos were counted together in government censuses of the

Table 1. Categories and Population Counts in Bolivian Censuses, 1846–1950

POPULATION	1846	1854	1900	1950
White and Mestizo	629,195	635,167	—	—
Indian	710,666	930,988	776,120	1,703,371
White	—	—	231,088	—
Mestizo	—	—	484,611	—
Tribes, Neophytes, and Noncivilized	—	760,000	91,000	—
"Indians and Tribes"*	—	1,690,988	867,120	—
Total with Neophytes	—	2,326,155	1,582,819	—
Total without Neophytes	—	1,566,155	1,491,819	—
Total (from Sources)	1,381,856	2,326,155	1,816,271	2,704,165

Due to the complicated nature of the census data, this table contains various totals. As a result, the columns do not always add up.

* This column and category do not appear in the original documents; we have included it to provide an estimate of the entire indigenous population which includes the category of Indians and the category of tribes, neophytes and noncivilized.

first half of the nineteenth century (see table 1). Only in the final decades of the century did officials begin to count them separately.

That mestizos and whites were grouped together in the census had important implications. It meant that whites could feel close to the mestizos or to the "former mixed castes." To a certain extent, whites considered themselves to be a mixture. For Baldomero, for example, whites were indeed something of a mixture. His logic was the following: European fathers had given rise to Creoles, "the country's children," who had in turn retained their fathers' physical characteristics, yet the Creole "color" was not "as white" as that of their fathers, nor did they have "all the energy, all the activity . . . of the conquistadors and dominators of Peru." Baldomero did think that Creoles had all the "intelligence, vigor, sharpness, and aptitude" that the Spaniards possessed, but he criticized them for not applying themselves to any type of useful work. Instead, he wrote, they viewed "other men as beings exclusively destined to serve them and as subject to their will and whims."[52] Baldomero was perhaps one of the first writers to view mestizaje in terms of a kind of demographic political plan that would only come into effect in the twentieth century. He urged his countrymen to develop "the white race and the mestizos, who are the children of European fathers and indigenous mothers."[53]

Perspectives on classification began to change toward the end of the nineteenth century. In this era, the combined grouping and counting of whites and mestizos was dropped and these two categories were separated in census records. We can explain this change in part by looking to the class dynamics of the Belzu era. During this "populist" period (1848–55), artisans acquired new political and economic importance. The new political panorama in turn produced a polarization of relations between the common people—the plebes, the *chusma*, and *cholos*—and the "aristocratic" groups, which could not accept the active political role that the common people were playing. Despite such opposition, however, the artisans' involvement would be a fundamental element of Bolivia's political dynamic from then on. In addition, the urban popular sectors gained a foothold in the government bureaucracy. As a result, they not only sustained successive governments but made up the "dangerous classes" that had to be controlled. In other words, the differences between whites and mestizos were reestablished and "mestizo" began to emerge again as an independent category.

At the end of the nineteenth century, then, Bolivian censuses began to distinguish between the white race, the mestizo race, and the Indian race (see table 1). The invention of the mestizo race—its separation from the white race—should be attributed to the growing importance of the artisans, which in turn contributed to the display of new social and cultural distinctions following a logic that was absolutely fundamental to nineteenth-century society. In a profoundly unequal and hierarchical society, social groups continually reinvented the differences and boundaries between themselves and others.

In general, census takers of the late nineteenth century assumed an equivalency between the mestizos and the middle class—in both the urban and rural spheres. In the cities, mestizos were practically synonymous with the artisans, while in the countryside they were the ones who lived in the villages. According to Rigoberto Paredes, an early twentieth-century writer and lawyer, mestizos were also farmers who grew coffee, coca, sugar cane, and rubber. Paredes felt that the mestizos were very close to the Indians—"whose customs they acquire"—and he pointed out that mestizos married "women of that race."[54] But for someone like Luis S. Crespo, a member of the Geographic Society of La Paz, the mestizos were instead very close to the "whites" as they dressed in the European style "with a hat, frock coat, cane, and gloves."[55] But who were the Indians, whites (or Spanish), and mestizos behind the government categories used in intellectual treatises and censuses?

The Social Content of Racial Categories in the 1881 Census of La Paz

Despite its rapid growth, La Paz still showed traces of an old divide in 1881: it was marked by a sharp contrast between Indian parishes and Spanish parishes. The Choqueyapu River divided the city into two sections at the time. The area around the plaza and the cathedral—the old Spanish parish—was called "within the bridges" or "intra-bridges." It represented a space of political and commercial power. The region "outside the bridges"—the territories of the old Indian parishes—in contrast, was defined by its distance and exclusion from the political center. This part of the city could only be reached by crossing the river.

The census of 1881, which was undertaken house by house and person by person, is an invaluable resource for analyzing the meaning of each of the racial designations.[56] One of La Paz's foremost intellectuals of the nineteenth century, Manuel Vicente Ballivián, was involved in this census. Ballivián held many important posts during the late nineteenth century and the early twentieth. He was a member of the La Paz Geographic Society, where social Darwinist ideas dominated and were disseminated.[57] Later he helped found the Geographical Society of La Paz. Most important, Ballivián served as director of the National Office on Statistics and as such took charge of the national census of 1900 and the departmental census of La Paz carried out in 1909.[58]

In keeping with the standard approach, the population of La Paz was classified into four races in the census of 1881. Three races predominated: the white race, which made up 32 percent of the population; the Indian race, which represented 21 percent; and the mestizo race, which was measured at 47 percent.

The census also revealed a clear gender imbalance: males made up 44 percent of the population while females made up 56 percent. Moreover, this imbalance varied depending on the "race." The ratio was relatively even for the Indian population (48 percent male and 52 percent female), but there was a very striking gender disproportion among the so-called whites and especially among the mestizos. Finally, the black population was not only more than 80 percent female but also more than 80 percent "domestic."

How can the gender imbalance among whites and mestizos be explained? In the case of the women who were called mestizas, it can be assumed that there was more female migration from the countryside to the city because of the demand for domestic servants. However, another factor reflected in the statistics is the fact that the women wore "distinctive" and emblematic clothing: the *pollera*, a layered skirt that differentiated them as much from white women as from indigenous women. The same was not true for the mestizo men: as Crespo noted some twenty years later, the men wore European-style clothing.[59] The women, then, were visibly "more mestizo," if we make use of Marisol de la Cadena's expression in a modified form.[60]

Of all the categories in the census, the ones concerning race and employment provide the most interesting data. Practically the entire indigenous population (70 percent) was concentrated in agriculture; in the census they were listed as *agricultores* (farmers) and *labradores* (farm laborers). In contrast, the whites involved in agriculture were classified by an entirely different employment category; they were known as *propietarios*, or landowners. Nineteenth-century landowners were mainly owners of haciendas, but the term was used in an even more limited sense by the officials in charge of the census, who defined landowners as "those who have demonstrated that they live off the income from their property without working in any trade or profession."[61] This restricted definition explains why there were just four "indigenous landowners" listed in the census.

Gender further defined and differentiated these social categories. In the section of the census that dealt with rural areas, one part of the rural indigenous population was grouped into communities while the other part lived on private haciendas and ranches. In both cases, the indigenous population was recorded in the classic way: every taxpayer was counted with his wife and children. This explains the relatively even number of men and women, with males predominating. The term "Indian" covered people in a number of different situations: *originarios* had land, yet were also attached to communities and haciendas, and *yanaconas* (debt peons) were laborers on the haciendas.

The few mestizo farmers who appeared in the census were mainly men. In other words, mestizo women were not farmers—or there were no female farmers who were considered mestizos. Nevertheless, women predominated as landowners, the other category related to agricultural activity. The reason why so many white female landowners appeared is that white men were engaged in many other activities: in teaching, in the church, and especially in the learned professions. As a result, a large number of the men's wives were listed as landowners, in place of their husbands. The men were mainly professionals, and the hacienda had become a secondary activity for them. A saying passed on orally by the descendants of female large landowners seems to have already been valid in 1881: "To the man, the profession, and to the woman, the hacienda."[62] At that time, men were professionals, especially lawyers, and their training as lawyers opened the doors of government to them. As the author of a census conducted in 1909 indicated, "The 'whites' only aspire to government positions . . . and all those occupations that do not cause a great deal of bodily fatigue, as is the case with all the learned professions."[63] Moreover, being a professional or a civil servant was much more prestigious than being a landowner. According to a female descendant of large landowners in La Paz, "Men like anything associated with honor." Female descendants also recalled that the women were the ones who administered the "property," and that such activities were viewed as an extension of their domestic responsibilities. The wives' role as administrators of rural property permitted the husbands to devote themselves to "public" life.[64]

Let us turn to the artisans. The few indigenous artisans who appear in the census were *hilanderas* (female spinners); out of a total of 179 indigenous artisans, 165 were female spinners. *Costureras* (seamstresses), in contrast, were mainly white; there were 793 seamstresses out of a total of 909 white artisans. In fact, there would not have been any white artisans if not for these female seamstresses. And so it was the mestizos who were the artisans par excellence. But there was a clear gender division among this group, with carpenters, *pollereros* (makers of polleras), blacksmiths, shoemakers, and hatters being male, and seamstresses, *juboneras* (makers of a kind of blouse or shirt worn by mestiza women), corn liquor brewers, and cigar makers being female.

The term "*comerciantes*" (merchants) used in the census had a very specific meaning and was applied mainly to whites and mestizos. According to Crespo, when the word "commerce" was used, it signified the importation of items from abroad or the trade and exportation of metals and agricultural products. Thus it was used with reference to those people known at the time as *agentes consignatorios* (consignment agents) and *almaceneros* (warehouse men), activities usually carried out by whites.[65] Crespo also indicated that these same people, due to their "limited interest in physical labor . . . only aspire to positions in government or commerce." The female equivalent to the merchants were the white *pulperas*, or storekeepers, the sales personnel in what today are *abarrotes*, or grocery stores (where nuts, sugar, oil, etc. were sold).

The mestizo occupations related to commerce were essentially female, but it is important to stress once again that the term "comerciantes" was not used to classify them. Instead they were known as *regatonas* (small-scale retailers) and *gateras* (retail sellers of fruits and vegetables in the markets), *mercachifles* or *chifles* (peddlers or hawkers of wares), and *pulperas* (storekeepers). Finally, another predominantly female occupation was domestic service. Seventy-three percent of the domestic servants were mestiza and 26 percent were Indian.

From this brief description of the census taken in La Paz in 1881, we can conclude that while the census categories were exclusively racial, they were closely related to occupation and economic criteria, criteria that were already imbued with a racial structure. As a result, the classification system used in the census expressed an evolutionary occupational hierarchy. At the top were white men who worked in the government, the learned professions, and commerce (that is, in imports and exports). The female equivalent of this high echelon was found in landownership or sewing. At the opposite extreme, male and female Indians were constructed and thought of not as landowners but as farmers and farm laborers. Finally, those in the middle were involved in manual occupations: artisanry, retail trade, and domestic service, a female subaltern activity mainly carried out by mestiza women.

*

The criteria for naming and classifying the Bolivian population as Indians, mestizos, and whites was never explicitly defined, not even in the national censuses of the late nineteenth century and the mid-twentieth century. In nineteenth-century Bolivia, where government officials were legally required to wear clothing that reflected the hierarchy of power, it is surprising that no clear statement was made about the criteria used to name and categorize people. This is because the indigenous population was already listed in the registries used for tribute collection, and also because the Indians no longer held a special legal status. The introduction to the census taken in the city of La Paz in 1909 states merely that "the 'white or Spanish race,' as we call it," signified the "descendants of European fathers and mothers, mainly Spanish," that the "*cholos* or mestizos" were the "descendants of an Indian/Spanish mix," and that the "Indians" were the "*originarios* of the area."[66] Nothing could be so clear and so vague, but also so static, all at once. And who could brag about having Spanish parents after sixty-five years of republican life in a country in which the population born in Spain had already become extremely reduced by the end of the colonial period, and where there was practically no influx of new migrants? Even though race was conceived of in biological terms of origin and descendants, in practice the criteria were occupational because occupations were themselves already racialized.

Each category of classification assumes and demands, as all categories do, certain relatively stable and permanent defining characteristics; once particular individuals no longer have those characteristics, they can be situated in other categories. This is the reason why the census of 1909 contains no Indians who were not farmers or rural laborers (*labradores*), and no farmers who were not Indians. The assumption behind this hierarchical structure is that it is impossible to conceive of a learned Indian or a white *regatona*.[67] Racial and occupational categories were so intertwined that a shoemaker would be considered a mestizo even if he were an Indian.[68]

In the end, this state-driven and static image of the social order was the product of a construction based on opposing ideals, on valued and non-valued extremes associated with "savagery" and "barbarism" versus "civilization" and "progress." The social order was woven together by racial, cultural, and social factors that placed the population, as part of the process of domination, on an evolutionary ladder in which Indians, mestizos, and whites occupied distinct positions. With this we return to what Fernando Fuenzalida and Enrique Mayer have argued: that the names "indio," "cholo," "mestizo," "blanco," and "criollo" established and described ideal positions at the extreme lower, intermediate, and extreme upper levels.[69] Nevertheless, this rigid, ideal system should also be understood in a context in which the criteria for inclusion in and exclusion from each of the categories was subject to dispute. This situation also led to the reinvention of the autonomous category of the mestizo, which in informal and less institutionalized language was known by the largely pejorative term of "cholo" or "chola." The mestizo category was an invention because, according to European intellectuals' traditional views about race, mixture has generally been considered a form of degeneration, resulting in the degradation of the race. The use of the term "mestizo" was a reinvention because this group once again began to be considered a separate category after its brief association with whites. At the same time, however, being mestizo meant leaving behind the defining characteristics of the category "Indian." This explains why the government's discourse on mestizaje in the twentieth century in the end implied both inclusion and exclusion via the dissolution of the indigenous sphere.

The "lower" categories have tended to be stigmatized.[70] They form part of the construction of a social order and its legitimization, especially in societies with a colonial past, in which the groups and the characteristics associated with those groups can be constantly reinvented in relation to the social dynamic. The loss of the war with Chile in 1879 and later the massive Indian rebellion of 1899—a century after the Katari rebellions of the 1780s—seem to have changed the principles of the nineteenth-century social order, which was based on difference, inequality, and hierarchy. The twentieth century would be the time for the "education of the Indian" and the quest for a mestizo nation. This idealized mestizaje was undoubtedly very distant from the racial, social, and occupational order of the nineteenth century.

Notes

This chapter has been translated by Jane Walter and edited by Laura Gotkowitz.

1. "Indio" is the colonial term; "indígena" began to be used in Bolivian legislation from the time of Bolívar's early nineteenth-century decrees (see Flores Moncayo 1953).

2. Wade 2000.

3. Todorov 1989.

4. Bourdieu 1990, 294.

5. There were, however, a number of attempts, in 1832, 1841, and 1845.

6. Law of November 9, 1872, cited in Ruck and Benedicto Medinaceli 1874 and Ruck 1875, No. 535.

7. Ruck apparently planned to publish a work with statistics on imports and exports, education, national and departmental income, etc. (see Miscelánea Estadística de Bolivia 1875, 535). The quote is from Ruck and Benedicto Medinaceli 1874, 19v or 2 and ANB Ruck 1875, No. 535.

8. Ibid., 20 and following.

9. ANB Ruck 1875, No. 535.

10. Oficina Nacional de Inmigración, Estadística y Propaganda Geográfica 1900.

11. *Informes del Director* 1902, 1–3.

12. Haenke 1901, 32, 255.

13. Matrícula de castas, quoted in Kubler 1952, 7, n. 22; José Serra, on taxes, in Kubler 1952, 2; Kubler, 1952, 7.

14. Kubler 1952, 5.

15. This does not mean that race was not spoken of previously. The term was already in use by early travelers such as J. B. Pentland, but the state and its representatives only adopted it later. See Pentland 1975, 41.

16. For example, in the case of the army it was said that "the National Army will maintain the best harmony with Citizens of all classes" (General Order of November 12, 1857, quoted in Flores Moncayo 1953, 172).

17. El Aldeano was the author of a description of the "state of the national wealth of Bolivia." El Aldeano's text and a series of commentaries on his work were compiled by Ana María Lema (1994).

18. Spanish law clearly distinguished the cacique from the "common Indian" (Real Cédula de 1697, quoted in Díaz Rementería 1977, 97–98). In civil cases, for example, the law held that the caciques could not be detained by any judge except the highest authorities (ibid., 102).

19. *Recopilación de Leyes*, Libro Sexto, Título I, 1.I, *Recopilación de Leyes*, T II, 1774: 194.

20. *Las Partidas*, vol. 4, Séptima Partida, Título XXXI, L. VIII: 709–710, in *Las Siete Partidas del Sabio Rey D. Alfonso el Nono*, around 1250–1851.

21. Solórzano 1739, Book V, chap. XIX, Tomo I.: 152.

22. For good government, the authorities could force citizens "to work and not stop being free because of it" (Solórzano 1739, Book II, chap. V, Tomo I.: 80–82).

23. Solórzano 1739, Book II, chap. IV, Tomo I.: 71, 77 and Book II, chap. VI, Tomo I.: 77, 80.

24. Ibid., 77.

25. Solórzano 1739, Book II, chap. XXVIII, Tomo I.: 203–05, 208.

26. Ibid., 211. For the spiritual sphere, see chapter XXIX.

27. This was the case because they were not considered people who could deceive (Solórzano 1739, Book II, chap. XXVIII, Tomo I.: 206–07; Book V, Título X and L.83, Título 15, Lib. 2, 1.: 10–13 and Título 10, Lib. 5 of the Recopilación).

28. Solórzano 1739, Book II, chap. XXVIII, Tomo I.: 206.

29. Ibid., 208–9.

30. An Order of the Concilio Limense II prohibited priests and Vicars from flogging Indians even when they were found guilty (Solórzano 1739, Book II, chap. XXVIII, Tomo I.: 207).

31. Ibid.

32. Ibid., 208.

33. *Recopilación de Leyes*, see p. 205 and Libro Sexto Título VI.

34. This was expressed in the Republic via Bolívar's decree of July 4, 1825. Cacicazgo is a system of Indian community government headed by a cacique. On the crisis of the *cacicazgo*, see Thomson 2002.

35. This encompassed those people who did not have a minimum annual income or profit of 200 pesos (Santa Cruz 1852, articles 751 and 763). Indians were explicitly included in the pobres de solemnidad category in 1853 (Order of November 14, 1835, in Bonifaz 1953, 51).

36. Bonifaz 1953, 16.

37. There were, however, short periods when the *protectores* were reestablished. See *Memoria del Ministerio de Relaciones Exteriores y Culto* 1837, 10; Santa Cruz 1852, Articles 64 and 69; *Compilación de las Leyes* 1890, Article 160.

38. Solórzano 1739, Book II, chap. XXVIII, vol. I: 206.

39. See Solórzano 1739, Book II, Chapter V, Vol. I: 72–74.

40. Royal Order of 1792, in *Mercurio Peruano*, 23 August 1792, No. 171. In ANB-BNB, Colección de Documentos Col. G.R.M., 1792–1820, 2768 ff. Haenke also reported that the term *"españoles europeos"* was beginning to be used at the end of the seventeenth century (Haenke 1901, 23).

41. In the early years of the nineteenth century, newspaper articles written in defense of América circulated in Buenos Aires. In response to allegations from de Paw, the authors of such works argued that they were men as good as those from the Old World (Chiaramonte 1997, 72).

42. The term "blanco" was already being used by Buffon (see Todorov 1989). According to Lockhart, the term appeared in América at the end of the eighteenth century (Lockhart 1984, 286). Haenke indicated in the final decades of the eighteenth century that "every white man" in Lima was called a gentleman (Haenke 1901, 24).

43. Articles in newspapers such as *El Iris* suggest a counterpoint, for even in the 1830s this publication called for separation from Spain.

44. Dalence 1975, 198.

45. *Diccionario* 1824.

46. *Nuevo Diccionario* 1883.

47. Ibid., 199–200.

48. Ibid., 200–201, 205.

49. Cortés 1858, 21.

50. Cortés 1861, 5.

51. In each department, Dalence compared the number of blancos with the number of "aborigines" (Dalence 1975, 201).

52. Baldomero Menéndez 1860, 116, 118.

53. Ibid., 120, 121, 132.

54. Paredes 1898, 111.

55. Crespo 1909–1910, 51.

56. The census, called a *padrón*, consists of nine books (each with approximately 120 pages), housed today in the Archive of La Paz. The census takers counted the population house by house in different parishes of the city. The objective was to impose a general personal tax (on the Indian and non-Indian population) or "head tax," as defined by the law of August 13, 1880 and D.R. of April 4, 1881 (in Ovando Sanz 1985, 297–98). The data collected for women (on the left-hand page) and for men (on the right-hand page) include house number, full name, marital status, age, race, occupation, and number of children. Although we know from the census of 1909 that other censuses of the city were taken in the nineteenth century, none of those censuses have been located. We also know that this particular census is incomplete since the population in it totals 20,000 while the census of La Paz taken in 1909 lists 56,849 inhabitants for 1886; 60,031 for 1902; and 78,856 for 1909 (Crespo 1909–1910, 24–25). The tables on which the following figures are based cannot be included here due to limitations of space.

57. Demélas 1981, 58.

58. Crespo 1909–1910, chapter 8.

59. Ibid., 51.

60. De la Cadena 1991.

61. Crespo 1909–1910, 64.

62. Qayum et al. 1997.

63. Crespo 1909–1910, 47.

64. Qayum et al. 1997, 37–57.

65. Crespo 1909–1910, 19, 47, 63.

66. Ibid., 44, 46. The only explicit instructions were: "In column 8 . . . the races or castes are to be recorded, with some sort of mark." And: "Note that in the statistical classification of races, only the four that have been listed will be accepted" (ibid., xii).

67. Likewise, in Bolivia's present-day censuses, it is difficult to conceive of a female-headed household: the man is listed as "head of household" except when the woman is divorced or a widow.

68. An artisans' newspaper stated that the "arts" were for "the man in a poncho, but also for the one from the workshop, who can use white gloves, and who by virtue of his education, his manners, his virtues, and learning is worthy of associating with the society's ruling class."

69. Fuenzalida 1970, 82–83.

70. See Barragán 1992.

Forging the Unlettered Indian:

The Pedagogy of Race in the Bolivian Andes

BROOKE LARSON

Ever since Angel Rama first bundled writing, imperial power, and urbanism into the powerful metaphor of "the lettered city," scholars have been fascinated by the role that alphabetic literacy played in the cultural and spatial colonization of the Americas.[1] The lettered city began as a blueprint of a classical polis, which the Iberian rulers would stamp onto the untamed landscapes of the New World. Each such city would serve as a citadel of Iberian civilization, as well as the locus of writing, law, and the monarch's overseas bureaucracy. As the Spanish empire built an administrative machinery, its urban spaces soon turned into "cities of protocols" producing laws, regulations, proclamations, certificates, propaganda—not to mention secular and religious ideologies to justify the imperial enterprise in the first place.

At the center of that knotted relationship between writing, power, and urbanity stood a tiny group of administrators, lawyers, and other educated men of letters (whom Rama identifies as "*letrados*").[2] As masters of the written word, these lettered men became a traditional force in Latin America's public life. Not only did they monopolize the symbols and instruments of imperial knowledge and power in radically heteroglossic, colonized societies, they conducted the day-to-day affairs of administration, justice, and extraction. The letrados were the flesh-and-blood agents who put into practice Antonio de Nebrija's famous dictum of 1492 that the language of Castile was "the companion of empire."

The link between writing, urban space, and legitimate rule only became stronger with time, as indigenous people appropriated Spanish writing in their ongoing protestations and negotiations before their colonial overlords. As indigenous subjects were drawn into the orbit of Spanish imperial justice, the lettered city reinforced its spatial and bureaucratic function as an internal metropole committed to the monarch's dual project of colonizing and evangelizing indigenous people in the empire's rural hinterlands. Particularly in the Amerindian highlands, where millions of rural peasants vastly outnumbered the urban enclaves of Hispanic and hispanizing populations, the lettered city became a focal point for ongoing colonization, an ideal polis that outlived its capacity to be an outpost of the Iberian empire.

In the mid-nineteenth century, the Spanish urban ideal was still the preserve of a tiny Hispanic elite monopolizing the dominant language. Around the turn of the twentieth century, however, Latin American cities were transformed by the social forces of modernization and by a new generation of letrados who, as journalists, literary nationalists, teachers, lawyers, and university professors, began to "broaden the exercise of letters."[3] Riding the circuits of nationalism in the early 1900s, the lettered city reached out into the countryside to rediscover its national heritage, interior landscapes, and vanishing folkways. At the same time, the lettered city sought to bring "public instruction," "universal education," or "national pedagogy" to the masses. These new letrados would seem to be the flag bearers of a universalizing nationalism, if not a revolutionary idealism, that would finally breach the colonial barrier by spreading access to literacy beyond the privileged few.

Yet, Rama's sweeping narrative of the lettered city never chronicles the city's demise. Despite the transformation of urban life under economic modernization and political flux, the lettered city still "retained a vision of itself as a cultural aristocracy," albeit one that "incorporated powerful democratizing cross-currents."[4] Jeremy Adelman has recently noted this subtle paradox in the work of Rama, where "*letrados* claim to be proponents of change, but wind up reproducing a seminal condition of Latin American history, which is the power of the city."[5]

One way to examine this enduring paradox is to probe the bitter ideological battles that erupted in the lettered city over the question of popular literacy. Because writing, specifically official and legal forms of writing, furnished a powerful cultural symbol and tool of legitimacy in a racially divided, radically unequal society, its surrender to the greater cause of universal schooling was inevitably going to produce controversy among those who had most at stake. Even dissident intellectuals who ushered in the era of cultural nationalism in the early twentieth century were traditionalists, simultaneously celebrating their nation's vanishing "folk traditions" and urban popular cultures, and fearing the democratizing forces that threatened to corrupt their cultural domain. Many worried, for example, about delivering literacy, cultural mobility, and the franchise to peasants, the laboring classes, or new immigrants beginning to flood into the cities. Blind adherence to universal norms was tantamount, in their view, to surrendering the terms of their own cultural authority, and ongoing debates on education called forth conservative challenges to European ideals of universalism, positivism, and democracy. But there were material and class interests at stake, as well. No generation of letrados was willing to surrender its privileged access to power and knowledge; none wanted to abandon its stake in cultural power and withdraw from public life, especially when membership in the cultural plutocracy continued to confer prestige and wealth to those who rode the circuits of power politics.

And yet, by the 1870s, the ideal of public education was beginning to spread beyond the vanguard reformers of Uruguay and Argentina into the heartland of the Andean nations, where liberal reformers turned to Europe and the United States for pedagogical models that might guide them in establishing national systems of education and inculcating civic values in the masses.[6] Even before many nations had established public schooling, the program to offer "education and instruction" to the masses became a source of bitter contention among factions of the lettered elite, each seeking to assert its authority over this new tool of nation-building and use it to advance its ideological, partisan, or class interests. By 1910, these intraelite squabbles were suffused with larger theories about national identity, race, and gender.[7] Increasingly, the very idea of educating the masses in order to bring them into the nation in various capacities (perhaps as enfranchised citizens, wage laborers, or patriotic soldiers) raised deeper ideological and pseudoscientific issues about the nation's capacity for "racial improvement," economic progress, and cultural homogenization. Literary nationalists, in turn, borrowed elements from German idealism to probe the nation's moral character, racial-cultural essence, and mythic past—all strategic forms of knowledge and power that might guide the nation's "apostles of education" to raise the masses and redeem the nation.[8]

The stakes were particularly high in the city of La Paz in the early 1900s, after it was transformed into Bolivia's seat of economic, political, and intellectual power. Its secondary role was that of internal metropole, home to writers and statesmen who were designing new liberal land reforms and civilizing projects for the Aymara population of the *altiplano*. The outlying provinces of La Paz, populated by some half-million Aymara peasants, were becoming increasingly attractive as an agrarian hinterland to land speculators and *latifundistas* (large estate owners), eager to capitalize on liberal land laws, railroads, urban food markets, and a growing reserve labor force of dispossessed ex-*comunarios* (member of a land-based community or ayllu). As the scramble for indigenous lands grew more ruthless, the city of La Paz experienced an influx of Aymara refugees fleeing rural violence and land divestiture. The metaphorical lettered city, in other words, was under assault by the forces of modernization. The Aymarization of La Paz intensified during the liberal boom years of the early 1900s, as the city became a refuge and place of protest for the ex-comunarios and a sprawling street fair for Aymara merchants and laborers. Such a jostling of ethnic-racial groups in downtown La Paz brought the city's lettered elites face to face with their Indian Other. And if such everyday encounters failed to alarm progressive members of the urban elite, then the specters of "race war" on the altiplano certainly did. All this combined to make the "Indian problem" more urgent to the urban architects of nationhood in Bolivia than to those almost anywhere else in Latin America.

Under such circumstances, Bolivian elites confronted a fundamental contradiction of postcolonial nationmaking—how to unify this weak and divided nation around universal principles of literacy, suffrage, and civilization while securing social peace in the countryside and protecting the lettered city of La Paz from litigious Indians and acculturating *cholos*? How would La Paz's liberal vanguard fashion a national pedagogy that might reconcile these contradictory goals of cultural hegemony and racial exclusion? Would educators promote the Spanish language and literacy so as to inculcate hispanist values, hasten Indian acculturation, and prepare the rural masses for their entry into national political life? Or would educational reformers seek to educate Indians in their "natural habitat," away from the harmful social influences of the city and its "degenerate" hybrid races? Would Bolivia's national pedagogues discover the "national soul" in a hispanized version of *mestizaje*, or in some recycled version of Indian redemption and racial purity?

Bolivian elites tried to confront such questions through the lens of rural school reform. The development of a separate system of Indian schooling privileged manual labor over literacy. Racial discourses played an important part in the imagining and engineering of a modern Bolivian society through pedagogic reforms. For it was in the production of race and educational discourses that we can perceive the techniques Bolivia's letrados used to defend their cultural authority against the challenge of literate and litigious Indians who were flooding the lettered public sphere with their own written and oral dispositions on land, justice, and citizenship. Educational reformers played a key role in the formation of a racial discourse impacting educational policy. By 1920, Bolivia had set in place a segregated model of rural Indian schooling that was to endure for almost fifty years. A dissident group of intellectuals hijacked the liberal ideal of universal literacy and schooling to push forward a model of Indian schooling that subordinated universal literacy to specialized labor. Bolivia's reformulated "national pedagogy" became a discursive tool for valorizing a new subject—the schooled, but unlettered, Indian.

The Politics of Possibility

Around 1900 Bolivia's writers and statesmen were eager to capitalize on the new liberal-positivist spirit of science, rationality, progress, and reform. Encouraged by the racial prognosis of the national census of 1900, and predicting the gradual racial assimilation of Aymara and Quechua peasants, a few *pensadores* began to toy with theories of race and environment to diagnose the essential character of Bolivia, Latin America's most Indian nation, and predict its destiny. Among a tiny vanguard of writers, educators, and politicians, new doctrines of environmental determinism opened the possibility of racial uplift and improvement. The idea that the Indian was a victim of nature, history, and deprivation gained currency in the writings of Bautista Saavedra, among others. After the murder of liberal soldiers by Aymara rebels in the 1899 civil war, Saavedra became the overnight expert on the Indian "collective psychology" in his role as the Indians' defense lawyer. Before the court and in the press, Saavedra vigorously argued that the Aymara's sociopsychic character was molded as much by climatic and social forces, as by biology. The Aymara's desire for revenge on Bolivian society, Saavedra contended, sprang from their centuries-long oppression. While this argument gave cold comfort to Indian defendants, it carried a hopeful message for educators and other reformers, who believed that medicine, technology, and schools would sanitize and improve the living conditions of the Indian race.[9] It was the possibility of racial regeneration that made the softer doctrines of environmentalism so attractive to Bolivia's new liberal vanguard. In his acclaimed 1903 essay on "the principles of sociology," Daniel Sánchez Bustamante, the university rector, endorsed the environmental doctrine, proclaiming that if the psychological character of a people (or a "race") were primarily the product of the environment, then that character could be positively shaped by environmental factors such as education.[10] For this young educator, public education would provide the antidote to "nature, which has been cruel to the uncivilized races."[11]

Here, then, was an early Bolivian expression of what Nancy Stepan has called Latin America's version of "pliant racism," a construct that privileged environment over blood and left open the possibility of "social agency and purposive action."[12] Bolivian liberals heeded the hopeful words of the rector. Upon assuming the Ministry of Instruction and Justice in 1904, Juan Saracho, a liberal, went before congress to proclaim the need to sacrifice everything for the cause of "consolidating Bolivian nationality . . . through moral, intellectual, and physical education." To educate was to "construct a new fatherland."[13]

Saracho issued this call to arms at a propitious moment. There was growing public awareness of Bolivia's disastrous state of primary education in the early 1900s. Thanks to official inspections, it was public knowledge that primary and secondary school curricula were still cast in eighteenth-century molds of "scholasticism," "verbalism," and mind-numbing memorization. The university continued to produce legions of lawyers and other *doctorcitos*, for whom oratory, writing, law, and bureaucracy constituted essential professional instruments, the same instruments of the colonial period. But where were the mining engineers, land surveyors, industrialists, and other stewards of capitalist development? Worse yet, the nation's primary schools, where they existed, were failing their pupils on all levels. According to the Ministry of Instruction, most students entering secondary schools did not know their letters or numbers. Academic standards were abysmal, but the state could not regulate curricular standards since 95 percent of the nation's primary schools were controlled by provincial authorities. Although the liberal state increased funding for education and established some sixty new rural primary schools over the course of the decade, it scarcely made a dent in the monopolies that municipal authorities and religious organizations exercised over schooling.[14] And, needless to say, Bolivia had one of Latin America's highest rates of illiteracy in the early twentieth century.[15]

The school inspector's dismal reports added a sense of urgency to the Liberal Party's project to build a federal system of compulsory education. Its first priority was to break down Bolivia's landlocked isolation by training a cadre of schoolteachers in the latest pedagogic philosophies and methods. In

1905, Saracho raised funds to send the first group of Bolivian students to study in Chile's Escuela Normal. Soon afterward, he recruited Chilean educators to change the outmoded methods and dangerous influences of Methodist missionaries working among Aymara communities on the altiplano. But it was mainly to Europe that Saracho looked for inspiration, and he found the perfect emissary in his esteemed colleague, Sánchez Bustamante. In 1908 the young writer and educator set out on his grand tour of teacher-training institutes in Chile, Argentina, Spain, France, Italy, Switzerland, Germany, England, and Belgium. In Brussels, Sánchez Bustamante finally found the man he was looking for: an avant-garde Belgian educator who was eager to shape school reform according to the latest pedagogic fashions and thereby bring Bolivia into the modern, "civilized" world. Upon his arrival in 1909, Georges Rouma became the liberals' chief architect of educational policies for the next eight or nine years.

Rouma's first task was to mobilize a professional corps of teachers who would carry his enlightened principles and methods into the new federal schoolhouses, which were supposed to proliferate throughout the cities and the countryside.[16] With the blessings of the Ministry of Instruction, Rouma established Bolivia's first Escuela Normal (teacher training institute) in Sucre in 1909. The school's opening was itself a foundational act, rich in patriotic symbolism. President Ismael Montes (holding office from 1904–9 and from 1913–17) consecrated the school's founding with utopian hopes for Bolivia's "second emancipation." Leading this spiritual-cultural revolution to genuine nationhood would be the teachers and professors, armed with new pedagogic knowledge.[17] Only slightly more circumspect, Daniel Sánchez Bustamante, the new education minister, viewed the Escuela Normal as the instrument through which the government could discover and mold "the Bolivian soul" and improve the race.[18] But as Rouma soon discovered, patriotic rhetoric was cheap, political alliances transitory, and financial support almost nil. In spite of these structural obstacles and political shifts, however, Rouma managed to turn the Sucre school into an enclave of literary, social scientific, and professional activities. By 1920, Bolivia had formed its first generation of *normalistas*, many of whom became leading public intellectuals and educators during the 1920s and 1930s.

Equally important was Rouma's move to establish the Escuela Normal as a catalyst of educational and scientific inquiry into the pedagogic subject. From his research on abnormal children in Belgium, Rouma now turned to the "psycho-social character" of Bolivian children, so as to be able to design an educational program to improve it. Based on empirical observations, Rouma's *"Les indiens quitchouas et aymaraes de haut plateau de la Bolivie"* depicted the collective character flaws of the nation: the lack of a scientific spirit, emotive excess, a lack of will power, and false patriotism. Rouma's prescription? Bolivia's pedagogic revolution had to mold *normalista* students into men of action, will power, and scientific spirit so they could carry these virtues into schoolhouses across the nation. Specifically, the Escuela Normal would instill in its students *"el espíritu docente"*: work ethic, self-confidence, responsibility, and commitment.[19]

Rouma's confidence in the power of pedagogy to mold men was scientifically confirmed in the anthropometric research of French scientist Arthur Chervin. Using hundreds of photographs and anatomical specimens, Chervin had compiled cranial measurements that shed new light on the country's prospects for racial improvement and economic development. Chervin's study was optimistic. Bolivia's racial destiny was bound to improve if the Indian races intermixed with the mestizos and the nation gradually whitened its racial stock through eugenic and cultural means.[20] His prescription for Bolivian racial progress was the prevailing one in most of Latin America in the early 1900s: whitening through the intermediate eugenic stage of mestizaje.

Rouma was encouraged by Chervin's findings. Not content to rely on the French scientist's evidence, however, Rouma conducted his own studies of bones and skulls dug up from graves at Tiwanaku in order to diagnose the "racial physiology" of Bolivian Indians, cholos, and mestizos.[21] His findings lent scientific authority to his overarching goal: to civilize and assimilate the Aymara and Quechua (and eventually the Guaraní) races into a unified, Spanish-speaking, mestizo Bolivia. Toward that end, Rouma's pedagogy would be organized around the principle of *"castellanización"*; that is, schooling all Bolivian children in basic moral and civic values through literacy and Spanish language instruction. All of Bolivia's primary schools would follow a uniform curriculum: "moral and civic education," "aesthetic education," drawing and music, physical education, writing, "national language," arithmetic, geography, history, and constitutional law, among other subjects. To integrate non-Spanish-speaking children into this curriculum, the country's rural primary schools would offer a two-year preparatory program designed to "initiate students into the everyday use of the national language," and "awaken their intellectual aptitudes and discipline."[22] These programs would then feed their graduates into regular primary school programs. The curriculum, although adjusted to local conditions, was designed to create a uniformly literate, acculturated, and moralized population. And Bolivia would leave behind its racial backwardness and enter the company of civilized nations.

Popular Literacy, Suffrage, and the Dangers of the Partisan Game

Liberal ambitions for spreading rural schools indicate how high the stakes were for them. Even without Gramscian theory to point the way, Bolivian state-builders were farsighted enough to realize that popular education might become an essential tool for building a national culture and political economy. They saw in the state's educational apparatus (were it to be built) the means of extending control over the nation's 2 million Indian peasants, so as to wrench them free of feudal servitude or "primitive" *ayllu* economies. Where priests and missionaries had served as agents of cultural reform, rural teachers were left to bring the next generation of Indians into the regulatory ambit of the state as productive laborers and consumers, and possibly even as hispanized citizens in the distant future.

Not all of this liberal fanfare had to do with the imperatives of cultural assimilation. There were powerful partisan interests behind the liberal push to spread literacy and suffrage into rural and urban areas, where the underclasses might become electoral clientele and be carted off to voting urns in town plazas across the altiplano in election years. Over the years, the Liberal Party had proved effective in capturing the votes of indigenous authorities, traders, and landowners in rural villages throughout the southern highlands of Chayanta and parts of the northern altiplano.[23] Patronage pactmaking was a fixture of rural politics throughout Latin America, so it should come as no surprise that the issue of popular literacy became linked to partisan politics and, more generally, to class and racial anxieties over Indian participation in national politics. Not only did Bolivia's party system (spurning the principle of the secret ballot) rely on the public urn, but the electoral system itself (charged with the responsibility of ratifying the presidential victor) turned congressional elections into bitter high-stakes contests between Conservatives and Liberals. Each party hoped to secure its succession by packing parliament with loyal partisans, and the reigning president could wield his power either to capture or dissolve the legislative body. Even as the Liberal Party ushered in a twenty-year era of strongman rule following its victory in the 1899 civil war, it continued to deploy familiar tactics of political pactmaking to secure control over elections.[24]

Liberals took advantage of the clamor for "public instruction" as an instrument to expand their network of electoral clients into nearby Aymara communities. Indeed, President Montes was the first political leader to turn the ministries of education and war into agents of political recruitment. Working through these ministries, Montes saw a unique opportunity to hasten language and literacy training (*castellanización* and *alfabetización*, respectively). His minister of instruction, Juan Saracho, sent ambulatory teachers into the countryside to teach reading and writing in local Aymara communities. Saracho also ordered all large estate owners to establish primary schools for the children of their *colonos* (servile laborers).[25]

In addition, Liberal Party officials hunted for literate Indians, or Indian school instructors, during the electoral season. In Omasuyos and elsewhere, rural people remember the era of Montes as a time of Liberal Party officials' roaming the countryside in search of semiliterate peasant voters. In 1905 and 1906, for example, an official from the ministry roamed the countryside looking for "more citizens to inscribe as voters in the general elections. Having information that Avelino Siñani taught literacy . . . , the official thought he would discover new [Indian] voters who would favor [the Liberal Party]."[26] As Siñani's daughter recounted, the official did track down her father, a bilingual man who taught reading in the villages throughout Warisata and other parts of Omasuyo. The state official offered Siñani two *billetes* for every "literate voter" he mobilized for the Liberal Party. For his own reasons, Siñani accepted the proposal and used the political pact to expand his own networks of schools—at the risk of violent opposition from local *gamonales* (rural-based strongmen). Over the next several years, Montes apparently cultivated the relationship with Siñani by offering greater rewards and honors (e.g., an invitation to visit parliament in 1909) for Siñani's help "preparing voting citizens."[27]

Lest we think that liberal-Indian pacts like this one created a broadly based party in rural Bolivia, we need only remember the turbulent rural context in which the Montes government operated. For it was Liberal Party rule that unleashed a wave of *latifundismo* (hacienda expansion in Indian lands) that engulfed many parts of the altiplano. Meanwhile, other state projects also intruded on rural life: the enforced conscription of young Indian men into the army, the crackdown on rural-to-urban migration, and the liberal's ultimate project of cultural assimilation. As Silvia Rivera, Carlos Mamani, and other historians have vividly chronicled, the Montes years intensified the threat to indigenous rights to communal landholdings, territorial self-rule, and other Andean-colonial entitlements.[28] Indigenous communities took advantage of the liberal campaign to spread rural schools, but they did so under increasingly disadvantageous conditions. More than ever, they needed to restore an indigenous elite with access to Spanish literacy to engage the federal bureaucracy in their ongoing struggle over land, tax, and labor impositions.[29]

It is no surprise, then, that in 1908 Minister Saracho discovered intense enthusiasm among Aymaras for his ambulatory school project. Finding the popular stereotypes of the indifferent Indian unfounded, Saracho was overwhelmed by indigenous offers of support for the construction and maintenance of village schools and the enthusiasm that greeted most itinerant teachers who visited local communities.[30] Montes, in turn, promised indigenous communities that the state would send school supplies and even a teacher to each school Indians constructed of their own accord. Without a federal budget, and facing obdurate landlords who forbade their colonos to learn letters, Saracho's promises of government support were hollow. But they spurred indigenous demands for protection against landlord retribution, as ayllus and communities began to build a network of primary schools and to instruct their own people in the rudiments of reading land titles and other documents vital to communal defense. The grassroots communal movement for literacy might have played into Liberal partisan interests, but it simultaneously aimed to empower a new generation of indigenous leaders and litigators charged with the responsibility of defending local land titles against liberal policies of land divestiture and outright usurpation. Just as had occurred with liberal-peasant political pacts, the rural literacy campaign that Montes and Saracho promoted could be turned against the elite in the long-term indigenous struggle for community defense and ethnic empowerment. Peasant literacy might produce more clients in moments of intense interparty rivalry, but it also threatened to inflate the ranks of litigious peasants, political meddlers, and cholo migrants crashing against the gates of the lettered city.

From its early years, the Liberal Party's flirtation with peasant political pacts created anxiety among its political rivals. Every parliamentary and presidential election exploded in partisan intrigue and public accusations, which spurred the enemies of Montes to denounce liberal policies and ideals.[31] Key political leaders began to break ranks with the party after 1910. Daniel Sánchez Bustamante occupied the Ministry of Instruction barely a year and a half (1908–1909), and briefly resurfaced in the ministry in 1919, at the end of the liberal era. But by then he had repudiated liberal ideals of universal literacy and education. Bautista Saavedra departed from the Ministry of Education after only two years (1909–1910). He went on to form the opposition Republican Party in 1914, and then emerged as a conservative and authoritarian ideologue of Bolivian (anti)democracy. Although Saavedra used patronage to court indigenous support, he was dead set against promoting popular literacy and schooling.[32] Against the liberal utopia of mass schooling in the countryside, there arose a dissident movement that repudiated the Liberal monopoly of political power, its corrupt pacts, and dangerous policies. To these dissident liberals, popular literacy had become a dangerous thing—it had come to symbolize the scratchings of an ignorant, illiterate peasant who was instructed and intimidated by Liberal teachers and politicians to sign his name in the electoral registry so as to vote for a caudillo Liberal candidate. In their repudiation of cosmopolitanism and liberal positivism, a few prominent Bolivian intellectuals also began to assemble an alternative vision of the nation's moral character and the sort of national pedagogy that was needed to uplift the nation and set it on the road to modernity and redemption.

Toward a Pedagogy of Race

Around 1910, La Paz produced a phalanx of critical ethnographers, novelists, and pedagogues, who aspired to spiritual and scientific leadership beyond dangerous partisan politics. These dissident letrados were immersed in politics, but they also used their writing to provide pitiless studies of social reality and sweeping normative principles by which Bolivia might redeem its Indian races. From his lofty perch as a celebrated writer in exile, Alcides Arguedas excoriated Bolivia's multiracial inheritance as the source of collective illness in his famous *Pueblo enfermo* (1909). Far more influential than Arguedas, however, were Bolivian writers who took part in public life during the liberal era, and whose debates reverberated widely in government circles and urban journalism. Manuel Rigoberto Paredes produced ethnographies of altiplano provinces while serving as a deputy in congress. Franz Tamayo, an obscure poet, gained overnight fame in 1910 when he used his newspaper column to formulate a "national pedagogy" for Bolivia.[33] Bautista Saavedra and Sánchez Bustamante served as philosopher-educators while participating in politics and government.

As their counterparts in other Latin American cities had been, Bolivian letrados were engrossed in the intellectual traditions of Europe, from French racial doctrines to a variety of political ideologies, including socialism, anarchism, and communism. But Bolivian letrados also warned of the risks the passive acceptance of Europeanization posed to Bolivia's own traditions. As the vogue of liberalism and modernization declined after 1910, elites arrogated to themselves three major tasks. The first was to attack the basis of liberal-republican norms (popular literacy, universal suffrage, democracy, etc.) in the Bolivian racial milieu. The second involved constructing the "authentic" Indian subject in his "natural habitat." Third, paceño elites would reorganize rural Indian education around a strict regimen of moralization and manual labor.

Most urgent was the democratizing challenge to the white city of letters, as popular literacy and suffrage spread among new rural and urban laborers. By the early 1900s, liberal critics deployed European and Argentine strictures against racial hybridism to explain and condemn the moral perversion of Bolivian democracy. Certainly this evolutionary paradigm linking racial and republican degeneracy was not an original formulation. By the 1880s, Gabriel René Moreno and Nicomedes Antelo, Bolivian race theorists, had adapted the ideas of Arthur de Gobineau and Hippolyte Taine to deplore the biocultural effects of mestizaje and to rail against the imposition of republican liberties in a racially and materially backward nation like Bolivia.[34] But only when faced with the threat of liberal populism and social reforms—specifically Saracho and Rouma's project to spread literacy and schooling throughout the countryside—did Bolivian writers take up the interlocking themes of degenerative mestizaje, *caudillismo* (strong-man politics), and the history of failed republicanism.

The emerging narrative of racial and national decline might have been lifted from any pessimistic race theorist in Latin America at the time. The story is familiar: a golden age of colonialism is shattered by the wars of independence; militarism and anarchy spread; white Spanish immigration dries up and the pseudorepublic withers into an anemic social organism plagued by petty violence, greed, and corruption. Writing from the provinces, Manuel Rigoberto Paredes sketched the ethnographic details of Bolivia's national descent into economic and moral decay. He described caudillo bands, especially the *cruzadas* that fled across the Peruvian border only to reinvade Bolivia in order to pillage border towns, making life in the countryside impossible. Abandoned by the *hacendados*, whole regions across the altiplano turned into desert, livestock died, artisan production declined, and hunger haunted every peasant dwelling. Fifty years of republicanism had turned the altiplano backlands of the new capital of La Paz into a wasteland, inhabited by only the worst social types—mestizo despots and predators given to drink, corruption, and brutality.[35] Alcides Arguedas crystallized the narrative of racial and republican decline in his early diagnostic writing on Bolivia as a "sick society," as well as in his later historical volumes on the "caudillo republic." He hung Bolivia's wretched history of caudillismo on the psychosocial character of the cholo: "The history of this country, Bolivia, is . . . in synthesis, that of the cholo in his different incarnations . . . as ruler, legislator, magistrate, industrialist, or businessman."[36]

By narrating national decline, these writers reorganized elite anxieties around the literate, politicized cholo ("scientifically" defined as the biocultural product of crossbreeding Indians and mestizos). As Bolivian elites tried to grapple with the ambiguous implications of biocultural mestizaje—did it signify the degeneration or regeneration of the future nation?—they reorganized the category of "cholo" as an acculturating, semiliterate, prerational political subject. Collectively, cholos represented Bolivia's counterpart to Gustave Le Bon's republican rabble.[37] As Saavedra had demonstrated at the turn of the century, the Le Bonian concept of "collective psychology" provided a powerful interpretive framework for indicting the Aymara "criminal mind" as well as republics overrun by raving Jacobins and other mobs.[38] Several years later, Paredes redeployed the concept to characterize the "cholo electoral mob" and its sabotage of Bolivia's system of parliamentary democracy.[39]

In his celebrated series of newspaper essays from 1910 on the need to create a "national pedagogy," Franz Tamayo consolidated these linked images of cholaje, popular politics, and political corruption. In Tamayo's mental world, to be a cholo was to be a social parasite.[40] Reconstituted as an atavistic *elector*, or servile political client, the Bolivian cholo thus assumed the historic burden of Bolivia's hundred-year failure of republicanism.

More importantly, treacherous liberal practices and misguided policies were actually *producing* cholos, who (by definition) were beginning to infiltrate the public sphere and engage the "gravest questions of the state." Through universal education and conscription, the Liberal Party had created the machinery to manufacture more cholos. The new conservative vanguard disagreed only about which was more dangerous to society: universal literacy or conscription, giving Indians access to their first letters or their first guns? Writing from the provinces, Paredes argued that the military was proving to be the most dangerous source of ethnic violence in the countryside: "There is no worse enemy of the Indian than the Indian converted into a soldier."[41] Tamayo, on the other hand, excoriated the liberals' project of universal primary education, which was uprooting and demoralizing the Indian. Once an honest laborer and miner, the schooled cholo now aspired to become a corrupt elector or public employee—that is, another "parasite" on the nation.[42]

Criollo uses, abuses, and fears of the *indio letrado* (reinvented as the politicized cholo) lay at the center of pedagogic debates about Indian education in the early 1900s.[43] Whereas the liberals under Saracho and later under Rouma tried to extend popular literacy as an instrument of partisan power-building and, more generally, as a strategy of castellanización, their opponents exposed the dangers of book-learning under the treacherous practices of liberal-populist pactmaking. Writing against the liberal establishment in 1910, Tamayo called for a "national pedagogy" to replace the liberals' indiscriminant application of universal literacy and suffrage. Indians needed civilizing and hispanizing; they needed instruction in the practical arts of agropastoralism; eventually they would need to be instructed in their letters. But Tamayo warned against the idea of organizing rural schooling around literacy and "intellectualism." Tamayo's warning reverberated through Bolivian writings on race, education, and nation over the next twenty years. By the end of the second decade, Bolivia's grand diagnosticians of democracy routinely called for laws that effectively restricted suffrage, and for education that downgraded literacy instruction in favor of work regimes in rural schools.[44] It fell to the *indigenista* writers and reformers to craft pedagogic goals and methods that hewed to Bolivia's indigenous environment and culture.

As La Paz's dissident indigenistas wrestled with theories of *raza y medio* (race and habitat), they invariably began to rearrange racial-ethnic categories —Criollo whiteness, Indianness, and variant racial-cultural hybridities. None of these race categories fared well under their critical gaze. Even Criollo whiteness was deemed contaminated because of the preponderance of "decadent Latin blood."[45] Mestizos and Indians ranked lower in the modern racial taxonomic order, both of them supposedly degraded products of racial and environmental conditioning over centuries of colonial despotism and republican anarchy. But whereas liberal ideologues promoted progressive whitening, La Paz's dissenters discovered in the "pure" Aymara Indian the authentic roots of Bolivian identity. As the new icon of racial purity and authenticity, the Aymara was counterposed to the degenerate hybrid races, which had led to Bolivia's nineteenth-century political nihilism.

Indigenistas reworked colonial idioms of Indian or mestizo and purity or pollution through a variety of literary and scientific genres. Out of this rich national literature emerged a new figure: the redeemed Aymara. Pure, stoic, potentially savage, yet also hard working, the indigenista's Aymara Indian was well adapted to the harsh conditions of life on the high plateau.[46] This positive gloss on the Aymara reflected the regional imperative to modernize highland agriculture on the altiplano. If the Aymara race were to disappear, Paredes warned in 1906, Bolivia would lose its high-altitude farmers because European immigrants could not tolerate the harsh climate of highland Bolivia.[47] Tamayo was more fervent about the Indian's essential role in the national economy. Alone among the races, he proclaimed in 1910, the Indian had managed "to produce, to produce incessantly in whatever form, be it agricultural or mining labor, rustic manufacturing or manual service in the urban economy."[48]

This emerging iconography of Bolivia's telluric and utilitarian Indian—the muscle power and perhaps even the soul of the nation—carried several implications. First, the Indian race belonged in its "natural habitat," where the primordial forces of nature had molded the Aymara race, and where it had become strong, autonomous, and autodidactic.[49] The Indian's racial and spatial fixity, and the metaphysical merging of raza y medio, provided the perfect foil against changes taking place in real life—escalating incidents of Aymara land despoliation, comunario mobilization, Aymara political trafficking in the tribunals, and the stream of rural-to-urban migration into La Paz. Second, the Indian's "natural attributes" rendered him useful to the nation in certain capacities. Arguedas appraised the Indian as a good and willing cultivator; as an excellent miner endowed with physical endurance and strength; and as a deeply regimented, brave warrior who could be turned into a superior soldier. Soldier, miner, farmer: this was the Indian's destiny in the modernizing nation.[50] Third, the enlightened conservative Criollos needed to protect and uplift the Aymara race, and prepare it for incorporation into the agrarian economy, while guarding against the dangers of Aymara rebellion, acculturation, and migration to the city.

In short, these indigenista literary truths fundamentally challenged the populist rhetoric and practices of Liberal Party reformism. The dissident elites shared many of the long-range goals of their "liberal enemies": to promote economic development, to integrate the national territory, and to subject rural Indian cultures to the modernizing norms of capitalist society. Yet they profoundly disagreed on the institutional means by which these nationmaking goals might be accomplished. The indigenista project boiled down to one negative prescription: Indians should not be allowed to crash the gates of the lettered city, either in metaphorical or real terms. The indigenista prescription called for "the education of the Indian in his own environment" and by 1920, it had become the mantra of Bolivia's Ministry of Instruction.

This redefinition of Indian education began even before the Liberal Party was banished from power in 1920. There were growing internal debates and power struggles over the issue of Indian education within the Ministry of Instruction. In his 1918 report to congress, the instruction minister provided the first official critique of Rouma's "imported pedagogy."[51] The ministry's critical stance reflected alarming reports from the field, where rural teachers confronted the risks of trying to convert pedagogy into practice. One of the more eye-opening reports came from a director and a teacher stationed in the rural normal school of Umala. They reported an unstable state of affairs and issued a sharp warning against liberal policies of universal instruction and conscription. These teachers worried about the effects of turning Aymara conscripts back into civilians armed with modern guns and political claims: "Militarized, the Indian has a broader concept of his rights and more audacity to react against the landlord who demands services that he no longer thinks is just."[52] The teachers warned against the rising tide of rural militarism, since Aymara exconscript rebels were seen deploying military maneuvers against the Bolivian infantry that they had learned in the barracks as conscripts. In villages around Lake Titicaca, Indians had caches of modern rifles, which they used with "extraordinary precision." Writing from the edge of the ethnic frontier, these rural teachers offered two dismal prophesies— the apocalyptic endgame of race war (as Indians acquired vigor, unity of thought, and an emancipatory agenda) or the nihilistic prospect of continual racial degeneration until the altiplano's 500,000 Aymara Indians (some 25 percent of the total population, they noted) gradually died off.

This alarming report reveals the multiple functions that rural teachers might have served in the expanding apparatus of state power—as civilizing agents, instructors, and spies. It can also be read as a barometer of agrarian tensions across the altiplano. The teachers' fear of armed Aymara mobilization is almost palpable, while their firsthand observations and field experience lend a measure of credibility to their alarm. Indeed, across the altiplano, indigenous communities were mobilizing under a network of *caciques* and *apoderados* (inherited chiefs and appointed authorities), who wielded ancient titles and petitions demanding the return of their colonial land rights.

Liberal dogmas of universal schooling and conscription must have seemed reckless when set against the social tremors registering so vividly in the schoolteachers' report.

Perhaps it is not surprising, then, that the Ministry of Instruction moved in 1918 and 1919 to tighten its control over rural schools and to revoke the liberal curriculum. The ministry discarded Rouma's pedagogic goal of universal castellanización in favor of an industrial curriculum whose central objective was to train the rural workforce. Specifically, the ministry's 1919 statute called for the conversion of rural normal schools into agricultural work-schools and for their relocation to remote areas, thickly populated by "pure" Indians. The new work-school model was the centerpiece of the tripartite cycle of rural schooling: the elementary cycle, the work-school cycle, and the normal. The work-schools would be the basis of the altiplano's economic recovery and the nation's defense against the onslaught of foreign manufacturing competition. They would be appendages of the rural normal schools, so that the two establishments could coordinate their curricula around manual labor training. The work-school would produce two sorts of graduates—skilled artisans and agriculturalists who would go on to practice their practical knowledge, and those students who would move into the third cycle of the normal. Eventually, Indian *normalistas* would become the purveyors of the new technical education—either by teaching in distant elementary schools or by participating as preceptors of "general material" in the work-schools. In either case, they would use apprenticeship methods to teach practical skills—in that way rooting out of the schools "all academic teaching that does not form manual laborers."[53] Thus conceived, castellanización was to be linked to practical knowledge, rather than to reading and writing.

Lest we attribute this effort at curricular reform simply to prevailing positivist modes of pedagogy, we need to relocate it in the larger arena of letrado debates about race, place, and the dangers of putting literate knowledge in the hands of peasants and plebes. The new rural pedagogy of race derived much of its rationale from its power to articulate two contradictory needs of the lettered city—to integrate the Indian masses into the modernizing nation-state as a subaltern labor force, and to deny them the power of writing, suffrage, and ultimately citizenship. The teaching of rudimentary ABCs could not be avoided if Indians were ultimately to be instructed in the Spanish language and values, morality and religion, patriotism and military drills. But a separate system of rural schools would be set up to monitor the types of knowledge taught and learned. And in line with the racial science of pedagogy, Indians would be taught in accord with their "natural fitness" for manual labor. The political significance of such pedagogic innovation was nothing less than to defend racial difference and caste hierarchy.[54]

*

In 1920 La Paz's lettered elites began to hammer their pedagogy of race into concrete form, by designing the ideal Indian work-school colony. In blueprint, the Indian work-school was an insular utopia of community and schooling, far removed from the threat of landlords or urban vices. It would take another two decades before a few educational reformers tried to put such plans into operation in Warisata and elsewhere. Educational reform was an emerging field of knowledge and cultural prescription, one that fashioned racial, spatial, and environmental truths to buttress the case for segregated Indian work-schools. This discursive project represents another aspect of the paradox of Angel Rama's lettered city. In Bolivia, national pedagogy provided an interpretive space for urban letrados to promote education to the rural masses, while at the same time letrados tried to protect the socioracial exclusivity of the lettered city. La Paz's new generation of literary nationalists, who reached into the Indian hinterland to produce a corpus of writing on Bolivia's authentic Indians, geographies, and psychic self, were the same men who sought to restrict the exercise of letters and, by extension, suffrage and citizenship. Although the physical ejection of the unruly indigenous masses from the city of La Paz was untenable, pedagogic reformers looked to education as the last best defense against literate, litigating, and politicizing peasants. By the same token, positivist, anarchosyndicalist, and utilitarian ideologies furnished complementary arguments in favor of vocational training for the masses over any other form of knowledge. A growing body of politicians and educators promoted agrarian-industrial training for the Indian children of the altiplano in the hope that they would form a future labor force of modern farmers.

In either case, to educate the Indian in his natural habitat became the prescriptive norm of Bolivia's new national pedagogy. It could be argued, then, that the debate over mass peasant schooling resolved itself, at least for the moment, in a state project to shore up racial, spatial, and class hierarchies rather than breach the boundaries of the lettered city and allow Indians to acquire literacy and citizenship rights. Such a project rested on the moral dichotomy between the pure Aymara and the plebian cholo, and between the lettered city and the unlettered campo. Thus the letrados of La Paz tried to bundle race, space, and pedagogy into a new relationship that would preserve social exclusivity of the city, politics, and public life.

It is not surprising, then, that as these pioneering pedagogues cast about for new paradigms of Indian boarding and work-schools, they turned their sights to the far north, where the United States had a century-long tradition of segregated schooling for its African and Indian populations. For Bolivian reformers, there was much to be learned from the famous black teacher-training schools of Hampton, Virginia, and Tuskeegee, Alabama. Their curriculum seemed to be compatible with Bolivia's new pedagogic goals: to instruct black and Indian students "to produce, not to know."[55] Felipe Guzmán, once the champion of Liberal Party reform, now adhered to the new precepts of separate and unequal Indian education, modeled after the Hampton Institute, the oldest vocational training school for African Americans. In 1922, he wrote that "the [educational] plan that Hampton has followed, with its retarded negroes and Indians, is almost identical to that which we propose for the education of the altiplano Indians. The system is, then, based on scientific prescriptions, according to which . . . industrial and manual labor is directly related to the mental agility that the Indian [race] has achieved in its evolution."[56] Although more blunt than many other government proposals, Felipe Guzmán's call for a Hampton-style Indian normal school had all the hallmarks of the conservative indigenista agenda: to create a disciplined and productive population of Aymara farmers and artisans, affixed to the land, and situated safely beyond the boundaries of the lettered city.

Notes

1. Rama 1996. See also González Echevarría 1990; Mignolo 1996; and Adorno 1986.

2. According to Mignolo, the term "*letrado*," in common use in sixteenth-century Castile, carried two meanings: someone who possessed scientific knowledge (scientific knowledge was associated with the written word) or an expert in law (including lawyers, notaries, and scribes). Rama uses the term for the high-ranking functionaries who performed the ideological and administrative work of Spanish colonial rule.

3. Rama 1996, 56.

4. Ibid., 112.

5. Adelman 2004, 230.

6. The historical sociology of education in Latin America goes well beyond the scope of this essay. Suffice it to say that scholars have long noted the testy relationship

among educational values, ideological and partisan interests, and social and popular pressures for change. But one narrative arc, generally recognized by scholars, traces the decline, in the face of growing skepticism, of the ideal of a universal literate public. After 1900, a range of educational reformers, on both the left and right wings of the political spectrum, began to question the function of schooling in under-developed societies radically divided by region, race, and class. See Britton 1994; Carnoy and Samoff 1990.

7. Stepan 1991.

8. Critical theorists of schools and other "disciplinary regimes" of the modernizing state borrow heavily from Michel Foucault. They approach schools not only from narrow institutional or pedagogical points of view, but as social and symbolic sites where new power relations, representations, and knowledges were formed in societies undergoing industrial transitions. See, for example, Levinson et al. 1996; and Giroux 1992.

9. Saavedra 1987.

10. Sánchez Bustamante 1903. See Francovich 2002, 20, 29–33; and Albarracín Millán 1978, 44–72.

11. Sánchez Bustamante 1903, 161.

12. Stepan 1991, 87.

13. Memoria del Ministro de Justicia e Instrucción Pública al Congreso Ordinario de 1904. Archivo Histórico de la Honorable Cámara de Diputados (AHHCD) 350.0035, M533 (1904), 52–53.

14. Calderón Jemio 1994, 70.

15. Tristan Marof, a socialist critic and writer, estimated that 85 percent of the Bolivian population was illiterate in the mid-1930s. See Marof 1934, 42. In 1955, the government's official rate of illiteracy hovered around 70 percent, with much higher rates in some rural areas. Clearly, these numbers represent a stark failure of the Bolivian government. Or is it too cynical to suggest that these statistics offer testimony to the government's historic indifference to popular illiteracy?

16. Calderón Jemio 1994, 56–57, 62–63.

17. Quoted in Suárez Arnez 1958, 233.

18. Ibid.

19. Ibid., 237.

20. Chervin 1908.

21. See Rouma 1911; Rouma 1928.

22. Rep. de Bolivia. Ministerio de Instrucción Pública y Agricultura. *Informe del Dr. Georges Rouma, Director General de Instrucción Primaria, Secundaria, y Normal* (La Paz: Imprenta Velarde, 1916), 6–7.

23. See Irurozqui Victoriano 2000.

24. Klein 1969, 51.

25. Choque Canqui 1994, 14–15; Martínez 1995.

26. Quoted in Siñani de Willka 1992, 128.

27. Ibid., 129. Tomasa Siñani de Willka (daughter of Avelino Siñani), interview by author, August 25, 1990.

28. Rivera Cusicanqui 1984; and Mamani 1991.

29. Ibid. On the importance of indigenous literacy and self-representation, see Condori Chura and Ticona Alejo 1992.

30. Martínez 1995.

31. Paredes 1911.

32. Both men produced ambitious ideological indictments of liberal-republican values. See Sánchez Bustamante 1918; and Saavedra 1921.

33. The term, "national pedagogy," was coined by Ricardo Rojas, an Argentine cultural nationalist who repudiated positivist materialism and other imported ideals in favor of a conservative idealist project that would restore the authentic ethno-cultural character of the Argentine nation by celebrating vanishing folk cultures (gauchesque and otherwise), the hispanist past, and other "authentic" features of the nation against the onslaught of European immigrants. See especially his foundational work, *La restauración nacionalista* (Rojas 1909). Bolivia's counterpart, Franz Tamayo, published a year later his celebrated *Creación de una pedagogía nacional* [1910] (1988). He used the idea of "national pedagogy" to produce a diagnostic and prescriptive essay on Bolivia's multiracial landscape. For an especially insightful study of Tamayo's national pedagogy, see García Pabón 1998, chapter 6.

34. See Zea 1963, 198–202; and Irurozqui Victoriano 1994.

35. Paredes 1965, 180–81.

36. Arguedas 1936, 62.

37. Paredes 1911, 2.

38. On French race theory and its political context, see Nye 1975.

39. Paredes 1911.

40. Tamayo 1988, 56.

41. Paredes 1965, 191.

42. Tamayo 1988, 69–70.

43. García Pabón 1998, chapter 6; and Irurozqui Victoriano 1994, 154–80.

44. See Carlos Romero 1919; Guillén Pinto 1919; Saavedra 1921; Pérez Velasco 1928.

45. Quoted in Paredes 1911, 197; see also Arguedas 1936, 62.

46. Larson 2005. Marisol de la Cadena develops a parallel argument in her study of Cuzco's indigenist literary movement under the powerful influence of Luis Eduardo Valcárcel (de la Cadena 2000, especially chapter 2).

47. Paredes 1906, 120.

48. Tamayo 1988, 64.

49. Ibid., 68; Paredes 1923, 587; Arguedas 1936, 36.

50. Ibid., chapter 2.

51. Rep. de Bolivia. *Memorias y Anexos del Ministerio de Instrucción Pública y*

Agricultura (La Paz: Moderna, 1919). For parliamentary debate on Indian school reform and public instruction more generally, see *Proyectos de Leyes y Informes de la Cámara de Diputados* (La Paz: Moderna, 1919).

52. Mariaca and Peñaranda 1918, 8.

53. Ibid., 262.

54. See, for example, Rep. de Bolivia. Ministerio de Instrucción y Agricultura, *Memorias y Anexos* (La Paz: Imprenta Moderna, 1918).

55. Litwack 1998, 70.

56. Felipe Guzmán, "La educación de la raza indígena boliviana" (Letter to the Ministro de Estado en el Despacho de Guerra y Colonización, dated October 21, 1922), 4. Typewritten and filed by Elizardo Pérez in his personal papers.

PART III ✳ Racialization and Nationalist

Mythologies in the Twentieth Century

Indian Ruins, National Origins: Tiwanaku

and *Indigenismo* in La Paz, 1897–1933

SEEMIN QAYUM

The storied archaeological site at Tiwanaku became the source of local, regional, and national appropriations and dissensions in early twentieth-
century Bolivia. A landscape of abandoned ruins was intellectually reconstructed into a political monument that stood for a potent past, a past imbued with nationalist meaning that salvaged the present from a history of
ostensible racial and civilizational decline. After generations of republican
debate over the relative merits of the Inca and Spanish empires, Tiwanaku
emerged as a compelling alternative to both Inca-centered and Spanish-
centered narratives of the past. The discourse and practice of archaeology
and history were instrumental in the reconstruction of the local and the
national even as they relied on "fabrication, invention, and imagination" for
their authentication.[1] The Geographic Society of La Paz, an institution on the
cusp of state and civil society, produced a body of historical and ethnographic
knowledge asserting the primordial status of ancient Tiwanaku as an Andean
and American civilization, and as fundamentally Aymara. The Society mar-
shalled the intelligentsia of the Liberal Party, which governed for most of the
first two decades of the twentieth century, its membership spanning the
upper echelons of Bolivian society, including statesmen, hacienda and mine
owners, scientists, and intellectuals.[2] Making manifest the "inseparability of
the spheres of professional and public knowledge, of academic and nationalist motivations," the cult of Tiwanaku symbolically condensed the Society's
vision of the Bolivian nation as projected from La Paz.[3]

A revealing source for understanding the symbolic potency of the site is a political tract published in 1897 that deemed Tiwanaku the origin of South American civilization and, therefore, the foundation for modern Bolivian nationality. The tract stands as one of the first definitive expressions of *indigenista* nationalism in Bolivia. By claiming Tiwanaku's precedence over the Inca empire, with its center at Cuzco, Bolivian indigenistas framed their nationalist project against Peruvian culture and society. Emphasis on the ancient archaeological site at Tiwanaku made possible an alternative version of Andean history, one that was Tiwanaku-centered rather than Cuzco-centered. According to this vision, the Bolivian nation and its Creole elites no longer had to summon up an imperial Inca past that was closely associated with Peru.[4] For the new century they had a glorious, primordial Aymara past situated geographically within Bolivian territory. Yet Bolivian Creole intellectuals also had continental pretensions, for Tiwanaku gave them an original claim to American identity. Through the use of scientific, racial, and civilizational discourses, the Geographic Society made Tiwanaku the cradle not only of Bolivian nationality but also of American civilization.

Tiwanaku was an ancient city-state located just south of Lake Titicaca on the altiplano, or highland plateau, of La Paz. Emerging around 200 C.E., Tiwanaku became the leading political and religious site within the Lake Titicaca basin by about 500 C.E. It subsequently became the center of an extended territorial and trade network expanding westward to coastal Peru, to the fertile valleys east of Lake Titicaca as well as to Cochabamba, and reaching as far south as northern Chile. Tiwanaku suddenly entered into decline and collapsed around 1100 C.E.[5] As the Inca state expanded in the fourteenth century, it sought legitimacy through symbolic links with the Titicaca basin and the prestigious Tiwanaku civilization. When Spanish chroniclers such as Pedro Cieza de León arrived in the region in the mid-sixteenth century, they collected Inca and local Andean origin myths involving this sacred site.[6] In the nineteenth century the ruins were visited by a long list of European travelers and scholars who published studies or memoirs of their stays.[7] It was on these foundations that turn-of-the-century *letrados* (the lettered elites discussed by Brooke Larson in this volume) associated with the Geographic Society of La Paz would construct their indigenista interpretations of the local and national significance of Tiwanaku.

Indigenismo has taken a variety of forms in twentieth-century Latin America. The term refers commonly to a reformist movement led by mestizo and Creole intellectuals and artists who sought to defend a marginalized Indian population and vindicate its cultural past or future potential. Indigenistas criticized the abuses of a backward, "feudal" order in the countryside, and their concerns helped to motivate social and agrarian reforms on the part of modernizing and populist state governments. In Mexico, indigenismo served the assimilationist aims of the postrevolutionary government and blended with the official national ideology of mestizaje, engendering the idea of a "cosmic race," as José Vasconcelos would have it. In Peru, indigenismo arose most forcefully in Cuzco as intellectual elites promoted a regional identity based on a celebration of the Inca heritage. It subsequently grew to become an important source of Peruvian national cultural identity.[8]

In the heyday of the movement, from the 1920s to the 1960s, indigenismo was never as developed as a cultural or political project in Bolivia as it was elsewhere. Yet Tiwanaku and Aymara civilization did provide raw material for Bolivian Creole intellectuals to develop a distinctive indigenismo that eventually served the nationalist project culminating in the 1952 national revolution.[9] This tentative development of Bolivian indigenismo reflects the fraught relation between liberal elites and the contemporaneous political mobilization of Aymara communities in the Lake Titicaca and La Paz regions. Some of the most forceful indigenous and "Indianist" movements in late nineteenth-century and twentieth-century Latin America emerged in these regions, beginning with the Zárate Willka mobilization during the 1899 Federal War and the *cacique-apoderado* movement for indigenous territorial and cultural restoration from the 1910s to the 1930s.[10] In the period discussed in this essay, there were both efforts at alliances between elite party officials and Indian leaders, and conflicts leading to the criminalization and repression of mobilized Indian community members.[11] It is beyond the scope of this essay to explore the relationship between indigenismo and Indian politics, but the hesitant, erratic nature of the relationship is suggestive of the ultimately nonhegemonic character of Bolivian indigenismo.

Local Politics and National Projections

In 1897 the representatives of the town of Tiwanaku on the shores of Lake Titicaca published a tract arguing against the transfer of the capital of the second section of the province of Pacajes to the rival claimant, the town of Viacha, located some distance inland near the departmental capital, La Paz.[12] Tiwanaku had gained the right to be the capital only five years earlier and was now faced with a counterinitiative from the pro-Viacha forces. The tract was intended to appeal to the rational and patriotic sentiments of the political representatives of Pacajes. It also sought to influence national opinion about the rightful place of Tiwanaku in politics, geography, and history.

That the *vecinos* or townspeople of Tiwanaku felt their political struggle had a place on the national stage in large part rested on the claim, unilaterally stated in the first paragraph of the tract, that Pacajes was the richest province of the Department of La Paz. This claim was borne out by the presence of the Corocoro tin mines and the port of Guaqui on Lake Titicaca. The province was rivaled only by the prosperous coca-producing province of Yungas. Moreover, it was noted in the tract that Tiwanaku constituted the geographic and historic center of the province and enjoyed considerable administrative efficacy, as evidenced by the healthy state of repair of its roads (no mean feat in the Bolivian highlands).

The tract identified several factors to justify the location of a provincial capital: administrative improvements, protection of international borders (in this case with Peru), access by towns and villages in the provincial section, historical precedents, significant livelihood possibilities, and good local facilities. It then examined each point systematically, establishing the merits of Tiwanaku over Viacha in every case. Individual declarations of support for Tiwanaku from the major towns in the section appeared at the end of the document, along with a rather beautifully sketched map of the section. But the most compelling reason given, and the one to which most of the tract was dedicated, was the ruins at Tiwanaku. The town council of Tiwanaku took credit for having established at the site the richest and most-visited museum in all of Bolivia, one surpassing the Museum of La Paz in scientific interest.

The Tiwanaku Anthropological Museum had attracted the attention of Bolivians and foreigners alike. European scholars had petitioned the national and local governments for permission to excavate the archaeological site, offering more than 5,000 bolivianos as an investment in the proceedings. However, since the intention of the would-be excavators was to take the booty off to Europe, these applications had been rejected for offending a sense of "national decorum." One of these learned visitors, the German archaeologist Max Uhle, had purportedly offered to purchase the holdings of the Tiwanaku Museum for a sum of 26,000 bolivianos, but had "naturally" been refused.[13] This keen interest on the part of European cognoscenti confirmed the riches of Tiwanaku and supported Tiwanaku's claim of being not only the section capital but the cradle of civilization in South America: "The scientific world grants more importance to Tiahuanaco than to any other city in Bolivia and only a barbarian would, as a means of taking away its right to be the section capital, attack the *cradle of civilization in South America*, the source of our nationality, and the arc which encloses our tradition."[14]

To buttress these remarkable assertions, a text was included—attributed to an unpublished manuscript, "The Aborigenes of Bolivia," by "M. R. P."—that reviewed the scientific world's opinion about Tiwanaku. This section, entitled "Historical Foundations," covered the following topics: the Aymara as a national factor, Aymara evolution in Tiwanaku, the etymology of "Tiwanaku," the ruins and learned opinion, sculptural interpretations, and national writers (as opposed to the "learned opinion" of foreign travelers and scientists covered previously). M. R. P. was probably Manuel Rigoberto Paredes, noted folklorist, ethnographer, historian, and prominent member of the Geographic Society of La Paz.[15] What can be thought of as Paredes's section of the manuscript begins with the categorical assertion that "three major factors have successively contributed to form the Bolivian nationality: the Aymaras, the Quechuas, and the Spaniards." This mixture, despite a history of mutual distrust, antagonism, and conflict, had, over time, taken on "a national and eminently creole character which can be distinguished from that of other peoples."[16] Though Paredes's assertion left out the entire eastern lowlands and Amazon basin ethnic groups, his matter-of-fact assumption of a tripartite national heritage, which did not necessarily invoke mestizaje or racial miscegenation, contrasted sharply with the racialized conclusions of the census of 1900, in which census director Manuel Vicente Ballivián categorically asserted that the indigenous peoples of Bolivia were slowly but inevitably dying out.[17]

Paredes's section of the tract invokes what could be termed the spatialization of the national question: the Quechuas in national territory were considered descendants of *mitimaes*, or Inca colonies, and the provenance of the Spanish element was obvious. However, the origins of the Aymaras were a recurrent problem in the historiographic, ethnographic, and archaeological literature.[18] To unearth the buried Aymara past, Paredes relied on the texts of Spanish colonial chroniclers such as Cieza de León and the writings of republican foreign travelers—foremost among them, Alcide D'Orbigny, the French scientific explorer who journeyed throughout the country from 1830 to 1833, and Bartolomé Mitre, the Argentine statesman who spent the years 1847–48 in exile in Bolivia.[19]

Basing his views on early chroniclers and philologists, Paredes concluded that the Aymara language and the Aymara people were the most ancient in America and the root of Quechua culture and all others.[20] He noted that

Figure 1. View of ruins of ancient monuments at Tiwanaku. Credit: Alcide D'Orbigny. *Voyage dans l'Amérique Méridionale.* 9 vols. Paris and Strasbourg, 1835–1847. Plate Antiquités 4. Collections of the New York Public Library, Astor, Lenox, and Tilden Foundations.

Cieza de León had recounted an Aymara myth of origin involving an "immense flood."[21] Paredes also cited D'Orbigny's opinion that the Aymaras were the first to have acquired "a degree of civilization" in America and must have also been the ancestors of the people who formed the Inca empire. Such evidence served to shift the focus away from an Inca and Spanish imperial view of the past to one that essayed a deepening of historical time and a concentration of national space at Tiwanaku: "It is in Tiahuanaco, says D'Orbigny, within the Aymara nation, that agricultural and pastoral life were developed, where social ideas were germinated, and where the first monarchical and religious government of Peru was born. But to arrive at this state required the passage of many centuries and generations and this very civilization is so remote that its vestiges have all but disappeared."[22]

For Paredes, the Aymara metropolis of Tiwanaku was the counterpart of the great sites of the European and Asian ancient worlds (in Egypt, India, and the Roman Empire). Yet he was also grappling with the classic quandary of perceived civilizational decline—that temporal arc from glorious past to degraded present. Paredes ruefully acknowledged that "the Aymara metropolis is forgotten; its origin and deeds are entombed in silence and shadow: its glorious monuments are destroyed, its population is decimated, degraded, returning to barbarism because of this law of retreat/backward movement that in animal species is known as a *throwback*."[23]

Despite the problem of a presumed indigenous decline, however, Paredes sought to convince readers that the town of Tiwanaku should acquire national significance based on its former history and culture.

A History of National Neglect

Paredes took pains to demonstrate in both of his texts on Tiwanaku that while foreign interest was intense, albeit sporadic, the official Bolivian preoccupation with Tiwanaku had been minimal in the nineteenth century. Republican governments after those of Antonio José de Sucre (in office 1825–28) and Andrés Santa Cruz (in office 1829–39) had been singularly unconcerned with the fate of the site. Paredes apotheosized Santa Cruz as one of the best to have governed in America after Bolívar and Sucre, as he was of the "legitimate stock of the Mallcus [Aymara lords] of Omasuyos who must have descended from the ancient sovereigns of Tiahuanaco."[24] It is not clear from the text what Santa Cruz actually did for Tiwanaku—but this was overshadowed by his power to ethnically represent Tiwanaku's potential as a national symbol. In the early postindependence period, Presidents José Miguel de Velasco (in office 1839–41) and José Ballivián (in office 1841–47), influenced by D'Orbigny's scientific collections, legislated and carried out, respectively, the project of establishing a museum of Tiwanaku antiquities in La Paz. Paredes recounted how stone monoliths were taken from the site to La Paz, how one of them was broken and abandoned en route and the other was placed in the museum. In this same period of activity, what we can assume was the Gateway of the Sun monolith was lifted out of the earth and made to stand upright. Paredes related the legend that on the night of the gateway's unearthing, a torrent of rain was unleashed and a bolt of lightning struck a jagged crack in the stone.[25]

The sort of incidental damage that Paredes decried was part of a larger history of state neglect and systematic destruction and looting. Throughout the colonial and republican periods, relics and stones were taken from the site to pave roads and construct buildings such as the church of Tiwanaku. Railroad construction would inevitably play its part in this destruction, as another member of the Geographic Society later observed.[26] The authors of the

Tiahuanaco tract argued that the designation of Tiwanaku as district capital was the only means to rectify the long neglect of the site and address its municipal ambitions.

> Shameful and even inexplicable would it be that the most celebrated and meritorious town in Bolivia, and precisely the one that had made the country known in the scientific world, were treated as a miserable village. Its intrinsic importance does not increase an iota by being the capital, . . . [but its recognition as the capital] impedes the total destruction of the precious ruins. . . . Even if Tiahuanaco does not merit anything good from Bolivia . . . at the very least do not commit the injustice of robbing the poor distinction [of district capital] that was awarded to this miserable town that was the cradle of Bolivian nationality.[27]

Although Tiwanaku's defenders marshaled an arsenal of political, economic, and historical justifications to maintain the status of Tiwanaku as district capital, and despite its claims to cultural prestige, Tiwanaku lost out to the commercial center of Viacha.[28] That the alleged cradle of Bolivian nationality and American civilization failed in the local political contest reveals the limits of an incipient indigenista-nationalist discourse.

Arturo Posnansky: The Great Proselytizer

The idea of Tiwanaku's grandeur would be more fully and successfully articulated by Arturo Posnansky. Of all the early twentieth-century aficionados of Tiwanaku, Posnansky was without equal.[29] An Austrian by birth, and a chemical engineer by training, Posnansky arrived in Bolivia around the turn of the twentieth century, lured by the rubber boom in Acre territory. He wrote dozens of articles and monographs on Tiwanaku archaeology, ethnography, and racial science and was both president of the Geographic Society and director of the Archaeological Museum. Although Posnansky was a controversial figure and his legacy rather equivocal, his biographer, the Bolivian archaeologist Carlos Ponce Sanjinés, considered him one of three archaeological pioneers in the Southern Andes, along with the German archaeologist Max Uhle and the North American anthropologist Adolph Bandelier.

According to Ponce, Posnansky did not undertake methodological excavations himself, although he consistently accompanied excavations conducted by others, beginning with his first visit to Tiwanaku in 1903 with the French anthropological Créqui-Montfort-Courty mission, and continuing through the North American archaeologist Wendell Bennett's field session in 1932. Posnansky was a popularizer above all, but he also *propagated* concepts and theories about the provenance and evolution of Andean peoples and civilizations, rather than merely make the ideas of other writers accessible.

From his very first acquaintance with the site, Posnansky became a zealous and jealous guardian of the monuments. In 1904, he joined Manuel Vicente Ballivián and others of the Geographic Society of La Paz in denouncing the excesses of the Courty excavation: "Even more damaging for the ruins of Tihuanacu than the devastating action of time, of natural phenomena, the work of builders of cities and the zeal of fanatic guardians of the Christian religion, have been the excavations of Georges Courty. Of all that which this inept and unscrupulous searcher may have disinterred in his excavations, there remains today not a stone in its place."[30] The collateral tiles and stones uncovered by the dig were carried off, according to Posnansky, by villagers and local hacienda estate agents, while the archaeological finds were sent to France via Antofagasta, a port city in northern Chile. The Geographic Society insisted that the Bolivian government seize the shipment and have the pieces returned to La Paz. Ballivián apparently made an inventory of the pieces to maintain some control over what was removed from the country by the French team. The trove was divided between Bolivian government museums and the French archaeologists; the latter's spoils eventually found their way to the Musée de l'Homme in Paris.[31] Posnansky noted with some satisfaction that action on his and Ballivián's part led to the building of a fence around the most important ruins to prevent all the stones from being removed from the site and a pavilion to house the pieces from the village museum. Posnasky did not report on the reaction of local authorities or villagers to the expropriation of the museum.[32]

Posnansky's first major piece appeared in 1911 and his best known work, translated into English by Columbia University professors, was published in a bilingual edition in 1945.[33] Over the course of forty years, he argued doggedly and avidly—even in the face of vehement opposition—for the conclusions he had reached in the first decade of the twentieth century about the primacy of Tiwanaku and its people: the origin of American "man" was in America, and had an evolution independent of the Old World. According to Posnansky, the point of origin of the great pre-Columbian civilizations of Peru, Ecuador, Colombia, Central America, Yucatán, and Mexico was in the Andean altiplano at Tiwanaku. Tiwanaku was an island in the middle of Lake Titicaca, which was then more of an inland sea that covered the altiplano. Tiwanaku civilization was of great antiquity, perhaps 10,000 years old, and was inhabited by two principal races, the Aymara-speaking *kolla*, and their inferiors, the *arawak*. After the cataclysmic destruction of Tiwanaku, due to seismic movements and resulting floods of Lake Titicaca, its people spread across America, carrying with them the intellectual, artistic, religious, and architectural achievements of their civilization. The diffusion of the "staircase sign," the leitmotiv of prehistoric civilization at Tiwanaku, was visible proof for Posnansky that the genesis of all great American civilizations, including Mexico's Aztlán, was in the altiplano.

Posnansky attributed the discrepancy between the imagined high culture of the remote past and the reality of the "miserable Indian who inhabits the altiplano today" to this emigration and to the loss of the memory of civilizational achievements by those who remained. He had no doubt that the indigenous population at the time of the Spanish conquest had a "relatively grand culture compared to that of the present-day Indian." In his view, sexual corruption, alcohol abuse, and religious oppression under Spanish rule caused the dramatic decline of the Aymara.

> The Andean Altiplano was not always, as it is today, a desolate, arid and cold region. It was not always extremely poor in vegetation and inhabited in part by groups of "apparently inferior" races, possessing scant civilization, like those who today speak Aymara, Quechua, Puquina, Uru, etc. These groups are completely devoid of culture at the present time; they scarcely know how to scratch the soil to provide themselves with their miserable daily bread. They weave coarse cloth to protect their bodies against the inclemency of the weather and they lead a wretched existence in clay huts which seem, rather than human dwellings, the caves of troglodytes. The dreary and monotonous life of these unhappy people, who lull their hunger with coca leaves, is interrupted at times during the feasts by flashes of a mournful joy, produced by the deceitful poison of alcohol.[34]

Posnansky dedicated several works to the study of race, distinguishing between "inferior" and "superior" races mainly by anthropometric methods. He believed that in the Andes, the most ancient part of South America in geological terms, there existed "pure races"—arawaks, puqinas, urus, chipayas, and kollas—with the last of these comprising most of the indigenous communities in the highlands. Even as he took some rhetorical steps to distance himself from German national socialist racial ideology, he nonetheless insisted on the fact of superior and inferior races: "I can only reiterate that not language, nor religious belief, nor geographic latitude, nor hundreds of other factors contribute to forming a 'race,' but I insist that there are true races and that there are superior races and inferior races. This fact must be very much taken into account, especially in Bolivia, when it comes to trying to educate, that is, to familiarize, to accommodate the Indian to our culture and to make him into a useful man for the state and the country."[35]

Posnansky argued for the intellectual, organizational, and moral superiority of the kollas in relation to the arawaks, referring to them as "*ur-rassen*," which he translated as a "German technical term that means 'fundamental race' or 'primordial race.'" Posnansky denied the existence of an Aymara or Quechua race, claiming that "a race cannot be distinguished in terms of the language it spoke or still speaks," and that there were kollas and arawaks among both language groups. From the remote past to the present, the kollas were the race of "*führers*," rulers and guides of superior intelligence and dynamism, and the arawaks constituted the mass of plebes, hardworking, obedient, and well led.[36]

Posnansky claimed that foreign travelers and most Bolivians were misled by their inability to understand the Aymara language and culture, and did not appreciate the "great intellectual treasure which sleeps in this disgraced race."[37] Yet for Posnansky, this treasure was only accessible through stone monuments, not living beings. Unlike his peers in the Geographic Society, or the pamphleteers of the nineteenth century, Posnansky did not cite the accumulated knowledge produced by centuries of European and Creole chroniclers and travelers. Posnansky's archaeological and racial ideas were severely disputed during his lifetime—published as they were during the era of Nazism, the Second World War, and, subsequently, the decline of racial science. His ideas were dismissed by later archaeologists, as Ponce exhaustively demonstrates.[38] It was among the lay public that Posnansky's diffusionist model of Tiwanaku civilization as the primal center of America gained "an astonishing number of acolytes in Latin America."[39]

Posnansky's Teutonic-inflected writings about superior and inferior races are a stark expression of the Creole predicament of coming to terms with the ostensible difference between indigenous Bolivians past and present. Tiwanaku served as a sort of centrifugal point for a nationalist "political cosmology," to use Fabian's term.[40] For the theoreticians of Tiwanaku, the conundrum to be solved was that Tiwanaku can be and must be "us." But how then to deal with the presumed descendants of the creators of *tiwanakota* civilization? Turning again to Fabian, we can say that time defined the content of relations between the Self and the Other, giving form to relations of power and inequality. In the conceptual construction of Tiwanaku, the contemporary Indian subject was constructed as out of time—as a throwback, as Mitre and Paredes would have it. The parallel maneuver—space giving form to power and inequality—was deployed in the Creole state's spatial appropriation of the site and its museum, and in the displacement of one of Tiwanaku's monoliths to the city of La Paz.

The Bennett Stela

In 1932 the North American archaeologist Wendell Bennett, during a short field stay in Bolivia, unearthed a monolith at Tiwanaku that had been initially discovered by Courty in 1903 and then reburied. Posnansky not only finished the job of excavation, but insisted that the only way to preserve the monolith would be to move it to a secure site in the city of La Paz. By this time, there had been repeated public denunciations of the looting and vandalism at Tiwanaku, and calls for the national government to take decisive remedial action. In 1906, following the massive destruction caused by the construction of the Guaqui railroad, the site had been declared state property and the national government had been charged with its protection and care. With the reappearance of the monolith, which came to be known as the Bennett Stela, Posnansky and his allies began a campaign to oblige President Daniel Salamanca (in office 1931–34) to act.

Posnansky embarked on a highly public crusade in the major La Paz dailies, unilaterally thrusting aside learned opinion that favored in situ conservation and maintaining the site intact for study, research, and tourism.[41] Condemning his opponents as complicit in crimes against civilization, Posnansky declared that only he and his onetime adversary, Dr. Uhle (he once accused Uhle of carrying off Tiwanaku relics to Europe) had the authority and expertise to decide about transporting the Stela to La Paz. The Friends of the City of La Paz were similarly excoriated for failing to permit the transfer of other important structures a few years before, leaving them to the destructive will of ignorant local authorities and communities that sold pieces to passing tourists. Two months later, President Salamanca declared that four zones of Tiwanaku canton would be expropriated to protect the national patrimony.[42] At the same time, Posnansky engineered a well-publicized excursion to Tiwanaku for the diplomatic corps, mostly Latin American and European, to demonstrate the need to move the Bennett Stela to La Paz.[43]

For the operation of removal, Posnansky had the authorization of President Salamanca and his minister of education, Remy Rodas Eguino. With the collaboration of the Guaqui-La Paz railway, which extended a branch to the site, the Bennett Stela was transported to La Paz to be installed at the end of the Prado (the city's main thoroughfare). Posnansky described in some detail the arduous steps taken to disinter the monolith and ready it for transport to La Paz.

> These preliminary steps having been taken for the salvation of this unique piece, arrangements were made with the President of the Republic, Dr. Daniel Salamanca, an understanding and studious man, and his Minister of Education, Dr. Remy Rodas Eguino, for the moving of this petrous page of prehistory to the city of La Paz, before the rough boot of the tourist and the "yockallas" of the village destroyed it any more . . . After the Indians of the region of Tihuanacu had celebrated the nocturnal and age-old ceremony of the "Kjucho" to their Pachamama, in which a white llama had to be sacrificed as a burnt offering, it was placed on a railroad car and the trip to La Paz was begun.[44]

A different version of events is offered in Paredes's account, which reveals that the local Indians opposed the excavation and removal of the monolith. Under the direction of a *yatiri* (ritual specialist), the community and especially the workers involved in the actual digging and removal undertook propitiatory rites for having committed this offense, including an all-night vigil to accompany the Stela as it lay partially in the earth.[45]

The Bennett Stela's arrival in La Paz in 1933 unleashed a storm of protest, led by the La Paz municipal council, against situating the monument on the Prado or in Sopocachi (an elite neighborhood nearby). Posnansky's proposal, which had government support, was to substitute the Bennett Stela for a statue of Queen Isabel the Catholic in a plaza at the southern end of the Prado, and this provoked a struggle between indigenista and hispanista factions.[46] The city council balked and the newspapers pressured the council to erect the Stela elsewhere so as to not offend the resident Spanish colony.[47] The entrance to the stadium—far removed from the elegant promenade of the Prado—was suggested as an appropriate site. Newspaper headlines declared: "A preincaic monument has been converted into an obstruction for the citizenry." "The monolith, a question of high politics." "The affair of the monolith will end in gunshots. The municipality mobilizes the urban troops." And "the councilors will not permit the erection of the gigantic monolith." In a letter to the city council, Minister Rodas expressed the need to make haste if the monolith were to be in place for the national holiday on August 6, but the city council paid no heed. The municipal police were called out to prevent workers from laying the concrete for the pedestal, and the minister, in turn, sent the police to protect the workers. Impotent in the face of such public opposition, Posnansky published an article in which he raged, "I, the supreme apostle of Tiwanaku, excommunicate you. I, the supreme apostle of Tiwanaku, curse you."[48]

Despite the furor, the monument was ultimately installed on a temporary pedestal in the Prado—but not at the site of Queen Isabel's statue. Paredes, always skeptical about Posnansky's enthusiasms, remarked that "the transfer and installation cost the sum of *seventeen thousand bolivianos* which would have been better invested in the conservation and restoration of the Tiahuanacu ruins."[49] Posnansky later had the Bennett Stela transferred to the stadium in the Miraflores neighborhood on the other side of the river, at a remove from the urban center. It stood there, corroded by intense pollution in a traffic roundabout, for another seventy years.

*

The Geographic Society of La Paz made a particular rhetoric of race and civilization tangible. "Race" was deployed not just to structure discourses of rights, citizenship, entitlement, and to mark difference (as has been well treated in the literature), but also to create spatial and temporal hierarchies. This can be seen in the gradual creation of Tiwanaku as a site of national political reverence, and in its construction as both a local and a national public space. The placement of the Bennett Stela in a symbolically significant site in the city of La Paz was the clearest expression of the spatial relocalization associated with the Geographic Society's national project. But the defeat of Tiwanaku's bid to maintain its status as district capital, and the unease of urban Creoles over locating a massive symbol of the Aymara past in the heart of the nation's capital, reflect the limits of incipient nationalist indigenismo. The intellectual and cultural exercises to recast the meaning of Tiwanaku, and to transfer it to the capital city, were part of a larger though also frustrated effort to found the Bolivian nation upon the ruins of the Indian past.

The Return of the Stela

But this was not the last time the site of Tiwanaku would take on a potent na-tional dimension. Carlos Ponce, one of the leading cultural cadre of the Revo-lutionary Nationalist Movement, effectively linked Tiwanaku and archaeology with revolutionary national identity in the 1950s and 1960s. And Tiwanacota motifs abounded in nationalist architecture and aesthetics. Tiwanaku, as a sign of ancient America, figured spectacularly on the 1992 quincentennial anniversary of the Spanish conquest. Aymara yatiris and other religious, cultural, and political figures organized commemorative events at the site for local, national, and international consumption. Twenty years earlier, the emerging *katarista* indigenous movement had chosen to call its first procla-mation the "Tiwanaku Manifesto," and once again the symbolic power of the ruins was mobilized to demonstrate Aymara cultural resilience over millen-nia, above all for having withstood conquest by the Inca and the Spanish crown.

In 1994, the vice-president of Bolivia, Aymara intellectual Víctor Hugo Cárdenas, called for the restoration of the Bennett Stela to its original site at Tiwanaku. A presidential decree passed in September of that year created a "National Committee for the Restitution of the Bennett Stela or Pachamama to Tiwanaku." Despite the good intentions of the government, concerned archaeologists, and indigenista groups, technical and financial obstacles pre-vented the Bennett Stela from being returned to Tiwanaku during Cárdenas's tenure. At the end of 1999, the press called the projected move a "tale without end," but announced that the year 2000 would witness the return of the monument to Tiwanaku, since Mexico had promised technical assistance for the transport and Spain had ensured the necessary financial aid.[50]

It was not until March 2002, with enormous difficulty and fanfare, that the *monolito*—as the Bennett Stela is commonly known—was uprooted from its pedestal in the stadium roundabout in Miraflores and returned to Tiwanaku. This time, the residents of Miraflores vociferously opposed the move, arguing that the monolith had become an integral aspect of the cityscape and their particular neighborhood. Nevertheless, public and political opinion—nearly seventy years after Posnansky faced down the city fathers to install the Ben-nett Stela in La Paz—now favored returning it and other collateral pieces to Tiwanaku and undertaking further restoration and improvement of the site. On the day of the monolith's departure, crowds gathered to witness the spectacle, and Aymara yatiris ritually supervised the proceedings. A caravan of over 100 vehicles accompanied the monolith on its journey, and Aymara communities along the route paid homage with offerings and prayers. It was received in Tiwanaku by the surrounding communities with brass bands and *morenadas* (festival dances): "Now we will stop suffering; the monolith will no longer punish us. Now the Aymara people will once again rule—the Pachakuti has arrived."[51]

At the site itself, the communities of Tiwanaku had taken matters into their own hands. Spurred by the Popular Participation Law of 1994, which decentralized political and financial functions to the local level, the municipality of Tiwanaku, in association with twenty-three surrounding communities, occupied the site in 2000 to wrest the administration of the ruins and museum away from the Ministry of Culture. Tiwanaku justified the takeover on the grounds that the site and museum had suffered from severe historical neglect by the national government. Moreover, argued the municipality and its allied communities, oversight of cultural patrimony—as well as income from ticket sales—belongs to the people who live in the area and have a genuine historical and cultural stake in the site.[52]

At the start of the new millennium, the site demonstrated a striking vibrancy after years of public neglect. A splendid new museum, built to house the monolith and other antiquities, received its finishing touches in 2002. The *mallkus* or traditional authorities of Tiwanaku's communities, on guard duty rotations of six months, patrolled the area and kept a watchful eye on wandering tourists. More than a hundred years after the 1897 conflict, the custodians of the site were no longer a local town elite, and the definition of Tiwanaku's public memory was no longer the exclusive province of Creole politicians and intellectuals from La Paz.

The community appropriation of local space and power anticipated a momentous shift in national politics. On January 21, 2006, the president-elect of the republic, Evo Morales Ayma, processed into the archaeological precinct, dressed in a tunic and headpiece styled according to ancient Tiwanaku patterns. For this ceremony before the formal inauguration the next day, he wielded an Indian staff of authority, as if in fulfillment of the expectation at the time of the Stela's repatriation to Tiwanaku in 2002: "The Aymara people will once again rule—the Pachakuti has arrived."[53] While the indigenista nationalism of Creole and mestizo intellectuals in the early twentieth century gained only limited purchase, in the early twenty-first century a new national project—this time with actual indigenous leadership—proclaimed its hegemonic pretensions upon the ancient Indian ruins.

Notes

1. Guha-Thakurta 2004.
2. On the Geographic Society of La Paz as a critical site for nation-building, see Qayum 2002a.
3. Guha-Thakurta 2004.
4. On elite appropriation of the symbol of the Inca during the national period, see Platt 1993; König 1984, 394–98; Flores Galindo 1987.
5. See Kolata 1993. For a critique of the explanations of decline, and an alternative argument for continuity, see Erickson 1999.
6. Pedro Cieza de León, *Crónica de Perú* (1553; Madrid: Biblioteca de Autores Españoles, 1947).
7. In addition to the figures mentioned here, other noteworthy visitors were Von Tschudi (1851), Comte de Castelnau (1850–61), Angrand (1866), Raimondi (1874), Squier (1877), and Weiner (1880).
8. For a general survey of indigenismo in Latin America (from a rather anti-indigenista standpoint), see Favre 1998. Indigenismo varied dramatically from country to country, even in the Andes. On Mexico, see Knight 1990; Vasconcelos 1997. On Cuzco and Peru, see de la Cadena 2000; Tamayo Herrera 1982; Kristal 1987. On Ecuador, see Muratorio 1994.
9. For a contrasting view, see Parrenin and Lavaud (1980), who claim that Bolivian indigenismo did not emerge out of any political relationship between elites and indigenous society; instead it represented a strategy on the part of new (nonindigenous) social sectors to distinguish themselves by criticizing the existing social order.
10. On the history of the early twentieth-century movements, see Condarco Morales 1983; Rivera Cusicanqui 1984; Taller de Historia Oral Andina, 1984; Condori and Ticona 1992; Mamani 1991; Choque and Ticona 1996; and Choque et al. 1992. On the movements later in the century, see Albó 1991; and Stern 1987b; Hurtado 1986; Pacheco 1992. "Indianist" in Bolivia is distinguished from "indigenismo" insofar as it entails a more radical ethnic agenda and is headed by Indian intellectuals and political leaders, rather than mestizos and Creoles.
11. This is the case for the alliance between Liberal General J. M. Pando and Zárate Willka around the time that the 1897 tract was written. It was also the case for the exploratory alliance between caciques-apoderados and the Republican Party leader Bautista Saavedra at the time of his own and Arturo Posnansky's promotion of Tiwanaku in the 1910s.
12. Anonymous 1897. After the 1899 Federal War, La Paz became the national

capital, replacing Sucre. The archaeological site and town have been spelled in a variety of ways. "Tiahuanacu" was the spelling used in the document analyzed. However, I follow current practice, based on the work of Aymara linguists, and use the spelling "Tiwanaku."

13. Anonymous 1897, 15. Uhle made his first trip to Bolivia in 1893, and visited Tiwanaku in 1894. He was appalled to find the Bolivian army using the ruins for target practice and wrote a letter condemning this willful destruction, which was published in the La Paz newspaper *El Comercio*.

14. Anonymous 1897, 86.

15. Much of this material was published posthumously in 1955 as part of the series of provincial monographs that Paredes produced over the course of several decades. See Paredes 1955. Pacajes province was divided into Pacajes and Ingavi in 1909.

16. Anonymous 1897, 16–18.

17. Oficina Nacional de Inmigración, Estadística y Propaganda Geográfica 1973, 36. On the 1900 census and its director, a long-time Geographic Society president, see Qayum 2002a.

18. Paredes would return to this question some twenty years later in his monograph on Kollasuyu, one of the four realms of the Inca empire (Tawantinsuyu) and the one comprising the Aymara kingdoms. In the opening pages, he asked, "Where does the mysterious inhabitant of the Andean altiplano come from?" See Paredes 1979, 7.

19. Bartolomé Mitre, poet, politician, general, and historian, was exiled by the dictator Juan Manuel de Rosas in 1846. He was invited to Bolivia by President José Ballivián (in office 1841–47) and was ordered to leave by General Belzu (in office 1847–55). While he was in Bolivia he worked as a journalist, and also wrote the novel *Soledad*. He visited Tiwanaku briefly under military escort as he was being marched out of the country toward the Peruvian border. Mitre returned to Argentina in 1852 and became president of his country in 1862. He founded the newspaper *La Nación* in 1870 and wrote several histories during his retirement from political life, including *Las Ruinas de Tiahuanaco* in 1879.

20. One Bolivian precedent for the idea of Aymara and American genesis may be found in the work of the archivist and bibliophile Vicente de Ballivián y Roxas, who in 1872 called for a comparative study of Aymara, Quechua, and Sanskrit (the "root of all the Aryan languages") that would confirm that "Aymara is the mother tongue of Quechua . . . and that the Inca civilization was only a subsequent development of Andean civilization, as the ruins at Tiahuanacu prove beyond a doubt." Vicente de Ballivián y Roxas, *Archivo Boliviano: Colección de documentos relativos a la historia de Bolivia* (1872; La Paz: Casa Municipal de la Cultura, 1977), 14.

21. Paredes undertook a more scholarly exegesis of the chroniclers—with similar conclusions—in *Tiahuanacu y la provincia de Ingavi*.

22. Anonymous 1897, 19, 41. In the colonial period, Bolivia formed part of "Peru." Paredes describes D'Orbigny as "the most profound and astute ethnographer and

archaeologist of the many who have concerned themselves with South American antiquities and peoples." During his stay in Bolivia, D'Orbigny was responsible for "awakening the country's interest in the natural sciences." Paredes 1955, 70–72. D'Orbigny's discussion of Tiwanaku, which he visited in 1833, can be found in D'Orbigny 1945, 1534–42.

23. Paredes 1955, 23. The use of this biological metaphor was all the more striking since Paredes's text did not otherwise refer overtly to contemporary racial science ideology or the burgeoning debate over mestizaje. He must have taken this Spencerian concept from Mitre. See Mitre 1954, 189–98. Given the context, I have translated "salto-atrás" as "throwback," meaning "a reversion to a former type or ancestral characteristic . . . an atavism." For Spencer's influence on Latin American intellectuals, see Hale 1984, 396–97.

24. Anonymous 1897, 39.

25. Ibid., 42.

26. Camacho 1920.

27. Anonymous 1897, 53–54.

28. Paredes 1955, 4. The law of October 16, 1897, restored the capital to Viacha, and in 1909 this district became the province of Ingavi—with its capital at Viacha.

29. Other important intellectuals held views similar to Posnansky's. Geographic Society member, lawyer, and future president Bautista Saavedra affirmed that Tiwanaku was superior to Inca civilization and underscored its Aymara origin. See Saavedra 1995, 51.

30. Posnansky 1945, 59–60.

31. The Geographic Society became involved because a commission of its members had visited the Courty dig to undertake a comprehensive study of the monuments that were being excavated. Manuel Ballivián, "Informe anual elevado al Ministerio de Instrucción Pública, sobre los trabajos efectuados durante el segundo semestre de 1903 y primero de 1904," *Boletín de la Sociedad Geográfica de La Paz* 5, nos. 7–9, 18, 19, 20. Ponce Sanjinés 1995, 115–16.

32. Posnansky 1945, 60.

33. Posnansky 1911; Posnansky 1945. The latter source—which contains much of the same material as the first—was republished by the Bolivian ministry of education in 1957.

34. Posnansky 1945, 33.

35. Posnansky 1942, 18–19. See also Posnansky 1937a and Posnansky 1943.

36. Posnansky 1942, 27–44.

37. Posnansky 1911, 46–49.

38. Ponce Sanjinés 1995, 76–80. See also Abecia Baldivieso 1973, 556.

39. Kolata 1993, 16.

40. Fabian 1983.

41. Buck 1933.

42. In 1937, well after the Bennett Stela controversy, Posnansky published a pro-

posal to turn Tiwanaku into a national park; the proposal contemplated the forcible relocation of several Aymara communities. Posnansky 1937b.

43. *El Diario*, May 3, 1933; *La Razón*, July 1, 1933, July 4, 1933.

44. Posnansky 1945, 187. Coming from an upper-class Creole, the term "yokalla" refers dismissively to local mestizo town residents as being juvenile and unrefined. In the original Aymara or Quechua, it means "youth."

45. For a description of the rituals, see Paredes 1955, 124–26.

46. Hispanism celebrated the Spanish, Catholic tradition and viewed the colonization of America as a great civilizing stage in world history. In the early twentieth century, it tended to be politically conservative, embracing organicist and corporatist ideology in opposition to liberal democracy and capitalism.

47. The conflict discussed here resembles that analyzed by Rudi Colloredo-Mansfeld in this volume.

48. *La Razón*, November 12, 1995, and from July 5 to July 18, 1933.

49. Paredes 1955, 126.

50. *La Razón*, December 23, 1999. On the monolith's return to Tiwanaku, see Qayum 2002b, chapter 6.

51. *La Prensa*, March 17, 2002, March 15, 2002, March 18, 2002; Marcelo Fernández, personal communication, June 2002. "Pachakuti" refers to an upheaval and transformation in time and space that issues in a new historical era.

52. *La Razón*, July 10, 2000.

53. On past and present cycles of indigenous political mobilization and the notion of pachakuti, see Hylton and Thomson 2007.

Mestizaje, Distinction, and Cultural Presence:
The View from Oaxaca

DEBORAH POOLE

On July 20, 2002, some 3,000 protestors headed by the Coordinadora Oaxa-queña Magonista Popular Antineoliberal (COMPA) marched through the tourist-filled streets of Oaxaca's historic center. COMPA's official list of de-mands covered an impressive range of issues including "opposition to the Plan Puebla-Panama, the Indigenous law approved by the Pri-Panista sena-tors, [then-president Vicente Fox's proposed] Added Value Tax on food, medicines and books, the proposed privatization of electricity, petroleum, education and healthcare, the proposed reform of the Federal Labor Laws, and the importation of agricultural products and genetically altered foods." In addition to these oppositional demands, COMPA also called for "compli-ance with the Acuerdos de San Andrés Larrainzar; respect for the alimentary, economic, political and cultural autonomy of our pueblos, a just exchange of goods and ideas, a development project that is egalitarian, popularly based and socially just, liberty for political prisoners, and the dismantling of para-military groups."[1]

For the purposes of the march, such a long list of demands proved un-wieldy. The organizers therefore focused the march itself on three local de-mands. The first involved fifteen indigenous peasants who had been unjustly jailed. The second involved a controversial law allowing the Oaxacan state legislature to "disappear" disloyal municipal governments. The third and most publicized concerned the unjust practices of the Guelaguetza, a large folklore festival through which the Oaxacan government promotes an image of the state as "the cradle of multicultural diversity in Mexico," in the words of a former governor.[2] The COMPA marchers focused in particular on the well-known (but seldom publicly acknowledged) fact that participation in the Guelaguetza often depended on party-based interests (usually PRI interests) at the municipal level. This particular grievance was directed toward the Authenticity Committee, whose responsibilities included selection of festival delegations, the policing of tradition, and control over who could speak for Oaxaca's seven officially recognized cultural regions.

The following year, COMPA again organized a march to coincide with the celebration of the Guelaguetza. They voiced a similar set of demands, including a more hostile denunciation of the authoritarian measures of the Authenticity Committee. This year, however, COMPA had competition from two larger demonstrations organized by an association of pineapple producers and a coalition of provincial peasant and indigenous organizations gathered under the umbrella of the Movimiento Unificado de Lucha Triqui (Unified Movement of Triqui Struggle) and Nueva Izquierda Oaxaca (New Left Oaxaca). Like COMPA's demonstration, both of these marches were held on the highway that provides public access to the amphitheater where the Guelaguetza is performed. Thus, although neither organization directly targeted the Guelaguetza, the timing and location of the marches speak to the political importance of folklore in a state that is home to at least fifteen ethnic and language groups.[3] Indeed, the Oaxacan press responded to the tense atmosphere with satiric representations of the heavily armed police forces that the government deployed to hold at bay the poor and indigenous Oaxacans who did not fit their criteria of "authentic" culture bearers. In one cartoon, the state governor, José Murat, carrying the dead body of "tourism" dressed as a Zapotec princess, laments that the "damn Indians" are driving tourists away. Another shows the police dancing on the Guelaguetza stage for an audience composed of the protesting organizations. The disputes also served to remind journalists and the public of the very small number of seats reserved for low-income spectators.

Such protests speak to the complexity of cultural politics in a country where government gestures toward cultural rights and indigenous self-representation have run up against the devastation brought on by the same government's economic policies. As home to over one-third of Mexico's indigenous municipalities, Oaxaca provides a particularly contentious example of this predicament. Along with Guerrero and Chiapas, Oaxaca is among the poorest of Mexico's states. It also has one of the highest levels of out-migration and remittance dependency.[4] At the same time, Oaxaca's PRI government has advanced constitutional reforms, electoral procedures, and legislation that favor, at least on paper, the recognition of indigenous cultural and political rights. Foremost among these reforms is the 1998 Law of Indigenous Rights, which recognizes the right of indigenous communities to elect local officials through *usos y costumbres* (traditional practices and customs) that operate independently of political party structures.[5] Along with electoral reforms, the legislation includes significant gestures toward the recognition of cultural rights and autonomies. Needless to say, with the exception of the politically expedient usos y costumbres clause, such laws have not implied the enforcement of cultural rights in any comprehensive or legal sense. Indeed, in 2002, when COMPA organized its march, Oaxaca was second only to Chiapas in the number of indigenous political prisoners and militarized, or semi-militarized, indigenous territories, and indigenous peoples continue to rank as the poorest sectors of the Oaxacan economy.[6] Until 2006, when opposition groups led by the teachers' union began to organize their own "Popular Guelaguetza," indigenous organizations and communities had been largely excluded from the folkloric spectacles through which the Oaxacan state produces its national and international reputation as "a cradle of multicultural diversity."[7] Such exclusions, of course, have a long history in Mexico, as they do elsewhere in Latin America. They confirm that double-edged sense of "pueblo," as the necessary collective grounding of a liberal polity *and* the unruly mass that must be kept at bay.[8]

Given the predictability of such exclusionary forms and practices in liberal governance and thought, what distinguishes the cultural and racial politics of neoliberalism in Oaxaca? By excluding Indians from popular cultural forms that supposedly derive from indigenous cultural expressions, were Oaxaca's PRI governments merely reasserting the old claims of Mexican mestizaje that presumed a new national identity would emanate from ancient indigenous cultures? Or does culture play a particular role in neoliberal multiculturalism? It is important to bear in mind that, in Mexico, mestizaje is the historically sanctioned identity claim against which *both* neoliberal multiculturalism and popular cultural movements, such as COMPA, allegedly speak. Take, for example, the reception of the recent wave of constitutional amendments ratifying the "pluricultural" character of both Oaxaca and Mexico as a whole.[9] By granting independent status and permanency to indigenous cultures, such official—and legally binding—declarations call into question both popular and academic understandings of mestizaje as the grounds from which a national identity could be imagined.

In most "popular" accounts (by which I mean textbooks, public histories, and the accounts I have collected from upper-class and working-class Oaxaqueños), mestizaje tends to be viewed as a historical process through which the different biological ("racial") groups and cultures of colonial Mexico have melded into the unmarked racial and cultural category of "mestizo." In some cases, this process extends far back in time. A man from one of the communities bordering the fourteenth-century archaeological site of Monte Albán told me that the ruins had been built by what he described as "a mestizo civilization" formed by the mixture of "three races: the Olmec, the Zapotec and the Mixtec."[10]

Most recent historical and anthropological accounts, on the other hand, locate mestizaje firmly within the *post*colonial history of Mexico. They describe mestizaje as the centerpiece of a national imaginary whose origin is most often traced to the eighteenth-century Jesuit, Francisco Clavijero.[11] Within this political project, mestizaje provided the language through which elites of the nineteenth and twentieth centuries—identified by themselves and others as white or mestizo—sought to construct a unified national identity by eradicating, denying, or devaluing the cultures and histories of the various indigenous, African, Asian, and Middle Eastern groups who have historically made up the Mexican population. In this view, the hegemonic status of mestizaje as a political project for revolutionary nation-building depends on the inherent *un*attainability of mestizaje as a process of racial and cultural mixture that is never complete.[12]

One way of thinking about this unfinished quality is to look at the administrative practices and institutional sites through which the Mexican state apparatus has produced and regulated the very diversity that mestizaje is supposed to undo.[13] Another complementary approach, which this chapter explores, is to think about how mestizaje resonates with the metaphysics of suspicion that underwrite liberal notions of identity and recognition. This notion of suspicion can be seen from two angles. First, anxieties about deception and authenticity haunt the visual practices and forms through which "culture" is claimed as a form of collective and personal property in the public spaces of state-sponsored festivals.[14] On a second and related level, uncertainties are produced by an identity claim—mestizaje—that is grounded in the impermanence of a historical process. The new politics of multiculturalism are most clearly distinguished from earlier modernist (or, in the case of Mexico, revolutionary) understandings of mestizaje, by the sense of completion, finality, or presence that now surrounds talk about culture and identity. The chapter begins with a look at understandings of genealogy and distinction in nineteenth-century Oaxacan debates about civilization, property, and race. I then discuss the reworking of the nationalist or revolutionary ideology of mestizaje in a festival sponsored by the Oaxacan revolutionary state. I conclude by returning to the contentious politics surrounding the Guelaguetza festival as they unfolded in the years between 1998 and 2003.[15]

Culture and Property in the Porfiriato

To understand cultural politics in Oaxaca, it is useful to begin by examining nineteenth-century liberal anxieties about property and culture. Oaxaca occupied a somewhat peculiar position within the liberal imagination of nineteenth-century Mexico. On the one hand, the state was home to Mexico's leading nation-builders—Benito Juárez and Porfirio Díaz—as well as to the Instituto de Ciencias, where many positivist, liberal intellectuals were formed. By the end of the Porfiriato (the period of Díaz's rule, 1876–1911), Oaxaca stood as the fifth largest recipient of the foreign (principally U.S.) investment that liberals imagined would fuel the progress of their nation. By 1907, it ranked second only to Guanajuato among regions receiving U.S. mining capital. The tropical cash crops produced in the Isthmus of Tehuantepec and Valle Nacional added to the illusion of progress surrounding certain regions of Díaz's home state.[16]

On the other hand, it was in Oaxaca that the liberal reformers had the least success in dismantling the corporate property forms that they considered obstacles to the formation of a modern national economy. Between 1856 and 1876, only about 600 nonchurch properties outside the Central Valley were affected by the liberal reforms, and these were concentrated in areas close to the capital city. In regions farther removed, the weak market in land coupled with sheer distance and the political strength of the indigenous communities prevented land reforms from taking hold. As a result, there were few haciendas in Oaxaca, and well over 70 percent of the state's population lived in autonomous municipalities where communal land-tenure systems remained virtually intact.[17] Furthermore, following the disentailment of church corporate landholdings and *cofradías* (religious cofraternities), the autonomous authority structures that typified indigenous communities were in many cases reinforced as the separate civil and religious hierarchies of colonial times merged into a single structure.[18] In short, Juárez's home-state emerged from the period of reform as a stronghold of the four things nineteenth-century liberals feared most: collective property, noncentralized forms of authority, racial heterogeneity, and strong ties to the "irrational" forms of popular Mexican Catholicism (if not always to the Catholic Church).

Under the presidency of Porfirio Díaz (1876–1911), indigenous communities successfully brokered continuing control over traditional forms of collective property in exchange for supporting local political elites.[19] One result of this relationship with local elites was the proliferation of municipalities, from 452 in 1883 to 1,131 in 1910. This expansion bolstered traditional indigenous authority structures while protecting collective property forms and territorial identities. As a result, Oaxaca's indigenous communities managed to defend and preserve traditional forms of local authority, succession to office, and landholding. According to one account, 99 percent of Oaxacan heads of household lacked individual private property.[20] Such factors also help to account for the fact that the 1878 Oaxacan census registers only 18 percent of the state's total population as mestizo, as compared to 77 percent indigenous.[21] The extent to which these demographics threatened liberal ideals of central government and control can be seen in the repeated attempts to regulate the proliferation of municipalities.[22] For the liberals in Oaxaca and elsewhere in Mexico, fragmentation was the ghost that haunted their dreams of crafting a modern polity. In Oaxaca, not only did the "backward" indigenous municipalities threaten the "progress" of capital and nation, but, even in the two regions where large commercial landholdings had been successfully established (the Isthmus of Tehuantepec and Tuxtepec), secessionist movements regularly came forward with plans to further fragment the state.

In this context, cultural variation presented the dominant classes with a problem that exceeded whatever anxieties they might have had about their own racial identities. For the intellectuals gathered at Oaxaca's Instituto de Ciencias, the enduring ethnic and racial variety of the state served as a material reminder of their failure to achieve the three things dearest to the liberal political project: private property, centralized control, and secular governance. This observation helps to account for the fact that neither "assimilation," nor the concept of mestizaje itself, was a topic of interest for any of Oaxaca's nineteenth-century intellectuals. Instead, Oaxacan liberals such as Manuel Martínez Gracida, Juan Carriedo, and Manuel Brioso y Candiani tried to imagine a way to build a liberal polity on the basis of what we might think of as "really existing diversity."[23] They did this through two techniques, each involving a qualitatively different understanding of the idea of culture.

The first technique employed archaeology and, to a lesser extent, physiognomy to uncover a genealogical argument for linking Oaxacan society and institutions with the cultural achievements of the pre-Columbian Zapotec civilizations in the Isthmus of Tehuantepec. Like proponents of other national projects in which archaeology played an important role, Oaxacan liberals described archaeological sites, deciphered existing codices, and analyzed their own collections of Zapotec cultural remains. The most ambitious of these projects was carried out by a political protégé of Díaz, Manuel Martínez Gracida.[24] In his historical accounts, Martínez Gracida combined the antiquarian interests of contemporary Oaxacan historians with the liberal vision of progress and governance that bound him to Díaz. He describes the ancient Zapotec kingdom of Didjazaa, for example, as "an autochthonous nation . . . in which people lived happily and independently with their own political state."[25] Martínez Gracida's account draws on the standard historical sources to portray a secular Zapotec kingdom that might serve as a model for Mexico's liberal state.[26] "Among these people, the State was separate from the Church, and this wise disposition led to the formation of two distinct classes, whose paths were neither confused nor conceived as obstacles to genius or valor: to this they owed their importance and respectability. Moreover, by regulating the Indians' conscience, religion established the peace and well-being of families, and contributed to the working and progress of the State."[27]

Much as the French philosophes looked to the Incas and Aztecs for examples of enlightened monarchies and a purer, deist religion, Martínez Gracida held up the pre-Spanish Oaxacan civilizations as models of a secular, progressive social order, civilizations whose vitality was demonstrated by their successful resistance to Aztec rule, as well as by their religion, which he described as both "reminiscent of Masonry" and distinct from that of the Aztecs in its disdain for human sacrifice.[28] As a Oaxaca City liberal, Martínez Gracida deliberately made assertions on Oaxacan civilization that were grounded in a genealogical claim that allowed for a connection, but not an identification, with the Zapotecs. This form of distancing was further reinforced by the gendering of Zapotec civilization. Martínez Gracida looked to photographs of Zapotec men for evidence of the physiognomic or racial characteristics by which they could be identified not just as Indians, but as descendants of the original Oaxacan Indians, the Zapotecs.

It was to images of Isthmus women, however, that Martínez Gracida looked for evidence of the Zapotecs' continuing status as an originary civilization. For Martínez Gracida, as for other contemporary travelers and authors, the ornately embroidered clothes, headdresses, and jewelry from Tehuantepec and Juchitán offered proof of the Zapotecs' cultural (and thus civilizational) vitality. In Martínez Gracida's descriptions of the women, this admiration is couched in the language of class. By describing the women represented in his plates as "rich," "upper class," or "aristocratic," Martínez Gracida suggests to his readers that the Zapotec civilization is rooted not only in the past, but in its continuing ability to generate class distinctions. Zapotec clothing was acknowledged to be a product of modern history, since the garments incorporated elements of contemporary European, Spanish, Indian, and Arab fashion.[29] While the claim to civilizational status may have rested on past achievements, the availability of Isthmus culture for projects like that of Martínez Gracida was in many ways due to the creatively hybrid, or mestizo, clothing through which the Isthmus women came to be elevated to the status of regional—and eventually national—icons. The *Tehuana* woman was appealing to the Oaxacan elite as a symbol of Oaxacan identity, and eventually her clothing was appropriated as fashion by Mexico City actresses and artists, including Frida Kahlo. But at least part of her appeal resided in the fact that the Tehuana—unlike other women from Oaxaca—was unproblematically seen as at once indigenous *and* mestiza.

The second technique Oaxacan intellectuals used to build a liberal polity was the description of forms of cultural variation in the present. Martínez Gracida's work can again serve as example of this approach. This involved the compilation of detailed inventories of the material culture, dress, languages, and (to a lesser extent) customs of the sixteen different "tribes" that made up the contemporary population of Oaxaca. To construct this inventory, Martínez Gracida commissioned watercolors and photographs of "ethnological types" for an ambitious—and still unpublished—ten-volume work entitled *The Indians of Oaxaca and Their Archaeological Monuments*.[30] In this work, Martínez Gracida's goal was not so much to uncover the hidden connections of a genealogy, as it was to make diversity legible and intelligible. Whereas his work on the Isthmus Zapotec relied on a notion of civilizational achievement that could be passed down through dynamic and ever changing cultural forms such as clothes and knowledge, in his ten-volume study Martínez Gracida invoked contemporary ethnological understandings of "culture" as simultaneously material and ephemeral. As a material property, culture was the product of human creativity—and especially, in the case of Oaxaca, culture comprised the dress, ceramics, and other products of local peasant society. In his map of cultural distinction, Martínez Gracida classified his subjects according to a rigorous calculus of type that Oaxaca's nineteenth-century positivists considered ethnological rather than racial. Ethnological types were identified by their use of narrowly defined—and historically stabilized—costumes, and by their association with particular assemblages of ceramics, basketry, weavings, and house-forms.

It is worth noting the distance that separates this understanding of culture from the idea of race. Martínez Gracida's understanding of ethnological types clearly rested on an understanding of culture *as something made up of things*. As such—and as his comments on the ethnological tribes make clear—his understanding allowed little room for an acknowledgement of the humanity of the people who either made or owned those things. His understanding of race, however, brought with it the possibility of articulating a genealogical claim of connection with the Other. Whereas ethnological types had culture in the form of costume, the Zapotec *race* had an ancient and enduring civilization. One way in which Oaxacan historians enforced this distinction was by designating certain tribes as foreign to Oaxacan Territory. The Chatinos were said to originate in Peru; the Mixes in Eastern Europe; and the Huaves in Nicaragua.[31] As "foreigners," these tribes were not seen as bearing distinctive forms of knowledge that could mark their relationship to a place. Rather, their claim to cultural distinction was restricted to the material and, for the most part, utilitarian products they made—primarily clothes, ceramics, and basketry. The Isthmus Zapotecs, meanwhile, were described by the historian José Antonio Gay and those who cite him as the first to have arrived at Oaxaca from Anahuac. The Mixtecos were thought to have come to Oaxaca shortly thereafter.[32] As the original inhabitants of Oaxacan territory, Zapotecs established a "culture" or civilization that was understood to reside in the forms of knowledge—astronomical, historical, and political— that bound them to the land, as well as in the highly creative and continually evolving dress style of the Isthmus women.

I have written about Martínez Gracida's representational and aesthetic projects elsewhere.[33] Here I want to make one simple observation about the relationships to the visible world that are implied in a classificatory or descriptive discourse of distinction, on the one hand, and a genealogical model of civilizational achievement, on the other. The calculus of distinction by which the Oaxacan liberal differentiated his own world from that of the Indians who surrounded him was based on the fixed cultural properties that allowed him to identify territorially locatable ethnological types. Because distinction was to be read off the visible surface of the world (principally clothing and material culture), culture carried with it a notion of descriptive excess or presence. Via its affiliation with the notion of race or descent, however, the genealogical claim to civilization lay hidden beneath the world of appearances. Archaeology and physiognomy were the operative technologies for uncovering genealogical truth and, with it, the racial affiliations of societies and individuals. In this sense, the Oaxacans' search for Zapotec roots resembles the Mexico City nationalists' understandings of mestizaje in that both were concerned with a historical process of descent and gradual disaffection from an originary indigenous type. In both cases, the "Indian" continued to figure as the uncanny reminder of the modern mestizo subject's historical origins, while anxieties about what we now think of as their "identity" revolved around the impossibility of knowing, with absolute certainty, when the modern, "liberal Oaxacan" emerged as distinct from his Zapotec ancestors.

Culture and Presence in the Revolutionary State

The Mexican Revolution of 1910 of course brought many changes to Oaxaca. Arguably the most important change concerned the approach to resolving the political fragmentation that Oaxaca's revolutionary governors had inherited from the Porfiriato. Faced with threats of political secession from both the Isthmus and the northern part of the state, and the heavily armed caciques holed up in the Mixteca and Sierra Juárez, the Revolutionary Government of Oaxaca made effective use of culture as a means to rein in the chaotic forces of disorder and "reaction."[34] Whereas Porfirian intellectuals had attempted to forge a distinctive identity for their state by uncovering the civilizational basis of Oaxacan culture in a single region (the Isthmus of Tehuantepec), revolutionary intellectuals sought to make diversity itself the consensual basis of a unified Oaxacan identity. In so doing, they uprooted culture from its affiliation with nineteenth-century notions of genealogy and civilization. They did this through creative appropriations of the Secretariat of Education's Cultural Missions, designed to promote a national mestizo culture, as well as through the creation of new music and art forms that could embody and disseminate the "Oaxacan soul."[35]

Perhaps the revolutionary intellectuals' most enduring contribution to Oaxacan cultural politics was the celebration in April 1932 of an *Homenaje Racial* (Racial Homage) in which "racial ambassadresses" from Oaxaca's six

Figure 1. Homenaje Racial 1932. Miss Oaxaca surrounded by delegation from the Isthmus of Tehuantepec. Credit: Juan Arriaga. Original in collection of the Fundación Bustamante Vasconcelos, Oaxaca de Juárez.

"racial regions" rendered homage to the mestizo city of Oaxaca in the person of "La Señorita Oaxaca." Organized by members of the state governor's office and education department as part of the fourth-centennial celebration of the founding of the City of Oaxaca, this predecessor of today's Guelaguetza festival was described by its director, Alberto Vargas, as a "great festival of the races to the Sultaness of the South." The performance itself consisted of the entry into Oaxaca of five regional delegations headed by *Embajadoras Raciales* (Racial Ambassadresses) and their indigenous "entourages" (see figure 1).[36] Each of these "gentile missions" was intended to represent a discrete cultural territory within the state. The entourages were composed of, in Vargas's words, "men and women who still conserved the autochthonous garments of their race." The ambassadresses, however, were not what we (or they, for that matter) would consider "Indians." Indeed, some such as Rosa María Meixuiero de Hernández, the embajadora from the Sierra Juárez, and daughter of one of the caciques of the Sovereignty Movement, represented the most powerful (and whitest) families of their respective regions.[37] Several of the ambassadresses further marked their distance from the dark-skinned entourages by whitening their faces with flour or powder (see figure 2).

Culture, in the form of dress, was even more central than race to the goals

Figure 2. Embajadoras Raciales, commemorative album, Homenaje Racial, 1932. Credit: *Album Conmemorativo del IV Centenario de la Ciudad de Oaxaca* (Oaxaca, Gobierno del Estado, 1932); photograph not credited in album, but the photographer is presumably Juan Arriaga. Album at Fundación Bustamante Vasconcelos, Oaxaca de Juárez.

of the organizing committee. In its instructions to the regional committees charged with raising monies and costuming the embajadoras and their entourages, the Central Organizing Committee in Oaxaca cautioned the regional committees to "make a careful selection of types" so as "to give a perfect idea of the moral, ethnic and social character of the race."[38] When the regional committees disagreed with the choice of costume or cultural affiliation for their region, the Central Organizing Committee moved to enforce its selection: if necessary, the committee instructed, costumes were to be borrowed from other places.[39] The important point was to police the territorial, administrative, and political boundaries that the festival would establish for both culture and race.

Clearly the sense of Oaxaca conveyed in this festival was, like that of its counterpart *el pueblo*, both exclusionary and inclusionary. A spectator watching the Homenaje Racial could look at the racial entourages as proof that different types of people lived in Oaxaca. In this respect, the festival built on that part of the nineteenth-century classificatory project that dealt with surface appearance, description, and presence. In the Homenaje Racial, however, the very fact that culture was performed as spectacle carried with it the uncanny tension between the idealized stability of the ethnological type as representative of a specific region or place, and the idea that the materiality of culture or "type" could be donned like fashion or a costume—by women (the ambassadresses) who were not racially distinct from the middle- and upper-class spectators of the Homenaje Racial. Indeed, it is during these same years (the 1920s and 1930s) that women from the City of Oaxaca began to pose for portraits in indigenous clothes.[40] At the same time, the visual spectacle of the Homenaje Racial made it clear that these regional "others" should be seen as radically distinct from one another *and* as the unstable raw material from which the mestizo could be forged. As both presence and excess, they were an uncanny reminder of the inherently unfinished quality of mestizaje, of mestizaje as a calculus of belonging in which claims to distinction could be defended only through the constant invocation of the Indian as both present and past.

Excess and Presence

Today's Guelaguetza is a direct descendant of the Homenaje Racial in 1932. As Oaxaca's leading tourist attraction and centerpiece for Oaxacan cultural allegiances—and political protests—the Guelaguetza retains many of the same formal attributes: delegations, representing the officially recognized "seven cultural regions" of Oaxaca, and the performance of dances considered autochthonous to their regions. The performance takes place on a large stage overlooking the Oaxaca Valley. Following their performance, the delegations offer gifts to the governor of the state, who sits on a dais at the center of the stage. The delegations then throw smaller gifts to the audience of tourists and Oaxacans who attend the spectacle. Among the elements that have remained unchanged since 1932 is the offering of gifts (now to the governor; then to Miss Oaxaca); the equation of regional culture with female dress; and the celebration of diversity as the basis of a unified Oaxacan culture. What has changed significantly is the name and the date of the festival. The original Homenaje Racial, held in April 1932, has been expunged from official histories of the Guelaguetza. The festival is instead said to be a descendant of ancient Zapotec and Mixtec rituals performed during the month of July and related to the maize cycle. In interviews conducted in Oaxaca in the late 1990s, state officials and participants alike denied that any sort of racial element might be attributed to their state's festival.

Indeed, at all levels of organization and public presentation, care is taken to mark the distance that (supposedly) separates the forms of cultural distinction celebrated in the Guelaguetza from any notion of genealogical, natural, or racial entitlement to separate identities. The delegations that perform are selected by the Committee of Authenticity, whose policing role is essentially the same as that of the 1932 Organizing Committee. The authenticity committee comprises distinguished senior members of Oaxaca's several folklore associations. Some months prior to the event, the committee members travel to each of the seven regions to preside over auditions for the group that will represent that region in the Guelaguetza. Members check for authenticity of clothing, shoes, musical style, choreography, and physical appearance. When asked on what basis these decisions were made, the head of the committee told me that no documentary or historical sources were consulted. "I just know," she assured me. "I can tell what is authentic or not, or when a costume is 'off.' I have lived in Oaxaca all my life. I just know."

Through such statements and practices, members of the authenticity committee effectively separate their "expert" knowledge of cultural distinction from the shared forms of life we think of as "culture," in the anthropological sense of the word. At the same time—and invoking the racial contours of mestizaje—they hint at a genealogy of affect linking the members of the committee (and their aesthetic sensibilities) to the cultures they authenticate as distinct. Residing at the limits of this calculus of recognition are those "ethnicities"—such as the "Afromestizos" from Oaxaca—whom the authenticity committee considers alien to its own genealogical imagination of Oaxacan cultural distinction and belonging. In an interview with me, the head of the authenticity committee lamented the unfavorable impression left by the Afromestizo dance group that the committee allowed to perform—for the first time—in 2000.

> The public did not like them because they lacked the attraction of regional costumes. They wore some ratty, old pants; it is a dance they dance on the coast the day of All Souls, in the cemetery. . . . It is not that we are racists but they have no attractive qualities to present in a spectacle. I do not care if, for example, they present the dance in the coastal dance festival, because there they have their own space where they present just dances. That is their space. . . . It is not that we disdain them, we want them to continue preserving [their customs], but they should conserve them in their own context, in their place of origin.

Similar remarks surface in newspaper reviews of the performance. "The blacks," wrote one journalist, "are a race, not a Oaxacan ethnic group. Moreover, they broke with the indigenous context and rhythm [of the event]."[41] For another journalist, the foreign character of black culture simply "provoked boredom among the spectators."[42] Excluded politically and culturally from the Oaxacan polity, the "Afromestizos" represent that which cannot be rendered "intelligible" within the grammar of distinction proper to the Guelaguetza. As the ultimate outsiders, their racial alterity offered no imaginable sentimental links to the forms of cultural distinction they represented. For these journalists, as for the authenticity committee, blackness is illegible as culture—it is legible only as race. It is therefore unavailable as a source of mestizaje, nor does it bear any viable genealogical connection to the place of Oaxaca and its Guelaguetza.

Even this brief overview of the attitudes and practices of the authenticity committee (which include, in addition to racial biases, preference for the delegations sponsored by particular political parties and factions of municipal governments) make it clear why the committee should have been a target of the compa demonstrators. On one level, the committee's strict control over the Guelaguetza limits the range of cultural actors and groups who can benefit materially and professionally from the tourism and folklore industry. On another level, the spectacle is the most visible manifestation of the Oaxacan state's claims to speak on behalf of its many different cultural and ethnic groups. The issue is not only *who* is allowed to authenticate culture, but, perhaps more importantly, how claims to cultural distinction and belonging can be made intelligible. Here it is instructive to look at the different ways that individuals and organizations negotiate the distinct temporal registers represented by the genealogical discourse of race and the classificatory discourse of distinction. Two final examples serve to illustrate.

The first example comes from an annual government-sponsored contest to elect the *Diosa Centeotl* (Maize Goddess). In this rendition of an Oaxacan beauty contest, women from Oaxaca's seven regions explain the composition and symbolism of their region's typical costume before a panel of judges headed by the director of the Institute of Oaxacan Cultures. Most striking in their oratory is the extent to which the costume itself has been abstracted or fetishized as the embodiment of ethnicity and region. In 2002 and 2003, when the state ceased to offer a scholarship to the winner, many of the contestants included in their speeches references to popular demands for cultural rights and the restoration of cultural programs sponsored by a previous governor of Oaxaca (see figure 3).

No matter how assertive their demands, all the women's speeches echoed a densely layered interpretation of the diversity-speak of the state, a language that is framed by the idea of mixture or mestizaje. Whereas the mestizaje of Mexican nation-building paints mixture as a form of resolution, the women sculpt the language of mixture as a defense of their particular forms of difference. In the 1998 competition, one woman began her speech by identifying herself and her region, and by placing them in relationship to the City of Oaxaca: "I am from the community of San Miguel Panixtlahuaca of traditional customs of the aroma of cafe. Through my person I send a fraternal greeting to everyone without distinction. The presence of my community is here with me today. We dress like this when we go to an important feast like the Oaxaca Guelaguetza." After describing in great detail her costume and its symbolism, she concluded her speech by invoking the colonial distinction between "the people with reason" and the "people without reason": "Thus barefoot or with sandals," she proclaimed, "we are people of many customs. We have reasons (*razones*) for our beliefs and we also love the people with reason (*gente de razón*)." Here "reason" (*razón*) receives a double charge: much like the terms "pueblo," "raza," or "culture," it references both an absolute racial and cultural distinction, and a more universal way of thinking in which even the Mixtecos have a right to be included.

Other contestants employed similar tropes to describe their region, their costume, and the forms of cultural presence that unite and distinguish them from the rest of Oaxaca. The representative from the coast, a region home to a dense population of Afrometizos, for example, said she was from the "coastal region where there exist ethnic groups like the blacks, Indians and mestizos." After a detailed description of her multiracial region's supposedly uniform costume, cooking, and culture, she concluded: "I say farewell by making a petition to the competent authorities for the rescue and conservation of our customs, roots, and traditions, that this great wealth that graces our coast won't die and with it all of our beautiful and historic Oaxaca." A Mazateca woman concluded her speech with a similar plea: "We offer you Huautla de Jimenez," she proclaims, "so that you can visit us and together we can forge a Mazatec ethnic group." Here the project of building or reinforcing ethnicity was clearly meant as an inclusive project requiring, minimally, an outside observer (the state, tourists, other Oaxaqueños) and the Mazatecos.

Figure 3. Diosa Centeotl contest, 1998. Credit: Deborah Poole.

Mazatec ethnicity was to be built through conversation with Oaxaca's other six regions, not as an exclusive essence.

In response to such pleas—which are themselves shaped by a historic language of type—the state speaks back with a version of the language of mestizaje that effectively undermines all claims to distinction. It does so by placing a historical (and marketable) value on distinction as a passing fashion to which the state nevertheless has a claim as the authority that decides who is the authentic Indian or mestizo. As one woman from the government's cultural branch explained to me:

> Today it is no longer fashionable to talk about mestizaje . . . this has meant searching for people's ethnic origins in the different towns, looking for their identity within the Zapotecos, even though they are mestizos . . . that is to say, that their parents were married with other people who were not Zapotec. And I don't mean they are always mestizos by [mixture with] Spanish or Europeans, but also mestizos from a Zapotec father and a Mixtec mother. Thus there you have a Mixtec and a Zapotec, or a Mixe and a Zapotec. So you have a mixture, but that is not what is important, what is important is the form in which the people identify with the ethnic group where they are living. There are many Mixes that are not Mixes by origin, and they think of themselves as Mixe . . . I think it is a form of looking in this town or that region for an identity and today mestizaje doesn't exist, it is not fashionable to be mestizo. It is fashionable to be Zapotec, Mazateco, etc. For that reason the government of the State of Oaxaca strengthens the identity. That is the idea. For that reason we reinforce the cultural identities in order to give greater relevance to the Oaxaqueño identity which is multiple. And that is something we have consciously done. It is a conscious act of our government.

Here "mestizaje" is taken as a broad process of cultural—and biological—mixture, between not only "Spanish" and "Indians," but between the different indigenous groups that collectively make up the category of "Indian"—a category that supposedly represents the cultural and biological antithesis of the mestizo.

In spectacles such as the Diosa Centeotl, *visual* markers are described (and possessed) through a language of presence in which the fact of distinction constitutes the means for claiming a place in a larger mestizo whole. For the women who participate in the Diosa Centeotl contest, this may mean that the available idioms of modern identity are images of costumes and types held up to them by a state that has a long investment in authorizing diversity. For the upper-class and, above all, middle-class and working-class Oaxacans who *watch* (and listen to) the contestants, the invocation of distinction to claim mestizaje reinforces an aesthetic of appearances in which the customs and costumes of different parts of their state are made available as markers of an undifferentiated Oaxacan identity. This mestizo subject is predicated not on a unified or homogeneous cultural subject whose "identity" is constituted (as in the European case) through its opposition to an absolute, excluded Other. It is formed instead in opposition to an Other that shares something of the substance of the mestizo self.[43] In this respect, the discourse of mestizaje shares the suspicion—but not the optimism—that marked the nineteenth-century genealogical project. In both instances, the surface appearances of culture must be scrutinized for evidence of the racial substance that might reveal a subterranean link between the mestizo self and the indigenous (excluded) Other.

The status of the genealogical discourse of race as a hidden substance in this metaphysics of suspicion surfaces even more clearly in the claims to cultural distinction made by some of the new cultural and indigenous organizations in Oaxaca. As an example, we might take the Ninth Annual Festival of Mixtec Culture, which I observed in December 1999. According to its organizers, the goal of this event was to "awaken in us the ancestral and genetic memory of affect and respect for the tradition that is preserved from generation to generation in the towns that make up the Mixtec nation; it is to grow closer and make more tangible our historical patrimony." One way in which organizers hoped to effect this closeness was by holding the event in the town of San Miguel Achiutla—the alleged "origin place of the Mixtec race." Another was by making their culture "tangible" through stylized reconstructions of forgotten rituals, didactic lectures on iconographic symbols drawn from sixteenth-century codices, and graphic visualizations and recitations about women's "typical" dress. Each performance was preceded by an impassioned lecture concerning the dismal state of Mixtec culture and the need to revitalize it through folklore workshops, school dances, and the dissemination of ritual and medical knowledge.

Faced with the daunting task of reviving a culture that, according to the event's organizers, no one actually practiced anymore, the speakers looked to their "genetic racial memory" as a repository of the sentiments and affects that constituted knowledge of their culture. The performance of a "secret ritual," for example, was said to "speak of the genetic memory that can serve as a basis for renewing the culture of our Mixtec race. Through this cultural work we unite ourselves in one race. . . . The resistance of the Mixtec culture reaffirms our genetic code." Even access to forgotten languages—in this case the Mixtec Codices—was tied to this genetic code. "Historians in Mexico have forgotten how to read these codices," one speaker explained, "but we Mixtecs carry that knowledge in our genes." This form of local—and apparently "genetic"—knowledge, they assured the audience, was necessary not just for the good of the Mixtec region, but as a contribution to Oaxaca as a whole. "Oaxaca," the festival coordinator explained, "is the state with the most biodiversity. It is therefore natural that it also have the most diversity of cultures."

For present purposes, I want to emphasize three points about the festival. The first is the organizers' view of culture as the invisible genetic code that forms the basis of a Mixtec nation. At a moment when Oaxacan intellectuals and the Mexican nation were at pains to erase the notion of race from the history of the nation, local culture-workers were busy resurrecting a racial theory of culture—or, to be more precise, a cultural theory of race. The second involves the vision of the Mixtec "nation" as a means to reinsert the Mixteca as a specific cultural region into the larger "diversity" of Oaxaca. Here we are reminded of the continual tributes to diversity as the basis for a uniquely Oaxacan identity—an identity that can serve, in the words of one Oaxacan writer, as "a national reserve in the face of the *extranjerismos* (foreign-isms) that are so alien to us Mexicans." The final issue involves the reliance on performed culture and stylized notions of "type"—in particular, women's indigenous dress—as the tangible forms of culture through which the genetic code is reaffirmed. As in the Guelaguetza, Diosa Centeotl, and other state-sponsored spectacles, these provincial and largely disempowered intellectuals looked to ritual performances and women's dress for the visual evidence of their cultural distinction. This evidence—not the more "elusive" genetic code—is the ground from which claims for cultural recognition can be articulated.

❋

For most Mexican indigenous organizations, the grammar of culture is a strategic language with which to negotiate more substantial grievances concerning resources, land, and political autonomy. Mexico offers many examples of this, including Oaxaca and Chiapas, where longstanding demands for political autonomy are now conjugated through the juridical—and hence state-controlled—language of "cultural rights" and usos y costumbres.[44] To understand the grammatical forms that make culture intelligible as a political discourse, however, we must look at the forms of life through which such concepts as culture, mestizaje, diversity, homogeneity, and distinction become recurring points of disagreement and debate (rather than settled meanings). In the case of Oaxaca, I have suggested that this debate was centered in the state's early moves to articulate a discourse of political unity based on the de facto fragmentation and indigenous control of Oaxaca's many municipalities. By offering a vision of state unity premised on natural "regions," and by mapping indigenous culture onto these political territories, Oaxaca's revolutionary state effectively staked a claim over the cultural identities of the many municipalities where state control had been rendered tenuous by indigenous traditions, authorities, and communal property forms.

The cultural politics of the neoliberal era build on this historical work, work that has linked cultural diversity with political legitimization and state-building. For the Mixtec schoolteachers with whom I spoke, this heritage comes through in their equation of cultural diversity with biodiversity. For the state itself, it is in the domain of politics and law that culture looms large. This sort of back and forth between states and the peoples whose cultures (or identities) they claim to represent is not, of course, unique to Oaxaca or Mexico. As neoliberal states across Latin America attempt to assimilate the new priorities of multilateral lenders, nongovernmental organizations, and other transnational organizations that favor direct funding to ethnic and community-based organizations, indigenous groups respond with heightened demands for control over the terms in which their own "identities" are to be promoted. The result is a tense dialogue between governments that promote multiculturalism as a backdrop for new forms of community-based governance, and indigenous or community-based groups who deploy the same language to claim something more substantive than culture alone. This dynamic will be familiar to anyone who has worked in Latin America in the last twenty years.[45]

Cultural recognition acquires a peculiar dynamic in a country like Mexico where the normative modern subject must define him or herself through reference to a process (mestizaje) rather than in terms of a finished national subject. By disaggregating the genealogical and descriptive dimensions of cultural discourse in Oaxaca, I have emphasized the distinct forms of temporality that characterize notions of "distinction" and "genealogy." Mestizaje has traditionally been seen as a *process* of assimilation or mixture that is clearly directed toward the future (as in Gamio's project of "forging a fatherland") and cultural distinction. But this is clearly a claim to presence whose authenticity is rooted in the past. In the new politics of multiculturalism, "the mestizo" emerges as just one of many different and allegedly fixed claims to identity. While modernist discussions of mestizaje were concerned with the genealogical claims that made it possible to establish an individual's (or group's) distance from Indian, Spanish, or African ancestry, in the language of neoliberal multiculturalism, mestizaje is one of many identity claims that are authenticated not by reference to genealogy or history, but by staking a claim to cultural properties in the present. Thus, while anxieties about identity once focused on appearance (race) and the highly mobile line separating Indian and mestizo forms of life, neoliberal anxieties about mestizaje center on the relative success with which indigenous groups have taken hold of a language in which culture is conceived of as a property that is simultaneously transhistorical and a product of continuous self-cultivation. Within this language of cultural belonging and recognition, the majority stance of mestizo enjoys little credence as an identity claim that is grounded in a historical process of differentiation and exclusion.

Notes

1. "Anuncian pueblos bloqueos a la Guelaguetza," *Noticias* (Oaxaca), July 19, 2002. The Acuerdos de San Andrés are the signed agreements between the EZLN and the Mexican government that include demands for cultural rights and partial political autonomy. The Plan Puebla-Panama is an international investment strategy initiated in 2001 to develop corridors for resource extraction and "capital integration" in nine southern Mexican states, as well as in Colombia and Central America.

2. Diodoro Carrasco Altamirano, quoted in "Presencia de Oaxaca en Paris: Oaxaca, principal nicho de la diversidad indígena de México," *Noticias* (Oaxaca), September 29, 1998.

3. On ethnic and linguistic diversity in Oaxaca, see Barabas, Bartolomé, and Maldonado 2004.

4. On Oaxacan migration, see Lewin and Guzmán 2003.

5. The practice of elections through usos y costumbres grew out of indigenous demands from the 1990s (Hernández Díaz 2001). By legislating a practice that had been in effect since at least 1995, Oaxaca's PRI government sought to ensure control over indigenous municipalities at a moment when the PRI hegemony was challenged by the PRD, an opposition party. Although the number of PRI-controlled munici-

palities dropped dramatically from 535 (in 1989) to 112 in 1995 (when elections were first run under usos y costumbres), the party continued to control municipal presidencies through clientelistic ties that link "nonpartisan" authorities to the PRI. On the history of usos y costumbres in Oaxaca, see Anaya Muñoz 2004; Hernández Navarro 1999; Nahmad 2001; Recondo 2001 and 2007; Velásquez 2000.

6. Amnesty International 1986; Human Rights Watch 1997; Human Rights Watch 1999; Red Oaxaqueña de Derechos Humanos, *Segundo Informe*, January 2001. In the years since this article was originally written, the human rights situation has significantly worsened under the administrations of governors José Murat Casab (1998–2004) and Ulises Ruiz Ortíz (2004–2010). See Comisión Civil Internacional de Observación por los Derechos Humanos 2008; Red Oaxaqueña de Derechos Humanos 2006.

7. On the Guelaguetza Popular, see Poole 2007 and Oaxaca Pie en Lucha, http://oaxacaenpiedelucha.blogspot.com/2007/07/la-verdadera-guelaguetza-es-la.html, July 16, 2007.

8. Agamben 2000, 29–36; Rancière 2001.

9. The Oaxaca Constitution was first amended to recognize pluricultural status in 1990. See Anaya Muñoz 2004; Martínez 2004; Velásquez 2000. The Mexican national constitution was similarly amended in 1992.

10. Monte Albán was occupied successively, but never concurrently, by Mixtec and Zapotec polities. Olmec occupation, however, came many centuries before Mixtec occupation. In this example, then, the temporality of mestizaje is imagined not as a mixing that takes place between contemporaries, but as a historical progression.

11. On Clavijero and the historical genealogy of mestizaje as national project in Mexico, see, among others, Basave Benítez 1992; Brading 1991, 450–62; and Pacheco 1976.

12. On mestizaje as national revolutionary ideology, see Alonso 2004. On racial and cultural diversity in Mexico, see Bonfil Batalla 1993.

13. Saldivar 2008.

14. On race and public space in Oaxaca, see Poole 2009.

15. Following the Oaxacan insurrection of 2006 (see Esteva 2007 and Rénique 2007) and the initiation of the annual Popular Guelaguetzas (see Poole 2007), the political disputes generated by state control over cultural representation have deepened. Because this chapter was written several years before the formation of the first Guelaguetza Popular in 2006, I deal with forms of protest leading up to (and foregrounding) the more formal contestations of the PRI-dominated "official Guelaguetza" that were voiced during the 2006-7 Oaxacan Insurrection.

16. On the Porfiriato in Oaxaca, see Chassen-López 2004; Dalton 1987; McNamara 2007.

17. Although Church properties were affected by the reforms, a third of these were sold back to Indians. See Berry 1981; Esparza 1988a, 269–330; on haciendas, see Cassidy 1986–90, 292–323.

18. Chance 1978; see also Traffano 2002.

19. McNamara 2007.

20. McBride 1923, 146.

21. Cited in Garner 1988, 25–39.

22. On municipalities in Oaxaca, see, among others, Pastor 1987; Velásquez 2000.

23. Carriedo 1847; Gay 1990; Martínez Gracida 1888; see also Dalton 1986.

24. Martínez moved to Tehuantepec with Díaz during Díaz's term as governor of the state of Oaxaca and remained loyal to Díaz throughout his career. Manuel Brioso y Candiani, "Biografia de Manuel Martínez Gracida," *El Mercurio* (Oaxaca), August 12, 13, 14, and 16, 1927. Manuel Brioso y Candiani, "Manuel Martínez Gracida," *El Centenario* (Mexico), 1910.

25. Martínez Gracida 1888, 2.

26. Martínez Gracida and subsequent Oaxacan historians relied heavily on the work of the seventeenth-century Dominican Francisco Burgoa and the work of their contemporaries. Gay (1990), Carriedo (1847), and López Ruiz (1898).

27. Martínez Gracida 1888, 2–3

28. Martínez Gracida 1888, 71–74. On eighteenth-century French philosophes' uses of pre-Columbian history, see Poole 1997. On Aztecs, see Keen 1984.

29. On the history of women's dress in the Isthmus of Tehuantepec, see Cajigas Langner 1954; Chassen-López 2004; Pérez Montfort 2003; Sierra 2000.

30. Manuel Martínez Gracida's *Los Indios oaxaqueños y sus monumentos* can be found in the Biblioteca de la Municipaidad de Oaxaca de Juarez. Though unpublished, this work has nevertheless served as a major source for all subsequent work on Oaxacan ethnology and history. Extracts from the work have been published by Esparza 1988b. For analysis of Martínez's watercolors and photographs, see Poole 2004b.

31. The argument about foreign origins was first put forward by Gay (1990, 9–15). Gay's history was the principal source for all other nineteenth-century historians.

32. Gay 1990, 26.

33. Poole 2004a; Poole 2004b.

34. On the revolution in Oaxaca, see Ruiz Cervantes 1986; McNamara 2007; Martínez Vásquez 1993.

35. On the cultural missions in Oaxaca, see Mendoza García 2004 and Poole 2004b.

36. "Argumento Escenificado del Homenaje Racial," *El Mercurio* (Oaxaca), April 20, 1932, and April 21, 1932.

37. The regional committees were expected to receive nominations for the embajadoras from the given regions, and then to raise money by *selling* votes for other candidates. Not surprisingly, the winners were representatives of the wealthier—and, for the most part, whiter—families of their respective regions.

38. Complaints about the problem of finding appropriate indigenous dress for the embajadoras surface in many of the letters from provincial subcommittees to the

Organizing Committee. See, for example, "Carta de Miguel Bennetts, Presidente Subcomité Yautepec, a León Olvera," [1932] and the reply, "Carta de León Olvera a Miguel Bennetts," March 15, 1932. Such exchanges reflect the confusion regarding how to map costume onto region in regions where ethnic boundaries overlapped. Correspondence cited is from the Archivo de la Municipalidad de Oaxaca, Documentos varios, IV Centenario, 1932.

39. "Carta de Leon Olvera del Comite Organizadora del IV Centenario a Alfonso Cuella del Comite Regional de Juchila," March 21, 1932; Archivo Histórico de la Municipalidad de Oaxaca.

40. Poole 2004b.

41. Rosy Ramales, "De Nuevo, la magia y el color de los dias cultivaron a propios y extraños," *Noticias* (Oaxaca), July 25, 2000.

42. Jesús García, "Guelaguetza, muestra del valor que da Oaxaca a sus tradiciones," *Noticias* (Oaxaca), July 25, 2000.

43. On European concepts of identity, see Asad 2000, 11–24; Connolly 1996.

44. Anaya Muñoz 2004; Poole 2006; Recondo 2007; Sierra 1998; Speed and Collier 2000.

45. On neoliberal multiculturalism in Latin America see Hale 2005; on neoliberal governance by community see Rose 1999.

On the Origin of the "Mexican Race"

CLAUDIO LOMNITZ

A few years ago I became interested in the following questions: How is national unity forged? What role does racialization—that is, naturalizing social differences—play in forming the national subject? What is the relationship between "race" and Mexican national identity? I was fascinated by the feeling of uniqueness, bordering on self-obsession, that many of us had in Mexico when I was a student in the 1970s. That feeling, that obsession with what Andrés Molina Enríquez, the ideologue of the Mexican Revolution, called "The Great National Problems" carried an ambivalent weight for me, insofar as it captured a model of the intellectual as a translator, mediator, or hinge who served to present outside ideas to a captive internal market that the intellectual considered his own. To a certain extent, the model for Mexican intellectual life paralleled the economic policies of the time, which also favored the development of the internal market. Even multinational corporations positioned themselves to develop the Mexican market: the Ford Company's Mexican division translated and transferred its patents and designs for the Mexican market to its factory in Mexico; its Brazilian counterpart did the same for Brazil.

The emergence of neoliberal globalization, which erupted in Mexico with the financial crisis of 1982, also presented a crisis for Mexican intellectuals. To my way of thinking, Mexico has been unlike Brazil, which was able to take advantage of globalization to exponentially expand its dialogue and influence with neighboring countries. Mexico's engagement in intellectual exchange with its most important neighbor, the United States, has not yet taken on the bold, confident tenor of Brazil's engagement with its neighbors, an engagement making Brazil a major power in South America. Rather, the exchange between Mexico and its neighbors has been arduous, and it has taken place in gradual, subtle, and equivocal ways. The parallels between Mexico and Brazil can be deceiving, because Mexico is not to North America what Brazil is to South America, nor does Mexico play the role in the Spanish-speaking world that Brazil does in the Portuguese-speaking world. The contrasts between these two countries clearly show that the current era of globalization forces us to think beyond the narrow frame of great national problems. What's needed now is not to go deeper into our supposed or real uniqueness but to put into play our viewpoints and worldviews. This exercise requires us to conceptualize not only what we sometimes still call, with exhaustion, *lo nuestro* (what is ours), with its overwhelming weight, but to also consider the meaning of our situation from a global point of view.

Mexico has a unique place in the history and geography of the Americas. Its uniqueness derives from the long border it shares with the United States. The border is central to the two nations' integration and provokes so much reaction and interaction that it merits comparison with countries sharing borders outside the Americas, for example, Ireland and England, Poland and Germany, or Korea and Japan. The uniqueness on the American continent of Mexico's border with the United States is linked to another particularity: Mexico's size and prominence in relation to other Spanish American countries. Mexico was the richest and most populous Spanish colony in America. It is the largest Spanish-speaking country in the world, and today it is large enough to accommodate a relatively robust public opinion, intelligentsia, and university system.

Mexico's unique position in the Americas is my point of departure for exploring the question of national unity and how it is forged. Until very recently, racialization, or at least the search for unity and a certain homogeneity, was a problem common to all nations. The first responses to the problems of national unity appeared in revolutionary France and in the United States after it achieved its independence.

How did the United States confront the problem of national unity? It created unity, first, by distributing the debt from its war for independence throughout the entire country. That is, it nationalized its debt, even though each colony was affected to a different degree by the war. Then the federal government constructed a political agreement that respected the states' representation.

How did France confront the question of heterogeneity? It created a national time, as the historian Mona Ozouf showed many years ago.[1] As Tocqueville demonstrated, the centralized administration that had existed since the reign of Louis XIV created a deep division between the people and the sovereign and eliminated the autonomous power of the aristocracy.[2] Once the sovereign was overthrown, it was necessary to homogenize the people, imposing not only a common language but also a series of synchronized rituals within the republic's institutions. Thus, for example, all children learned everything together in a measured, coordinated way, from multiplication tables to the "fact" that their ancestors were Gauls, even if they were, in fact, from Italy or Germany.

In Mexico, as in much of Spanish America, the formation of the national subject was a difficult process. In the years following independence, only two institutions had a national reach: the church and the army, and the power of the latter was counterbalanced by state militias. The population was multilingual, and no single class dominated at the national level. Thus, when Mexico went to war with the United States, some states in the federation declared themselves neutral in the conflict. Though Mexico had abolished slavery in 1829, foreign travelers and national authors traded in a baroque repertoire of common "Mexican types" depicted in racialized detail. These types represented occupational groups that were marked by caste, race, and sex, and they reflected a heterogeneity that challenged the idea of the existence of "the Mexican" as a common or universal type at a national level.

The local censuses carried out between the time the Mexican Society of Geography and Statistics was formed, in 1833, and the first national census was carried out, in 1895, refer to the "races" of each region in very different ways. For example, the prefect of Tixtla, Guerrero, noted that out of a population of 25,000 inhabitants, 20,000 were Indians. He complained, however, that the remaining 5,000 inhabitants had merged with the Indians in an effort to exterminate the "Hispano-Mexican race," which at the time seemed foreign to the region. The prefect of Querétaro offered a less original classification, closer to that proposed by Baron von Humboldt in 1803. According to von Humboldt, Querétaro consisted of Creoles, *mestizos*, and Indians—fine up to this point—but then he separated the Creoles into two classes: the good and the bad. The prefect of Soconusco, Chiapas, divided the population into four races: *ladinos* (Spanish-speaking Indians), Indians, blacks, and *Lacandons*. He believed that the Lacandons belonged to a different race than the Indians. E. B. Tylor, who would later found the discipline of anthropology at

Oxford University, traveled to Mexico in 1856 and identified three different races of Indians: "red Indians" (corresponding to those called "barbarous Indians" in Mexico), "brown Indians" (roughly corresponding to the Mexican peasantry) and "blue Indians" (corresponding to General Juan Álvarez's troops, who at that time had taken Mexico City, and who frequently suffered from a skin disease known in Mexico as *mal de pinto* or *pinta*).[3]

The practice of dividing the Mexican people into multiple, picturesque races and castes lasted until the beginning of the twentieth century, and not only on the postcards that had begun to circulate among tourists. In 1901, Julio Guerrero, a positivist criminologist, published an important book about crime in Mexico City, in which he proposed classifying the capital's society into eight different types. Guerrero configured his ethnographically interesting typology according to salary, racial origin, occupation, and private consumption habits. Taken together, his types reflected a vision of a racially and culturally disparate Mexican society, even in the capital of the republic itself. Nationally, physiologists sought to distinguish physical differences among Mexican types, as the ethnographer and explorer Carl Lumholtz had begun to do.

Yet during those same years, around the beginning of the twentieth century, references to a "Mexican race" surfaced in colloquial usage. How does the notion of a unified Mexican race emerge in such a diverse and fragmented environment?

Before attempting to answer this question, it is important to consider the phenomenon of race itself. Is the idea of a national race really so unique? The process of racializing citizens has occurred in many places where the construction of the nation has involved a form of mestizaje. The Spanish people, for instance, have been seen as a fusion of Iberians and Romans, or as a fusion of Iberians, Romans, Arabs, and Jews. Brazil and Cuba have hybrid images. The British have pictured themselves as a fusion of Anglo-Saxons, Normans, and Celts. In other cases, race was determined by exclusion. In the France of the Dreyfus era, for example, national identity was racialized through anti-Semitism. In the United States after 1882, the racialization of national identity justified the exclusion of the Chinese.

While the case of the Mexican race is not unique, two factors distinguish it from others. First, the Mexican race rarely proposes itself as a superior race, but rather as a race ideally suited to the specific environment of Mexico.[4] Second, the representation of Mexicans as a race is deeply rooted in the popular imagination. For example, in northern Mexico and the United States, the word "*raza*," or "race," is used to mean "us"—the "raza" is going to the movies, for example. It parallels the way in which "*a gente*" ("the people") is used in Portuguese. However, in Brazil, another American country known for its mestizophilia, the "Brazilian race" has tended to be identified as a project for the future, not as an existing empirical reality. For example, a statue of the "Brazilian man," designed for the patio of the building that housed the Department of Education—constructed by Le Corbusier in Rio de Janeiro in 1930—was never built, because a committee of experts on race decided that the subject's physical characteristics were too frightening for the taste of the age.[5] In contrast, in early twentieth-century Mexico, the nation became identified with a race in a relatively extensive (and perhaps generalized) way. How and why did this occur?

At any given moment, three factors have advanced the idea of mestizaje and its transformation into a national race. The first factor, shared by other nations, is found in a government's public policies. When a political regime fails to achieve effective citizenship based on equality before the law, it uses race or origin to define the citizen and thus form the national subject. In Mexico, as in all of Spanish America, the initial goal was to create a citizenry on the basis of equality before the law. For example, in 1822 the congress of the state of Jalisco justified its new agrarian property law as follows:

> If one desires to do away with the source of the Indians' isolation from the rest of the nation, and to prepare their amalgamation with it, so that it acquires the homogeneity that it lacks—and this is the main obstacle impeding our complete social regeneration—we have no choice but to adopt the following measure: to circulate an order to all provincial, district and subordinate town governors for them to issue a proclamation requiring the Indians to proceed to their respective town councils to provide information about the lands that may compose their original legal estates, and of other lands that they may have bought with community money, so that, by dividing them equally among the families of the Indians who now exist, each family may take ownership of the property that belongs to them.[6]

Initially, the Mexican citizen was to be constructed on the basis of equality before the law, and the idea of a national race was rejected as a distant or impossible goal, if not an outright recipe for what were then called "caste wars." The caste wars called for the extermination of the minority of European origin (or later, for the extermination of the Indians, as happened in the campaigns against the Yaquis and Apaches or in the War of the Desert in Argentina). However, two policy failures contributed to rethinking citizenship in Mexico. First, political liberalism failed to provide a formula for forming a powerful state. Second, the migration policy of the Porfirio Díaz dictatorship failed to attract Europeans to Mexico on a large scale. In this way the policy was unlike the policies of Argentina, Uruguay, Brazil, Chile, Cuba, or Venezuela. As a consequence, a wholly Mexican racialization of the citizen was adopted by leveling out the general population into one emergent category: the mestizo.

The politics of forming a mestizo national subject found its most successful ideologue in Andrés Molina Enríquez, who wrote *Los grandes problemas nacionales* in 1909. While he argued that the history of Mexico was the history of the rise of the mestizo, this was not his most innovative proposal, nor was it in itself an original thesis. Rather, his most innovative proposal was that Mexico's central problem, land ownership, would be resolved by giving land to the mestizo.[7] For Molina Enríquez, the independence process, which had been consolidated in the mid-nineteenth-century reform wars and the struggle against French intervention, would only come to an end when lands were distributed among the mestizo race. Benito Juárez left the process unfinished when he gave church lands to the new Creole bourgeoisie instead of handing them over to the mestizos. Agrarian reform was declared in the Mexican constitution of 1917, and its agrarian law—article 27—was drafted in part by Molina Enríquez. It served to consolidate the idea of the mestizo as a national class, and the revolution as the "Mexican's" final arrival to power.

The second factor that consolidated the racialization of the national subject was economic dynamism. Economic developments broke down categories of identity and created a basis for new identities that, while different from the original ones, still retained a racial discourse. This process began in the colonial period and was enormously important in Mexico, in part because the principal mining centers, in contrast to those in Peru, were far from the centers of the indigenous population. Mining cities such as Zacatecas, San Luis Potosí, and Guanajuato, and the haciendas that fed them, were centers of mestizaje from their inception. The expansion of mining into northern Mexico also required the establishment of free towns settled by *colonos*, who were granted land in exchange for participating in the struggle against the "barbarous Indians," that is, the Apaches. These towns, eventually known as "free frontier" towns, were also spaces of mestizaje.

By the end of the nineteenth century and the beginning of the twentieth, the accelerated pace of building the Mexican train network and large-scale capital investments in mining, textiles, petroleum, and agriculture generated waves of migration, both inside Mexico and to the United States. These migrations contributed to the phenomenon of mestizaje, because the identities that are called indigenous today were almost all based on location at that time. One identified as an Indian from Xochimilco or Tlaxiaco much more than as a "Nahua" or a "Mixtec." The Mixtec speaker from Tlaxiaco who moved to Mexico City or who worked on the railroads in the isthmus merged with the "plebeian class" or the "people" as soon as he learned a little Spanish. Capitalist growth, with its dislocations, facilitated the consolidation of a mestizo ideology.

Why did people come to identify the new mestizaje with national identity? A third and final factor, which seems to me comparatively rare, is undoubtedly the most interesting in terms of its implications for Mexican thought: the racialization of the Mexican as a product of the logic of the border between Mexico and the United States. This history begins with the racialization of the Mexican in the territories annexed by the United States after 1848, a process which had two central axes. The first was the formation of a racialized labor force in Texas, which became a southern slave state after its annexation. This meant that Mexicans living there occupied an intermediary place between whites, who were the conquering group, and black slaves. The second axis can be understood clearly through the case of New Mexico, a territory where Mexicans were still more numerous than whites for many decades. In New Mexico the racialization of the Mexican as inferior was used to keep the territory from becoming a state until an "Anglo" majority could emerge.[8] The racialization of the Mexican in the United States responded, on the one hand, to a strategy of Mexican integration into an ethnically segmented labor market (which predominated in Texas), and, on the other, to a white strategy of political marginalization (especially relevant in the territory of New Mexico). The Mexican was first considered a member of a unified race in the United States.

As the Mexican was racialized in the southwestern United States, another practice emerged: that of paying Mexican workers less than Anglos, for example, in Arizona's copper mines. White sharecroppers and tenant farmers were replaced by Mexican laborers who accepted lower salaries on Texas's cotton plantations.[9] The practice of dividing the workforce according to race was exported to Mexico at the end of the nineteenth century. The new foreign companies—especially the railway, mining, petroleum, and brewing companies—paid Mexican workers less than European or North American workers.[10] In the Cananea mine, for example, U.S. and European workers earned between 60 to 100 percent more than the Mexican workers doing the same job.[11] "The Mexican race" came to have a practical and tangible meaning in the border regions.

Salary contributed to the racialization of Mexicans in the United States and in Mexico, and political exclusion had the same effect in the United States. Yet, another factor explains the dissemination of the idea of the Mexican race: the international border, which the U.S. and Mexican governments designated to signal the beginning of one "regime of value" (to use Arjun Appadurai's term), and the end of another.[12] Little by little, the border turned into a magical threshold, through which one passed, or should pass, from one world to another. The border became a threshold between languages, currencies, relationships, peoples, and even times.[13]

Perhaps the most dramatic illustration of the border as threshold in the Porfirian era can be found in the life of Teresa Urrea, known as the Saint of Cabora. This *curandera,* or faith healer, a girl from Cabora, Sinaloa, became the emblem of several millenarian revolts among the Maya and Yaqui Indians and the mestizo settlers of the Tarahumara mountain ranges in Chihuahua, who were confronting the dislocation caused by runaway modernization. These rebellions—the most famous was in Tomóchic—have some parallels with the famous Canudos rebellion in Brazil during the same period. During the Brazilian rebellion, a holy man, Antonio Conselheiro, led a movement against the republic. This movement was described by Euclides de Cunha in his famous book *Os sertões (Rebellion in the Backlands).* In Tomóchic, as in Canudos, the rebels triggered alarm in the capital when they defeated the federal army on a couple of occasions, before the rebels were finally annihilated. Tomóchic became a national scandal, as did Canudos, a symbol of fierce resistance as well as the army's and government's vengeance and iniquity. The charismatic Brazilian leader Antonio Conselheiro was executed, whereas the Saint of Cabora was deported. She ended up living in the border region, and the government was content for her to remain a saint. It did not want her to become a martyr, too.

Teresa's story took an interesting twist when she arrived in the American section of the city of Nogales. There she was received by the mayor and a delegation of merchants who offered her free hotel lodging and a series of gifts, because they knew that Teresa would attract Mexican pilgrims to Arizona, seeking her miraculous cures. Teresa was good business in the United States.

From Nogales, Teresa left for Los Angeles, where a publicist paid her the extravagant sum of $10,000 to tour the United States. On tour her cures became a circus attraction. Teresa even appeared in Barnum's famous theater in New York. When Teresa, a messianic and politically dangerous figure, crossed the border, she turned into a freak-show attraction.[14]

Political refugees from the Mexican Revolution also experienced the effects of the border's magical threshold. In the novel *Los de abajo (The Underdogs)*, written in 1915 by an officer in Pancho Villa's forces, Mariano Azuela, an opportunistic intellectual who accompanies the Villista revolutionary forces emigrates to San Antonio. He starts a Mexican restaurant there and invites Venancio, a truly bloodthirsty soldier, to play the guitar as a mariachi. This kind of transformation is not just a literary ploy: General Felipe Ángeles, one of the most important and educated figures of the revolution, worked as a waiter during his New York exile.

Crossings in the other direction, from the United States to Mexico, also wrought magical transformations. Practically any white North American could adopt a new, aristocratic identity in Mexico. For example, Ralph Ingersoll, a mining engineer who wrote about his experience in the mines of Cobre de Jesús, Sonora, described the attitudes of the North American colony that prevailed around 1920:

> I have read of Englishmen who go out into the wilderness and, living there, dress for dinner, play cards in the evening, and build golf-courses on Sunday. The point to remember, however, is that these men were accustomed to do these things before they left civilization and that they are trying, by means of preserving their customs and games, to keep themselves in touch with the lives they have left. The American exiles, on the other hand, were simulating something they never knew. They did not play Mah Jong and bridge because they had learned, in their youth, to love them, but because they suffered from an inferiority complex which they were endeavoring to dispel by imitating people who played these games. The effect was peculiarly insincere, and they must have felt it, for they entrenched themselves behind the barriers of formality on every possible occasion.[15]

The movement of people between Mexico and the United States produced radical transformations on each side, but what the Mexican nationalists wanted, and what the government of Mexico also may have wanted, was for the nations to be more symmetrical. Mexican nationalists wanted the North

Americans who went to Mexico to submit to the Mexican regime in the same way that Mexicans had submitted to the North American regime. For that reason, Mexican nationalists were determined to strengthen Mexico's own regime of value, represented by its national currency, language, laws, customs, and so on. At times, though, these norms were only maintained with great effort or they were not maintained at all.

For example, in 1901 the district prefect of Naco, on Sonora's border with Arizona, complained that U.S. currency circulated in his district instead of Mexican currency, and that the English language dominated in public transactions. In response, he ordered that the metric system be used on the Mexican side and that all signs be in Spanish. It was difficult to enforce the idea that a different system functioned in Mexico than in the United States. To assert that difference, Mexican authorities used everything from Spanish to the metric system as identity markers.

Even so, during the Porfiriato, Mexicans were subordinate to North Americans on both sides of the border. In this regard, the threshold of the border lacked all magical power. The most humiliating cases were like the one in the Cananea mines in Sonora, where even in Mexico Mexican workers earned less than North Americans. Worse yet, in the Mexican border states, Mexicans sometimes subsisted in economic conditions worse than those experienced by races considered the lowest in the United States, for example, blacks or Chinese. This, in particular, irritated Mexican nationalists of the era. A pamphlet published in Cananea in May 1906, during the disturbances that were later considered precursors of the revolution, declared: "Damn the idea that a Mexican is worth less than a Yankee, or that a black or a Chinese can be compared with a Mexican! . . . Mexicans, arise! The country and our dignity demand it of us!"[16]

Mexicans on the North American side of the border suffered discrimination because of their "Mexican race," but they also enjoyed the advantages of the United States, including higher salaries than they received in Mexico, better public services, and, in some cases, even better legal protection. Ingersoll draws an interesting contrast between Mexican miners in Arizona and Sonora:

There is, however, a wide variance in the attitude taken toward the so-called "elevation of the race." In southern Mexico no attempt is made to change the status of the peon laborer: he is taken for what he is. He is fed and given money to buy alcohol, and his shortcomings are sworn at but accepted. Over the line, to the north, in camps that employ nothing but Mexican labor, where a Mexican city is literally transplanted from its own soil to ours, systematic attempts are made to raise the standard of living. I was told that it takes four years to complete the Americanization of the Mexican—to teach him to bathe every day, to sleep in clean rooms with plenty of air, and to curb, in a measure, his ferocious appetite for spirits. Also it is an accepted fact that the results are highly satisfactory, and that increased output goes hand in hand with physical and mental improvement.[17]

Though working conditions in the United States may have been better than those in Mexico, Mexicans north of the border suffered discrimination, and the "Americanization" of which Ingersoll speaks did not take place in either the political or the social arena. The struggle against the Díaz dictatorship and for social reform in Mexico was imagined on the border as a struggle for the liberation of the "Mexican race." For example, in 1911, at the beginning of the Mexican Revolution, Prisciliano Silva, a general aligned with the Magón faction, wrote after his first victory—the capture of an arsenal in Guadalupe, Chihuahua: "With these arms we will avenge the humiliation our race has suffered."[18]

This use of the term "race" to refer to the Mexican people was common in the writings of the Magón faction during the prerevolutionary period and at the beginning of the revolution. Porfirio Díaz was accused of being a "murderer of his race," whereas John Kenneth Turner, "the Yankee," was said to have been "a very good friend of our race and of our liberties, as were Mina, the 'Spaniard,' and Victor Hugo, 'the Frenchman,' in other fateful times."[19] The revolution was imagined as a full recovery of symmetry on the border, and that is why the revolutionary slogan par excellence was "Mexico for the Mexicans" (as the United States already was for the North Americans). That slogan ran as a banner headline across the front page of the newspapers *Regeneración* in Los Angeles and *El Ahuizote* in Mexico City.

Furthermore, the qualities belonging to the mestizo race came to be invoked even in private, to aid Mexicans in the United States in times of need or to understand or explain the psychology of Mexicans in that country. In a private letter, Ricardo Flores Magón described a visit he received in jail from the Mexican consul, Antonio Lozano. Flores Magón recalls how Lozano tried to convince him to betray his cause: "The lackey has come to tempt me with his base, Jesuit cunning. My life of misery and suffering, of anxiety and danger will undergo a radical transformation. . . . [a]s soon as I shake hands with Díaz, the hand that has wiped out my brothers' lives, the bloody hand, the vile hand that is strangling my race." Then Flores Magón explains his internal psychological struggle, also in racial code: "In those moments, my Indian blood gave me the necessary calm to listen, restraining the rebellions of my other, Spanish blood, that bade me to spit on my strange visitor."[20]

The "mestizophilia" that characterized Mexican nationalism of the twentieth century—the so-called revolutionary nationalism—was not, as is sometimes believed, exclusively a state-directed project to form the Mexican citizen, one mobilized in Porfirian times by intellectuals such as Justo Sierra, and during revolutionary times by figures such as Andrés Molina Enríquez, Manuel Gamio, or the Hispanicist José Vasconcelos. Mestizaje was also a lived experience, which later became a state project shaped by experiences on the border. The combination of the state's need to form a national subject, and the racialized experience of national identity on the border, is what gives roots and credibility to the Mexican racial mestizo identity.

The discourses concerning the idea of the Mexican race flow into the same ideological-scientific matrix that once circulated throughout the Americas and, indeed, the world: Spencerism, eugenics, and a positivist discourse of adaptation and progress were embellished first in the 1920s with heterodox versions of cultural relativism (already adapted to mestizo nationalism) and later in the 1980s, with a certain multiculturalist spin.

Throughout Spanish America, Latinist thought—formulated in racial code by José Vasconcelos—was fuelled by the ascent of the United States as the empire that would rule the American hemisphere throughout the twentieth century. Nonetheless, Mexico constructed a racialized image, in large part out of the border dialectic described here, of a national subject whose deep roots and specific referents are without parallel in the Americas.

Moreover, the processes of defining the citizen had far-reaching psychological consequences. The idea of national liberation and unity as the story of a national race's arrival to power (captured in the slogan "Mexico for the Mexicans") had its corollary in the restriction of public support for intellectual work that explicitly sought solutions to the so-called national problems. Knowledge of "the race" remained limited to a more modest space than the enlightened universalism—still Porfirian—imagined by Justo Sierra, and even the Vasconcelist "Arielism," which was ultimately pan–Latin American. If the motto of the National Autonomous University of Mexico had been in harmony with the racial ideology of revolutionary nationalism that legitimized the university's budget, the motto would have been, "Through my race the great national problems will speak."

The creation of a Mexican race had important positive social implications. It was the basis of revolutionary nationalism with its particular ideology of land redistribution and popular education, but it also placed long-term limits on the cultural horizons of Mexico when it defined the Mexican race as a people suited only for Mexico. On the other hand, the friction caused by the border with the United States, which has been so troubling since its inception, will continue to be a vital source of creativity, criticism, and broadening horizons. Perhaps the time has come to move away from an idea of race whose definition derives from a first line of defense and toward proposals that are more ambitious and free.

Notes

Translated by Eileen Willingham and Janet Hendrickson, this chapter first appeared in Spanish as "Por mi raza hablará el nacionalismo revolucionario (Arqueología de la unidad nacional)," in *Nexos* (Mexico City), February 2010.

1. Ozouf 1976.

2. Tocqueville 1952.

3. E. B. Tylor, *Anahuac; or, Mexico and the Mexicans, Ancient and Modern* (London: Longman, Green, Longman, and Roberts, 1861).

4. Some public figures have claimed that the Mexican race is superior to the "Anglo" race in the United States, but such views have generally emerged in reaction to representations of the inferiority of the Mexican. This was the case when the border rebel Catarino Garza alleged that "we Mexicans consider ourselves to have purer blood than the Americans, given that in our country there is only a mixture of Spanish and Indian, and they [the Americans] are generally descendants of Irish adventurers, Polish beggars, Swiss, Prussians, Russians and more than anything else filthy Africans" (Young 2004, 50). The idea that mestizo is the race best suited to the Mexican environment was defended by Andrés Molina Enríquez. See Lomnitz 2009a.

5. Jaguaribe 1999.

6. *Colección de acuerdos, órdenes y decretos sobre tierras, casas y solares de los indígenas, bienes de sus comunidades y fundos legales de los pueblos del Estado de Jalisco* (2nd ed., expanded), vol. 1, Cromotipografía del buen gusto, Guadalajara, 1876, xiii.

7. Lomnitz 2009a.

8. For a discussion of the racialization of the Mexican in New Mexico, see Gómez 2007; for a description of racist language in Texas in the nineteenth century, see León 1983.

9. On Texas, see Foley 1997, 130–31; on Arizona and Sonora, see Tinker Salas 1997.

10. Brown 1993.

11. Gonzales 1994, 662.

12. Appadurai 1988.

13. For a study of the relationship between border dynamics and temporality, see Lomnitz 2009b.

14. Teresa Urrea's story is narrated in Vanderwood 1998.

15. Ralph Ingersoll, *In and Under Mexico* (New York: The Century Co., 1924), 146.

16. Esparza Valdivia 2000, 62.

17. Ingersoll, *In and Under Mexico*, 116–17.

18. Ricardo Flores Magón, "Francisco I. Madero es un traidor a la causa de la libertad," *Regeneración* 26 (February 25, 1911).

19. Lázaro Gutiérrez de Lara, "1810–1910," *Regeneración* 2 (September 10, 1910); Antonio I. Villarreal, "John Kenneth Turner: Su labor," *Regeneración* 2 (September 10, 1910).

20. Ricardo Flores Magón to Elizabeth Trowbridge Sarabia, February 21, 1909, in *Obras Completas de Ricardo Flores Magón*, 511–12.

PART IV ❋ Antiracist Movements
and Racism Today

Politics of Place and Urban Indígenas in Ecuador's Indigenous Movement

RUDI COLLOREDO-MANSFELD

The 2002 restoration of the Bennett Stela, "a massive symbol of the Aymara past," from a traffic roundabout in La Paz to the ruins of Tiwanaku near Lake Titicaca captures in a single event many currents of contemporary Andean native politics. The repatriation was championed by an indigenous intellectual and politician, supported by international funders and technical experts, and facilitated by allies in the national government. In the course of the move itself, Aymara ritual specialists consecrated the monolith's departure from the city, and indigenous political activists presided over its reincorporation at Tiwanaku's ruins in the country. If this event signaled the rise of a new politics, one that would culminate in the election of Bolivia's first Aymara president, it also affirmed an old premise: native authenticity and authority properly reside in the countryside.

In Ecuador, a national indigenous movement found its footing by promoting the needs, heritage, and identity of provincial municipalities and rural *comunas,* or formally recognized peasant communities with territorial jurisdictions that have been registered with the state. Led by the Confederación de Nacionalidades Indígenas del Ecuador (CONAIE), with its provincial organizations, native peoples mobilized to secure land for small-hold farmers, political autonomy for communities, and constitutional recognition for native cultures. *Levantamientos* (uprisings) throughout the 1990s initiated specific negotiations with the state over land reform, water rights, and bilingual education. They also provoked a national discussion about civil rights and collective identity. For all its activism and skilled maneuvering, though, the movement surged, in part, because potential political rivals faltered. The historic, urban popular movements that had attracted a measure of indigenous support struggled in the 1990s. Industrial economies of cities lost ground during the post-1982 economic crisis, and neoliberalism's promises of personal advancement began to shape a new populist turn away from class-based solidarities.[1] Mass emigration further harmed older political activism, as some 2.5 million Ecuadorians moved abroad rather than struggle for change at home.[2] Summarizing the changes, Kim Clark writes, "The processes of globalization have left behind the space for [an indigenous national project,] shifting the locus of subordinate organizing and political engagement out of the cities and into the countryside" and—in her analysis—away from poor and middle-class mestizos and toward the indigenous population.[3]

The equation that links countryside, indígenas, and political momentum does not always add up, however. Two of the native organizations I have worked with are instances in which the urban bases of indigenous activism seem more robust. For example, the peasant comuna of Quiloa, Cotopaxi, is located on a high ridge in the valley of Tigua. With between eighty and a hundred households, Quiloa has at times actively promoted its own development, securing government or NGO funding for soil-building projects, a communal house, or reforestation efforts. Local residents, though, have tired of the bad schools, the lack of water, and the poor access to the provincial highway, and many have moved on to either the provincial capital or Quito. Population has declined to the point that remaining residents can only attempt their famous Three Kings or Corpus Christi celebrations if outside donors provide the resources. Meanwhile, in Otavalo, the artisan association known as the Unión de Artesanos Indígenas del Mercado Centenario de Otavalo (UNAIMCO) represents over 1,000 members who work on three different continents and in trades ranging from hand knitting to industrialized manufacture. In the 1990s, UNAIMCO orchestrated a way to host the costumed dancers of the Fiesta of San Juan in the heart of Otavalo's artisan district, promoting indigenous culture in a space once reserved for mestizo-run events. In the early 2000s, several leaders of the organization went on to win municipal and provincial elections. Briefly put, the urban, artisan association is in an expansive mode; the peasant sector is contracting. Though CONAIE professes to be rooted in the rural zone, its most vociferous supporters and well-resourced indigenous backers are often in the city.

And yet, for all the differences, and for all the apparent gains of the trade organization, it shares much with the peasant comuna. Since the early

1990s, both the Quiloa community council and UNAIMCO leadership have carried out business for a core membership that combines informal trade with stripped-down subsistence farming. The leaders of the community council and UNAIMCO often choose to live in provincial cities, rather than the countryside or the capital, Quito. Both groups concentrate on economic development issues but seek to ensure that the projects they sponsor build work or trades "with identity," or are marked explicitly as Kichwa.[4] And the national indigenous movement magnifies the cultural and economic claims of both rural community and urban union. Put another way, if there were two popular, public spheres in Ecuador, an urban one linked to informal markets, working-class neighborhoods, and trade-based organizations, and a rural one of peasant communities and provincial federations, Kichwa people would be comfortably at home in either. This raises a key question: why has indigenous politics assumed a rural territorial identity?

Indeed, for all their apparent naturalness, the territories and jurisdictions of Andean identity politics—communities, parish associations, provincial umbrella organizations—were forged at a time when huge numbers of native people were not just living and working in cities, but working to legitimize their claims on the city. Translocal careers, decentralized development programs, and a strengthening indigenous movement all reinforced peasant jurisdictions. As it became a political vehicle for those whose ambitions reached beyond the day-to-day responsibilities of a rural council member, "placemaking," or the political defense, cultural celebration, and material improvements of a rural community, became a tactic in making a new, countrywide indigenous public sphere.

Amid this rural activism, however, urban indigenous cultures continue to grow. A politics of place has inspired a new kind of urban Kichwa mobilization. In Otavalo, city-based activism has expanded from direct economic concerns to support for commemorative statues and beauty pageants. As new causes launch new candidates into municipal politics, indigenous people assert more clearly than ever before the significance of the city to their identity. This new politics collides with long-established mestizo prerogatives—and with the privileged position of native leaders who have worked up through the ranks of peasant organizing. It is the ambiguity of the urban, indigenous political field that has brought it to the forefront of problems of indigenous self-representation, creating a space "where alliances shift, definitions are reworked, entities are named and authority rethought."[5] The interplay between Otavalo's peasant federation and its artisan association has shaped two civic fiestas, a generation of public office holders, and an urban indigenous commercial district. Over time, the contests over space have helped to turn the personal urban odysseys of indigenous men and women into a meaningful collective experience.

Circulation, Comunas, and Careers

The growth of Ecuador's big cities did not drain peasant sectors in the same way urban migration elsewhere in Latin American did. To be sure, a generation before the rise of the indigenous movement, indígenas themselves had worn a path to the city. Between 1962 and 1982, over 1 million people, mestizos and indígenas, migrated to the cities.[6] But the growth of the urban economy did not relocate whole reserves of destitute small-hold farmers to the city so much as shore them up in the countryside. Migration took the form of circulation.[7] In the early 1970s, oil revenues trickled down through urban wages to highland peasant men, whose regular returns to home parishes meant that their income translated into goods for rural households—furniture, blankets, school uniforms, and household contributions to community development projects. With more years of schooling than their nonmigrating neighbors, more Spanish skills, and a network of urban contacts, these men were not only geographically mobile but were advancing socially as well.[8] Their itineraries secured some of the trappings once reserved for white Ecuadorians, gains that often left them more exposed to the racist taunts of teachers, classmates, employers, and neighbors in the city.

The consequences of this circulation assumed political shape during the late 1970s and the 1980s, through the politicization of state-sanctioned peasant comunas. Since the 1964 agrarian reform law that freed peasant settlements from labor obligations to *haciendas* (landed estates), many communities had organized to gain state recognition.[9] Initially, the material results of such efforts were minimal, as communities recovered little of the land lost to haciendas. In the 1980s, however, the reasons to seek official status multiplied. As the state struggled with its debt, development programs stalled, leaving a void sometimes filled by nongovernmental organizations. Well-established comunas with official councils could attract both sporadic state development funds and NGO investment far better than unofficial neighbors.

Collective development intersected with personal lives in this council formation. City life in the 1970s had always placed ambitious migrants in a bind. As León Zamosc writes, "These better-off artisans, petty merchants, and peasants are caught in a contradiction between expectations raised by their economic mobility and the persistence of their negative valuation of their Indian condition by whites and mestizos."[10] In the aftermath of the fall in oil prices and the financial crisis beginning in 1982, many men lost their foothold on the lower rungs of Quito's economic ladder and had to find new resources for their households and new channels for their careers. Rural communities attracted fresh interest as men embraced councils and created public lives in the pursuit of development projects. Election to community office bestowed recognition for bureaucratic know-how and intercultural skills. Local leaders could fight back against the slights and discrimination experienced in mestizo-dominated workplaces by celebrating indigenous life, by "relearning Kichwa, returning to Indian dress, [and] founding cultural clubs."[11] There were also economic benefits to holding elected office. Development projects often yielded council members privileged access to water, electricity, and roads or brought them other material benefits. As the recession deepened, renewed community struggle for stalled land cases held out the hope of getting desperately needed pastures and cropland.

The community of Quiloa, in Guangaje parish, Cotopaxi, illustrates how peasant councils can grow from urban roots. The first and only legally recognized association representing rural Quiloa within official domains was the Association of Small Traders, set up in 1983 by José Vega, who lived in Quito and sought vending space in an urban park for his paintings and other artisanal goods. Throughout the 1980s, Vega never made much money as a trader. However, he continued for ten years as president of the association's council and obtained a forestry project, a soil improvement project, a communal house, and a private housing improvement project, all for his rural sector. Even as he tapped these projects to rebuild his own home in Quiloa, he and his family never gave up their residence in the capital city.

Subsequent presidents refocused the association's identity. In the mid-1990s, they changed the name to the Association of Indigenous Painters and Artisans of Tigua-Quiloa, emphasizing indigenous artisanship, not commerce. Furthermore, they affiliated formally with the province's indigenous movement and other peasant sectors in the parish. What began with entrepreneurial ambitions eventually transformed. By the late 1990s, the association served primarily to keep a rural parish sector connected to agricultural development initiatives, bilingual programs, and indigenous political organizing.

The Quiloa council's trajectory from translocal trade association in the early 1980s to provincially oriented peasant-farming organization a decade later was linked with a wider simplification (and intensification) of indigenous political space. While politicking for community autonomy, control over development, and cultural investments, activists recuperated and promoted identity—"a distinctive social memory, consciousness, and practice"—as a key characteristic of organizational form.[12] "Council," "community," "consensus-building," and "place stewardship" coalesced as pan-Ecuadorian indigenous values and expressions that gave transcendental significance to material objectives. That is, because the movement opened up new ways of being indigenous, it selected narrowly among practices and symbols that communicated that identity to national audiences.[13]

Language offered a place to start. Norman Whitten, for example, comes close to defining indigeneity in terms of language when he describes the movement's growth in the 1980s: "Bit by escalating bit the people who spoke indigenous languages as first languages and those who identified with them by parentage or other persuasion increased their ranks."[14] Indeed, when CONAIE formed at a national level in 1986, it chose to fight first for bilingual education as a common need among all indigenous peoples. Few cultural activists stopped there, though. Along with language instruction, groups revived dances and created entirely new "organization-sponsored cultural festivals and anniversaries."[15] They also fought racism by reteaching history. Pre-Columbian dynasties and colonial revolts fueled workshop discussions in the 1980s, when activists began to challenge an official history of conquest and passive subordination.[16]

Language, dances, fiestas, and history, however, never strayed far from rural place as the foundation of Indian distinctiveness. The history of an ancient indigenous dynasty mattered in Cacha, Chimborazo, for instance, because it demonstrated the territorial unity of the modern parish's subdivided sectors.[17] And while language performance broadcasted indigenousness far beyond native communities, official language-instruction programs eventually institutionalized Kichwa in country classrooms. Quiloa children seeking Kichwa lessons, for example, could not find them in their Quiteño barrios and had to return to Cotopaxi for them. A new indigenous beauty pageant in Imbabura also emphasized a return to the countryside in cultural terms as judges appraised contestants on their knowledge of the local staple crop.[18] Not surprisingly, individual leaders cut their own rich experience down to the agrarian bone. When recounting his personal development, the former president of CONAIE, Luis Macas, downplayed his flight from seminary and his university degrees. Instead, he dwelled upon time spent in his own community: "What is important is that half my life was in the community plowing, working."[19] Cultural practices, whether collective or personal, could most easily be legitimized by linking them to the soil, its fertility, and the unity of those who work it.

Thus an understandable irony: a generation prior to the modern movement, Ecuadorian schoolbooks rejected indigenous peoples as a degenerate race precisely because of their intimacy with the land.[20] In response, diverse mestizo intellectuals labored to defend indigenous people, often by making a virtue of nature and a vice of modernization.[21] Luis Monslave Pozo, for example, championed Indians in *The Indian: Questions of His Life and His Passion* by divorcing them from all things modern.

> The Ecuadorian Indian, flesh, blood, and spirit of America lives in this book as he does in nature . . . without pretensions of novelty, without traces of a new order. Naturally.
>
> Thus the landscape and the natural world. Rude. Magnificent. Dramatic. And in the middle of the landscape as the son of this natural world, in its center and its grip . . . the Indian.[22]

Now, eschewing patrons from outside their communities, Indians defend themselves. They worked for a generation to connect collectivities and back their own indigenous leaders, who in turn have demanded "a new order." Still, in doing that work, Indians remade their identity "in the middle of the landscape," narrating their lives closer to nature than to novelty.

The flip side of this restricted, rural identity, though, has been political clout. The Levantamiento Indígena Nacional of June 1990 stemmed from the reorganization of parish life and launched indigenous identity politics on a national level. While ultimately driven by CONAIE's leadership, the strike of 1990 came from local peasant initiative. As Zamosc put it, "thus abruptly and without warning, CONAIE was forced by pressure from below to take up agrarian demands not central to its agenda and also to change tactics, shifting from pleading and lobbying to a more assertive stand backed by popular mobilization."[23] The national leadership abruptly moved from negotiating language programs to demanding the constitutional redefinition of Ecuador as a plurinational state and the widespread return of land to autonomous communities.

CONAIE's power over the next four years blossomed as the leadership of the organization continued to respond to and nurture a politics of land. In 1992, the Confederación de Nacionalidades Indígenas de la Amazonía Ecuatoriana (CONFENAIE), an affiliate of CONAIE, organized a march from their base in the Amazon to Quito, demanding legal recognition of their territories. Two years later, in a protest that paralyzed the country for twenty days, CONAIE fought an agrarian reform law that would have opened community land holdings to the marketplace. Led by the indigenous lawyer Nina Pacari, CONAIE arrived at the negotiating table with a full indigenous legal team, video cameras, and their own media specialists to ensure fair coverage. Pacari negotiated important concessions and cemented CONAIE's political identity in the defense of indigenous territories—the rainforests of Amazonian peoples and the pastures and cultivated fields of highland comunas. Never before had such diverse indigenous peoples sustained a pan-Ecuadorian unity, and never before had the national government dialogued on equal terms with indigenous representatives. Momentum carried through 1998, when Ecuador's new constitution enshrined the basic tenets of plurinationalism demanded in 1990: recognition of indigenous and Afro-Ecuadorian nationalities and traditional forms of organization, and the exercise of community-based authority.[24]

In this sketch of the indigenous movement and its rural base, I am not arguing that embracing rural territory was a contrived political strategy. For all their mobility, many indigenous people continue to see community lands as the irreplaceable base that "a community . . . or an indigenous nationality occupy and in which they develop their particular lifeways."[25] And outside forces, from state privatization programs to transnational oil companies, were the interests sparking land struggles, not indigenous political careerists. Even so, today's territories are just as much artifacts of men's and women's soured urban careers, truncated development programs, and a national movement's tactical decisions as they are primordial cultural homelands. Usurping language's role as CONAIE's vehicle for a plurinational society, territory has helped to engineer tighter connections between base and leaders, sustain the movement's unity over more than a decade of major popular uprisings, and preserve cooperation between Sierra and Amazonia.

These organizational gains have also entailed regularizing Kichwa society into bounded political units at a peculiar historical moment of recessions, circulatory migration, austerity measures, NGO-led development, and neoliberal schemes of decentralization. Inevitably, the material rewards of this organizing have been uneven. Some have gained through the confines of peasant jurisdictions—men savvy in peasant and urban cultures, artisan intermediaries, diversified, small-capitalist producers. Others have lost—urban indigenous households, women within base organizations, and outlying peasant sectors. Women's losses are particularly ironic. Women had taken on increasing responsibility for the subsistence economy since land reform. Yet their labor did not translate into power. Although a comuna potentially accepts any adult man and woman as formal members, in the mid-1980s less than 10 percent of listed comuna members were women.[26] In an analysis of 2,253 comunas and over 3,000 other base organizations, the Ministry of Agriculture and Livestock found that women made up less than 1 percent of the leaders.[27]

Finally, though, the labeling of winners and losers fruitlessly implies a stable culmination of a single line of political development. Since 2000, the economy, Ecuador's weakened governments, and the fragility of the alliances among social movements has at times amplified the indigenous movement and at other times curtailed it. A "panoply of political programs and positions," to use Gow's and Rappaport's descriptive phrase, characterizes the indigenous political sphere.[28] The indigenous movement's acceptance of different nationalities and political and economic concerns may mean that the movement is open to remaking its program and goals. And one of the reasons for the movement's unsettled politics is the challenge of incorporating explicitly urban native groups and political projects.

Otavalo offers a glimpse into the way indigenous politics is susceptible to reworking from within as well as outside. Not only does the city sustain a vast, explicitly indigenous commercial economy, but the men and women who have recently led the town's most active trade association, UNAIMCO, came of age politically through skirmishes over the city's core spaces.

Kichwa Town and Country Politics

The town of Otavalo and its rural environs host two powerful indigenous organizations: UNAIMCO and the Federación Indígena y Campesina de Imbabura (FICI), one of CONAIE's more effective regional affiliates. In the popular imagination, UNAIMCO represents the town's market and enjoys the backing of *los ricos* (wealthy, indigenous merchant-artisans), while FICI is rooted in the countryside and taps a militant popular base. Once again, though, these differences are overdrawn. Both organizations occupy headquarters within a block of each other in Otavalo. Their leaders draw from the same class of university-educated, indigenous professionals. Membership does indeed differ. Associates in UNAIMCO number about 1,250 and have a livelihood that relates to Otavalo's handicraft market, the Plaza Centenario, or the Plaza de Ponchos, as it is colloquially known. On the other hand, FICI claims to represent members of the peasant comunas surrounding Otavalo, perhaps 20,000 to 30,000 people. But the majority of artisans live amid their farm plots outside city limits, and nearly all peasant communities around Otavalo have a big economic stake in the Plaza de Ponchos.

Amid such overlap, peasant and artisan organizations have each developed projects that clarified a constituency and the organizations' ability to lead it. For example, FICI defined itself culturally by organizing the fiesta of Colla Raymi, a "cultural encounter" initiated in 1992 to challenge the official annual municipal fiesta of Yamor.[29] Dismissing Yamor's beauty pageant for the daughters of the town's white-mestizo elite, FICI lobbied for and received municipal funds to hold alternative events.[30] These revolved around a pageant to elect an indigenous *Sara Ñusta* (Corn Princess), as well as folklore dances and community exchanges connected to the autumnal equinox. Although the money came from city coffers, FICI channeled it to the countryside. In rejecting the city, FICI leaders sought to leave behind the "asymmetric and exploitative association" with the Yamor fiesta and to instead stake out "an autonomous realm of indigenous tradition."[31] In doing so, FICI abandoned any Otavaleño who claimed both the city and indigenousness as their heritage.

In contrast, UNAIMCO began in 1988 as a caretaker organization for the Plaza de Ponchos. Artisans had been relocating from surrounding communities into the town of Otavalo since the 1940s, pushed by demographic pressures on the crowded peasant sectors and drawn by the business opportunities of the Saturday textile market.[32] This weekly event took place in an open, paved square on the northern edge of town and lasted for less than half a day. Beginning in the 1980s, though, tourist volume and transnational Otavaleño resellers augmented the Saturday market. By 1992, vendors were out there every day of the week.[33]

As an economic setting, the plaza is the "epicenter" (as the directors of UNAIMCO put it) of an economy with annual sales estimated as close to $50 million in the late 1990s.[34] Once, at a board meeting of UNAIMCO, I pointed out that the magnitude of selling is a problem for foreigners who tend to see sales to tourists as inauthentic in contrast to production for native use, which was seen as "real." Directors of the organization instantly disagreed. Far from seeing it as problematic, the president described the market as a "space of indigenous power." Indeed, UNAIMCO itself is a product of this power, coming into existence only when market activities reach a critical mass of almost daily operations involving over 100 regular vendors. UNAIMCO first busied itself with the arrangement of stall space and the distribution of trash cans. By the end of the 1990s, though, the president met regularly with European ambassadors to Ecuador to lobby for the rights of vendors overseas and coordinated with the Ministry of Foreign Trade to promote exports. Culturally, UNAIMCO made its stand in the plaza as well. Beginning in 1996, it organized the activities of the annual San Juan fiesta, bringing scores of both formal and informal dance groups into the city. In the first year, UNAIMCO received about fourteen groups at the temporary hearth they set up on the corner of the Plaza de Ponchos. In 2001, they calculated that over 100 groups danced around the plaza.

The daily congestion of unregulated smalltime vendors vexes Otavalo's older indigenous families almost more than its mestizo ones. This established indigenous bourgeoisie of artisan-merchants speak of the plaza as the antithesis of the branded, orderly handicraft trade they are trying to engineer. "In the plaza there are no guarantees," the owner of one of Otavalo's largest textile shops said—speaking ambiguously about both the quality of a product to be found there and the business practices of the persons selling it. To work in the plaza is to feel relatively powerless, to suffer from too much competition, low sales, and low margins. Yet for shop owners and producers, to be "in the plaza" is to be undisciplined, disruptive, and in effective control of the reputation of Otavalo's trade—the popular space pitted against the trademarked artisan-merchant sphere. Indigenous self-representation crops up again as a problem. While representing the plaza once meant working on behalf of all indigenous artisans, in recent times it has meant choosing sides within a growing, class-divided urban society. The need to reclaim common ground has raised the stakes for the cultural and political projects tackled by local leaders.

Corn Princesses and Indian Generals

As CONAIE leaders did nationally, members of UNAIMCO's directorate have maintained credibility by defending indigenous claims to places. In 1996, the challenge came during the mestizo elite's most cherished performance of its identity, the selection of the Queen of Yamor. Verónica Barahona was the candidate who set things in motion. An indigenous woman from the wealthy Otavaleño community of Peguche, she followed in the footsteps of her college-educated parents to enroll at a university in Quito. Her interest in competing in the pageant of that year's fiesta drew the backing of several organizations and activists. Signed by a coalition called *el Comité Interinstitucional*, as well as Mario Conejo, a sociologist and elected council member in nearby Peguche, her application was peremptorily rejected by Mayor Fabián Villareal. The refusal made national headlines. Indigenous groups, high government officials, and even the new president Abdala Bucaram excoriated Villareal and the town council as racists. Standing firm, the mayor insisted that each ethnic group had its own pageant—Yamor and the new Colla Raymi fiesta set up by FICI—and declared that to accept Barahona's application "would terminate that tradition and custom that the Otavaleño people have lived for years."[35]

Barahona's backers bought none of this. Germán Manuela, a member of the Comité Interinstitucional, told the national newspaper *Hoy* that the Sara Ñusta "is not something of ours." He insisted that it had its roots in mockery: "The mestizos got a hold of the indigenous women who they had as maids to make a show of the same nature as the Queen of Yamor, but with the singularity that they were ridiculing the indigenous woman. They were making her up and obliging her to blow kisses."[36] While they credited FICI's indigenous organizers with taking over the Sara Ñusta and recovering indigenous values, the committee did not think this went far enough. Another committee member and future UNAIMCO officer, José Manuel Quimbo, stated, "The matter was not balanced in that for the election of the Queen of Yamor, there was all of the infrastructure and the municipality put up all of the economic costs. For the Sara Ñusta there was none of that."[37] Or as Quimbo put it to me in an interview, "Yamor was in the best hotel in town; Sara Ñusta was in a gym." The spatial separation played out all year long. At important events, the Queen of Yamor presided; the Sara Ñusta sat idle, except for sporadic indigenous celebrations. "If we pay taxes, we have duties and rights," argued Quimbo, "why shouldn't we feel represented?"[38]

As the events played out, the comité organized a symbolic launching of Barahona's candidacy in Peguche with a huge fiesta featuring the region's most popular Andean music groups. Any formal invitation to Barahona for Yamor events would be rejected, they announced. Yet, while they planned several counter-fiestas for Barahona during Yamor itself, committee members in the end decided not to call for outsiders to boycott Yamor. Rather they wanted "to demonstrate to Otavaleño residents, to national tourists and to foreigners the potential that they have organizationally and that their activities would be the best of the fiesta."[39] Gone were the days when indígenas had to abandon the city in order to uphold their values. Now, only a massive infusion of Kichwa music, dance, and indigenous fiesta-goers in the streets of Otavalo could properly defend indigenous culture.

The fight over a young woman's civil rights had thus become a contest over settings and venues. Anthropologists have argued that Latin American beauty pageants get social force for the way women in them offer performances of identities that can be used "to reinterpret social relationships, contest relations of inequality, and, in some cases establish new hegemonies within subaltern groups themselves."[40] But much of this power lies not with the contestants, but with the institutions that decorate the ballroom, assemble the audiences, and set up the spotlights that direct spectators' attention.[41] In the eyes of the comité, its political peer (and rival), FICI, had been haggling in the margins when it rewrote the beauty criteria and consigned the winner to country events. Barahona, Manuela, Conejo, and Quimbo did not so much want the Queen's sash and roses; they wanted the wider civic world that gave the pageant its weight and received the pageant's grace. While the woman from Barahona never competed, the ordinance that prohibited her participation was struck down. Inevitably, the other casualty of this activism was FICI's Sara Ñusta pageant, which went on hiatus after the rules were changed.

Mayor Villareal fired up interethnic tensions again two years later by proposing the removal of the statue of the "Indian General" Rumiñahui from Otavalo's main plaza, the Parque Simón Bolívar (see figure 1). Back in 1983, the city had received a statue of el Libertador Bolívar for the plaza as a donation from the government of Venezuela. Yet a massive bust of Rumiñahui has gazed out across the passersby, shoe shiners, and weary citizens relaxing on benches in the park since 1956. Villareal decided it was time for the Indian to go.

Ironically, nonindigenous citizens of Otavalo had been responsible for the original placement of Rumiñahui. A group of mestizo intellectuals erected the monument hoping to demonstrate "the necessity of uniting the races of a nation to the racial mixing given as a consequence of the Spanish presence in America and with faith in the future of this Indian people."[42] In their own way, these men were bringing the larger Latin American project of mestizaje home. In Mexico, the monumentalization of indigenous culture offered images of a past native culture for a contemporary project of national identification.[43] Memorializing an Indian general in Otavalo similarly allowed leaders

Figure 1. Statue of the "Indian General" Rumiñahui, main plaza of Otavalo, Parque Simón Bolivar. Credit: Rudi Colloredo-Mansfeld.

to use native culture to stage a mixed and shared (nonnative) national identity. However, in the decades that followed the installation of Rumiñahui, the province's Kichwa communities affirmed and renewed their own culture. Rather than attest to the national glory of a unified Spanish-speaking culture, the statue increasingly marked difference, ethnic pride, and a plurinational possibility for Ecuador.

For fifteen years after the rival Bolivar statue arrived, Otavalo's mayors left well enough alone and consigned the Venezuelans' gift to the ornate main meeting room of city hall. Villareal, however, had embarked on a plan to rationalize civic space among Otavalo's ethnic groups. He saw this project as a commitment to indigenous peoples and himself as one who "has offered homage to the Indian race with monuments such as 'La Danza Indígena'"—a garish statue standing in a roadway roundabout depicting three figures in an awkward foot-waving pose.[44] Having memorialized Indians as tourist folklore, his administration committed approximately $12,500 to a new park on the outskirts of the city, next to "La Danza Indígena," that would be called "El Parque Rumiñahui." Out in the margins of the city, the Parque Rumiñahui would get the head of Rumiñahui. In the center, the Parque Bolívar would get Bolívar, and a racial civic order would finally be restored.

Enraged by the plan, over 1,000 indígenas took to the streets to protest, rallied by the "Commission for the Defense of the Monument to Rumiñahui." A member of the commission, the sociologist Mario Conejo (previously active in the Yamor protests), publicly declared that the mayor's park scheme was "a new type of racism" that was a response to the city's becoming an area populated by indígenas and their businesses.[45] Another member of the commission and UNAIMCO board member, José Manuel Quimbo, proclaimed that the statue connected them to the city: "Here in the center of the city, the Indians, we feel ourselves proudly represented by General Rumiñahui."[46] He argued from the cosmopolitan perspective of the international handicraft vendor that he was and asked rhetorically, "How is it possible that the martyr and Indian general could be admired in Moscow and whom we encounter in the Barajas airport in Cuba, nevertheless in Otavalo, there is an authority who has no idea what Rumiñahui represents in the Ecuadorian national context."[47] Rumiñahui, that is, anchors indigenous culture at the center of the city while simultaneously elevating Otavalo's indigenous legacy as a national heritage and international symbol of resistance. In the end, Rumiñahui (Kichwa for "stone face") did not budge.

Indigenousness Unbound: The Evolving Public Sphere

The Plaza de Ponchos, beauty pageants, and the city's central park have been settings for stories—about growing exports, racist city politics, indigenous history—that have received national coverage. Yet even as it deems Otavalo's municipal battles newsworthy, the press too quickly writes them up as the "reflections of the interethnic problems existing in Otavalo," in which protest boils down to culture, and the stakes remain local.[48] The political drama stirring here goes unreviewed. Nevertheless, for the first time, a consistent, urban, indigenous voice orchestrates changes in civic life and politics.

Certainly, in the fight for a spot in the local beauty pageant, an Otavaleño sociologist, craft intermediary, and marketing student built on the credibility achieved by the national movement in order to frame their protest. At the same time, they have been breaking out of the movement's implicit spatial governmentality. For all its real accomplishments, Ecuador's indigenous movement simplified the political landscape into the historic antagonism that arranges mestizo cities against Indian countryside. This ethnic rationalization paid off. Community authority grew; indigenous intellectuals reconnected with wider constituencies; and indigenousness itself achieved modern currency. In Otavalo, however, the diverse constituents of the Indian city—young vendors, competitive manufacturers, middle-class wholesalers—had little interest in reclaiming the country in order to advance political goals that were explicitly connected to living in the city. While not opposed to CONAIE-backed positions—FICI and UNAIMCO members in fact worked together in 1996 and 1998 to fight Villareal—urban members of the indigenous movement nevertheless consistently stood apart from those policies. Consequently, the growing municipal power of Otavalo's urban indigenous population has weakened programs, such as the Sara Ñusta Pageant, that FICI pioneered.

In recasting the public sphere, activists have expanded the places in which indigenous leaders can seek victories and have begun to redefine how place and territory can work for indigenous communities. Too often in the analysis of social movements, place gets pigeonholed as "territoriality," implying bounded terrain, a cultural homeland, or a political object to be defended.[49] While central to indigenous political strategy, defending boundaries is only one way that physical settings can propel politics.[50] In Otavalo, leaders have fought every effort to isolate Indians in particular zones, and they have done so, in part, by claiming open-ended places, crossroads, and town squares. The Plaza de Ponchos offers a model of a fluid, unbounded space, with its weekly spillover of vendors into surrounding streets, and the seasonal flight of intermediaries to Santiago, Montevideo, Barcelona, Chicago, and beyond. As global artisan entrepreneurship does, urban indigenous politics finds power through physical ground that enables interconnectivity rather than exclusivity. José Quimbo pointed out as much when he argued that connecting with Rumiñahui in downtown Otavalo meant reaching out to Quito, Russia, and Cuba. Militantly rejecting Mayor Villareal and his simplifying scheme, indigenous Otavaleños insisted upon the mingling of Rumiñahui with Bolívar in Otavalo. Centrality, not territoriality, defines a new politics of place.

＊

The new force of the urban artisan sector's politics materialized in Otavalo's 2000 mayoral race. With only a few months to go before the election, Mario Conejo, the indigenous sociologist active in both the Yamor and Rumiñahui controversies, entered a two-person race that pitted the controversial incumbent Villareal against the president of FICI, an indigenous woman named Carmen Yamberla. Conejo received the backing of UNAIMCO, whose vice-president at the time was José Manuel Quimbo. Rather than splitting the indigenous vote, as many had feared, Conejo won. As Otavalo's first indigenous mayor, Conejo has supported the expansion of UNAIMCO by earmarking funds for the construction of a new, multistory artisan training center on the edge of the Plaza de Ponchos.

UNAIMCO has continued to work more closely with its popular base. Seeking to halt rapid cost increases that were putting small knitters out of business in 2000, it organized a boycott nearly a month long of yarn factories based in Ambato, Ecuador. Furthermore, the group's leadership has connected with the national movement. José Manuel Quimbo, who had been elected president of UNAIMCO in 2001, was chosen by CONAIE's electoral arm "Movimiento de Unidad Plurinacional: Pachakutik Nuevo País" to run on their slate for the office of *Consejero Provincial* in the October 2002 elections. He won after a grueling campaign. Once blithely ignored by white-mestizo town fathers and indigenous peasant activists alike, the urban artisan sector now sets the pace for indigenous politics in the province of Imbabura.

In attempting to account for Conejo's election, local and national analysts put it down to the power of indigenous capital: once "los ricos" from UNAIMCO backed a candidate, the politician from the CONAIE affiliate did not stand a chance. True enough. The mayoral election does represent an indigenous bourgeoisie newly concerned with politics. But reducing Conejo's victory to money slights the political innovation that has taken place in Otavalo. The recovery of cultural authenticity downtown bucked a colonial narrative of people-in-place that both white-mestizo elite and indigenous militant organizations profited from. In forging a new way, activists paralleled the way the indigenous movement consolidated its rural bases in the 1980s. Urban indígenas publicized and fortified cultural pride by identifying with specific locales (the Plaza de Ponchos, Rumiñahui in the central park) and annual placemaking activities like the one in Yamor.

Otavaleños have now shown that an urban popular sector can regain its political footing through the politics of place. Moreover, this popular sphere also self-consciously identifies as Kichwa. At various times undermining, reinforcing, ignoring, or serving the national movement's agenda, urban activists have complicated the politically effective indigenous cultural location of the early 1990s. Such is the price of indigenous politics' new maturity.

Prying indigeneity from the grip of the natural world, a segment of new indigenous leaders are working to position native politics much closer to the settings of their constituents' lives.

Notes

1. De la Torre 2000.
2. Rodas Martínez 2001.
3. Clark 1997, 25.
4. Kichwa refers to the version of the Quechua language that is spoken by highland indigenous people in Ecuador. Many Andean peoples also use the word to name their ethnic identity.
5. Warren and Jackson 2002, 28.
6. Whitaker and Greene 1990.
7. Brown, Brea, and Goetz 1988.
8. Preston, Taveras, and Preston 1981; Weismantel 1988.
9. Korovkin 1997.
10. Zamosc 1994, 56.
11. Pallares 2002, 79.
12. Hale 1997b, 568.
13. Selverston 1994.
14. Whitten 2003, 5.
15. Pallares 2002, 86.
16. Meisch 2002, 26; Pallares 2002, 132.
17. Pallares 2002.
18. Ibid.
19. Macas, Belote, and Belote 2003, 223.
20. For an example, see Neptalí Zuñiga, *Fenómenos de la Realidad Ecuatoriana* (Quito: Talleras Gráficos de Educación, 1940).
21. De la Cadena 2000, 24.
22. Monsalve Pozo 1943, 32.
23. Zamosc 1994, 63.
24. Gerlach 2003, 77.
25. Consejo de Desarrollo de las Nacionalidades y Pueblos del Ecuador 2000.
26. FIDA 1989, 166, cited in Deere and Leon 2001.
27. Deere and Leon 2001, 52, n. 40.
28. Gow and Rappaport 2002, 49.
29. Rogers 1998a, 60.
30. Ibid.
31. Ibid., 61.
32. Chavez 1982.

33. Meisch 1998.

34. Meisch 2002; Meisch 1998.

35. "Un Tema Difícil," *Hoy*, September 1, 1996.

36. "Una fiesta que nos impusieron," *Hoy*, September 1, 1996.

37. Ibid.

38. Ibid.

39. "No se insistirá en la candidatura," *Diario del Norte*, August 22, 1996.

40. Rogers 1998b, 12.

41. Wilk 1995.

42. Mora 1998.

43. Alonso 2004.

44. Ibid.

45. Javier Izquierdo, "'Aquí dejamos nuestro corazón,' dicen los indígenas imbabureños: 'Caipicmi ñucanchipac shungo,'" *Hoy*, September 1, 1998.

46. Mora 1998.

47. Ibid.

48. "Rumiñahui vs. Bolívar en Otavalo," *Hoy*, September 1, 1998.

49. Grueso, Rosero, and Escobar 1998, 211.

50. De la Cruz 1995.

Education and Decolonization in the Work of the Aymara Activist Eduardo Leandro Nina Qhispi

ESTEBAN TICONA ALEJO

Through his work in education in the late 1920s, the Aymara intellectual Eduardo Leandro Nina Qhispi developed a remarkable proposal for an intercultural and decolonized Bolivian nation. Although Nina Qhispi did not use the word "racism," his work was antiracist in the sense that he sought intercultural equality and respect, a *convivencia de igualdades* (experience of equality). The driving principle of his work was renovation or refoundation, the refoundation of Bolivia through equality, brotherhood, and respect. Although Nina Qhispi has not yet received the recognition he merits, his wisdom resonates today.

Nina Qhispi was born in the *ayllu* Ch'iwu in Canton Santa Rosa de Taraqu (Ingavi province) on March 9, 1882. He was the son of Santiago F. Qhispi and Paula Nina de Qhispi, who had come, respectively, from Ingavi and Pacajes provinces (La Paz).[1]

The documents that exist about Nina Qhispi may be found primarily in the Archive of La Paz among the files of the Prefecture and the Superior Court. These sources refer mainly to the consolidation and activities of the *Sociedad República del Kollasuyo* (Society of the Republic of Kollasuyo) and the *Centro Educativo Kollasuyo* (Kollasuyo Educational Center).[2] One of the main objectives of these institutions was to establish schools in ayllus, communities, and rural haciendas for all the Indians in the country. Nina Qhispi was one of the administrators and directors of this center in 1930.[3]

On the specifics of the educational proposal of the Sociedad Kollasuyo, only oral sources are available to us from the testimony of Leandro Condori Chura, who was one of the main *escribanos* (scribes) of the *caciques-apoderados* (an early twentieth-century network of indigenous leaders). In an autobiographical text written jointly with me, Condori Chura recalled: "I met [Nina Qhispi] in 1925. He lived in my uncle's house, where I was also living, as his tenant. He would talk to the Indians there. We communicated well because he was an Indian from Taraqu. He had been . . . [a] servant, a hacienda Indian, a hacienda slave. Because of that he became an *apoderado*, in order to defend himself. He was grown up, and I was just young."[4]

Don Leandro, who was from Tiwanaku, shared with Nina Qhispi the experience of being an Indian who was expelled by the large landowners, of being a victim of land seizure. According to Don Leandro, Nina Qhispi was forced to flee his community because of an eviction order against his family: "'I'm in contact with the authorities, I'm continuing the fight, damn it. The bosses have expelled me, they've thrown me out,' [Nina Qhispi] told me. Nina Qhispi had been expelled from his estancia. This was the 1920s, ['21, '22, '23]; in those years Indians were being thrown out everywhere."[5]

According to documents in the Archive of La Paz, the territorial conflict between haciendas and communities culminated in the 1920s with a general uprising that took place mainly in areas near Lake Titicaca. The Taraqu, Waqi, and Tiwanaku revolts of 1920–22 and the Jesús de Machaqa revolt of 1921 were part of the general unrest.[6]

Meanwhile, the land grabbers sought to obtain judicial orders to evict their "tenants." These legal judgments would be used by the landowners to justify their acts of aggression and to make up for the supposed damages and harm caused by the Indians, who resisted the obligation to provide unremunerated services on the haciendas. The seizure of Indian land by the feudal-mining oligarchy was linked to a project of indigenous education that "consisted of civilizing and enlightening the Indian from a perspective of Western-Creole cultural ethnocentrism, in order to incorporate him into 'Bolivian nationality' as an efficient producer. However, for this the land should not be in the hands of the 'ignorant and backward Indian,' but rather in those of enterprising Creoles."[7] This is the general context in which Nina Qhispi was expelled from his ayllu and established residency in the city of La Paz. Condori recalled some aspects of Nina Qhispi's personality and style of work during this period:

> He lived in Ch'ijini, that's why I visited him freely. Because of the reasons I already gave, he had migrated to the city. At the time, I was young and

didn't understand what he was fighting for, besides this the landowners were destroying the estancias and many Indians were migrating. When I met him he was still young, barely forty.

He was short, like I am; however, he was talkative, he talked a lot and spoke well about everything, he talked like a woman. . . . He was talkative, small, and thin . . . , intelligent and talkative, that's also why he had that position, because of those talents. He spoke Spanish, although not very well; I mean he didn't speak proper Spanish. He also knew how to write; I mean that he didn't do it perfectly.[8]

This description of Nina Qhispi highlights some special characteristics of his personality, those on which his leadership was based. What stood out most for Leandro Condori was Nina Qhispi's "talkative" nature. While this trait, according to Condori, made Nina Qhispi similar to women, it was also essential for the role he was to play as a representative to and mediator with the dominant mestizo-Creole world. There is just a brief reference to Nina Qhispi's childhood in the available sources, one reflecting his extraordinary will and ability to find out about the Creole world by learning from a Spanish primer on his own. A journalist asked him, "In what school did you learn how to read?" Nina Qhispi replied, "Ever since I was little I noticed gentlemen buying newspapers and finding out things that way about everything that was going on. So I thought about learning how to read by using a primer that was given to me. Night after night I began to recognize the first letters; my tenacity meant that soon I could hold a book in my hands and know what it contained within."[9]

Education of the Indian: The First Phase of the Struggle

To study Nina Qhispi's struggle to provide Indians with access to education, with access to literacy, is an opportunity to recuperate an educational experience rooted in the culture of Bolivia's indigenous peoples. It also allows us an understanding of the arduous struggles undertaken by Aymaras, Quechuas, and other native peoples who were seeking access to school. As Karen Claure stated: "None of those precursors of indigenous education escaped punishment, jail, threats, taunts, and sometimes death."[10]

In the second half of the 1920s and the early 1930s, Nina Qhispi began to propose that the liberation of the Aymaras, Quechuas, Tupi-Guaranis, Moxeños, and other native peoples from this part of the Americas would be possible through a genuine form of education and literacy, one based on their own cultures. It was in this frame of mind that Nina Qhispi began to carry out his educational work in the city of La Paz.

Commencing in the colonial period, *gremios* (associations of Indian artisans) based on the old ayllus began to be created on the outskirts of the city of La Paz. These associations were strengthened by Aymara migration to the city, which intensified in the 1910s and 1920s as a result of the repression by large landowners. In this way, powerful Indian organizations emerged, such as organizations of masons, milkmaids, stonecutters, butchers, or slaughterers. It was in the slaughterers' union that Nina Qhispi established the main base for organizing the Sociedad República del Kollasuyo and the Centro Educativo Kollasuyo in its first stage of development between 1928 and 1930.

The government and church of that time, which were advised by social-Darwinist intellectuals, tried to put into effect policies for indigenous education through the *Gran Cruzada Nacional Pro-indio* (Great National Crusade for Indians), which sought to "civilize" Indians and erase their indigenous cultural identity. Priority was placed on teaching Spanish as a means of "preparing the Indian to learn to read and write."[11] Despite being influenced by the Cruzada Pro-indio, Nina Qhispi began to form an Aymara school in his own home. Most of the children of the slaughterers attended this school. Nina Qhispi recalled this experience as follows:

> When the Gran Cruzada Nacional Pro-indio began, I read about it in the newspapers. On the street I would stop in front of the posters, and then I thought: Why can't I support this work? I am so familiar with the sadness of the gaunt and defeated Indian. I myself have felt the cry of a humiliated race sobbing in my heart. I visited the houses of some of my fellow workers, helping them to understand how beneficial it would be for us to get off the rugged roads of servitude. Time passed. My little ranch was the meeting place for the butchers' union. They agreed to send me their children so I could teach them how to read.[12]

Before long, this effort was welcomed by important government authorities and radical intellectuals. The former group assumed that Nina Qhispi's enterprise coincided with their own educational project. The latter group instead saw the effort as an indigenous response to the government's approach to Indian literacy and education.

By these means, Nina Qhispi came to be a spokesman and leader of the ayllus and communities in different parts of the country, with broad powers to represent Aymaras, Quechuas, and Tupi-Guaranis before whatever government was in office. His constant concern for the good of his brothers and sisters allowed him to open other spaces for teaching. Nina Qhispi himself told of this: "My house was small, so I thought of asking the municipal government for a more appropriate place to teach my classes. I went in person to follow up on this. Often I would wait for a while at the door, because my social position did not allow me to speak up and I was afraid of being thrown out. I felt my eyes becoming moist, and that is what pushed me to keep on."[13] Nina Qhispi's efforts were crowned with success when a classroom in one of the municipal schools was provided so he could continue his work:

> Finally I was successful in getting them to give me a classroom in the night school at 150 Yanacocha Street. Bursting with happiness, I told the good news to my students, and before we took over the room we performed the *challa* (offering to the Pachamama, Mother Earth) so we would have good luck to guide us. And so it was that every day there were more and more pupils. The inspector, Mr. Beltrán, gave me some notebooks, books, and a small amount of teaching materials. As a result, seven months later it was possible for my students to participate in an exhibition with other schools.[14]

At the end of the first academic period Nina Qhispi taught, the result of the academic experiment with the Aymara children was that there were fifty-seven students attending classes regularly. By the end of the school year of 1928, the pupils who attended the classes in Nina Qhispi's school had not only begun to emerge as good students, they were capable of competing with the regular students in other municipal institutions. A certificate given by the Technical Inspector of Municipal Education indicated: "In conjunction with the municipal educational establishments, in October 1928 [Nina Qhispi] presented an exhibition of the work done by his students in the Municipal Theater. The exhibition was praised by the press, the members of the town council, and the public."[15] These activities were accomplished without any funding from the government, for Nina Qhispi's time alternated between his unpaid work as a teacher and his daily effort to earn a living: "I work in a bakery during the day, and at night I work with my students along with my son, Mariano, who has the qualities to one day become a respected and well-to-do man."[16]

The president at the time, Hernando Siles (in office 1926–30) was aware of the results of Nina Qhispi's work. In fact, Nina Qhispi met personally with the president and gained the government's sympathy and support:

> One of my fondest memories was my visit with the president of the Republic. I entered the palace very timidly, but after I started chatting with Mr. Siles my fear disappeared. I explained my goals to him, and he congratulated me on my work and promised to help me in every way. When I said good-bye, he embraced me affectionately. His words gave me so much encouragement that I joyfully told my students about my meeting, making them see that the highest authority was now a great supporter.[17]

Nina Qhispi's educational experience with Aymara children and his good relations with high authorities, intellectuals, and community leaders helped his thinking mature. In 1928 he was already planning to create the Sociedad República del Kollasuyo and the Centro Educativo Kollasuyo. The manner in which his literacy work was carried out also matured, in such a way that illiterate Aymaras themselves played a leading role in this activity, for it was thought that they ought to be educated in accordance with their own national and cultural reality. Nina Qhispi described his projects this way: "I intend to form an Indian Cultural Center and will ask intellectuals to come weekly to enlighten us. I also want to do a publicity tour in the altiplano and bring together everyone who is illiterate. At the start of the new year I will issue an invitation in the press, asking all Indians who want to learn how to read to come to me. With this effort I will have the satisfaction of passing on to them my limited knowledge."[18]

The Conceptualization of Education and Literacy

The proverb, "*jach'a jaqirus, jisk'a jaqirus jaqirjamaw uñjañaxa,*" which can be translated literally as "people both big and small need to be seen as people," conveys one of the ethical principles of Aymara culture. The saying means that people must respect each other regardless of age or social position, and that communication must be respectful in any kind of social interaction.

We believe that Nina Qhispi applied this Aymara ethical principle to his work educating children and teaching literacy to adults. It became the ideological basis of his educational plan. He said, "The first thing I teach is respect for others. I explain to them the meaning of the word, 'justice,' making them see the horrors caused by alcoholism and theft, and the consequences of these vices."[19] This statement shows that Nina Qhispi not only concerned himself with literacy but with the complete education of his pupils in the context of the ethical and ideological principles of their culture. He sought through his teachings to raise Indians' consciousness of the reality of oppression and injustice, to present a kind of "liberatory education"—but one that emphasized decolonization. Nina Qhispi's teachings thus focused on the topic of "justice," which was an advanced and dangerous idea at the time, since his Creole enemies saw his school as a focal point of "communist" training and Indian rebellion. His struggle against oppression and exploitation by large landowners became explicit in his petitions to government authorities. Consider, for example, the request he submitted to the senate with the indigenous teachers Pedro Castillo, Adolfo Ticona, Feliciano Nina, and Carlos Laura: "As indigenous teachers who have devoted our efforts for quite some time to literacy work with our people, we turn to the Honorable National Senate to respectfully seek the passage of laws and legislative resolutions to protect our degraded race . . . from the wicked exploitation of it by large landowners who look only to their own benefit without any regard for us."[20]

The framework of acute racism that marked and still marks the Creole oligarchy's position toward indigenous societies helps us understand the difficult context in which Nina Qhispi proposed and defended his ideas. It was in this environment that the *Sociedad de Educación Indigenal Kollasuyo* emerged on September 23, 1929. The society's main objective was to circulate messages of liberation while promoting the literacy and education of Indians by Indians.

At first the society had the support of several members of the dominant social sectors, such as priest Dr. Tomás de los Lagos Molina, who was named honorary president of the society. The press emphasized that the society was founded in a school that had been supported by the Parish of San Sebastián: "Yesterday the Centro de Educación Indigenal was solemnly inaugurated at the former site of the San Sebastián Secondary School. Indian representatives from many different cantons attended the ceremony."[21] With the founding of the Centro de Educación Indigenal, Nina Qhispi proposed that the solution to illiteracy would come when Indians themselves gained awareness and began to participate actively in the process of education. The newspaper account highlighted Nina Qhispi's speech on that occasion:

> The teacher, Eduardo Nina Qhispi, opened the session saying that since all indigenous patriots wished to contribute to the training and education of

all the indígenas in the Republic, it had been decided to proceed with the formation of the Centro de Acción Educacional. Its goal, [Nina Qhispi stated, was] the broader diffusion of literacy for the Indian, for which purpose each canton would have a representative. . . . After Nina Qhispi finished speaking, the other representatives elaborated on these ideas.[22]

The main methodological principle of the society, which sponsored countless schools throughout the country, was the active participation of Aymaras, Quechuas, and Guaranis (Izoceños and Avas) in the educational process. This was seen as a way to guarantee that the educational program would not be disconnected from the cultural reality of the communities and that it would allow them to strengthen their collective social and territorial demands. The members of the society—which included the *caciques* (indigenous authorities) of Cordillera Province in Santa Cruz and Gran Chaco Province in Tarija —were involved in strengthening the organization and took part in the legal struggles of the communities, ayllus, and *cabildos* (indigenous councils) to achieve the long-awaited justice proposed in the society's documents and in the education it imparted.

In this sense, and in order to better systematize the ideas of the indigenous teachers, Nina Qhispi proposed that a conference of teachers and Indians from different communities in the altiplano, valley, and eastern parts of the country be held in July 1930. The newspaper account told of the upcoming event in the following way:

> Eduardo Nina Qhispi, the tireless leader of the indigenous movement, has visited our office accompanied by representatives of the different cantons and "ayllus" who will soon inaugurate the conference of Indian teachers. Our visitors, who have come from remote areas, told us about their desire for each Indian to learn once and for all how to read and write. For this reason, they are involved in organizing this conference, which will take place during the upcoming July vacation.[23]

The activities of the Centro de Educación Indigenal were backed by a government decree of 1926 that established the basic concepts and programs for the education of Indians in the country's communities and haciendas. The agenda for the conference of teachers and Indians included consideration of "the petition they will take to the Supreme Government, [which asks] that the Dirección General de Instrucción Pública ensure that the Decree of 1926 be carried out, in the sense that basic guidelines and programs for educating the Indian race be established; . . . [that] a special item for free schools be included in the [national] budget. . . . [and that] *pongueaje* (unpaid personal services on haciendas) [be eliminated]."[24]

The Sociedad República del Kollasuyo

Nina Qhispi founded the Sociedad República del Kollasuyo in Chuqiyapu marka (the Aymara name for La Paz) on August 8, 1930.[25] This society became a center where new ideas could be generated, and where it would be possible to fight against the prevailing system. It was established just as government authorities were trying to set up rural normal schools in the Andean region of the country, especially in Caquiaviri and Warisata, and while the Catholic and Evangelical churches sought to indoctrinate Indians and give them "some sort of trade." The Indians themselves, that is, Nina Qhispi or the indigenous activists associated with the parallel *Centro Educativo de Aborígenes Bartolomé de las Casas*, thought about how the "education of the Indian" could contribute to teaching about, defending, and restoring the territory that belonged to the ayllus, those that were threatened with expropriation or had already been turned into haciendas.

From the time it was founded, the Sociedad, or Centro Educativo Kollasuyo, became engaged in many different kinds of activities. A few days after it was inaugurated, Nina Qhispi expressed the following view in the weekly publication, *Claridad*: "For the greatness of the Kollasuyo region, devoting all its attention and energy to it, so that it will rise again."[26]

The Centro Educativo Kollasuyo was a community organization of ayllus and *markas*, and it extended from La Paz to various departments in the republic, such as Potosí, Oruro, Cochabamba, and Chuquisaca. During the Chaco War, it even reached Santa Cruz, Beni, and Tarija.

The Chaco War and Prison

When the Chaco War with Paraguay broke out in 1932, Nina Qhispi recognized the traps that had been laid by the government's enemies. He sent a note of support to the president of the republic, Dr. Daniel Salamanca, informing him that he was concerned "about the momentary lack of understanding on the part of some impressionable people who have gone so far as to show disrespect for your authority." President Salamanca's response was not long in coming. He wrote: "It is a pleasure to tell you that I am very thankful for your voice of protest, as it is inspired by an unselfish sense of patriotism."[27]

Nina Qhispi had cultivated good relations with important political and cultural figures of the period, such as the archeologist Arturo Posnansky.[28] However, the *Legión Cívica* and other organizations involved in national security fought fiercely against Nina Qhispi and the Sociedad República del Kollasuyo. In a report to the Prefecture, the commander of the Legión Cívica, Justiniano Zegarrundo, lodged the following accusations against Nina Qhispi:

> The Legión Cívica, which commenced a difficult campaign against the Communists and anticipated the last Indian uprising, has taken action against a person calling himself nothing less than the President of the Kollasuyo Republic. That person's name is Eduardo Nina Qhispi. He is an Indian who—using his position as the founder of rural schools—has managed to assert his authority over the enormous indigenous race and undoubtedly is weaving together a vast subversive organization. This Indian and his followers—who we have actively investigated—are currently being held in the panopticon on the basis of sufficient proof.[29]

It is clear that the role of the Legión Cívica, which specialized in repressing Indians in the countryside, was to deal with anything considered contrary to "national security" on the "domestic front"; the organization obviously supported the interests of large landowners and reactionary sectors of the government. The war with Paraguay helped accusations like the one mentioned above to have the desired effect: the point was to quiet Indians' educational work and dissent, and to jail the leaders of the indigenous organizations.

The Political Proposal to Renew or Refound Bolivia:
The Republic of Kollasuyo

In one of his most important documents, *De los títulos de composición de la corona de España*, Nina Qhispi presented a proposal to renew Bolivia. The complex interpretation developed in that manuscript begins with colonial land titles, the most forceful tool of the indigenous movement in its mobilizations to defend and restore the Andean ayllus.

In a letter to President Salamanca dated September 14, 1931, Nina Qhispi requested the following: "The society I am honored to preside respectfully requests that, in fulfillment of the legal provisions currently in force (copy enclosed), [your government] take administrative control of the land that was acquired by Indians via colonial composition titles. Almost all of this land has been violently expropriated from its indigenous owners."[30] This passage clearly shows that the territory of the ayllus had been legalized via colonial land titles and that those titles granted full landowning rights to the ayllus and markas of the era. This was the central argument the indigenous movement used when it demanded the government's immediate administrative takeover of the land on behalf of the ayllus.

How to Renew or "Refound" Bolivia?

In *De los títulos de composición de la corona de España*, Nina Qhispi included information about Bolivia in the 1930s, including its territory and administrative divisions. For Nina Qhispi, and for the indigenous movement more broadly, taking an interest in the historical and territorial patrimony not only involved attention to the Andean ayllu and marka but to the entire national territory. Nina Qhispi stated: "In the communities of the Republic, at borders or boundary markers, the Centro Educativo Kollasuyo of America can be found. Our national territory has the United States of Brazil as its boundary on the north."

Nina Qhispi was considered the equivalent of a world leader by indigenous peoples in Bolivia and was recognized by them for his work as an educator. Through his educational activities and defense of the territory of the ayllus and markas, Nina Qhispi clearly pursued the idea of refounding Bolivia in its own territory. He said, "All Bolivians obey in order to preserve freedom. The indigenous race speaks Aymara and Quechua; the white and mestizo races speak Spanish. They are all our brothers."[31]

It is evident that Nina Qhispi thought that Bolivia would have a better future if that future were based on the recognition of indigenous peoples— and on the recognition of non-Indians. This is what today would be called the search for multicultural coexistence.

In 1934, as president of the Sociedad Centro Educativo Kollasuyo, Nina Qhispi included the Guarani, Mojeño, and Chiquitano indigenous peoples of the departments of Santa Cruz, Tarija, and Beni in his request for a general demarcation of Andean territory. Others joined in his request: Casiano Barrientos, *capitán grande* of the Izozog, Saipurú, and Parapetí area in Cordillera province, Santa Cruz; Guardino Candeyo, Tiburcio Zapadengo, and Manuel Taco, from Tarija; José Felipe Nava and Sixto Salazar de Rocha, from Beni.

The most interesting of Nina Qhispi's ideas was this coming together again of Andean and Amazonian peoples. Research on this alliance has yet to be done.

*

The official history of Bolivian education recognizes the experience of the non-Indian educator Elizardo Pérez, who played a leading role in the creation of the controversial indigenous normal school in Warisata in the early 1930s. To some extent, the official history also recognizes the experience of Pérez's indigenous collaborator, Avelino Siñani.[32] However, to date, history does not recognize the experience of other indigenous educators such as Nina Qhispi. In order to understand and affirm the significance of these pioneering efforts, there needs to be more in-depth research on the educational struggles of the indigenous population. Nina Qhispi's educational work was part of a process in which illiterate people became aware of their rights.

The indigenous schools promoted by Nina Qhispi and the Sociedad Centro Educativo Kollasuyo represent yet another instance of the Aymara people's resistance to Creole oppression and discrimination. In these schools, the connection between education and the struggle for the territorial and cultural demands of native peoples was always present. An interest in strengthening traditional forms of organization and authority, strengthening indigenous cultural identity, and recognizing the value of Aymara thought was also taking place in these schools.

Nina Qhispi's ideas did not remain on a strictly educational plane. They had a political undercurrent, as is evident in his proposal for renovating or refounding Bolivia.[33] Nina Qhispi called for the renovation of Bolivia because, although the country was independent, it continued to be a land that belonged to the few. He was actually asking for the decolonization of the nation, so that native peoples would gain equal status and a new national state would be built. With the electoral triumph of Evo Morales and the *Movimiento al Socialismo* (the Movement Toward Socialism, MAS) in December 2005, and following two years of government by MAS, a project with some characteristics of Nina Qhispi's plan for decolonization has begun. But what does decolonization mean today? The pillars of a decolonized Bolivian state should be its indigenous roots—Andean, Amazonian, Eastern, and Chaco. Mestizo influences could join these influences, just as useful aspects could be taken from the Western world. What decolonization really involves is not only the recognition of indigenous people but the recognition of indigenous people's thought. Nina Qhispi played an important role in the struggle for such recognition. He was one of the most extraordinary Aymara visionaries of the twentieth century. His ideas have great relevance today.

"*Jichhapi jichaxa*," or "now is when," was the electoral slogan of Evo Morales and MAS. In this new postelectoral period, we must add on to this phase: "*jichhapi jichaxa mayaki sartañani jan jisk'achasisa*," or "now is when we have to walk together, but without discriminating against each other."

Notes

This chapter was translated by Jane Walter and edited by Laura Gotkowitz. The bulk of this chapter appeared as "La educación y la política en el pensamiento de Eduardo Leandro Nina Quispe," in Esteban Ticona, *Lecturas para la descolonización, taqpachani qhispiyasipxanani, liberemonos todos* (Cochabamba: Agruco-UMSS/Universidad de la Cordillera, 2005), 101–16. A shorter version was published as "Conceptualización de la educación y alfabetización en Eduardo Leandro Nina Qhispi," in *Educación indígena:¿Ciudadanía o colonización?* edited by Roberto Choque et al. (La Paz: Ediciones Aruwiyiri, Taller de Historia Oral Andina, 1992), 99–108.

1. Eduardo Nina Quispe, "De los títulos de composición de la corona de España. Composición a título de usufructo como se entiende la excensión revisitaria. Venta y composición de tierras de origen con la corona de España. Títulos de las comunidades de la República. Renovación de Bolivia. Años 1536, 1617, 1777 y 1925," 1932, 1. Archivo de La Paz (hereafter ALP), Expedientes de la Prefectura (hereafter EP), Caja 346. Quispe was used at the time; Qhispi is in accord with Aymara usage now.

2. Nina Qhispi first created the Centro Educativo, and later the Sociedad. The latter had a more explicit political function.

3. Choque 1986 and 1996.

4. Condori and Ticona Alejo 1992, 118. "Montes" is a reference to Ismael Montes, president of Bolivia from 1904–09 and 1913–17. An apoderado is a legal agent. Taking advantage of favorable republican legislation, indigenous leaders of the late nineteenth century and the early twentieth served their communities as apoderados who defended community interests before state authorities and in the courts.

5. Condori and Ticona Alejo 1992, 118.

6. Mamani 1991; Choque and Ticona Alejo 1996.

7. Claure 1989, 37.

8. Condori and Ticona Alejo 1992, 118–19.

9. *El Norte*, October 28, 1928.

10. Claure 1989, 21.

11. Ibid., 36.

12. *El Norte*, October 28, 1928.

13. Ibid.

14. Ibid.

15. Nina Quispe, "De los títulos de composición," 1932, 1, ALP, EP, Caja 346.

16. *El Norte*, October 28, 1928.

17. Ibid.

18. Ibid.

19. Ibid.

20. Nina Quispe, "De los títulos de composición," 1932, 4, ALP, EP, Caja 346.

21. *El Norte*, September 24, 1929.

22. Ibid.

23. *El Norte*, May 11, 1930.

24. Ibid.

25. A marka is a group of ayllus and the term for an Indian town.

26. *Claridad*, 1930, 4.

27. 10/5/1932.

28. For more on Posnansky, see Seemin Qayum's article in this volume.

29. ALP, EP, 1934.

30. Nina Quispe, "De los títulos de composición," 1932, ALP, EP, Caja 346.

31. Ibid., 5.

32. On Warisata, see Choque et al. 1992; Larson 2003.

33. This paragraph and the next paragraph are taken from Miguel E. Gómez Balboa's interview with Esteban Ticona: "El fenómeno descolonizador," *La Prensa* 2 (April 2005). See also Esteban Ticona Alejo, "Avances y retos del triunfo de Evo Morales," *La Prensa* 22 (January 2006). For more on decolonization in the current conjuncture, readers may wish to consult these articles.

Mistados, Cholos, and the Negation of Identity in the Guatemalan Highlands

CHARLES R. HALE

The mistado are an intermediate social group in the Guatemalan highlands, a group increasing in size, and whose members refuse both of the region's major identity categories, "indigenous" and "ladino." Guatemala's "ethnic ideology" has transformed, especially in the postwar decade of the 1990s. When the war began some three decades earlier, the ethnic ideology was well established and characterized by a strict bipolarity between two all-encompassing categories, which are sharply differentiated and separated from one another by a chasm of enduring inequality. This ideology did not fully capture the way people experienced racial and cultural difference: there were always ambiguities, transgressions, and exceptions to the rule; the arrangements were always unstable and subject to change.[1] Nevertheless, the contrast between then and now is crucial. The ethnic ideology then served to organize social relations, discipline transgressors, and shape perceptions of cultural difference, whereas today it does so to a dramatically lesser extent. The effects of that ethnic ideology are constrained by a striking increase of quiet dissent and active contestation. Today it is increasingly threadbare and the growing prominence of intermediate social groups—those who refuse identification as either ladino or indigenous—are both a symptom and a force of change.

The established ethnic ideology can be summarized with the familiar phrase, "separate and unequal," although the particularities are distinctly Guatemalan. The dominant racial category, "ladino," and the process by which members of the subordinate category became ladinos (i.e., through *ladinización* or "ladinization") cannot be confused with "mestizo" and the process of mestizaje in other Latin American societies. The terms *Ladino* and *mestizo* correspond to two distinct ethnic ideologies that organize and give meaning to social relations in different ways. These differences are especially evident now, as Guatemala's established ethnic ideology begins to unravel. As a result of this unraveling, the chasm between the two established categories is turning into a social space that increasing numbers of people occupy. Yet neither this space, nor its occupants, have an overarching collective identity or voice, or even a generally agreed upon name. To those who still rely on the established ethnic ideology, members of intermediate groups are misfits, in transition. Surprisingly, the emergent state-endorsed discourse of multiculturalism, which affirms cultural difference with equality, has little time for these intermediate groups, either. When politicians court these groups at election time, they avoid identity-specific language and favor generic social categories such as "popular classes," "workers," "Guatemalans," or "*chimaltecos*" (i.e., residents of Chimaltenango).

This largely anonymous intermediate sector, I fear, could become the Achilles heel of the Maya cultural rights movement. Despite much convergence in experiences and political sensibilities, Maya activists and members of these intermediate groups have diametrically opposed discourses of identity. The intermediate groups could align themselves with the vaguely populist political projects of the right, which offer very little to the Maya in the way of substantive collective rights. Yet the intermediate sectors also have qualities that point in a radically different direction: toward critique, even transformation of the racial hierarchy of times past; toward an inclusive, pluralist identity politics—what might be called a "mestizaje from below"— combined with an equally broad and heterodox class consciousness.

My use of the term "ethnic ideologies" requires a brief explanation. The term refers to a collection of historically constituted social categories, which people use to locate themselves, to describe others, and to mark boundaries between "us" and "them." It is *ethnic* ideology because, although race and racial premises deeply infuse the categories, the default idiom defining and differentiating these premises gravitates toward culture and ethnicity. It is ethnic *ideology* because these racial categories are overarching representations of complex social processes, which inevitably simplify experiences and ways of thinking, advancing certain interests and subordinating others.[2] Although a comprehensive analysis of any ethnic ideology would have to take a dual (or multiple) perspective examining the standpoint of those who occupy all the different ethnic categories, such an approach is beyond the scope of my analysis. Ladinos (i.e., the dominant category in the established binary) and their relationship to the emergent intermediate sector are the focus here. A parallel analysis from the standpoint of the indigenous majority will have to come from elsewhere.[3]

To study a group situated "in between" existing categories of the established ethnic ideology poses a problem. By naming the intermediate group, are we not creating a category for the purposes of our own analysis?[4] The ethnographer, in this sense, may confront a version of the same dilemma that scholars found when they explored questions of identity in regard to civil registry officials in the townships of Chimaltenango.[5] These officials, mostly ladinos, told researchers that in past times filling in the blank corresponding to "race" in the forms to record marriages or births previously posed little problem, because the officials always knew who was who. For many reasons (migration, culture change, etc.) this task has become more difficult. Surprisingly, none of the ten officials who were interviewed resolved the problem in the way an uninitiated outsider might have considered obvious: ask applicants, "How do you identify?" "Oh no, that is way too sensitive a question," one responded. "It could be offensive to do that." Instead, officials simply look at the person, and silently decide what to fill in, or (increasingly) they leave the line blank. This problem is not related primarily to "mixed marriages"—still relatively rare—but to entire mixed neighborhoods. Nor is it the result of occasional anomalous responses to the identity question; fully one-third of two high school classes identified as "mestizo" rather than indigenous or ladino. The relative invisibility of this group heightens the urgency to better understand members of the group as social actors, as critics of the established ethnic ideology, and as potential contributors to alternative political visions in Guatemala. As a modest response to this urgency, I introduce the "cholos"—the largest gang in Chimaltenango—into the ethnographic record. As the etymology of their name suggests, the cholos occupy the intermediate space between the two established categories—with all the cultural-political creativity, and all the risks and pitfalls, that this positioning entails.

Three questions guide my inquiry. First, why are these intermediate social groups emerging so prominently now, in postwar Guatemala? Carrying out a genealogy of the intermediate space and its occupants during the second half of the twentieth century substantiates the assertion that intermediate groups are growing. Second, why does this intermediate sector lack a narrative voice to represent and advance its collective interests? The implicit contrast is with politics in Peru and Bolivia, where groups roughly parallel to those in Guatemala have acquired a collective political identity.[6] Third, what are the consequences of the unraveling of the existing ethnic ideology, and of the growth of the intermediate groups? The standard assumption, which I believe is generally correct, is that movements to contest racism and achieve cultural rights and racial justice in Central America will be populated and led primarily by self-identified black and indigenous peoples. Yet this begs the question: how, if at all, do the intermediate groups articulate with such struggles?[7]

Knowing Who Is Who: The Established "Ethnic Ideology"

In the entrance to Leonidas Mencos Ávila high school in Chimaltenango hangs a plaque that commemorates the first graduating class of accountants, in the year 1960. When I discussed the plaque with a teacher who works at the high school, I learned that those first graduates had been all or mostly ladinos, in sharp contrast to today, when "the great majority is Indian." My interest piqued, I began to investigate when and how this change had taken place. I made a quick count of the Indian and ladino last names in each year since 1960. Last names are no certain indication of identity, but with the help of a teacher who had been at the school since its founding, I was able to increase the accuracy of the judgment. This old-timer helped me learn how certain names, such as "Pajarito," although ostensibly Spanish, were unmistakably Indian, while other names, such as "Ovalle," could be Indian or Spanish (and so you have to know which Ovalle family the student is from). Although he generally placed students as indigenous or ladino with great surety, in a few cases he would hesitate, "*Ah, Usted, aquél es mistado*" ("Oh, he is mistado"). The first time I heard this designation, I pushed for greater clarity: "OK, but what was his identity?" My informant hesitated and then responded, "Who knows . . . *supongo que agarra por lado del padre* I suppose he would incline toward the father."

"Mistado"—a term I heard with some frequency, especially from those of the older generation—is not simply a synonym of "mestizo." Its meaning is more restricted: both terms invoke biological mixture, but "mistado" ends there, foreclosing the possibility that cultural processes following from the mixture could result in a distinct identity. Instead, the assumption is that the mistado would incline toward the identity of one parent or the other. Given this logic, the mistado has no good option: he (or she) could resign himself to the indigenous identity of one parent, or begin the uphill battle to gain the acceptance of ladinos. While elderly people can cite cases when such acceptance was achieved, these cases are few and much scrutinized by ladinos who are deeply invested in the identity boundaries. The mistado who successfully becomes ladino has generally drawn on unusual resources—economic position, political power, professional status—to seal the argument. The possibilities for marshalling these resources, in all likelihood, are the best predictors of which side the mistado will be inclined toward: a few fortunate mistados have entered the ladino world, while the rest stayed knocking at the door, amid racial ambiguity. Ultimately, if only by default, these others remained much closer to the indigenous.

The established ethnic ideology was eminently local: it thrived in a society where everyone knew "who is who." Such local knowledge is crucial when phenotype is central, but not determinant, in placing people within the racial hierarchy. Ladinos pay great attention to physical characteristics—skin color, height, hair, body type, facial features—and make their racial categorizations accordingly. Indian characteristics were systematically denigrated and European ones desired. According to the established ethnic ideology, however, these phenotypic assessments did not yield definitive judgments about an individual's identity. You had to know something more. Previously, knowing "who is who" involved a strong spatial dimension: the central streets of town, especially the "*calle real*," were reserved for ladino families, while Indians lived in the peripheries. Spatial differentiation tracked with other characteristics, such as clothing, employment, facility with the Spanish language, and even body language, which implied submission or dominance. Above all, there was the use of *corte* (indigenous female clothing) among older women and knowledge of one's family background, a background suggested by a last name. In essence, knowing "who is who" was to know a person's family of origin. As long as this was clear, the mistado could be fixed in place not as a generic mestizo but as the anomalous offspring of a ladino and an Indian.

This deep knowledge about everyone, as long as it prevailed, helped ladinos resolve the central contradiction of the established ethnic ideology. How could ladinos be "direct descendants of the Spanish," and yet live with the ubiquitous insinuation that ladinos were racially mixed? The ultraelite Guatemalans of the capital city who claim strictly European descendance (Euro-Guatemalans) immediately suspected ladinos from Chimaltenango of having

"Indian blood," due to their proximity to Indians. Quiet talk after a baby's birth—generally restricted to the doctor and close family members—reported on whether or not the newborn had the "*mancha mongólica*" (a patch of darker skin around the hip area) supposedly proof of Indian admixture. There was also grumbling about ladinos who looked too Indian to possess unquestioned status in the ladino identity group.

The inquisitive anthropologist brings these insinuations into public discourse with seemingly straightforward questions, such as, "Do you have indigenous ancestry?" Rather than the definitive "no" prescribed by the established ethnic ideology, the response is often ambiguous. This ambiguity is consistent with the broader pattern. As long as no one digs up counterevidence, and as long as one's credentials as ladino are otherwise solid, a previous status as mistado fades. The contradiction is never actually resolved, but it does turn mild, and, most importantly, it escapes public scrutiny.

In recent times, however, this contradiction has come to the fore. Maya activist intellectuals enjoy probing the hypocrisy of ladino denial; or, in the language of the established ethnic ideology, they enjoy obliging ladinos to acknowledge the extensive presence of mistados in their midst and among their ancestors. Take, for example, a ladina named Yolanda, who was one subject of my Chimaltenango ethnography. In response to my standard question, "Do you have indigenous ancestry?," she answered yes at first and went on to affirm her affinities for the emergent "mestizo" category. A few days later, Yolanda asked to return to that interview to review her responses. In the intervening days, she had talked with her parents and other family members and recounted her response to my question. They responded with indignation, and provided Yolanda with an extensive genealogy lesson, complete with family names and marriages going back generations, to prove that they had always been ladinos, with no indigenous intermixture. "There surely was some mixture in the remote past," Yolanda concluded, wanting to lay the matter to rest, "but that has no influence on us today. For generations we have lived completely separate, and we have created two completely different cultures, with very little in common. My parents are right . . . better put me down in your study as ladina."

A small group of intellectuals, mainly in the capital city, have self-reflexively opted for the term "ladino" (rather than "mestizo") on the grounds that they are better positioned to confront the legacy of racism in Guatemala as ladinos. The term "ladino," they argue, downplays phenotype and other racial markers, and instead revolves around cultural precepts that all group members share. This image of ladinos as a phenotypic rainbow would be reinforced by a snapshot of any random grouping of ladinos in Chimaltenango, especially if the person looking never scratched beneath the surface or asked deeper questions about how particular individuals became members of the group, about their relationships with one another. This image also encapsulates one important way that Guatemala's racial hierarchy is different, for example, from apartheid South Africa or the southern United States in the time of Jim Crow. The identity category ladino embodies an ideal of cultural commonality in the face of vast phenotypic variation, which contradicts any social system that maps race onto color, and segregates racial groups accordingly. To understand how the ethnic ideology operates *among* ladinos, it is crucial to look more deeply, especially in regard to the darker-skinned members of the group. Under what conditions have darker-skinned ladinos, widely perceived as being "closer to the Indian," gained full membership in the group? Were they or perhaps their parents subjected to scrutiny or disdain as mistados who were trying to pass? If so, does the pain, resentment, or anger that this scrutiny generated live on? Where do those feelings reside? One can ask such questions of a particular individual, and one can ask about the aggregate effects of many individual experiences on the collective "ladino" category. The phenotypic rainbow, in short, has a social history that is obscured by the assertion that everyone belongs.

This line of inquiry brings forth the debate on "ladinization," a term that figures prominently in the established ethnic ideology. Although Richard N. Adams did not coin the term, his work played a central role in its elaboration. Fifty years later, he cannot shake free from his association with the term. As Adams explains in a recent essay, he did not use the term with theoretical pretensions; his objective was to give order to empirical observations on culture change in the Guatemalan highlands.[8] The scheme he created consisted of a typology that he called a "continuum of transculturation." Depending on the extent of observed culture change, he placed "indigenous" highlands inhabitants in one of four categories: traditional Indians, modified Indians, "ladinized" Indians, and new ladinos. Viewed with the benefit of fifty years of hindsight, the scheme appears to have glaring defects, which Adams himself has acknowledged. It presumes that cumulative "transculturation" leads to identity change, and that both processes are unidirectional and irreversible. The deeper problem, however, is the absence of a systematic analysis of the ethnic ideology that prevailed at the time, and of the relationship between that ideology and Adams' scheme. Adams documented culture change, but he did not scrutinize the dominant institutions and actors that played a central role in making the change and giving it meaning.

If we redirect the analytical gaze away from indigenous people and toward dominant institutions and actors, an intriguing hypothesis emerges, which I hope will motivate further research. Adams implicitly assumed that Guatemala's established ethnic ideology was, or would soon become, one of the many variants of mestizaje ideologies that prevailed in most of Latin America. Although the state-endorsed mestizaje ideologies vary widely, they share a key feature: the ideal of a single national identity forged from diverse cultures and traditions. Proponents of mestizaje ideologies actively promoted social integration, which did not eliminate racial hierarchy but did rest on the idea that as people conformed to the national identity norm, they would become full-fledged citizens of the nation. In contrast, it is now clear that Guatemala's ethnic ideology in the post-1954 period rejected the mestizaje ideal, maintained a deep chasm between ladinos and Indians, and made it difficult for Indians to cross the divide. While some Indians certainly passed for mestizo, and a few entire communities made the transition, these were exceptions to the rule; they remained suspect, on the margins of ladino acceptability. Framed by this peculiarly Guatemalan ethnic ideology, Adams' scheme acquires a different meaning: these categories (traditional, modified, etc.) depict Indians who have adopted a variety of individual and collective strategies in response to generalized racialization, with no necessary relationship to the evolutionary course of cultural change toward being ladino. Rather than being an inevitable outcome, "becoming ladino" is a vigorously discouraged possibility, achieved at considerable sacrifice.

A comparison between these two ethnic ideologies—that of "mestizaje" and that associated with the ladino-Indian binary in Guatemala—suggests a paradox. The established ethnic ideology in Guatemala may place more emphasis on equalitarian relations among those who belong to the ladino category, while the mestizaje ideology, which opens wider doors of membership, maintains a greater racialized hierarchy among those who are or become mestizo. While Guatemalan ladinos with Indian phenotypes are subjected to the opprobrium of being "too close to the Indian," they are offered a path to greater acceptance: sharp repudiation of the "Indian within," and full psychic investment in the chasm that keeps Indians and ladinos apart. In contrast, ideologies of mestizaje turn that chasm into a blurred line, which makes it easier for Indians to pass, but offers less relief from continued racial opprobrium for those who do. If this basic contrast holds up against systematic comparative analysis, a fascinating corollary would follow. Ethnic ideologies of mestizaje, grounded in the ideal of universal citizenship and relatively fluid boundaries between Indian and mestizo, make it more difficult for people to organize around Indian identity and collective rights to cultural difference. The segregation perpetuated by the "separate and unequal" principle inherent in the Guatemalan ethnic ideology, in contrast, leaves Indians with limited options: a few individuals might successfully cross the chasm, and gain acceptance as ladinos; for the rest, segregation—however odious for its premise of racial inferiority—lays the groundwork for collective cultural self-affirmation, organization, and autonomy.

This paradox, in turn, might contribute a complementary explanation for the widespread repudiation, by ladinos and Indians alike, of Adams's scheme. The catalyst was the perception that Adams was not just documenting culture change, but subtly promoting a new ethnic ideology for Guatemala, replacing separate and unequal with an official state-endorsed mestizaje. Many ladinos, whether of left-wing or right-wing affinities, if presented with this proposal, would have perceived it as a threat to the racial privilege that the established ethnic ideology protected. The ideal of equality between Indians and ladinos, the centerpiece of the mestizo ideology, would have been unacceptable to ladinos. For different reasons, Indian intellectuals would have found Adams's scheme just as threatening, especially with the emergence of the Maya movement in subsequent years. Indian intellectuals rejected the established ethnic ideology's foundational premise of separate and unequal, but they also rejected the ideology of mestizaje for its tendency to dismantle the borders between Indian and ladino, and by extension, to undermine Maya demands for autonomy. Not until the 1990s did a significant sector of ladinos, faced with a vibrant Maya movement, belatedly endorse mestizaje ideology and its assimilationist vision for Guatemalan society. In Chimaltenango, as elsewhere in the highlands, middle-class ladinos have begun to abandon the ethnic ideology of separate and unequal, to repudiate the racism of times past, and to promise the Maya majority an updated version of the mestizaje ideal: cultural equality and full participation in a society still largely controlled by ladinos. While certainly attractive to some, this promise is essentially backward-looking. By the 1990s, throughout Latin America—and Guatemala is no exception—ideologies of mestizaje had lost their prodigious hegemonic appeal, because they were undermined by indigenous resistance, on the one hand, and the global rise of multiculturalism, on the other.

The Logic of Denial

I returned some while later to the high school where I had discovered the existence of the mistado to facilitate a discussion about "intercultural relations" in a class of about fifty seniors. To initiate the discussion, I administered an anonymous questionnaire, which began with the identity question. My previous calculation, based on indigenous last names, had yielded a steady increase in the percentage of indigenous students, from 10 percent in 1960 to about 55 percent in 1994. The teachers I spoke with, all ladinos, insisted that the current percentage was more like 75, and that last names had become a less precise index of identity. My questionnaire, carried out in 1997, produced the following results: 17 percent ladino, 45 percent indigenous, and 38 percent mestizo. A similar questionnaire, administered to a group of university students attending weekend classes in the Chimaltenango branch of San Carlos University, produced similar results.

These quantitative data fit nicely with more qualitative ethnographic research carried out in 1998 in a peripheral neighborhood called Buena Vista. I asked Paula, a young woman of twenty-one years who lived in Buena Vista, about the identity of the young people in her neighborhood, and she responded: "Everyone is part indigenous, but they are mixed . . . They are not exactly indigenous, they are a mixture of indigenous and ladino, and they generally deny their origins . . . Indigenous culture is just not preserved here . . . because there is so much mixture. . . . This neighborhood could not be designated territory of either the indigenous or the ladino race: they're all mestizos."[9]

Paula identifies herself as mestiza. When I asked her about her indigenous ancestry, she paused, and yelled to her mother, who was working in another part of the house: "Mami, we are part Maya, aren't we?" Her mother responded: "Yes dear, I am indigenous from Cobán." Paula then turned back to me with her answer: "Pues sí [yes], . . . because we are Guatemalans and we are Mayas . . . I think of myself as Maya and I like it . . . My mother used [to wear] indigenous clothing from Cobán, but it just became too expensive . . . This clothing that comes from factories is much cheaper. Many people deny their indigenous ancestry . . . I say I am Maya, because that is our ancestry, and I will never denigrate our origins." Paula is Maya, but also mestiza, and both complement an identity with multiple dimensions that do not fit easily into a single category.

The central question here—why have these intermediate social groups arisen with such prominence in this particular historical juncture—begs a prior question: How do we know that this prominence is actually new? Could it be that this intermediate category always existed in Chimaltenango, and the difference now is that people have decided to bring it to light? I am convinced that a novel process of identity change is underway, but I must admit that the supporting evidence is mostly indirect and anecdotal. The most convincing proof is the constant flow of complaints I heard from ladinos of the older generation, who cling to the established ethnic ideology. "Before we always knew," they say with indignation, "who was who. Now, you just can't tell." The growing inclination for people to situate themselves in the middle, and the breakdown of the established ethnic ideology, open space for new expressions of identity that adamantly refuse the two established categories. There is no better example of this refusal than the "cholos," a youth gang to which Paula once belonged.

The Cholos at a Glance

Everyone in Chimaltenango knows the basics about the cholos: they emerged in the 1990s as the city's largest *mara* (youth gang). They wear baggy clothing, paint gang-like graffiti on walls in public places, and have marked tendencies toward violence, drugs, and delinquency. Beyond these accounts, drawn mainly from third-hand sources that rely on gossip and gross generalizations, knowledge of the cholos is minimal. When I expressed interest in investigating the cholos, ladino friends cautioned that they were dangerous people, with powerful leaders linked to the military, and drug-related economic interests to defend. When a coincidence later provided an entrée into the world of Chimaltenango's gangs, I found these assumptions to be superficial and in some respects plain wrong. Regarding the cholos, two observations are especially salient. First, although I never found out much about their nighttime activities, I confirmed that by day they were anything but delinquents who lived lives of crime. To make a date with Johnny, the leader I most wanted to interview, the biggest obstacle was actually finding a time when he was *not* working. Second, and even more surprising, the status of leaders like Johnny is achieved and maintained through dance, a particular kind of dance that combines gymnastic jumps with break-dance-type moves and goes by the name "*mortal.*" The verb is "*mortalear.*" Not everyone can do it. One must learn in order to gain position and assert leadership within the gang; the leaders of the cholos *mortalean* with widely recognized ability and grace.

In my first interview with Johnny, he recited the words of a rap the group had composed and recorded, with "*pista*" (background music) from a famous song from New York. Both observations noted earlier are nicely reiterated in the song's principal message:

Keep listening to what I'm going to tell you,
if in this country we'll be able to live.
People don't sleep with so much delinquency,
it's because of that we all lose our patience.
They think we have guilty consciences,
and they are led astray by appearances.
Just because we wear loose trousers,
they believe that we are thieves.
Or because they see that we like to dance,
they think we are out to mug them.

Sigan escuchando lo que les voy a decir,
si es que en este país podemos vivir;
La gente no duerme con tanta delincuencia,
es por eso que a todos nos pierde la paciencia;
Piensan que tenemos sucia la conciencia,
y se dejan guiar por lo que ven en apariencia;
Sólo porque usamos flojos pantalones,
Ellos consideran que somos ladrones;
O porque ven que nos gusta bailar,
piensan que también nos metemos a robar.

This same interview disabused me of some theoretically driven speculations, which sparked my interest in the cholos in the first place. In the Andean countries and the southwestern United States, the term "cholo" signifies an intermediate space: between indigenous and dominant social groups in the Andes, and between Anglo and Mexican cultures in the United States. It would be interesting, I thought, if Chimaltenango cholos could also be shown to be quintessential "border crossers," busily at work forging a new, intermediate mestizo identity. But in a long and rich interview, the only questions that seemed to squelch discussion were those concerning identity: Did the cholos invite both indigenous and ladino to join? "Of course," Johnny replied. Did Maya culture play a role in their thinking? ("No.") What are relations like between indigenous and ladino cholos? ("Good, normal, we walk together; like I told you, inside the group, no one is more or less than anyone else.") A similar answer followed when I asked about the origins of the mortal:

> Once Donis said to Chino, "Let's go to my house to see a movie." The movie that was rented happened to be *Sólo el Más Fuerte Sobrevive* [*Only the Strongest Survive*] and [another one called] *Duro de Matar* [*Hard to Kill*]. That was where they found out about the dance; afterward they went to get us and they told us, "Hey, look at that," . . . and we began to train . . . and the group really took off. Then everyone started to train. It was based on the dance in the movie that the group formed.
>
> At first we called it "the *fachosos*" [odd-looking ones], because they were already wearing loose clothing . . . but "fachoso," as it's used in Chimaltenango, means someone who doesn't have clothes to change into or who doesn't dress well. Then a friend came from the United States and he said, "You look just like cholos." We changed the name for it from "fachosos" to "cholos," and that's how the name came about.[10]

Although they are proud of their ability to dance and sing their own songs, the cholos emphasize that the creative impulse for their art comes from outside Guatemala. In regard to identity, they are very interested in forging and reinforcing group loyalties; beyond this, topics such as indigenous identity, ladino racism, and cultural rights don't seem to move them.

Ironically, both Mayas and ladinos criticize the cholos' tendencies to borrow cultural practices from the north. This is a sore point for ladinos, who have been disparaged (by Mayas, foreign academics, and to some extent other ladinos) for lacking an authentic culture of their own, for being inclined to imitate others. Maya intellectuals, in turn, tend to view the cholos as the epitome of alienation, whereby an outward orientation leads to identity loss. With both groups of *chimaltecos*, I faced an uphill battle to convince them that cholos were involved in a creative process, an identity politics that could enrich efforts to move beyond the standoff between indigenous resistance and ladino racism. Then again, the cholos themselves didn't provide much support for this battle. If their ascendancy as Chimaltenango's largest gang is indeed indicative of a third space in local identity processes, the politics of this space includes little inclination to participate in Maya-ladino contention. Instead, their stance regarding the established identity categories, and the contention between them, is one of disinterest and refusal.

Why Now?

Maya contestation is the most prominent force that has brought these inter-mediate social groups to the fore. The critique of racism and demands for rights grounded in cultural difference have exerted a profound influence on the political sensibilities of Guatemala's dominant sectors. While organized Maya political pressure has played a crucial role, equally important has been the uncoordinated forms of indigenous agency carried out by people who belong to no organization but have absorbed enough of the new sense of empowerment to know that they no longer need to remain silent. One way to gauge the effects of this contestation is to consider the fate of the founda-tional principle of the established ethnic ideology: separate and unequal. The public spaces where ladinos can get away with explicit affirmations of indige-nous inferiority are few and rapidly diminishing; two or three decades ago these spaces were ubiquitous.[11]

Maya contestation has contributed to the emergence of the intermediate space, mainly through its impact on the ladino identity category. The estab-lished ethnic ideology rested on a stark and relatively impermeable boundary between "Indian" and "ladino," reinforced by social hierarchy and spatial differentiation. Efforts to break down that hierarchy, to question ladino racial privilege, have destabilized established notions of what it means to be ladino. This contestation also affects ladino practices of boundary maintenance, whereby those considered too close to their Indian background are denied entry into the ladino category. I asked a ladina friend about the identity of someone who seemed to straddle this boundary and she responded, half-joking, "We have no idea any more who is who. In any case, Demetrio Cojtí [a prominent Maya intellectual] has told us that people must be able to define their own identities. If that guy says he's ladino (even if I have my doubts), he's ladino and that's that." The point is not, of course, that status differences between Maya and ladino have disappeared, but that ladinos like my friend are less inclined to invest so much energy in policing the identity boundary on which the persistence of the racial hierarchy ultimately depends.

This increasing fluidity of the once rigid boundary between "ladino" and "Indian" gives rise to a paradox. As it gets easier for outsiders to enter and occupy the ladino identity category, the privilege associated with being and becoming ladino declines. Previously this privilege had a dual point of ref-erence: racial superiority for Indians and a higher position in the socio-economic hierarchy. Maya contestation has called the former into question, while the latter has also lost persuasive power. Young inhabitants of poor neighborhoods in Chimaltenango, for example, see increasing numbers of middle-class Mayas who have passed them by; even though aggregate national-level change has been slight in particular local settings like Chimaltenango, ladinos' nearly monopolistic grip on the local economy has loosened to the point where the association between ladino identity and economic privilege is no longer convincing. While class differentiation among ladinos is nothing new, previously even those at the bottom could find an enormous substratum of indigenous people below them. Now that same substratum has a more ambiguous relationship to the Indian-ladino binary: members of the substratum could be ladinos (no one will tell them they cannot be), but with little or no recourse to the racial privilege that being ladino previously entailed and with a deep sense of social distance from the "real" ladinos, who exude superiority through the clothes they wear, access to prestigious consumer goods, attendance at good private schools, etc. Part of the impetus to carve out a third, intermediate space of identity, then, is the awareness that being ladino comes with fewer guarantees than it once did. And for many poor, urban youth, actively affirming an identity as Maya holds little attraction. To be involved in Maya identity politics, these youth explain, requires educational and economic levels they lack; and, moreover, in their immediate surroundings they find indigenous culture to be lacking in vibrancy, *aguada* (watered down).

Referring to spaces in the indigenous-majority highlands where indigenous culture is aguada sounds odd, especially since these same spaces (or adjacent ones) are home to prodigious Maya cultural activism. It is crucial to avoid the evolutionary connotations "aguada" could take on in connection with the long-standing assertion that indigenous culture and identity, in the face of the rigors of modernity, are destined to disappear. In fact, the term has so much noxious baggage, I find it uncomfortable to use. But there has to be some way to interpret what people from these poor, urban neighborhoods consistently say about the culture change in their vicinity. When asked about indigenous language, they reply: "We don't hear it anymore." About practices associated with *cofradías* (religious brotherhoods) or the corn harvest: "Once upon a time, but not anymore." About cultural values (like respect for the elders)? "Yes, but some have them, some don't, just like everyone else." About the Maya *cosmovisión* (worldview)? "the what?" A young Maya woman who works with a youth organization in the barrio was the first to use the term "aguada" with us; in a discussion of such responses to our questions, she said:

"Indigenous culture is weak, superficial here; it doesn't motivate people . . . it's become *aguada*."

Without question, one factor contributing to this waning vibrancy of *lo indígena* (indigenous identity and culture) is continuing anti-Indian racism. Maya contestation of this racism has much more impact in middle-class arenas than in places like the poor neighborhoods of Chimaltenango. A young man in his late teens, with an indigenous mother and ladino father, explained to me how this racism operates:

> If you go around with a girl "*de corte*" (wearing traditional indigenous female dress), the others start bothering you. I don't like to go out in public with someone dressed like that. You act in that way because of what the others would say. When I was in afternoon [classes], I would some-times take a girl [de corte] home. When I passed a group of ladino guys they would bother us: "Look who he's going around with," and all that.[12]

In mixed company, commentary from ladinos frequently disparages the indigenous corte, as the same young man added, "Put on a skirt, so you can show off how pretty you are," and when the indigenous woman obliges, the commentary would be, "Now you're really looking good." This racial dis-paragement does not focus only on girls; it can also take place in conversa-tions about men. The same young man went on to explain:

> If you're dark-skinned, [ladinos] despise you more. I have a brother who's taller than I am, and whiter. He has much more influence among the ladinos because of that. One day we went together to that guy's group and he introduced me. They saw me and said, "You don't look like him. . . ." They were checking out my skin color. What happens is that they decide what group you belong to by the color of your skin. If two guys are trying to get the same job, the one with the white skin is always going to be preferred. The blond one always has the advantage. Even though you may have better ideas, experience, and everything, that doesn't matter.

People need a strong dose of self-confidence and reliable support networks to resist the painful effects of this kind of racial disparagement. Many are not that fortunate.

However, the aguada character of indigenous culture in poor barrios of Chimaltenango should not be understood solely as a result of responses to racial oppression. This would elide the sense in which affinity with the inter-mediate space of identity is also the result of creative initiative and political agency. The cholos' intense group identification, fortified by their cultural production in song and dance styles, is one example; another example can be taken from people not aligned with the gangs, who have developed their own individual strategies to get by and get ahead. I talked with a young indigenous woman and her mother about clothing preference, which continues to be a key identity marker. "When I go to church or to some family gathering, I wear indigenous clothing," the young woman explained, "but when I go out on the street, screwing around [with my friends], I prefer pants."[13] Her statement evokes a central (and, I contend, growing) tension between racist social pressure to abandon distinctive indigenous clothing, and creative initiative on the part of Indian youth to resist orthodoxies of all sorts and create something new. Yet the tension has also yielded a grey area, where it is not completely clear which of these two forces of change predominates. This young woman—and many like her in these poor barrios—apparently prefer it that way.

In Search of a Narrative Voice

The state appears to be absent in the poor barrios of Chimaltenango, the fertile ground of the cholos, but appearances can be deceptive. These barrios are the last areas to receive public utilities, and the first to lose them when problems—such as the drought of 1998—arise. The barrios lack public spaces, apart from dusty, unpaved streets. Even the schools tend to be of the "cooperative" variant, which means that parents have to help pay for their operation. Absent in most ways, the state exercises authority mainly by enforcing political and economic ground rules: government agreements with the owners of *maquilas* is one good example; the government's blocking the investigation of the assassination of a Maya human rights activist is another. The threat of widespread repression is always present, and, given the recent experience of horrendous state violence, this threat must be taken as anything but idle. In recent years, however, state violence has been selective and generally overshadowed by the drastic increase in what is known as *delincuencia común* (common violence). Given the levels of social misery and embattlement, active resistance from members of the intermediate sector is surprisingly rare, and much more individual than collective. To the extent that collective responses do prevail—as in the case of the cholos—the message is outright refusal of the conventional terms of political contention, rather than explicit political intervention of any sort. Most fascinating, but also a source of concern that signals the need for further research, is the utter anonymity of this sector, and the absence of a political force that could "represent" them—in both senses of the term.[14] Part of the explanation for this absence lies in the version of multiculturalism that the Guatemalan state has advanced since the mid-1990s.

Those who endorse this ideology of multiculturalism speak of indigenous people (or Maya) and ladinos; they invoke the interests of the Guatemalan nation and (at least in the more left-leaning versions of the ideology) of the popular sectors; but they have no language to refer to mestizos, or otherwise to identify those who occupy the intermediate spaces. Even as the ideology of multiculturalism calls for the free expression of identity, it encourages little exploration beyond the "four peoples" (of whom the Garífuna and Xinca are very small and politically marginal). In the absence of an identity category that could describe and provide a home for the mestizos, everyone proceeds as if mestizos do not exist. One assumes that Guatemala's political elite would have been open, at least in theory, to a version of the ideological formula applied in the rest of Central America and Mexico: an official ideology of mestizaje that downplays distinct identities and their associated cultural-political rights, an ideology that affirms a single national identity forged through the fusion of the two principal strands of racial-cultural heritage. At the level of public political discourse, however, this formula is no longer possible. On the one hand, the global rise of multiculturalism—the image of a society composed of diverse identity groups, each meriting recognition and bearing rights—works directly against the image of inextricable mixture on which mestizaje rests. On the other hand, the political ascendancy of Maya rights activism has made it more difficult for state-aligned forces to recognize and promote the mestizos.

Intellectual-activists of the Maya movement generally consider mestizos to be products of the assimilationist policies of the dominant institutions, policies that are vehemently opposed by the Maya movement. Shortly after my arrival in Chimaltenango in the mid-1990s, a Maya activist gave me a clear answer in response to a general question about the demographic composition of the city: "The great majority is indigenous" he affirmed, "but in terms of consciousness, there are very few, perhaps 5 percent." This activist further noted the multiple forces of change and their impact on indigenous culture and identity—from large-scale employment in the maquilas to new patterns of global consumption; the words that he and others typically use to describe the results of these changes have an unambiguously negative ring: "displacement," "loss," "alienation." These same Maya intellectuals have argued, with considerable success, that there is no contradiction between, for example, maintaining strong indigenous identities and using computers, wearing Nike shoes, and driving SUVs. But for this much-celebrated hybridity to fit within a vibrant Maya movement, its protagonists must advance a heterogeneous and capacious notion of Maya identity, one that embraces people who live in diverse class and cultural contexts. Otherwise, those such as the cholos, who have contact mainly with a "watered down" indigenous culture, who are forging multiple identities that include but are not limited to "*lo maya*," are apt to be ignored or deplored. A difficult dilemma underlies this contrast: how to critique the facets of these mestizo sensibilities that reflect racism and assimilationist pressures, while at the same time affirming the aspects that are creative, critical, and even potentially liberating.

Judging from the two neighborhoods of Chimaltenango where I worked in 1998, the only organizations that show an interest in the mestizo inhabitants are NGOs funded especially to work in these areas. An NGO called Solidarity with Youth and Children (SNJ) is illustrative. Founded in the mid-1990s to carry out education and training among youth in poor neighborhoods, SNJ's methods involved the formation of youth groups focused on raising self-esteem, reinforcing a sense of collective identity, and generating alternatives to drugs and gangs. The organization had been well funded of late, thanks to the optimism of the times (especially the recently signed Peace Accords) and the energy of its coordinator, a ladino from eastern Guatemala named Gabriel. For their funding from USAID, SNJ had agreed to do a "diagnostic" of the neighborhoods where it was working. Perplexed by the number of respondents whose declared identities did not fit the standard ladino-indigenous binary, and pressured by an upcoming deadline imposed by the funding agency, Gabriel asked me to help. With two young SNJ promoters as guides, I spent about a month exploring two neighborhoods, documenting the life conditions of their inhabitants.

After leaving school, young people from these neighborhoods confront two paths of social organization: the gangs and the evangelical churches. These options offer strikingly similar solutions to the problems that youth confront: affirmation once the individual has joined and agreed to respect basic norms; a sense of community and a support network; a doctrine and strong leaders to respect and follow. In short, the gangs and the evangelical churches offer barrio youth an identity, one more concrete and meaningful than the abstract identity categories of indigenous and ladino. These concrete identities fit nicely with the image of an intermediate space—indeed they help to constitute that space. But for this very reason, they offer little in the way of a unifying message. To the contrary, they foster internal conflict and fragmentation: gang members criticize the authorities, but they also fight incessantly among themselves; evangelical churches proliferate and often enter into direct competition with one another. Beyond these similarities, of course, the gangs and the evangelicals are separated by mutually affirmed differences in values and morality—yet another impetus for fragmentation. Organizations like SNJ had nothing serious to offer in the face of this heterogeneity—Gabriel and his staff had their hands full discharging minimal commitments to guarantee the next disbursement of funds. To imagine a narrative voice that could speak across this heterogeneity to the basic commonality of conditions in these barrios, one would have to look beyond present political horizons.

Consequences: A Mestizaje from Below?

Belonging to the cholos affirms a local identity. Members obey group norms (such as clothing and lines of authority), learn specific cultural practices (such as the mortal), and enjoy the benefits of membership (solidarity, mutual aid, and equal treatment). In addition, becoming a cholo allows the member to critique marginalization at the hands of the dominant society and to refuse the established ethnic ideology. It is as if members were saying, "We do not care if we are indigenous or ladino, either way, we would be equally marginalized." Among those who occupy these intermediate spaces, there are many specific identities that have nothing to do with cholos; but members of intermediate groups may share the cholos' diffuse critique of the dominant society and their refusal of the ethnic binomial. Beyond this diffuse critique, and beyond the widespread identity category confusion—among civil registry officials, NGO operatives, and the like—what social and political consequences follow from the rise of this intermediate sector? Rather than provide a definitive answer to this question, I offer four possible scenarios: continued anonymity, absorption within the logic of neoliberal multiculturalism, articulation with a project of right-wing populism, and, lastly, an alternative political vision I will call "mestizaje from below." I cannot discern which scenario is more likely, given the preliminary character of the research, and the relative novelty of the social process under study. Needless to say, my own political sympathies lie with the image of mestizaje from below.

Given the potential support for the "four peoples" model and the associated multiculturalism ideal, it seems unlikely that intermediate categories like "cholo" or even "mestizo" will soon congeal as collectively assumed identities, widely recognized and viewed as bearers of rights. While it is true that the established ethnic ideology—separate and unequal—is in decline, its ascendant replacement conveys an image of distinct identity groups, each with its own bounded culture and associated rights, each enjoying formal equality in regard to the others. This ascendant ideology—which I have called neoliberal multiculturalism—leaves little space for collective mestizo agency. Granted, those who occupy the intermediate spaces need not ask for permission to speak. However, as long as they lack a narrator, a collective political voice, their agency will remain limited and relatively anonymous. In my judgment, the great losers in this scenario, in addition to the mestizos themselves, are the protagonists of the Maya movement. A strong collective political assertion on the part of the "mestizos" could include a direct challenge to Guatemala's persisting racism, a central goal of Maya cultural activists as well.

A second scenario involves absorption within the ethnic ideology of neoliberal multiculturalism, which has been on the rise in fits and starts since the early 1990s, and especially since the signing of the Peace Accords in 1996. In regard to cultural rights, neoliberal multiculturalism sends an ambivalent message: recognition of the four peoples and their associated rights, but opposition to the more expansive demands of the Maya movement. Neoliberal multiculturalism endorses the full and free expression of Maya identity, but within limits, without calling into question the basic tenets of the political-economic system. The great hope embedded in this emergent ethnic ideology is that the recognition of difference will lead directly and promptly to a higher principle of unity—a refashioned "multiethnic" and "pluricultural" nation with which all Guatemalans could identify. Those positioned in the intermediate spaces, even if they lack recognition as one of the four peoples, could claim citizenship rights directly, by virtue of belonging to the nation. In this scenario, the neoliberal state needs the absence of powerful counterdiscourses more than it needs active endorsement from the mestizos. The absence of a counternarrative is especially important among inhabitants of poor barrios, whose dissatisfaction is so close to the surface and combustible. To the extent that the mestizos are absorbed within the project of neoliberal multiculturalism, the articulation will retain two principal sources of instability. First, as mestizos particular identities continue to be ignored and denied, except in the most general sense of their belonging to the Guatemalan nation, multiculturalism for them will lack credibility. Second, their precarious material conditions will constantly be threatened by the neoliberal economic model, which makes them feel disposable and redundant.

For these very reasons, the third scenario seems more likely, and even more worrisome: the mestizos could become active adherents of a right-wing populism that capitalizes on deep resentment toward political-economic elites, but stops short of racial or class empowerment. The administration of Alfonso Portillo (2000–04) had strong tendencies along these lines. In his presidential campaign, Portillo promised to support and advance the Peace Accords, but his close alliance with the most recalcitrant and brutal sectors of the armed forces told a different story. Portillo's stance toward the Maya movement was similarly conflicted, a strange combination of the inclusion of key Maya intellectuals in his government (e.g., Demetrio Cojtí, Virgilio Alvarado, Otilia Lux de Cojtí) and opposition to many of the most cherished Maya demands (e.g., constitutional reforms proposed in the "Consulta Popular"). The ambiguity surrounding Portillo's commitment to multiculturalism extended to neoliberalism as well. Some of his policies and much of his administration's discourse took on a decidedly antioligarchic tone, which enraged those identified with the capitalist class and thrilled many of the popular sectors; yet he stopped far short of substantive redistribution and strayed very little from neoliberal orthodoxies. The best encapsulation of Portillo's populist appeal can be found in an effective campaign phrase, which emerged as he capitalized on a colossal political error of his principal rival, the Party of National Advancement (PAN). In an unguarded moment, a spokesperson from PAN referred to the Republican Guatemalan Front (FRG) as the "party of the *xumos*" (a deprecatory term for Indians or lower class ladinos), a phrase that the FRG then readily adopted to whip up support among the poor and marginalized majority. Many Mayas apparently decided that if elites from the ruling party disparaged the FRG as "xumos," their support for the FRG should follow. Yet the term "xumo" is ambiguous, combining a specific racial connotation with a more general meaning—out of place, lumpen, disreputable—precisely the characteristics associated with intermediate groups. Perhaps if the Portillo administration had not been so corrupt and inept, and so directly associated with the perpetrators of war crimes during the previous decade, the FRG's appeal as the party of the xumos might have soared, capturing the imagination of intermediate social groups like Chimaltenango's cholos.

Finally, it is possible that those who inhabit the intermediate spaces might forge a collective political voice of their own. It is a striking characteristic of the present moment that no established political force has stepped forward to play that role. In the absence of an official discourse of mestizaje, possibilities emerge for a mestizaje from below with the potential to mobilize without having to homogenize, to challenge racism and economic marginalization without having to discipline boundaries and pledge loyalty to a given collective identity and politics. This scenario is deeply attractive but highly contradictory; for its potential to be realized, the most serious contradictions would have to be addressed. The signature characteristic of these intermediate social groups is their refusal of the identity binaries, their insistence on local and multiple forms of identification. How can an aggregation of people, positioned in this way, mobilize the political power necessary to effect change without affirming a minimally homogeneous group identity? This question evokes the famous phrase of José Carlos Mariátegui from the 1920s: "The indigenous people of Peru await their Lenin." The Lenin that the cholos of Chimaltenango might await would have an improbable collection of qualities: she would wear the cholos' signature *ropa tumbada* (baggy clothing) without denigrating the indigenous corte; she would mortalear with the graceful charisma of Johnny and Chino; she would participate fully in patterns of global consumption while also affirming a distinctive local identity. Most importantly, she would have found a way to cultivate creative expressions of rebellion against injustice, without recourse to the identity orthodoxies that the cholos so adamantly refuse.

Notes

An earlier version of this chapter was published in Spanish in *Memorias del mestizaje: Cultura política en Centroamérica de 1920 al presente*, edited by Darío A. Euraque, Jeffrey L. Gould, and Charles R. Hale (Antigua: CIRMA, 2005). This chapter was written in the late 1990s and is grounded in that particular political moment: the immediate aftermath of Guatemala's three-decade civil war. This chapter does not consider how recent political developments may have influenced or altered the role of the intermediate social groups discussed here, but it does raise questions about a cultural and political process that has ongoing significance in Guatemalan society.

1. This heterogeneity is so great that scholars have doubted whether all those categorized as ladinos would actually identify as such. Analysts such as Martínez (1971) and Guzmán Bockler and Herbert (1971) have emphasized that white Guatemalans (also called *criollos*) often denied any connection with the ladino identity category, which they disdained. Analysts such as Adams (1956) emphasized the other side

of this heterogeneity: persons and communities supposedly in "transition" from indigenous to ladino. A parallel observation of heterogeneity could of course be made regarding the generalizing category "indigenous."

2. An example of this approach to the problem of ethnic-racial relations, with good results, would be the work of Williams (1989 and 1991). Also influential is work in the tradition of critical race studies, such as Smith (1995), Gilroy (1987), Hall (1996), and Omi and Winant (1987).

3. This omission can be justified, in part, by the fact that indigenous perspectives on this and related topics have been so extensively documented, while minimal ethnographic work involves efforts to "study up." Two important exceptions are Casaús Arzú (1991) and Schirmer (1998). The first made a major contribution to our understanding of the established ethnic ideology; the second somewhat less, given her primary emphasis on the political logic of military rule and her limited ability to move interview questions in directions that her military informants might have found uncomfortable.

4. This problem of the relationship between social science representation and political process is taken up and analyzed masterfully by García and Lucero (in this volume) in regard to anthropological representations of indigenous politics.

5. Field research carried out in Chimaltenango, together with Silvia Barreno, my research assistant. For more information, see Hale 2006.

6. See Quijano 1980 and 2000.

7. I must acknowledge the central influence of the historical research of the Center for Research on MesoAmerica (CIRMA) team, coordinated by Dr. Arturo Taracena Arriola, on my thinking here. See especially the major volume, Taracena 2002, and his chapter in this volume.

8. Adams 1994.

9. Paula is a university student in social work who lived in the neighborhood where the research was carried out, May 1998.

10. Interview with Johnny, one of the leaders of the Cholos, in Chimaltenango, May 1998.

11. Correspondingly, the widespread spatial separation between Indian and Ladino still exists, but is much diminished.

12. Interview with Edgar, who lived in one of the marginal neighborhoods of Chimaltenango, May 1998.

13. This young woman lives in a marginal neighborhood of Chimaltenango. The interview was conducted in May 1998.

14. The two meanings of "representation" are delineated nicely in Spivak 1994.

Authenticating Indians and Movements: Interrogating Indigenous Authenticity, Social Movements, and Fieldwork in Contemporary Peru

MARÍA ELENA GARCÍA AND JOSÉ ANTONIO LUCERO

In May 2003, we traveled to Cochabamba, Bolivia, to present a cowritten paper at a conference on Indigenous movements and the state in Latin America. Our paper examined recent Indigenous mobilization in Peru and responded critically to assertions, common among scholars (and funders) of Indigenous movements in Latin America, that Peru represented a surprising case of Indigenous movement "absence."[1] Our contention was that most analyses of the Peruvian case ignored the richness of Indigenous politics in the country, choosing instead to focus on the apparent inability of Indigenous organizing to coalesce nationally.[2] Amid the explosion in the past decade of conferences and publications addressing the "return of the Indian" in the region, the Peruvian case appeared only as a question mark; an exception to the more general rule of rising Indigenous political visibility.[3]

Our presentation drew from two sets of fieldwork experiences in Peru: García's dissertation research (conducted between 1996 and 1999) on the politics of intercultural education aimed at Indigenous highland communities, and a joint research trip (in June 2002) focused on exploring the politics of Indigenous organizations. Much of the paper's empirical evidence was based on fieldwork carried out in 2002. During this trip, we learned about important new organizations, such as the National Coordinator of Communities Affected by Mining (CONACAMI) and the Permanent Conference of the Indigenous Peoples of Peru (COPPIP).[4] We were already familiar with mobilization at both local and transnational scales, but what struck us immediately was how much was happening at a national level. In addition to the emergence of CONACAMI and COPPIP, a new state agency, the National Commission for Andean, Amazonian, and Afro-Peruvian Peoples (CONAPA), headed by former first lady Eliane Karp, seemed to promise at least the possibility for real change.[5] In the midst of this effervescence of political activity, there were, of course, tensions within and between organizations.

In the paper we presented in Cochabamba, we looked favorably upon the organizations that used the transnational social networks that recent scholarship has celebrated.[6] We were much more skeptical of organizations and individuals that seemed to retain elements of *Indianista* ideology, that is to say, those who proclaimed a more essentialist and radical Indian nationalism.[7] Though the paper was well received by many of the conference participants, the commentators on the panel, an Aymara leader from Peru and a Kichwa leader from Ecuador, were clearly bothered by the choices we had made, which cast some organizations in a more favorable light than others. While both commentators agreed with our critique of the prevailing descriptions of Peruvian absence, they were highly critical of the voices we had privileged. The leaders we found professional and representative, they saw as politically compromised and "inauthentic." The leaders we described as Indianista and isolated, they saw as organic and legitimate.

Our encounter with Indigenous commentators raised questions about the ideas behind their criticism and the role of "authenticators" of Indigenous identity and politics.[8] What counts as an Indigenous movement? Who is a "legitimate" representative of Indigenous demands? How do we, as social scientists, engage with, investigate, and write about Indigenous movements?

Approaching Peru: Writing Against Absence

As has been widely documented, the two decades between 1980 and 2000 in Peru were years of violent political conflict and authoritarian rule.[9] This violence and terror produced by the war between the state and leftist opposition forces, most notably *Sendero Luminoso* (the Peruvian Maoist organization known as the Shining Path), exacted a human toll that the recent (2003) report of the Truth and Reconciliation Commission puts at close to 70,000 deaths. This context of conflict and repression has been part of the explanation that scholars give for the relative absence of political mobilization among Indigenous populations in Peru. Compared to its neighbors (Ecuador and Bolivia, in particular), Peru seemed to lack the visible national presence of Indigenous confederations like the Confederation of Indigenous

Nationalities of Ecuador (CONAIE) or the Confederation of Indigenous Peoples of Bolivia.

This lack of social-movement activity, some scholars argue, had much to do with a much more hostile political environment in Peru than in other Andean countries and thus a less hospitable political opportunity structure.[10] Other scholars looked less to explain absence and more to capture the particular cultural dynamics that have characterized racial and ethnic relations in Peru historically. For instance, the use of leftist labels in forging rural "peasant" identities, the appropriation of Inca histories and mythologies by elites, and the complex nature of Peruvian racial mixture and internal migration that produced various interstitial identities that defied easy classification as simply Indigenous.[11] Indeed, the contested nature of Peruvian racial identities (who is really "Indigenous"?) is at the heart of recent debates over Indigenous politics. As a self-identified Quechua intellectual commented, "[In Peru] we have a long way to go. Before we can organize as Indigenous peoples, we must *be* Indigenous people."[12] Unlike Ecuador, where *indígena* has become a political identity common to both highland and lowland groups, Peru's racial and regional landscapes are characterized by unstable and shifting labels, including *campesino, andino, mestizo, nativo,* and *indígena.* The complexity of racial identifications in Peru has been read by many scholars as a lack of a consolidated Indigenous identity, which makes speaking of an Indigenous movement difficult.[13]

While these observations contained many persuasive elements in their analysis of the contrasts among Andean republics, to our eyes, the accounts of Peruvian exceptionalism had some important drawbacks. By privileging national social-movement organizations, scholars often tended to minimize the importance of local or regional actors that did impact national and transnational Indigenous politics. From García's research on education policies, we learned that Quechua parents in local communities, as well as Indigenous intellectuals in transnational institutes, were connected in important struggles over the content and implementation of intercultural education policies.[14] Other scholars had similarly documented the ways in which local peoples engaged and transformed transnational development agendas, often in dramatic ways.[15] Moreover, Amazonian organizations had a longer history in Peru than in many places in Ecuador or Bolivia, with the Amuesha Congress, established in the 1960s, being among the first Indigenous organizations to form in the continent.[16] In the highlands, Indigenous people had organized in peasant federations, as well as *rondas campesinas* (self-defense community organizations), during times of political unrest.[17] Thus, labeling the variegated and complex patterns of Indigenous politics as "absence" or "failure" seems to miss important parts of the story.

This skepticism about Peruvian exceptionalism was reinforced by political developments, as the fall of the Alberto Fujimori regime seemed to suggest the beginnings of a democratic opening in post-Sendero Peru. Moreover, the work of the Truth and Reconciliation Commission (2001–2003) brought to national attention the horrors lived primarily by Indigenous peoples and gave way to a national conversation over the rights of Indigenous Peruvians. While we believed that these openings would influence Indigenous politics in the country, we wanted to resist the teleological talk of observers who saw Peru as simply "catching up" with the regionwide "return" of Indigenous actors to national politics. Still, we went into our short field trip to Peru expecting to find a landscape of Indigenous politics that contrasted with the barren vistas of some prevailing scholarly accounts.

This expectation was also nourished by the fact that Oxfam America, an important actor in the transnational network of Indigenous politics in Latin America, had its regional office in Lima, Peru. In our previous work, we gained a deep appreciation and respect for the work of Oxfam, one of the first funders of organizations like CONAIE.[18] Oxfam professionals had been key informants in Lucero's and other scholars' research on Ecuadorian and Bolivian Indigenous movements.[19] We had also previously met with the Oxfam team on a research trip in 2001 and had subsequently invited members of the team to participate in a conference held later that year at Princeton University on Indigenous politics and development in Latin America. As could be expected, we counted many members of the Oxfam team not only as helpful professionals but also as friends. Thus it was no surprise that the office of Oxfam was almost our first stop in Lima when we arrived in June 2002.

Given that we were only staying in the country for a few weeks, we were very glad to accept Oxfam's help in setting up interviews with many of the Indigenous organizations, both new and old, working in the country. We were interested in Oxfam's and these organizations' perspectives on the changing state-society matrix in Peru. The picture we found is provided in greater detail in the paper we would later present in Cochabamba, but a brief discussion of the role of the state and the emergence of new Indigenous actors can help contextualize the conflicting views that emerged in Bolivia.

Relying on interviews and secondary sources, we realized that the period after the fall of Fujimori but before the election of Alejandro Toledo was a crucial moment for Indigenous advocacy. The interim administration of Valentín Paniagua responded to the demands of Amazonian Indigenous leaders by creating *"mesas de diálogo"* (forums for dialogue) that convoked experts and Indigenous leaders from throughout the country to discuss the needs and demands of various Indigenous communities. This period was described as a "window of opportunity" for Indigenous rights, one that seemed to close (somewhat surprisingly) with the election of Alejandro Toledo in 2001.

Despite making much of his Andean ancestry, especially with an unprecedented special ceremony at Machu Picchu as part of his inauguration, Toledo seemed to give Indigenous issues less attention than his predecessor had. Toledo's wife, Eliane Karp, played a much more visible role in the elaboration of a state response to Indigenous demands by heading the new agency for Indigenous and Afro-Peruvian affairs, known by the acronym CONAPA and often referred to as the *"comisión* Karp."[20] CONAPA sought to channel the new international funds (notably a $5 million World Bank loan) in a new development agenda for Indigenous and Afro-Peruvian communities. She also sought to establish a space for Indigenous representation in the Toledo government and advance the discussion over multicultural constitutional reforms. Some, including Oxfam director Martin Scurrah and many Indigenous leaders, saw Karp's commission as an important and visible space for Indigenous issues.[21] Others, however, were critical of the paternalism that came in such practices as Karp's naming the members of the commission herself and of the potential danger of the state's co-opting Indigenous organizations.[22]

In addition to new changes in state policies, there were also important developments in civil society. Joining older Amazonian organizations like the Inter-Ethnic Association for the Development of the Peruvian Jungle (AIDESEP), CONACAMI, a new highland organization, gained prominence in discussions about Indigenous mobilization. CONACAMI was primarily concerned with the impacts of mining on highland communities and was hardly a replica of the kinds of ethnic federations found in the Peruvian lowlands or in other countries. However, as CONACAMI represented many Quechua-speaking highland communities, many actors, including Oxfam, described CONACAMI as an important highland Indigenous counterpart to lowland federations. Interestingly, Oxfam and other international nongovernmental organizations funded exchanges between the leadership of Ecuadorian, Bolivian, and Peruvian organizations that included CONACAMI and other more "established" Indigenous actors like CONAIE and CONAMAQ, a new federation of ayllus in Bolivia. CONACAMI, along with AIDESEP and others, became part of a new national organization that was known as the Permanent Conference of the Indigenous Peoples of Peru (COPPIP).

Reporting these findings to our Indigenous and non-Indigenous colleagues in Cochabamba began a discussion over the precise nature of these new national developments and organizations. Our Indigenous critics allowed us to gain a more complex appreciation of the "filling" of Peruvian absence. Moreover, their critique put in high relief how our own position in social networks influenced our narrative of Peruvian Indigenous politics. One important lesson about ethnographic positionality came when we realized that COPPIP was not one organization, but rather two. The tensions between these two COPPIPs, and our initial failure to see them, say much about the process of "authenticating" Indigenous actors and the importance of engaged and self-reflexive research.

Indigenous Responses: Lessons in Ethnographic Uncertainty

We first learned about the existence of COPPIP, a national Indigenous organization and the very thing that most scholars claimed was absent in Peru, through interviews at Oxfam and the highland organization, CONACAMI. These interviews suggested that while still in the early stages of its development, this "permanent conference" offered the possibility of a larger pan-regional organization like those found in other countries. To find out more about what this organization was about, we set up a meeting with the new technical secretary of COPPIP, Jorge Agurto. Agurto, a non-Indigenous advisor, had a history of collaboration with Indigenous organizations on legal and political matters and was very well versed in the international and regional contexts for Indigenous politics. His office was in the headquarters of AIDESEP, the Amazonian organization, and his authority as an important advisor was evident to us. He received us warmly, provided detailed answers to all our questions and recounted the evolution of COPPIP. His narrative of COPPIP's trajectory was echoed by the accounts we were offered by our contacts at Oxfam, CONACAMI, and the Instituto del Bien Común, a relatively new NGO headed by Richard Chase Smith, formerly head of Indigenous programs for Oxfam.

The narrative, in broad strokes, went as follows. COPPIP was conceived during a meeting in Cuzco in 1997. It was established as a "conference" that would provide a non-hierarchical space in which a variety of Indigenous organizations could come together, without ceding their autonomy or identity, and discuss matters of common concern. Because it was a possible articulating space for highland and lowland organizations, it attracted considerable transnational attention and support from North American and European funders. Things began to get difficult, however, when Agurto resigned his post as technical secretary and was replaced by Javier Lajo, a controversial self-identified Quechua intellectual. In this story, Lajo was cast as the villain. As numerous people informed us, Lajo was affiliated with an old Indianista organization known as the Indian Council of South America (CISA). During the 1970s, CISA claimed to speak for Indigenous communities, though critics argued that the organization had few links to the rural countryside and had a radical discourse that shared more with the anticolonialism of thinkers like Frantz Fanon and Fausto Reinaga than the demands of local Indigenous leaders.[23] As several scholars have noted, Indianista voices were often loud, but not representative.[24] Moreover, in Peru, where ethnic identities are often the subject of debate, doubts over the authenticity of Indigenous identities can have politically significant consequences. Many students and funders of Indigenous organizations believed the Indianista currents in Lajo's work were the sins of his past. His sins of the present had to do with his alleged closeness to Eliane Karp and what critics thought was his use of political connections to secure jobs and funds for those close to him. According to Agurto, Smith, and others, Lajo's mismanagement of COPPIP resulted in a loss of international support and funds, including the help of Oxfam. It was not until Lajo left his post and Agurto returned to the post of technical secretary that COPPIP's transnational resources were re-established. This was, more or less, the story we told in Cochabamba. As it would turn out, this was (as we should have known) only one version of the story.

The conference we attended in Cochabamba was in some ways the ideal venue for a discussion of Indigenous politics. Unlike so many academic conferences on Indigenous questions, this one was held in a place where Indigenous people were not simply the subjects of papers but active participants in discussion and debate. The conference was sponsored by several local NGOs and a postgraduate program for Indigenous students from various South American countries. Because of the conference's sponsors and its being held in Bolivia, where approximately 60–70 percent of the population is Indigenous, the panels and presentations were more than simply academic. Indigenous presenters and commentators made the conference an exciting and slightly intimidating space for sharing our still tentative conclusions about Peruvian politics. Despite the horizontal and participatory nature of the conference, some participants still worried about lingering colonial legacies in a space where many of the panelists were foreign professors, often from the United States or Europe, and many of the discussants were Indigenous students. Moreover, there was a distinction between Indigenous activists (many of whom were now in an Andean graduate program) and students of Indigenous politics (most of whom resided in various parts of the "First World"). One of the Indigenous participants remarked during one of the conference sessions, "It is one thing to make a journey of a thousand kilometers and then tell others about it. It is another to talk about the journey without ever having made it." While never hostile, remarks like this one served to challenge the authority of "outside experts."

Still, this kind of encounter between Indigenous, non-Indigenous, Latin American, North American, and European observers and activists promised to be the kind of space that anthropologists have rightly begun to insist upon, one that seeks to decolonize the ethnographic and academic divide between the "field" and the "academy."[25] In this spirit, we were eager to hear the reactions of the conference participants and commentators on our panel.

We met briefly with our commentator, Brígida Peraza, a young Aymara Peruvian leader from the National Union of Aymara Communities, and she hinted that she had some strong reactions to our paper, a case of Aymara understatement if there ever was one. While agreeing with our central complaint about the prevailing academic account of Peruvian failure, she took issue not only with the narrative we crafted about the rise of COPPIP, but the voices we relied upon to relay it. The Oxfam sources, she suggested, were hardly the most objective or reliable. In addition, she contended that the Indianismo of Javier Lajo was not as unrepresentative as we seemed to imply.

The other commentator on our panel, Luis Maldonado of Ecuador, also had several reactions to our paper. Maldonado was one of the better-known Indigenous leaders at the conference. He had been an important member of CONAIE's inner circle and had "jumped scales" to lead state and multilateral institutions. In Ecuador, he had been named to the cabinet-level position of executive secretary of the Council for the Development of Indigenous and Afro-Ecuadorian Peoples. He had also been named Minister of Social Welfare. Later, he had been selected to head the multilateral Indigenous Fund, based in La Paz. He was part of the relatively recently formed group of transnational Indigenous elites. He echoed many of Peraza's concerns and was particularly bothered by the ways we had characterized older leaders like his friend Lajo.

In the question and answer session that followed our panel, there were several favorable reactions to our paper, many of which came from our North American colleagues. Moreover, Peraza's comments helped generate a healthy discussion about previous writings on Peruvian politics and our own provisional conclusions about recent changes. Upon hearing the comments and criticisms of the Indigenous commentators and other participants, many of the shortcomings of our research became quickly apparent. While we stood by many of the conclusions of the paper, we recognized that the more critical sections of the story should not have been personalized, blaming one or two individuals like Javier Lajo, with whom, regrettably, we did not speak during our brief research trip. We assured both our commentators that the present version of our paper was only a preliminary exploration and that their comments would be very much a part of the next draft, which we began writing upon our return to the United States.

Within days of our return, however, we received an e-mail message from Luis Enrique López, the director of the Andean graduate program that hosted the conference. With a tone of concern and urgency, López informed us that he was forwarding a response to our paper from Javier Lajo, something that López encouraged us to "take seriously" before we published the piece. We had no problem taking seriously Lajo's or anyone else's comments about our paper, but we were unprepared for the criticism that Lajo made of a draft that we had never intended for circulation. Lajo clearly had taken our paper seriously, though. Not only did he write an angry missive, he wrote an extended thirteen-page review essay on our paper, which he titled "Commentary on 'Un País Sin Indígenas' (UPSI): Indigenous Invisibility in Peru" (published later as Lajo 2005). Before summarizing the extensive dialogue that emerged from this correspondence, we should note that the tone of our exchange quickly evolved from one of personalized anger to one of civil reconsideration and friendly collaboration. One is tempted to say that this "review process" was more helpful and enriching than the ones usually privileged in academic circles. But it didn't begin that way.

Lajo's initial letter informed us that our paper was sent to him by the "Indigenous brothers and sisters" that had been at the conference, and who were alarmed by the content of what he came to abbreviate as UPSI (from the Spanish title of our paper). Contending that many of our claims were "false or inexact," he stated that he felt he had to respond since he had been cast in the "worst role of the film" and been the victim of "libelous and malevolent accusations, something very odd in an academic presentation." Moreover, according to him, we had cast Richard Chase Smith, Oxfam America, and other "foreign agents" and "yanqui anthropologists" as the "saviors" of Indigenous people. In his letter, addressed to López, he asks for our addresses so that he can respond directly to those who seek "to liquidate, bomb, and bury the Indianista perspective in Peru and South America."

The news that we were liquidators of anything was in itself a shock, and the idea that we had sided with the forces of imperialist anthropology against local Indigenous people did provoke an emotional response of our own. We felt misunderstood and maligned. But then this was precisely how Lajo described his own reaction to our paper. Rather than give in to feelings of academic defensiveness, however, we tried to make our way through the misunderstandings and take advantage of the opportunity to clarify our position and to learn more about his. In our response to Lajo, we recognized and apologized for our failure to get his or any other Indianista perspective during the course of our interviews. Moreover, we emphasized our own previous work with Indigenous communities and organizations in Ecuador, Bolivia, and Peru to make it clear that we took very seriously his indictment of a "yanqui" social science that was more concerned with the professional demands of the "North" than the realities of the "South." Finally, we asked for his assistance in correcting the biases that he saw in our account, while making it clear that we probably did disagree on some important matters of interpretation. We learned much in our correspondence with Lajo about the turbulent trajectory of COPPIP, gained a new perspective on the debate over the role of indianismo, and deepened our central contention about the authenticating power of NGOs and social science.

Rethinking Indigenous Representation: The "Other" COPPIP

One of the more important findings we offered in our Cochabamba paper was on the emergence of COPPIP, a national Indigenous organization in Peru that articulated highland and lowland organizations for the first time. As we reported above, our interviews suggested that this "permanent conference" was born in Cuzco in 1997, that it lost international funding due to leadership problems at the end of the decade and then was reconsolidated in 2002 under new leadership that re-established important transnational ties. We would learn after the Cochabamba meeting that the conference would be "promoted" to the status of "*coordinadora*" giving the loose assemblage a more institutionalized presence. The "new" COPPIP was headed by Miguel Palacín, who was also president of CONACAMI, the new highland federation. COPPIP and CONACAMI were, in our estimation, important elements of the new Indigenous representation in Peru. While this view was shared by other regional federations (like AIDESEP) and transnational NGOs (like Oxfam), other sectors of the Indigenous movement in Peru had different opinions.

In the course of our correspondence with Lajo, we learned of another competing account of the changes in COPPIP. Contradicting the story we heard of a "*conferencia*" becoming a coordinadora, Lajo and others suggested a narrative of schism, not evolution. Soon we found ourselves on the electronic mailing lists of two organizations, both using the same COPPIP acronym. Puzzled by this, we wrote to the "other" COPPIP, the one not headed by Palacín or supported by Oxfam, and asked if someone could clarify this apparent case of double identity. The response from a member of COPPIP (the conferencia) came quickly and sharply (and it is worth quoting at length):

> The differences between the *false* COPPIP-Coordinadora and the authentic COPPIP-Conferencia [are the following]: 1. COPPIP-Coordinadora is a Puppet-COPPIP, a puppet of the North American funders that in a temporary alliance (from August 2000–May of 2002) with the Karp elites attempted and accomplished the division of the Permanent Conference of the Indigenous Peoples of Peru. Now this corrupt alliance has ruptured and we are living its consequences: two factions disputing control of a $5 million World Bank loan. 2. Our Indigenous organization was founded in December 1997, in Cuzco with the name of Conferencia. 3. In contrast, the Coordinadora (False COPPIP or Puppet COPPIP) was founded just last year [2003] through a registration in the Public Registry in Lima where four organizations, one Indigenous organization (AIDESEP) plus three NGOs (ADECAP, CHIRAPAQ, and CONACAMI), painfully expropriated our acronym, COPPIP, one that we had already reserved . . . 4. This irregular behavior, odd in any Indigenous organization, takes place because foreign organizations, like Oxfam-America, control them. They are able to lobby "indigenista" funders and mining companies. They want to manipulate Indigenous people to allow them to become authenticators of environmental questions, allowing them to choose who approves or rejects permits and environmental impact studies . . . [26]

This response continues for several pages and goes on to request our help in investigating their indictments against "foreign" actors in general and Oxfam in particular. Explaining that a serious study is needed of Oxfam's work, the message asked us as social scientists to explore the accusations that Oxfam subverts the highland movement in order to keep Indigenous movements isolated in the lowlands, that it works in coordination with mining companies, and that it not only controls individual leaders, but seeks to set the criteria for Indigenous legitimacy and authenticity. The letter urges us to compare Oxfam's ideology with that of well-known Indianista thinkers like Javier Lajo and Indianista leaders like Felipe Quispe, the Aymara leader of Bolivia who has called for the creation of a separate Indigenous state. Aranwan, the author of this letter, explains:

> The theorists of Oxfam-A[merica] assure us that the projects of these [Indianista] Indigenous movements are not authentic. For example, they claim that CONAMAQ, a confederation in Bolivia [of ayllus] that is financed and controlled by Oxfam, is authentic. But this is baffling. How could a political force be more radical than Felipe Quispe? All this is to say, the North American funding agencies and controllers are judging who is Indigenous and who is not. A scientific study of this would be worthwhile.[27]

We are not attempting to answer the call for an investigation of Oxfam here, nor do we claim to be able to settle which account of the emergence and division of COPPIP is the right one. We do, however, want to explore some of the important themes that this controversy offers.

Reflections on Frameworks, Models, and Methods

In a 1983 paper on Indigenous organizations, Richard Chase Smith suggested that ethnic, campesino, and Indianista organizations varied in terms of their identity, autonomy, and representativity. Because Smith was for many years one of the guiding hands at Oxfam-America, his typology is helpful for understanding the partnerships and decisions that Oxfam-America, and perhaps other international NGOs, made in regard to supporting Indigenous causes. In his typology, the collective identities of "campesino" and "Indianista" organizations were refracted through the ideological oppositions of class analysis (workers versus capital) and anti-colonial radicalism (colonizers versus colonized). Ethnic federations were less tied to such grand theories and had more plural notions of identity. In terms of autonomy, all organizations responded in some degree to "outside" interests, though Indianistas were most vocal in refusing "to make any alliance with outside groups which may be 'tinged' with non-Indian domination."[28] As for the last criterion, representativity, Smith made it clear that, unlike ethnic or campesinista federations, the usually urban Indianista organizations tended to lack connections with rural bases and were therefore the "least" representative of the three types of movements. Smith's typology suggested that representative Indigenous organizations should be independent from rigid ideologies and the tutelage of political parties or outside actors, and should connect leaders at the top with communities at the base.

The controversy over COPPIP seems to raise questions about the political and cultural workings of the selection processes of international funders who rely on typologies like Smith's. Perhaps most significantly, development agencies' own choices over whom to support carry crucial representational weight. For example, Oxfam's decision to support an organization becomes part of the formula others use to evaluate that organization's credibility. That is, Oxfam's conferral of legitimacy "from above" serves a methodological and political shortcut for others trying to make judgments about a particular organization. One need not go as far as suspecting Oxfam of colluding with mining companies to suggest that it does play a role in the transnational politics of authenticating Indigenous actors. In our own case, the "Oxfam connection" did have an important influence on shaping our view of what the important organizations were. This had little to do with the conspiratorial logic suggested by some at COPPIP-Conferencia. Rather, Lucero's previous work in Ecuador and Bolivia relied on Oxfam as one of the central reference points for Indigenous politics. For example, Oxfam had been supporting the most powerful Indigenous confederation in the Americas, CONAIE, from the very beginning of CONAIE's political life. Oxfam's work in a variety of urgent fields including poverty, malnutrition, and health gave it a kind of moral authority that made its altruism fairly clear to us. Oxfam was the kind of organization we had always thought we would work with, if not for.

We should have been more attentive to the fact, quite obvious in retrospect, that other actors may not have the same estimation of Oxfam's role in this kind of "development encounter." In resource-scarce settings, altruism may not be enough to deflect suspicions of imperialism, or at least paternalism. More generally, the very structure of the encounter, as Talal Asad, Edward Said, and Arturo Escobar would warn, often serves to hide the ways in which "development operates as an arena for cultural contestation and identity construction."[29] We certainly knew that Oxfam and others were part of a regime of representation, but we were not as careful as we should have been in interrogating our own complicity with the same regime.

Recently, Richard Chase Smith has begun to make the same kind of reflective thinking part of his own analysis of Peruvian Indigenous politics.[30] As we spoke in his Lima office about a study he was completing on the identity of a lowland Indigenous group, he suggested that Indigenous people were often very conscious of the kinds of performances that had begun to be expected by NGOs and other actors. As many anthropologists do, Smith saw that Indigenous people were very savvy in cobbling together various discourses from a variety of sources in the articulation of a voice that they believed would be seen as "authentically" Indigenous and attractive to development funders.[31] Interestingly, ideas from Smith's own previous work among other groups in Peru were now being re-presented back to him. After so many years of helping craft a discourse of Indigenous autonomy and self-determination, Smith now was trying "to step out of and question the discourse."[32] So were we, though not as quickly as we should have. This does not mean that we were wrong to believe what people at Oxfam said, but only that these research findings called for more comparative inquiry into the other discourses that may not have fared as well within the regime of representation we had accepted and reinforced. In particular, the Indianista critique of Lajo and others from COPPIP-Conferencia certainly demands greater attention and study. The contentions cited above are themselves interesting statements on the ways in which an Indianista regime of representation might work.

First, there is an anti-imperialist assumption that casts "North American" assistance as almost inherently suspect. Economic interests, whether extractive (like mining companies) or developmental (like Oxfam) are part of the basic colonial contours of world politics that undermine Indigenous self-determination. Leaving aside the fact that Indianista organizations in the past certainly accepted their fair share of "Northern" funds and that Indianistas themselves called for "self-criticism," the nationalism and anti-imperialism of contemporary Indianismo should be taken seriously.[33]

The second component of what an Indianista perspective would emphasize is the following equivalence: real Indians are radical Indians. This is most clear in the example Aranwan gives about Felipe Quispe in Bolivia. Quispe, a former member of an armed Indianista movement (an involvement for which he was imprisoned) and leader of the Confederation of Rural Workers of Bolivia and the Pachakutik political party, is certainly one of the more radical Indigenous voices in the Americas today. Quispe calls for the creation of a separate state, whereas virtually all other major, national Indigenous leaders in the Andes do not. When Aymaras in neighboring Peru lynched a local mayor in 2004, Quispe called for Aymaras in that country to join forces with Aymaras in his.[34] His tactics and rhetoric are confrontational. The controversial coca-farmer leader Evo Morales (whom the United States publicly opposed in the 2002 presidential elections) sounded like the voice of reasoned diplomacy in comparison with Quispe, something that helped Morales win a historic victory in the 2005 presidential elections. While Quispe has been eclipsed by Morales, the political resurrection of Quispe, also known as El Mallku (the name for traditional Aymara leaders), is somewhat of a puzzle for those who see Indianistas as anachronistic or as isolated, unrepresentative ideologues, as Smith does. Quispe's being selected as head of a national rural federation represented the marriage of a broad-based campesino organizational structure with an Indianista discourse, a hybrid that Smith's typology did not anticipate. Moreover, in times of crisis, where the politics of rage compete with the politics of compromise, Quispe has shown himself to be a figure to be reckoned with. As Aranwan put it, "How could a political force be more radical than Felipe Quispe?" In the Indianista perspective, radical and authentic often become synonymous.

Rather than simply accepting one version of Indigenous legitimacy over another, interrogating both sets of claims and the conditions that produce those claims makes sense. For many members of the international development community, the criteria for evaluating Indigenous actors involve thick membership in Indigenous worlds, but also the ability to translate across the divide between local demands and external expectations of project efficiency and results. Indianista and anti-development critics, however, believe that the Indigenous organizations that work closest with NGOs become trapped in Foucauldian regimes of discipline and lose the ability to truly speak and act for themselves.[35] These different accounts of Indigenous authenticity and representation are not simply differing opinions on the same sets of practices and discourses. Rather, they are themselves political stances that are enacted by local and global actors that do the work of authenticating and legitimating some actors over others. Within all social movement organizations, there are ready epithets for those that "sell-out" the movement, as well as for the "ideologues" who put politics before pragmatism. Outside of social movements, there are opponents and allies who engage, strengthen, and weaken various voices within the movements in intentional and unintentional ways. Scholars like all interlocutors are part of this process.

In the complex dialogical formation of Indigenous representation, ideas and claims about who "really" represents Indigenous interests and identity will always be contested. It is critical for scholars to recognize that this is as important politically as it is methodologically. Indeed, to move toward the "decolonization" of academic field research, research projects must become increasingly multivocal and include multiple Indigenous responses to scholarly arguments and representations. In our case, an Indianista critique allowed us to gain a fuller understanding of a controversial and complex ideological and political landscape.

✳

In contemporary Peru, as in other countries, the range of Indigenous politics is vast. Despite reports of the failure and absence of movements, there is little question that Quechua, Aymara, Asháninka, Amuesha, Anqara, and other Indigenous peoples have long been politically active. We do not claim any originality in making this case as other scholars have found rich evidence of Indigenous politics in the context of conflicts over water, the establishment of rondas campesinas, and resistance to U.S.-supported coca eradication, among other conflicts.[36] That these struggles, and older struggles in the Amazon, have not produced a cohesive, national movement shouldn't simply be labeled a failure. Indeed, this label says more about the scholarly models for what counts as a "social movement" than it does about Indigenous activism. As many scholars have warned, the myths and models of "single" and "unified" movements often obscure the fragmented and conflicting elements that are at work in all fields of contestation.[37] What we wanted to say in our Cochabamba paper was simple: once something becomes a "negative case," in which something has not happened (as Peru had become for students of Indigenous movements), scholars often cease to explore what actually is happening. What we have learned since giving that paper has allowed us greater insight into the models of authenticity that are often silently at work in the processes of development and the practices of fieldwork.

Some of these models come from academic archaeologies, which seek to

sift the uneven and messy fragments of politics and culture into neatly ordered categories for the purpose of analysis and theory-building. Smith's
typology, for instance, which separated campesino, ethnic, and Indianista
organizations, was a helpful starting point for us in that it recognized the
plurality of politics while imposing some order onto an otherwise unruly
Andean and Amazonian mix. Yet, like all typologies, this scheme was an
artificial and provisional way of understanding complex dynamics, and it
was only one possible model among others. As Indigenous actors have now
become established parts of Latin American political systems, there have
evolved a variety of regimes of representation for understanding them. These
regimes, institutionalized through national and transnational policies, situate
various Indigenous actors in ways that make some more authentic and con-
sequential than others. As multiculturalism becomes "official," legitimated by
transnational ethno-development agendas and new constitutional frameworks, certain Indigenous actors are re-presented as legitimate partners in
multicultural development while others are tainted by "radicalized" stances
that are less amenable to contemporary neoliberal political and economic
orders.[38] While some might see this as the familiar and inevitable divide-and-
conquer strategy of dominant power, it is also a deeper and more interactive
process that does not only work from the top down. Radicals and reformers
alike negotiate the shifting constellations of political opportunity and representation. The division in COPPIP reflected not only contrasting styles of
radicalism and pragmatism, but competing and contested notions of Indianness and politics authenticated by a transnational field of actors.

Finally, this experience has helped us appreciate the benefits and importance of making tentative research findings public, especially when they are
controversial, and even when they might be wrong. Our narrative of the rise of
a national organization in Peru, COPPIP, had the advantage of providing a neat
example of how much other scholars had missed in talking about Peruvian
absence. Yet, our acceptance of one version of the history of COPPIP, influenced by our own position in the networks of social science and professional
advocacy, caused us to miss many parts of a story about continuing Indianista
critiques of "mainstream" transnationalized Indigenous organizations. We
spoke to one important sector of the Indigenous movement in Peru, a movement full of groups that articulate local communities and their struggles
with broader national and transnational agendas. CONACAMI and COPPIP-
Coordinadora, with the help of NGOs like Oxfam America, are becoming
important voices in civil society. They have been vocal about the dangers

Indigenous people face and the risks involved in collaborating with perhaps well-intentioned state agencies like CONAPA, which critics see as diminishing the autonomy of Indigenous organizations. Later, we found that we had neglected another Indianista sector of the Indigenous movement, COPPIP-Conferencia, that had its own critiques of the state, but also of NGOs that the organization claimed were equally dangerous to Indigenous autonomy.

So who is right? And who is more representative? In many ways, these questions invite more research, more reflection, and more debate. More profoundly, though, these questions also invite us to find various ways of seeing Indigenous projects as fragmented, contradictory, and multivocal, as all projects are. This way of seeing is central to the study of Indigenous movements, as questions over who is "really Indian" and doubts over who really speaks for whom are a constitutive part of Indigenous politics in Peru and elsewhere. In Ecuador, Bolivia, Peru, and elsewhere, certain Indigenous voices will emerge over others through the politics of Indigenous representation.[39] Our own normative and political sensibilities will always inform our evaluations of which voices we think are most persuasive, most influential, and right. Still, as we introduce our own voices to the conversation and listen ethnographically and self-reflexively to criticism and contradiction, we can better understand why and when some voices are broadcasted transnationally and nationally while others resonate in smaller spaces. Previous studies of Peruvian "absence" were explanations of silence, but not ethnographies of it. With ethnographic patience and curiosity, one can appreciate what poets already know about silence:

> It is a presence
> it has a history a form
> Do not confuse it
> with any kind of absence[40]

❋

Since writing this article, we have found that the "problem" of the two COPPIPs has continued to evolve. In 2006, the organization that had been COPPIP-Conferencia held a congress in Ayacucho in which it reconstituted itself as the Confederation of Indigenous Nationalities of Peru (CONAIP) and incorporated other sectors, including organizations of rondas campesinas and coca farmers. Meanwhile, the "other" COPPIP, COPPIP-Coordinadora, still composed of CONACAMI and AIDESEP, has become much less visible. Though CONACAMI and AIDESEP are more influential politically than the new CONAIP, no organization can claim to be pan-regional or nationally representative.

The year 2006 provided new opportunities for contentious politics as Indigenous organizations took positions on presidential elections and the issue of a free-trade agreement with the United States. In terms of political visibility and representation, the results have been mixed for the actors mentioned in this chapter. COPPIP-Coordinadora made almost no public pronouncements on either issue. Though its constituent members, CONACAMI and AIDESEP, were very visible in protests against the free-trade agreement, they were more silent on the elections. CONAIP (the former COPPIP-Conferencia) was also opposed to the free-trade agreement, but it was less visible in the organizational efforts against it. In July 2006, CONACAMI co-founded a transnational Andean coordinator of Indigenous organizations from Bolivia, Colombia, Chile, Ecuador, and Peru, further integrating itself into the transnational network of Indigenous organizations supported by NGOs. The 2006 election of Alan García and the implementation of his pro-mining development agenda have created new obstacles for Indigenous organizations and their allies. A particularly tragic example of these new tensions was the conflict in the Amazonian town of Bagua in 2009, when police clashed with Indigenous protesters, resulting in many deaths. This tragedy generated transnational criticism of the state which forced the Peruvian government to put many of its extractive projects in the Amazon on hold. Operating on various scales and involving multiple Indigenous actors, Indigenous representation continues to be dynamic, challenging, and very much up for grabs.

Notes

1. María Elena García and José Antonio Lucero, "Explorando un 'País Sin Indígenas': Reflexiones sobre los movimientos indígenas en el Perú" (paper presented at conference "Movimientos Indígenas y Estado en América Latina," Cochambamba, Bolivia, May 23, 2003). A version of the paper we presented in Cochabamba was published in English, García and Lucero 2004; an updated and corrected version was published in Spanish, García and Lucero 2005.

2. Gelles 2002; Remy 1994; Yashar 1998.

3. Albó 1991; Albó 2002.

4. There are two organizations that use the COPPIP acronym, though they each represent quite distinct philosophies. We expound on these differences later in the chapter.

5. In 2004 Karp resigned her leadership in the face of accusations of misadministration of World Bank funds. CONAPA has also undergone substantial changes and has been moved from the purview of the first lady's office to a ministerial agency now known as the Instituto Nacional de Desarrollo de los Pueblos.

6. Brysk 2000 and 1996; Keck and Sikkink 1998.

7. Smith 1983; Albó 2002.

8. Warren and Jackson 2002; Mires 1991; Wade 1997.

9. See, for example, Poole and Rénique 1992; Manrique 2002; Stern 1998.

10. Albó 1991 and 2002; Yashar 1998.

11. Degregori 1998; Gelles 2002; De la Cadena 2000. For a fuller discussion of these explanations see García 2005; García and Lucero 2004 and 2005, and Albó 2002.

12. Quoted in García 2005.

13. The peculiarity of Peruvian racial formation is beyond the scope of this chapter, but as de la Cadena (2000 and 2001) and several contributors to this volume note, the various discourses of racial mixture in the Andes and Mesoamerica call for continued comparative study as the constellations of race and nation are varied and complex. While all identity boundaries are fluid, the opposition between mestizo and Indigenous identities, for example, is much less marked in Peru than in Mexico or Ecuador.

14. García 2005.

15. Gelles 2000; Edelman 1999.

16. Smith 1983 and 2002; Greene 2006.

17. Starn 1999. The organization of the Asháninka army and the rise of rondas campesinas challenge the view that violence is always an obstacle for Indigenous organizing. Political violence can often be a catalyst for Indigenous organizing as a form of self-defense. See, for example, Manrique 1998 and Starn 1998.

18. For the sake of brevity, we will sometimes refer to Oxfam America simply as "Oxfam," but it should not be confused with Oxfam International or other Oxfam actors like Oxfam Great Britain.

19. Lucero 2002; Lucero 2008; Andolina 1999; Andolina et al. 2009.

20. For more on Toledo's complicated negotiation of Andean identities, see de la Cadena 2001 and García and Lucero 2008. Karp is often identified as a "Belgian anthropologist," an identification she does not reject. While she did study anthropology as an undergraduate and speaks Quechua, her graduate studies at Stanford (where she and Toledo met) were not in anthropology but in French literature. Disciplinary identities, like ethnic identities, carry a certain amount of cultural and political capital.

21. Martin Scurrah (director, Oxfam America), interviewed by authors, June 4, 2002, Lima, Peru.

22. Benavides 2001; Richard Chase Smith (former director, Oxfam America), interviewed by authors, June 6, 2002, Lima; Patricia Oliart (consultant, Oxfam America), interviewed by authors, June 5, 2002, Lima.

23. Albó 2002; Smith 1983 and 2002.

24. Albó 2002; Smith 1983 and 2002; Montoya 1998.

25. See, for example, Stephen 2002; Warren 1998a.

26. Aranwan, email message to the authors, July 2, 2003.

27. Ibid.

28. Smith 1983, 34.

29. See Asad 2000, Said 1979, and Escobar 1995; Escobar 1995, 15.

30. Smith of course is not alone in this regard. In addition to scholars like Warren, Hale, Jackson, and others, Joanne Rappaport (2005) provides a particularly insightful account of the possibilities and limits of engaged and collaborative anthropology.

31. See, for example, Jackson 1995; Li 2000; Rappaport 2005; Warren 1998b.

32. Richard Chase Smith (former director, Oxfam America), interviewed by authors, June 6, 2002, Lima.

33. Lajo expressed the need for Indianista self-criticism in an interview with the authors in Lima in August 2005.

34. This is not the place to review the events at Ilave that triggered a national political crisis in Peru. However, the framing of Ilave (in a wide range of press outlets) evoked images of Aymara violence and radical separatist movements. These representations are of course contested.

35. Patzi 1999.

36. On conflicts over water, see Gelles 2000. On rondas campesinas, see Starn 1998 and 1999 and Yrigoyen 2002. On coca eradication, see Rojas 2003. For an excellent recent discussion of the importance of Amazonian Indigenous organizing, see Greene 2006.

37. Warren 1998b; Rubin 1997; Alvarez, Escobar, and Dagnino 1998.

38. Hale 2002; Gustafson 2002; Mires 1991; Patzi 1999; Wade 1997.

39. Lucero 2008.

40. Rich 1978.

Transgressions and Racism:

The Struggle over a New Constitution in Bolivia

ANDRÉS CALLA AND KHANTUTA MURUCHI

Bolivia's Constituent Assembly was inaugurated on August 6, 2006, following a protracted process of social mobilization and the election of Evo Morales, the nation's first indigenous president.[1] In the city of Sucre, 255 delegates came together to draft the nation's new constitution. The delegates had been selected in a special election held just one month before, in July 2006. The composition of the delegates was extremely diverse in social, cultural, political, and geographic terms. Of the 255 total representatives, 88 (35 percent) were women; 119 (47 percent) spoke a native language (in addition to Spanish); 142 (55 percent) self-identified with an indigenous group; and 20 percent were local political leaders. The ruling party, the Movimiento al Socialismo (known as the Movement Toward Socialism, or MAS), gained 53.7 percent of the seats, while PODEMOS (Poder Democrático y Social), the principal opposition party, acquired 28 percent; the remaining seats were divided among small political groups.[2] The diverse composition of the delegates gave the constitutional process great significance. The social organizations represented by the MAS delegation—both peasant and urban-popular—had displaced the traditional political actors who previously controlled the government, making it possible to begin to construct a new institutional structure for the state.

Once the assembly was initiated, the delegates engaged in two types of work. First, they took part in plenary sessions, which were held in the Gran Mariscal Theatre. All of the delegates participated there with voice and vote to define the internal regulations that would govern the organization and operation of the Assembly. Second, the delegates were divided into twenty-one commissions to work in depth on the specific articles of the constitution.[3] These sessions were held in the Colegio Junín.

On August 17, 2007, following various phases of consensus and disagreement—and a decision to extend the time frame of the Assembly by four months—the Assembly's work was blocked by opposition groups' efforts to introduce into the agenda a debate on the return of the full capital to Sucre.[4] In a context of increasing conflict, plenary sessions were suspended and the struggle over the constitution moved to the streets. Students from the Universidad San Francisco Xavier de Chuquisaca and members of other institutions of Sucre initiated a series of mobilizations in defense of the *capitalía plena* (return of the full capital to Sucre), mobilizations that became laced with violence and racism.

"Leap or you're a llama! Leap or you're a llama!" Students chanted this refrain in their marches and rallies, to add their voice to the Constituent Assembly's discussion of the demand that the Bolivian capital be shifted from La Paz to Sucre. Why a llama? The llama is the emblematic animal of Bolivia's Altiplano region and is thus associated with the indigenous people of the Andes. "Llama" is used as an insult referring to peasants or indigenous people.

After Bolivia inaugurated the Constituent Assembly in Sucre on August 6, 2006, other manifestations of racism surfaced in the city's central plaza. Why has overt racism emerged more frequently since the Constituent Assembly was convened? How did it advance from insults to blows? What is the significance of the settings—the sessions of the Constituent Assembly and the central plaza of Sucre—for these increasingly common expressions of overt racism?

In posing these questions, we assume that Bolivian society has been marked historically by a silent racism of a structural and quotidian nature that has involved discrimination against indigenous people and peasants. We call this discrimination silent racism because until recently the everyday exclusion of indigenous people and peasants has been naturalized by Bolivian society, and because silent racism, in its structural form, can be hidden.[5] During the last five years or so, racism has become openly visible and been accompanied by physical violence.

The political conjuncture following the inauguration of the Constituent Assembly has been marked by the shift from a silent racism with structural characteristics to forms of open and violent racism. These open forms of racism are the product of a series of symbolic transgressions associated with the Constituent Assembly. In fact, the Assembly itself constituted a transgression of symbolic spaces and positions of power because the elaboration of a new constitution, demanded by social movements, emerged as an opportunity to alter the foundations and norms of the state. For many Bolivians, the Assembly augured a change from a state dominated by a small elite to one that has sought to include historically excluded sectors. A particular political situation—in this case an increasingly contentious struggle over a new constitution—gave rise to open forms of racism and acts of violence against perceived political enemies. While some of those "enemies" were identified in partisan terms, others were considered to be members of a race. To understand the turn to overt racism in present-day Bolivia, an understanding of the close relationship between politics, violence, and a history of racial discrimination is needed. The physical violence that has accompanied racism in Bolivia varies in intensity according to the degree to which longstanding social hierarchies and spaces of power have been transgressed.

We do not mean to suggest that the course of the Constituent Assembly was marked exclusively by tension or intolerance. While the plenary sessions of the first phase were quite tense, the various political groups in attendance did engage, at times, in dialogue and achieve compromises. Generally speaking, the political process that brought Evo Morales to the presidency has made people more conscious of including representatives from indigenous, peasant, and impoverished urban sectors in state institutions and policies. The work of the Constituent Assembly is an ongoing process. Levels of racial violence may or may not change as a result of the approval of the new constitution (in January 2009) and its subsequent implementation. But one thing is clear: the legal changes will lead to new forms of inclusion and a greater indigenous presence in government—or these changes will call attention to indigenous peoples' absence.

Political Ruptures and Symbolic Transgressions

Bolivia's presidential elections of December 2005 were won by an absolute majority by Evo Morales. Since then, state structures of power and control have experienced a series of ruptures that have deeply affected the political imaginary of Bolivia's diverse social sectors. We call these political ruptures *transgressions* because they have altered a hierarchical order of symbols, spaces, positions, and identities. The most significant of such transgressions has had to do with political "positioning" or "repositioning," that is, the dislodging of an economic-political elite (and its neoliberal tendencies) from the government and the state.[6] Some of these spaces of power may be occupied by historically excluded sectors, but they may also be filled by a segment of the middle class that identifies with the inclusive, proindigenous political project advanced by the Morales government. In addition to the strong presence of indigenous delegates in the Plurinational Legislative Assembly (formerly known as Congress) and the Constituent Assembly, there are Aymara representatives in the executive branch, such as the foreign minister, David Choquehuanca. Evo Morales's election to the presidency would seem to represent the symbolic transgression of an entrenched political order. The question of whether indigenous peoples have truly gained significant influence in spaces of power is nevertheless a subject of much debate.[7]

A related type of transgression has to do with the legislative process. Constituent Assembly delegates who are peasants, indigenous, or members of other impoverished sectors now possess political power: they were elected members of an assembly to rewrite the constitution. Their newfound situation has positioned them as actors on the same level as the traditional politicians who have wielded power in the past. For members of the previously excluded majority—indigenous people, peasants, and urban-popular sectors —the changes taking place today signify the possibility of their acceding to spaces of political power that have long been denied to them. The testimony of a female Constituent Assembly delegate, granddaughter of the indigenous leader Santos Marka T'ula, underscores this sense of possibility:

> I had hope because of something my grandfather used to say: "An Indian like us is going to come to govern, and at that time there will be a fight, a struggle, but we are not going to let ourselves be defeated. One way or another, we are going to win and we are going to govern." And that has come to pass. I have said: "My grandfather's words have been fulfilled. Now I *do* have to work, now I *can* go as a Constituent Assembly delegate, now I can be a representative, I can work in any office for which the people deposit their confidence in me, because this is an Indian government, a native indigenous government.[8]

Another Constituent Assembly delegate commented on the tensions that have accompanied the recent political changes: "For the first time, men from the countryside, indigenous leaders, women in *polleras*, people from the middle class, and intellectuals have sat down in the same place. The first sessions [of the assembly] have been marked by intense confrontation, by insults, by provocation and fighting. But with time these problems are being resolved, although some people still don't understand. This process should make us understand that people who have been marginalized have rights, they have the voice to decide."[9]

As the course of the Constituent Assembly makes clear, these transgressions of the traditional political order were accompanied by overt forms of discrimination. A significant number of the people we interviewed felt that open expressions of racism were most intense in the Constituent Assembly's initial plenary sessions: "In the beginning, it was a very stressful encounter. . . . In the first sessions it was funny to see how the female delegates from Santa Cruz would enter and say: 'Move over, son, I'm going to enter the assembly hall.' It turns out that the 'boy' or 'girl' were delegates just like they were."[10]

Once the work of the Constituent Assembly shifted from the plenary sessions to the commissions—much smaller working arenas—relations among the delegates changed. According to one delegate, the work of some of the commissions was characterized by respect: "[The Constituent Assembly] has had several stages. The first [was] characterized by the greatest racism . . . because you could feel discrimination in the air, depending on whether you wore a tie or a pollera. When we've worked in the commissions, I must admit that good relations have existed, depending on the commission. We have come to esteem each other. In the work of the commissions, we have been relating to each other based on dialogue."[11]

The work of the commissions, then, was characterized in some cases by genuine exchange. In other instances, however, hidden tensions emerged. The expressions of overt racism that marked the initial plenary sessions—expressions based on visible markers such as clothing or language—gave way in certain circumstances to a more subtle experience of discrimination rooted in hierarchies of knowledge and mastery (or lack of mastery) of the legal and juridical aspects of the work involved in writing a constitution. Essentially, the commissions required the construction of agreements about the new articles of the constitution and the delegates felt "obligated," in a certain way, to debate and confront diverse ideas and forms of knowledge. One way that a kind of discrimination manifested itself in this context was through command of the technical knowledge and codes necessary for writing the articles of the new constitution. This knowledge was possessed by delegates from the intellectual elite, and it prevailed in many cases over the life-based knowledge of the indigenous and peasant delegates.[12] As one delegate recounted: "In my commission there are people with doctorates and masters degrees, and I've been a domestic worker. . . . Why can't we be in the same hierarchy? Now we are. Although we are not professionals, we've still come to the Assembly to fight."[13]

As the conflict over the question of the capital intensified (from August to November 2007), another kind of discrimination became apparent, one that was associated with the perceived transgression of a particular public space: Veinte-cinco de Mayo Plaza, the central plaza of the city of Sucre. Since colonial times, this plaza has symbolized elite power. Yet, at the same time, it is a place where street vendors, shoe shine boys, newspaper vendors, gardeners, and street sweepers work—and, at times, relax—in some cases accompanied by their children. The perceived transgression of this space occurred when indigenous delegates entered it in a position of political authority. They were not there as workers, vendors, or passersby, but as elected political representatives. As one interviewee noted: "They have insulted us in the plaza. When we walk in the plaza wearing our hats, they say, 'This guy is a delegate, a peasant.' When we'd walk carrying a little woven bag [filled with coca leaves], they'd insult us. That's what it was like to walk through the plaza. . . . They would always humiliate those of us from the countryside."[14]

Expressions of overt racism were thus directed toward indigenous or peasant delegates, or against those who "seemed" to be indigenous or peasants, due to their clothing, language, or facial features. They became targets because they entered a particular public space in a political role—at a time of rising political tensions. Clothing and other symbols of authority played an important role in the construction of social distinctions and hierarchies in this context.[15] In Bolivia, certain articles of clothing serve to identify a figure of authority or social representative. The *guardatojo* (a helmet worn by the leaders of the mineworkers), the whip of the rural indigenous authority, and the hat of the *mama t'alla* (a female community leader) identify mineworkers or indigenous and peasant delegates. The clothing worn by indigenous authorities is a sign of distinction that garners legitimacy and respect for these leaders within their communities. Nevertheless, in the city of Sucre, as the struggle over the capital and the Constituent Assembly intensified, clothing and other symbols of authority that differentiated rural delegates from members of urban society were used as a means to discriminate against, and even punish, rural delegates who were also political opponents.[16]

Racialization and the Turn to Violence

"Racialization" is a form of representation that creates stereotyped categories of the other (ugly, dirty, ignorant) from the fictitious category of race.[17] In the case at hand, those who discriminate often lump together all peasants and indigenous people based on their clothing and skin color. In some cases, delegates from PODEMOS were confused with delegates from MAS on the basis of phenotypic characteristics. As one PODEMOS delegate stated: "[In the mobilizations in defense of the capitalía plena] they have mistaken me, they have thought that I was the leader of MAS, [laughter], I've been given a kicking.... Luckily . . . the press and some friends have appeared. [They said]: 'No, not him . . . he is fighting for unity.' They didn't know what to do."[18] The people who rescued this delegate from his attackers were able to pick him out because he was a delegate for PODEMOS, a party that backed the demand to return the full capital to Sucre; "unity" refers here to the defense of the capitalía.

We can thus begin to see how the turn to violent forms of racism was the product of specific political conflicts, and how violence, in this context, began to be directed against people because of the color of their skin, the cultural symbols they displayed, or the region they presumably hailed from. The violent attacks forced people to take precautionary measures. For example, a delegate who is a miner decided to stop wearing the guardatojo, and a female delegate stopped wearing clothing that denoted her indigenous authority. She felt forced to change her clothing for strategic purposes. In the midst of the conflicts over the capitalía, one delegate related the following testimony: "Yesterday they insulted me; they didn't allow me to have lunch because I was dressed in a pollera. [They said,] 'Indian pigs, mules, go back to Oruro. You people from La Paz, get out of here.' "[19]

As the mobilizations over the question of where to locate the capital grew more violent, transit through spaces such as the central plaza of Sucre became more dangerous, especially for indigenous and peasant men and women.[20] But they were not the only victims. In the course of the protests in defense of the full capital that were carried out by some sectors of the city of Sucre, the motives for attacks against particular individuals were political as well as racial. This was ever more the case as the struggle over the capital intensified, and with it, regionalist affinities and hostilities. In the majority of cases, those who were subjected to discrimination and violence were, or "seemed" to be, indigenous or peasant delegates because of their clothing or the color of their skin. In some cases, however, middle-class delegates who identified with MAS were also attacked for political and regionalist motives.[21] Nonetheless, we should emphasize that expressions of violent racism were directed more frequently against indigenous people who supported the government's political position and opposed the return of the full capital to Sucre.

In addition to attacks against particular delegates, mobilizations over where to locate Bolivia's capital prompted manifestations of a kind of political and ethnic mockery among some of the students at San Francisco Xavier University. These students held a *farándula* in November 2007 to celebrate the founding of one of the departments of the university.[22] A supplement of the newspaper *Correo del Sur* demonstrated that conservative sectors and the middle class of Sucre viewed this farándula as a "form of protest" characterized by "humor and wit." In reference to images of students dressed in polleras and Evo Morales masks and costumed as delegates in donkey masks, the supplement reported: "These images show that it is also possible to protest with humor and wit. On the other side, there are people with complexes who believe that this is an insult, and they take advantage of this comic parade to offend us and to show how uptight they are [by denouncing the parade] in some of the media."[23]

While some observers may have described this protest as innocent because it was a festive event, the farándula clearly demonstrated stereotypes and prejudices against indigenous and peasant men and women. As we observed during our stay in Sucre, the farándula made its way to the Gran Mariscal Theater, where civic leaders, along with Constituent Assembly delegates from Sucre and university students, stationed themselves to "protect" the theater's doors. Their objective was to prevent the initiation of the Constituent Assembly's plenary sessions unless the question of the full capital was addressed. The students who participated in the farándula were greeted there with applause and laughter. Later, they headed to the main plaza, where people welcomed the costumed students in the same manner. As photographs published in the local newspaper show, young people, the majority of them men, donned ponchos, polleras, and donkey masks to represent indigenous and peasant delegates. Specific references to Silvia Lazarte, a former leader of the coca growers and president of the Constituent Assembly, were common. In addition, a stereotyped image of Evo Morales appeared: the Bolivian president was represented by a mask that exaggerated his facial features, especially the nose and cheekbones. He was shown wearing the clothing of the television personality Chavo at Eight, who affects a naive, slow, and childlike persona. Other young people were dressed as Evo Morales in polleras. The pollera, in this case, was used to convey a derisive image of indigenous femininity. Sexist references, such as the exaggerated size of the men's genitals, were combined with ponchos, polleras, and donkey masks. These symbolic referents conveyed a racialized and feminized perception of indigenous and peasant men and women that belittled them.

Part of the population perceived these expressions of racism in a joking way precisely because they seemed "natural." That is to say, the symbolic representations observed in the farándula are familiar ones; they are representations that have been created and reproduced historically in the imaginary of Bolivian society. While the farándula presented derogatory perceptions of peasants and indigenous men and women, it should also be noted that some of the symbols employed by the university students correlated directly with political elements of mockery that have been used against the current MAS government. For example, some of the students carried signs that said "Evo lackey, Chávez boss," or they held oversized checks made out to Evo Morales and drawn on the "Bank of Venezuela." There were also students dressed up as Evo Morales and Hugo Chávez who walked hand in hand and carried suitcases stuffed with "bills," bolivianos and dollars. In this particular context, such political critiques were combined with the mockery of ethnic symbols.

*

The essence of the political project of Bolivia's historically marginalized sectors—peasants, the indigenous, and the urban impoverished—is to change the structures of exclusion, to "decolonize" Bolivian society from within the state apparatus. There is a social and, above all, a political resolve for change in Bolivia in favor of peasants and indigenous people. This desire for change has provoked expressions of racism that are sometimes combined with attacks against political opponents, such as the aggression against indigenous— and in some cases nonindigenous—delegates to the Constituent Assembly.

On the other hand, the shift from one type of racism to another, from the hidden to the overt, depends on the spaces in which those types of racism develop. The case of violence and discrimination involving the Constituent Assembly reveals a movement from open intolerance in the plenary sessions to more subtle forms of discrimination in the work of the commissions, and a final shift to violence and racism in the streets as the conflict over the capital raged. Open expressions of racism have surfaced because hierarchical spaces and positions are being transgressed at the same time political futures are being battled over.

These forms of racism are deeply connected with the political conflicts that are being waged in Bolivia during the period of Evo Morales's presidency. Violent forms of racism are directed against indigenous and peasant people who are MAS representatives, and not against indigenous people who oppose MAS. However, in moments of intense and uncontrolled violence, the latter group may be confused with MAS supporters due to their facial features, and they may also be assaulted. Politics can in turn become a form of social or ethnic differentiation, and in the popular imaginary indigenous people tend to be associated with MAS. However much racist violence in contemporary Bolivia may be structurally rooted in a long history of exclusion and exploitation, its peculiar forms and effects cannot be understood unless they are placed in the charged and conflictive context that has defined Bolivian politics in the first decade of the twenty-first century.

Notes

This chapter was translated by Eileen Willingham and edited by Laura Gotkowitz. An earlier version appeared in Spanish as "Transgresiones y racismo," in Observatorio del racismo en Bolivia, Área de Investigación, *Observando el Racismo: Racismo y regionalismo en el proceso constituyente* (La Paz: Defensor del Pueblo y Universidad de la Cordillera, 2008). The article forms part of an ongoing research project that is being carried out by the Observatorio del Racismo of the Universidad de la Cordillera in La Paz. The project commenced in 2007 while the Constituent Assembly convened in Sucre; fieldwork was carried out between August and November 2007. During that time, the research group conducted 130 semistructured interviews with Constituent Assembly delegates, technical advisers to the delegates, and leaders of Sucre social organizations.

1. The proposal for the Constituent Assembly surfaced in 1990, during the march for "Dignity and Territory" of lowland indigenous peoples from Trinidad (Beni) to La Paz. The "Water War" of 2000 in Cochabamba, the march of 2002, initiated by social organizations in the eastern lowlands, and the mobilizations of 2003 in La Paz and El Alto (which led to the resignation of Gonzalo Sánchez de Lozada from the presidency), solidified the call for the Assembly on a national level.

2. Albó 2008. In 2005, after the ADN party lost its legal status, the citizens' group PODEMOS was created with the goal of participating in that year's election. The characteristics and objectives of citizens groups are much the same as those of political parties.

3. Some of the most important commissions were Vision of the Nation; Organization and Structure of the New State; Departmental, Provincial, Municipal, and Indigenous Autonomy, Decentralization, and Territorial Organization; and Natural Resources, Land, Territory, and Environment.

4. As of 2010, Sucre is the site of the judicial branch of the government only. Supporters of capitalía plena have wanted the legislative and executive branches, which are located in La Paz (the seat of government), to be returned to Sucre (the nation's capital).

5. On structural racism, see Wieviorka 2002.

6. With Decree 21060 of 1985, neoliberal measures began to be implemented in Bolivia. These reached their fullest expression under the Gonzalo Sánchez de Lozada government, which privatized public enterprises.

7. For example, Pablo Mamani and others maintain that President Morales is surrounded by a white-mestizo leftist elite that is committed to a project of state nationalism and that belongs to a culturally western civilizing matrix, not to the popular indigenous-native-Afro milieu. See Mamani 2007.

8. Interview by the authors with female delegate to the Constituent Assembly, November 7, 2007, Sucre, Bolivia. Santos Marka T'ula is well known in Bolivian history as a member of the organization of the *caciques-apoderados*, one of the groups of early twentieth-century indigenous leaders discussed by Esteban Ticona in this volume.

9. Interview by the authors with male delegate to the Constituent Assembly, October 12, 2007, Sucre, Bolivia. The pollera is a type of skirt worn by indigenous women in the western part of Bolivia.

10. Interview by the authors with a journalist, November 1, 2007, Sucre, Bolivia. The term "son," which continues to be used today, implies a paternalistic relationship between nonindigenous and indigenous sectors and a view of indigenous peoples as minors.

11. Interview by the authors with male delegate to the Constituent Assembly, October 11, 2007, Sucre, Bolivia.

12. For in-depth treatment of this subject see Paz 2008; Zegarra Siles 2008.

13. Interview by the authors with female delegate to the Constituent Assembly, November 7, 2007, Sucre, Bolivia.

14. Interview by the authors with representative of peasant organization, November 8, 2007, Sucre, Bolivia.

15. For in-depth treatment of this subject see Núñez Reguerin 2008.

16. Espósito Guevara 2008.

17. See Wieviorka 2002.

18. Interview by the authors with male delegate to the Constituent Assembly, October 10, 2007, Sucre, Bolivia.

19. Interview by the authors with female delegate to the Constituent Assembly, November 7, 2007, Sucre, Bolivia.

20. For more on the debate over moving the capital, see Espósito 2008.

21. These attacks were observed during field work in Sucre on November 9, 2007.

22. The farándula is a form of theatrical street festival; it is generally used by high school and university students to celebrate the anniversary of the founding of a school.

23. *Correo del Sur* (Sucre), November 16, 2007.

Epilogue to "Transgressions and Racism"

Making Sense of May 24th in Sucre:

Toward an Antiracist Legislative Agenda

PAMELA CALLA AND THE RESEARCH GROUP

OF THE OBSERVATORIO DEL RACISMO

Every 25th of May, Bolivia marks the anniversary of one of the first revolts in the long process that culminated in independence in 1825, the revolt that took place in Sucre in May 1809. Almost like a paradox of history, one year before the bicentennial of the uprising, a shameful incident took place in front of the doors of the Casa de la Libertad (House of Liberty) in Sucre, where Bolivian independence was declared. This incident was at odds with every principle of liberty and equality that Bolivian history has known. On May 24, 2008, about forty people of indigenous and peasant origin were dragged into the main square of Sucre and publicly punished and humiliated there as a symbol of "surrender" and submission. Forced to their knees, trampled on, subjected to blows and verbal abuse, and threatened with sticks and stones, the indigenous and peasant people were obliged to remove and burn the symbols of their collective cultural and political identity, and to kiss the flag of Sucre as a sign of surrender.

How should we understand the cruel episode that took place in Sucre on May 24, 2008? What feelings circulated in the consciousness of the groups that engaged in this violent attack? What consequences will the attack have on the lives of those who were attacked? How can we prevent such acts from being repeated in the future? How should we define and assign burdens of responsibility for the attack?

Some people have said that this cruel episode of violence and humiliation was a response by members of the local population to the three deaths that took place in Sucre in November 2007 during a confrontation between government security forces and supporters of the demand to return the full capital to Sucre. Others see the attack as a reaction to Sucre's frustrated demand to be the nation's full capital; the government's refusal to take up the topic of capital status in the Constituent Assembly added anger to this frustration. While the struggle over the constitution, regional power, and the capital matter greatly, we believe that an explanation based on these issues alone is incomplete. The perceived transgressions associated with the election of Evo Morales as Bolivia's "first indigenous president," and the convocation of a Constituent Assembly that granted decision-making power to men and women who self-identified as indigenous, are of course key contexts for understanding the tragic events of May 24.[1] But much remains to be learned about the short-term and long-term causes of the violence that took place that day—causes that are social, cultural, and political—so that Bolivians may begin to make sense of the event that the country witnessed on May 24.[2]

Partly in response to acts of discrimination and violence (such as those discussed by Calla and Muruchi in this volume), an antiracist agenda began to emerge in Bolivia during 2007. Following the events of May 24, 2008, in Sucre, that agenda gained powerful momentum. As racism became linked with public and physical violence, Bolivian society began to express an antiracist potential in its social organizations, universities, nongovernmental organizations, and within the institutional spaces of the state. People who were victims of racism visited the National Congress as a group to present their formal complaints. A support network came together for them and others who had experienced similar forms of aggression in the polarized political environment that has characterized Bolivia in the era of Evo Morales. This antiracist network includes both state and nonstate entities, and that combination has given the network a national reach.

Efforts to create an antidiscrimination law have been central to the work of the network. In the effort to forge an antiracist legislative agenda for Bolivia, an advisory board made up of representatives from congress, the Ministry of Justice, the Ombudsperson's Office, the Office of the United Nations High Commissioner for Human Rights, and several groups from civil society was established. As legislative options have been debated, two different positions emerged, presenting a dilemma that remains unresolved. One legislative agenda was proposed by the Ombudsperson's Office, the Ministry of Justice, and Commissions of the National Congress (those on the constitution and indigenous affairs). Another legislative agenda has been proposed by the most activist and least institutionalized members of the antiracist network, such as the Assembly of Human Rights and other civil society groups. Those backing the first agenda proposed a general antidiscrimination law that would include various "populations"—as defined by disability, gender, ethnicity, sexual orientation, etc. Proponents of the second agenda called for an antiracist law that would respond directly to the events that took place in Sucre and would be defined in terms of ethnicity exclusively. The two positions are themselves the product of a process of negotiation that has been characterized by confrontation, struggle, and compromise, in an overall context of political polarization. These complex conditions have shaped—and will continue to shape—the effort to reach consensus on an antiracist legislative agenda.

To achieve an agreement about an appropriate legislative agenda, one of the challenges that remains is the unfinished work of analyzing what happened in Sucre on May 24th, so that Bolivians will be able to "name" the violence that took place in the main square and explain it in relation to incidents of racism on a global level. This is important given the resurgence of similar acts of hatred worldwide.

In order to settle on an appropriate legal classification of racist acts, we must also examine the antiracist legislation of other countries as well as Bolivia's own legal traditions. One key task is to define the burdens of responsibility, individual and collective, intellectual and political. That is, Bolivians must decide how to assign responsibility for different types of participation in acts of humiliation, hatred, and violence. One possible conceptualization, which might allow Bolivians to be alert to and prevent a recurrence of this kind of act, is the idea of hate crimes that originated in the civil rights movement of African American people in the United States in the 1950s and 1960s.[3] The notion of hate crimes may help us resolve the legislative dilemma of creating an antiracist law in particular or an antidiscrimination law in general. This concept has also aided the research group of the Observatorio del Racismo in its efforts to contribute to the difficult process of analyzing and "naming" what happened in Sucre. With this concept in mind, in a second issue of the journal *Observatorio* the research group put together a chronology that contextualized the events of May 24th in space and time.[4] We based our timeline on film footage, extracts from local Sucre newspapers, and interviews with the victims who came to the National Congress to report and condemn the act. The recovery of their experiences and points of view, as well as the chronological and detailed description of what happened, has allowed us to consider when and how the violence in Sucre was eminently political, and when and how it was permeated with racism against the indigenous-peasant other. We have also sought to understand the scorn of the urban-popular sectors that participated in this act of humiliation and abuse against those who—according to some of the victims—could have been the attackers' own parents, siblings, or nieces and nephews.[5]

As of June 2010, two distinct positions remain on the legislative agenda: the antiracism position based particularly on ethnicity, which was proposed and shaped by networks of human rights activists; and the antidiscrimination position, which takes into account not just ethnicity but other dimensions of identity such as gender, sexual orientation, disability, etc. The second position was presented to congress in late 2008 by the ombudsperson, the Ministry of Justice, commissions of the National Congress, and other institutional bodies, and was revised throughout 2009. One key point of discussion regarding both positions has to do with the limited outcomes of penalizing acts of discrimination, and the need to focus more broadly on public policy and its implementation, as well as on education and consciousness-raising. The law is of course crucial, but the law is not enough, and the challenge, ultimately, is to forge communities and forms of public life that will allow Bolivians to achieve a more racially just society. This would in turn require that the law itself be made accessible and comprehensible, so that a process of public reflection and debate can take place. The greatest challenges are yet to come and can only be addressed once a law is approved and begins to be implemented. The pursuit of an antiracist legislative agenda in Bolivia will be integrally linked with the broader struggle to transform the state, redistribute resources, and democratize practices of everyday life.

*

In the year since this article was completed, a "Law against Racism and All Forms of Discrimination" was approved by the Asamblea Plurinacional of Bolivia (national legislative body, formerly known as Congress).[6] The law is one piece of a comprehensive agenda; following the reinauguration of Evo Morales as president, in January 2010, the governing party (MAS) intensified its pursuit of a new legislative program in order to implement Bolivia's new constitution. While many laws have been debated and approved since Morales commenced his second term, no other law produced as much dissent and strife as the law against racism of October 2010.

The law has been criticized from diverse angles by distinct sectors of society. One key criticism has to do with the highly punitive nature of the law. And in this context, observers have suggested that the law will have limited effects. For example, a representative of the anti-racist network, Roberto Choque, a historian and Bolivia's first Vice Minister of Decolonization, noted that law and punishment alone would not prevent racist acts from occurring and, more importantly, would not necessarily facilitate an effective fight against racism in all its manifestations.[7] A second criticism has to do with the emphasis on the role of public officials in the antiracist struggle, at the expense of a more holistic approach that would involve diverse sectors and organizations of civil society. A third criticism, one that galvanized Bolivian society as a whole, has to do with the law's infringement against freedom of expression.

According to the Andean Information Network, the new law "strives to make Bolivia a more equitable society both by attempting to prevent racism and discrimination, and by criminalizing racist and discriminatory behavior."[8] Thus the law combats racism but also protects individuals from discrimination based on gender, sexual orientation, age, and physical disability. In its preamble, the law uses international accords on racism and discrimination to address the long history of discrimination and racism in Bolivia. The preamble also mentions Bolivia's new constitution and its mandate for equal social, economic, and cultural opportunity for all citizens. The racist backlash that followed the election of Evo Morales in December 2005 is another focus of attention. Following this preamble, the law then sets the legal parameters for the protection of victims of racism and discrimination. The measures to achieve this include disciplinary action against public and private institutions that commit racist or discriminatory acts. Article 23 of the law, the one contested by the press, defines racism and discrimination as criminal acts and outlines legal consequences for racist or discriminatory organizations, communications media, and for public officials and others who publicize racist or discriminatory ideas. The most severe penalities delineated in this article are reserved for public officials. Article 16 of the law, which was also contested by the press, states that communications media that authorize and publicize racist or discriminatory ideas will be subject to economic sanctions and the suspension of operating licenses.

Two months before the law was approved, a public debate took place that revolved around articles 23 and 16. Communications enterprises and the principal union of journalists claimed that the law was a gag law that violated their rights of expression. Independent and unionized journalists commenced a signature campaign in an effort to change the two articles of the law that restricted these rights. They took their campaign to international forums, including the Organization of American States. A great debate ensued in Bolivia, one that involved blogs, newspaper editorials, meetings, and a hunger strike by journalists. Although the journalists gained nationwide attention, they were ultimately unsuccessful in achieving their goal. The articles in question were not changed and the law was approved as written. The fate of the law, which was beginning to be implemented when this book went to press, remains to be seen.

The law against racism of October 2010 mobilized the various sides of the political divide because it goes to the core of the decolonizing agenda set out by Bolivian social movements. In order to meet the historic demands of the social organizations that brought Evo Morales to power, the government will need to move this larger agenda forward. It will need to take into consideration the diverse criticisms of the law against racism. Thus far, the government has approved a decree that delineates the rules for the implementation of the law.[9] These rules clarify what the penalties will be for violations of the law by the Bolivian communications media. The decree also calls for educational programs to combat discrimination, and includes guidelines that will be used to address racist and discriminatory actions that may be committed by public officials. Bolivia's anti-racist law provoked great conflict and debate because it is integrally linked with the broader struggle to create a more democratic society.

Notes

This chapter was translated by Eileen Willingham and edited by Laura Gotkowitz. An earlier and longer version of this chapter appeared in *Agenda Defensorial* 13, "Observando el Racismo: Racismo y regionalismo en el proceso autonómico: Hacia una perspectiva de clase" (Defensor del Pueblo y Universidad de la Cordillera, 2009). The version of the chapter provided here was written collectively, with initial contributions to the first paragraphs by Carla Espósito and the research team; the rest was written by Pamela Calla. The Observatorio del Racismo was established in July 2007 on the basis of an agreement between the University of the Cordillera and the Ombudsperson's Office (Defensor del Pueblo, a governmental human rights organization). The Observatorio has combined research on racism and violence in Sucre and other cities with efforts to help forge an antiracist agenda in Bolivia. The team of young researchers in the research group of the Observatorio includes Isidora Coria,

Khantuta Muruchi, Bethel Núñez, Andrés Calla, Eduardo Paz, and Martín Torrico. Pamela Calla is the director of the research group and María Lagos is currently the group's coordinator. The Observatorio coordinated its activities with the Ombudsperson's Office and other relevant entities, such as the Office of the United Nations High Commissioner for Human Rights and activist networks in civil society.

1. For an in-depth discussion, see the chapter by Calla and Muruchi in this volume.

2. For a chronology, see the introduction by Gotkowitz in this volume.

3. Use of the term "hate crime" to characterize the act of hatred that took place in Sucre was suggested by Laura Gotkowitz in a conversation about the difficulties facing the advisory board created by the Ombudsperson's Office as it sought to come to a consensus on a proposal for a law.

4. *Agenda Defensorial* 13, "Observando el Racismo: Racismo y regionalismo en el proceso autonómico: Hacia una perspectiva de clase," Defensor del Pueblo y Universidad de la Cordillera, 2009.

5. In a seminar on discrimination and racism toward women, organized by the Vice-Ministry for Gender (which was previously part of the Ministry of Justice), a woman from a rural area of Chuquisaca expressed this concern and asked, "What is wrong with the education system? It makes our children leave school and mistreat their parents."

6. The text of the law is available at http://www.lostiempos.com.

7. Capítulo de Derechos Humanos, June 2008.

8. Andean Information Network, October 15, 2010 and February 4, 2011.

9. Estado Plurinacional de Bolivia, January 5, 2011, "La Asamblea Legislativa Plurinacional, Decreto Supremo No. 0762, "Reglamento a la Ley Contra el Racismo y Toda Forma de Discriminación." Cited in Andean Information Network, February 4, 2011.

PART V ✳ Concluding Comments

A Postcolonial Palimpsest:

The Work Race Does in Latin America

FLORENCIA E. MALLON

In the past generation, the linguistic turn's emphasis on the constructed nature of all categories and forms of explanation has grown to dominate much intellectual discourse. Those of us still committed to politically relevant analysis have repeatedly faced a similar quandary. True, all social, cultural, political, and symbolic terms and relationships are constructed, and it is no longer possible to take them at face value. But what happens when, in the midst of a political confrontation or crisis, individuals or social movements deploy reified categories or images as motivation or explanation for action? Can we limit ourselves to criticizing, from an intellectual vantage point, the limitations of such a discourse? Or do we need to take seriously the ways in which such categories and images are being (re)inscribed, in a sense, as social realities?

These questions are especially salient when the subject of analysis is race. In the twentieth century, especially after the Second World War, notions of biological race entered into intellectual and political decline. In Latin America, there is also an enduring belief that the region's systems of racial classification have historically been more flexible. At the same time, in recent years, many of the region's most dramatic conflicts—civil wars, human rights abuse, struggles over resources in an increasingly globalized world, demands for regional and political autonomy—have been perceived as having a racialized component. To what extent, then, can we understand Latin America as different? And to what extent can we dismiss more fixed notions of race as historically "passé" or "superseded"? The essays in this volume attempt answers to these questions by considering, as Laura Gotkowitz explains in her introduction, what Thomas Holt has called the "effects" of race, or the "work race does."

Given Bolivia's emblematic place in recent political events—the Water Wars in Cochabamba in 2000; numerous popular uprisings in El Alto, the predominantly Aymara city bordering La Paz; the electoral victory of Evo Morales in December 2005, making him Bolivia's first indigenous president; and the violent conflicts in Sucre and Santa Cruz over political reorganization and regional autonomy—it is perhaps not surprising, and in some ways very appropriate, that Bolivia is the subject of more than half the volume. Indeed, Bolivian history—especially in its more recent alternative periodizations that highlight the continuities of Aymara mobilization—emerges as an implicit plotline around which the other cases are interwoven. With conquest and colonialism as a starting point, this narrative pauses at key junctures important in the Bolivian story: the colonial crisis of the 1780s; the late nineteenth-century civil war over the location of the nation's capital; the conflicts over education and "civilization" in the 1920s and 1930s; and recent attempts to "refound" the Bolivian nation with the Constituent Assembly of 2007. The rest of the essays in this book, more or less evenly distributed in their focus between Mexico and Guatemala on one side and Ecuador and Peru on the other, serve as confirmation, contrast, and counterpoint to the chapters on Bolivia.

The juxtaposition of a Bolivian narrative with narratives in other Latin American countries suggests a path of broader generalization about how race is constructed, performed, and contested, tracing how racial struggles are reburied in a widening palimpsest of memory, only to be disinterred once again in another historical moment, reconstructed yet again and redeployed. By focusing in depth on specific cases that dialogue and reverberate among themselves, we can reflect on the intricate ways in which race interacts with and is constructed by other relations of power. As a result, however, this is a volume not so much about race as about the construction of indigeneity. The one exception is the essay by Kathryn Burns on the colonial period, which places notions of purity of blood, lineage, and religion into a context that includes Moorish, Jewish, and African-descendant groups.

The depth and breadth of historical analysis that this focus permits also provide stimulating suggestions about the work race does, suggestions that can be useful and informative in other contexts.

Colonial Roots and Reconstructions

In her analytical efforts to unfix colonial notions of race, Kathryn Burns explores the ways in which, in the context of the Iberian military expansion against Islam, notions of purity of blood became connected to questions of lineage and religious belief. As part of an effort to define boundaries between groups in the context of military and religious confrontation, the unease associated with "in-between" populations helped articulate race with religion and lineage, and in a sense to equate conversos, moriscos, and mestizos as dangerous because they were supposedly impure, hard to define, and thus hard to control. By placing the construction of race at the militarized boundaries between societies and cultures in conflict, Burns explores the multiple elements associated with racialization as a system of border fixing. In such a context, race becomes an especially salient category when borders are unclear or loose, when too many people are in-between, when too much territory is up for grabs. And even though her perspective is developed in the context of the early colonial period, it connects in interesting ways with Lomnitz's notion that Mexican constructions of a "national race" in the postcolonial period are distinguished in particular by the dramatic and conflictive nature of U.S.-Mexican interactions along the two countries' extensive common border.

Historicizing race relations during the crisis of a mature colonial system, Sinclair Thomson argues that race is salient at times of change and instability in part because war and crisis clarify relations in a society and make it easier for a historian to see them. He also demonstrates, however, that in addition to becoming clearer at moments of conflict, race relations also change. During the course of the Andean civil war in the 1780s, Thomson argues, the separation between indigenous people and Spaniards became more racialized, as terms used socially to denote Spaniards and their allies, such as "*pukakungas*" (those with red necks) or "*q'aras*" (naked or bald ones), became coded as "white." This happened, Thomson suggests, essentially for political reasons. In the earlier part of the conflict the nonindigenous people pardoned after Túpac Amaru's victory in Sorata were obliged to dress as Indian and call themselves "Qollas." This blurring of racial boundaries was impossible once it became clear that Spaniards, or "Creoles," were not willing to become part of one larger community of "Americans."

One important benefit emerging from the historically contingent and constructivist approach offered by Thomson and Burns is that it helps us understand powerful but alternative meanings associated with race, such as "people," "nation," and "community." As forms of collective identity that contain memories of historical struggle, racialized categories such as "Indian" or "black" have political and cultural resonances that we ignore at our peril. An additional example of this, in Spanish-speaking populations, would be the notion of "La Raza," one of the central topics of Claudio Lomnitz's essay.

Although Lomnitz's essay focuses rather specifically on the evolution of a notion of "la raza mexicana" within Mexican history and in relation to the U.S.-Mexican border, we can broaden the lens to consider the wider implications of the notion of a "national race" by comparing Mexico to other parts of Latin America. Two cases where the question of peoples of African descent comes up most notably are those involving Brazil and Cuba. To Lomnitz's discussion of the failed project to construct a statue of "Brazilian man" we might add the famous notion of racial democracy attributed to Gilberto Freyre, and the debates around Brazil's "three races" set into motion by Oswald de Andrade's "Manifesto Antropófago." In this context, it is especially interesting to note that in a recent article about Freyre, Thomas Skidmore emphasized the importance of Freyre's years in the United States to the formation of his thought about race and Brazilian culture.[1] And Andrade's controversial notion of cultural cannibalism, developed in the 1920s, struggled with a triangulation of race that would come into play more fully in Mexico only at the end of the twentieth century, with the expansion of work on and debate around the historical role of the Afro-Mexican population.[2] In Cuba, however, as Aviva Chomsky has recently suggested, notions of "national race" combined a romantic narrative of Indian extermination through resistance with the development of a capacious Cuban identity that folded in certain forms of "civilized" Afro-Cubanness while rejecting immigrants of African descent from other parts of the Caribbean.[3]

A consideration of Brazil and Cuba in relation to Mexico, then, allows us to see how the Mexican case may not be quite as unique as it seems at first glance. In a variety of countries without a long border with the United States, the racialization of a national identity as a mixture of European and non-European—or, one might more accurately say, an incorporation of the non-European into the European through education and "civilization"—was crucial to the emergence of national states at the beginning of the twentieth century. But there is another way in which the Mexican case can help us think through the multiple variations of the work race has done in Latin America.

In 1904, Chilean medical doctor Nicolás Palacios published his extremely influential *Raza chilena*, in which he argued that Chilean nationality was superior precisely because it was a mixture of a race of Spanish conquerors whom he called *godos* (Goths) and the courageous and militarily superior Araucanos, or Mapuche.[4] These ideas were taken up by Chilean nationalist intellectuals in the 1920s, and by Chilean national socialists in the following decade. Despite the controversy associated today with these ideas, a controversy due especially to their adoption by the Chilean Nazi party, we might consider, in relation to the Mexican case, how a frontier—a frontier not necessarily or only with another nation-state in a process of expansion, but also with unpacified and militarily resistant indigenous people—might have an important effect on the way in which the nation, as a racialized form, emerges historically.

A complete consideration of how the racialization of the nation occurs, however, needs to include not only an analysis of elite statemakers, but an analysis of the evolution of popular forms of national identity. In the case of the U.S.-Mexican border, for example, we find that the term "La Raza" was also used by the Mexican Americans more generally, and especially by the Chicano movement. And as my current research is uncovering, some Mapuche activists in southern Chile in the 1920s and 1930s used the same term to denote the Mapuche people as a whole.[5] How these various forms of racialization—from above and from below—took shape across the nineteenth century and the twentieth must be understood in the context of postcolonial statemaking and the battles over citizenship that it entailed.

Postcolonial Statemaking and Exclusionary Citizenship

After the colonial crisis of the late eighteenth century and the early nineteenth century transformed notions and practices of racialization that had themselves been transformed by the construction of a colonial system, the exigencies of statemaking in the mid- to late nineteenth century yielded attempts to fix and harden racial categories in the interest of political consolidation. As Rossana Barragán demonstrates in her essay on late nineteenth-century Bolivia, the state was a crucial actor in the construction of race through the process of "naming and classification" at the center of census activity. The interplay of race and ethnicity with geographical mapping, and the crucial role of gender and class differences in the constitution of racial categories, emerge in Barragán's analysis as essential tools in the kit of state control.

By tracing the ways in which the postcolonial state constructed race in nineteenth-century Guatemala, Arturo Taracena's essay provides an excellent counterpoint to Barragán's. In Taracena's rendering, a system of exclusionary citizenship developed in Guatemala through segregation. The separation of Indian and ladino was justified, despite formal adherence to a liberal discourse of citizenship, through a narrative of Maya decadence. Because a previously great Maya civilization was in dramatic decline when the Spanish arrived, conquest and domination—as well as ongoing exploitation—were implicitly justified and explained because of cultural "degradation" and "decay."

In Seemin Qayum's analysis of elite Bolivian intellectual discourse, the Aymara ruins of Tiwanaku become a symbol of a late, great civilization nurturing Bolivian nationality and the representation of a "usable past" that explains why Spanish conquest was inevitable. This analysis dovetails dramatically with Taracena's discussion of Guatemalan elites' version of Maya "decadence." Indeed, in the two cases the selective reconstruction of a great indigenous past defines a new American "nationality" and explains why this nationality cannot be rooted in native traditions. Elite statemakers in Bolivia and Guatemala thus articulate notions of indigenous decline to the spatial construction of race and the geographical separation of racial groups, bringing us back to Burns's suggestion that racialization finds an important impetus in elites' political anxieties and their need to set boundaries as a form of control. And the idea that mapping race, culture, and ethnicity provides an answer to elites' sociopolitical and racial anxieties also lies at the core of Brooke Larson's and Deborah Poole's essays.

Larson considers how the rural-urban, "uncivilized"-*letrado* divide was reconstructed in early twentieth-century Bolivia. As part of a reaction to Aymara participation and violent protest within the 1899 liberal-conservative civil war, elite fears of mob violence mixed with notions of improperly educated Indians, first *cholos* and later *caciques-apoderados*. The response by a generation of reformist intellectuals was to map through education the "appropriate" locations for Indians and whites. The "work schools" reformists elaborated, clearly modeled on U.S. projects for African American and Native

American education, envisioned training for Indians that would take advantage of their "natural" propensity for high-altitude rural occupations and limit their presence in the city.

For her part, Poole analyzes how in the Mexican state of Oaxaca, where comparatively powerful indigenous communities largely resisted nineteenth-century liberal efforts to privatize indigenous lands, elites used cultural representation, festivals, and rituals to map the region's ethnic and racial relations in culturally safe ways. During the Porfiriato, for example, archaeologists traced the genealogy of the region's indigenous populations and, in ways reminiscent of the efforts of Guatemalan or Bolivian intellectuals, honored both the late greatness of indigenous civilization as a prelude to "American" nationality and emphasized the past nature of such greatness. At the same time, however, as Poole also shows, in postrevolutionary Oaxaca elite cultural politics changed and, through the Homenaje Racial of 1932 that served as precursor to today's Guelaguetza festival, ethnic and racial relations were reorganized into a form of controlled multiculturalism.

Taken together, the Barragán, Taracena, Qayum, Larson, and Poole essays provide a fascinating perspective on how intellectuals, policymakers, and states intervened in the construction of racial categories through the mapping of power relations. That racial and ethnic boundaries and categories are in part the product of this kind of deployment of power has been discussed in the African Studies field for years, and more recently has taken on a larger presence in the literatures on colonialism and postcolonialism.[6] Bringing these themes into the discussion of race in Latin America, therefore, is most welcome. At the same time, as Poole implies in her discussion of indigenous resistance to liberal reforms, race is constructed at the juncture of elite efforts at social control and subaltern attempts at cultural and political mobilization and unification. In this sense, recalling Thomson's suggestion that race can also be constructed as "people," "community," or "nation" is particularly relevant here.

In part due to the regional and temporal focus of this book, indigenismo, as an elite attempt to deflect subaltern mobilization, receives less attention. One of the two essays on Mexico, by Deborah Poole, provides us with a fascinating example of regional multicultural policy but focuses on a part of Mexico where participation in the 1910 Revolution was relatively peripheral and therefore does not treat the region's relationship with the central state. Claudio Lomnitz gestures to the crucial role of notions of national race in the development of postrevolutionary social policy, but his essay focuses less on these policies than on demonstrating the limits of postrevolutionary Mexican intellectual production.

In the other cases addressed in this volume, the presence of indigenismo seems to have been less central. In Guatemala and other parts of Central America, indigenismo came later, and was less organically connected to a national-popular project. As Larson shows, in Bolivia the vexed relationship between indigenous mobilization and elite responses in the twentieth century began as a project of educational segregation. Even after the revolution in 1952, Bolivian policymakers did not forge a Mexican-style indigenismo, in part, Qayum suggests, because of the specter of autonomous Aymara mobilization.

Esteban Ticona's essay on Eduardo Leandro Nina Qhispi provides us with a further reminder on this point. A laudatory biography that focuses on Nina Qhispi's efforts toward Indian education in Bolivia in the 1920s, Ticona's chapter also seeks to find in Nina Qhispi's political and cultural project a precursor for contemporary Bolivian efforts at decolonization. When placed side by side with the Larson and Qayum essays, Ticona's chapter is a much-needed companion piece highlighting the nature and importance of Aymara mobilization and, most notably, the movement of the caciques-apoderados.

The important dynamic between elite and subaltern cultural and political imaginaries that can be gleaned from these essays also brings to the foreground a missing piece in our consideration of the nineteenth century. What happened in the years between the colonial crisis and independence wars of the early 1800s and the state-driven efforts at control through racialization of the latter decades of the nineteenth century? If we start with Thomson's idea that the Andean Civil War in the 1780s was, in a sense, a missed opportunity, when a dream of multiracial and multiethnic "American" community came unraveled, we must wonder how this moment of political opportunity was experienced in other parts of the continent. Were there echoes in the first decades after independence, before newly consolidating states remapped territory and racial difference into a system of social control? Research carried out over the last decade and a half in a variety of regions suggests that there were.

On the elite side of the equation, Rebecca Earle has recently explored some of the ways in which Creole insurgents in early nineteenth-century Chile, Colombia, Ecuador, Guatemala, Peru, and Mexico deployed images of indigenous pre-Columbian nationhood as part of their narratives of and justifications for independence. In ways that were partially similar to the efforts of reformist intellectuals discussed by Taracena and Qayum, these patriots sought the origins of their unique national identities in a utopian rendering of preconquest indigenous societies.[7] In a sense, we may see this as the elite counterpart to Túpac Amaru's dream of a multiethnic American future, the difference lying precisely in which side of the "multi" was thought to be hegemonic.

In such a context, the conflicts and civil wars of the first half of the nineteenth century take on a deeper meaning, as the ultimate failure of this multiethnic project worked its way through the social fabric of the newly independent Latin American societies. And indeed, as work on Colombia, Peru, Mexico, and late nineteenth-century Cuba has shown, subaltern groups took seriously the promise of this project and, by making claims on emerging national polities, called into question elite hegemony. This challenge from below then prompted the closing of opportunities and the redrawing and remapping of social and political boundaries through racialization.[8]

Taking this broad perspective, we might suggest that a recurring dynamic emerged between the vision of American identity deployed by subalterns and indigenous groups on the one hand, and elite Creoles on the other. While both groups seemed to agree that the contribution of the original indigenous Americans and their polities was crucial to the emerging nations of the continent, the mobilizing power of this insurgent Enlightenment liberalism proved too dangerous for Creoles. Thus, by the late nineteenth century, as Barragán, Larson, Poole, Qayum, and Taracena all demonstrate, techniques of state domination were combined with intellectual discourse and representation to reinscribe the racial and geographical boundary between dangerous plebes and national elites.

As the layers of previous struggles were added to the growing palimpsest of race in Latin American history, an ongoing pattern of contestation emerged. On one side was a multiethnic vision of community articulated with the more egalitarian versions of the Enlightenment project, most notably insurgent liberalism and, especially after 1848, emerging forms of socialism. On the other side was a more exclusionary version of Enlightenment ideology, increasingly tied to positivism, in which race was deployed to reestablish the boundaries of a more hierarchically organized nation-state. Of course, as we know and as the Ticona essay suggests, the new revolutionary opening of the early twentieth century once again resuscitated and reconstructed earlier, more radical meanings of multiethnic community, not only in the caciques-apoderados movement, but increasingly in the form of new popular and leftist imaginaries and coalitions.

The Enduring Power of Postcolonialism in Twentieth-Century Latin America

The second period of multiethnic experimentation in postcolonial Latin American history, the revolutionary and socialist movements of the first three-quarters of the twentieth century, is lightly treated by the essays in this book. One way to explore the overall importance of this period to our understandings of race in Latin America may be to place it in a broader transnational perspective. The defeat of insurgent liberalism by liberal elites favoring consolidation in the nineteenth century created the conditions for a rearticulation of racial boundaries in Latin America; but the rise of anarchism and socialism also generated, at a world level, a twentieth-century version of earlier egalitarian imaginings. As Greg Grandin and Jeffrey Gould have argued in regard to Central America, the promise of this new socialist imaginary was that it explained oppression—and the ability to transcend it—through recourse to a historicized vision of exploitation and class struggle, rather than a naturalized and thus inherent difference between races.[9] The power of such a vision became clear throughout the world, in the period between the Mexican and Russian revolutions of 1910 and 1917, and the decolonization movements after the Second World War. Indeed, as recent work has begun to examine, the broad claims to equality that the socialist vision made possible were also taken up by indigenous movements in coalition with leftist or revolutionary movements.[10] By the 1980s and 1990s, however, this vision had come apart under the combined pressures of the Cold War, military dictatorships, and the fall of the Soviet Union. Once again, Latin America's postcolonial palimpsest was inscribed with the defeat of a new attempt at multiethnic egalitarianism.

It is in the context of this new moment that we see across the world the reemergence of indigenous militancy, in part as a response to the failure of earlier multiethnic experiments. The rest of the essays in the volume deal, from a variety of perspectives, with this current moment. In different ways, they all bring to the fore the deep anxieties and potential for violent confrontation that emerge when apparently stable alignments of race, geography, and power are once again called into question.

The Calla and Muruchi chapter and the essay authored by the Observatorio del Racismo are especially dramatic in this regard. As Andrés Calla and Khantuta Muruchi make clear, when the system of domination in Bolivia was called into question by the election of Evo Morales, what had been a relatively stable, structural, and silent racism was quickly transformed into a virulent, open, and confrontational racism. The Observatorio essay's treatment of the racially motivated violence against indigenous people in Sucre dramatically calls into question the erosion of biological and phenotypical definitions of race. Taken together, these two essays highlight how, at moments of dramatic sociopolitical change, layers long hidden in the palimpsest of race can suddenly be seen again and reinscribe conflict with an essentialist material reality. Particularly striking in this regard is the reemergence of Sucre's demand for "capitalía plena," articulated historically with the 1899 civil war and the specter of race war.

At one level, these recent confrontations in Bolivia can be seen as the culmination, in a situation where an indigenous president was elected, of the many challenges to existing structures of power that indigenous movements have presented throughout Latin America over the past generation. The remaining essays, by Colloredo-Mansfeld, Hale, and García and Lucero, also deal with these challenges. In similar ways to what Barragán, Larson, Qayum, and Taracena found for Bolivia and Guatemala, Rudi Colloredo-Mansfeld shows that in Ecuador, indigeneity had been mapped as rural. At the same time, he explores how an emerging urban indigenous group has attempted to empower itself culturally and politically by reinscribing indigeneity onto an urban landscape.

Charles Hale's essay, reflecting at the regional level in Guatemala after the end of that country's bloody civil war, attempts to move the discussion beyond the politicization of Maya identity to what he considers a new form of ethnic ideology, in which the boundaries between Indian and ladino have become blurred and the placing of individuals in particular categories much more difficult. To a certain extent, Hale's assessment of the situation in Guatemala runs counter to the historical trends observed elsewhere, in which the results of war were, rather, to highlight or harden boundaries between racial groups. Even in Guatemala, the emergence of a pan-Maya political and cultural movement after the civil war has been viewed by scholars as an example of how violent conflict contributed to a rearticulation and reorganization of racially and culturally based identities.[11] By examining a specific mixed-race stratum of urban poor at the regional level, however, Hale supports the conclusions reached by Lucero and García, that when dealing with the construction of race it is important to focus on regional complexities, lest we think that national-level generalizations can tell the whole story. At the same time, his suggestion that this new trend in Guatemala may be a "mestizaje from below" opens up the possibility that we may be on the verge of yet another chapter in the complex history of race in Latin America.

Given recent trends toward self-reflexiveness in the academy, it is perhaps surprising that only the essay by María Elena García and Antonio Lucero takes a self-critical stance on the ways in which we produce knowledge. The payoff of such an approach is high, for it allows us to look inside the conflicts over authenticity that exist within indigenous movements and between activists and academics. The stakes are high, as well, since they involve not only the access to international funding that most movements require, but also the prestige of leaders and organizations on the broader international scene. And as they focus on the case of Peru, García and Lucero also allow us to get a glimpse of the ways in which the Shining Path war has transformed the consciousness and relevance of struggles for indigenous rights.

*

Taken as a whole, this volume demonstrates that it is precisely at the present moment of intensifying indigenous mobilization and hardening racist reaction that the full meaning of indigenous political identities must be sought in a careful historical analysis of the earlier types of work that race has done. Putting Latin America's postcolonial palimpsest on a broader transnational canvas allows us to more fully understand the continuities and changes that underlie the role of indigenous peoples in coalitions for social change. While I do not presume that such reflections apply equally well to people of African descent or other racial groups, it is my hope that some of the more general notions contained herein might echo more broadly.

The colonial history of Latin America helps us understand how the notions of race that emerged at the dawn of the "modern" era were deeply interlaced with questions of conquest, religious conversion, and geographic boundarymaking. Moreover, in Enlightenment Europe, during the eighteenth century, imperial interest in profit, most notably from the slave trade and the export economies of the Americas, ran counter to the more egalitarian imaginings of insurgent liberalisms. As Elizabeth Colwill has suggested for the case of the French Revolution, the difficult negotiations of French revolutionaries with proslavery interests in the context of empire, especially in the case of Saint Domingue, yielded a vision of revolutionary citizenship in which "proslavery paternalism" and "antislavery Jacobinism" could agree on the need to "gently draw the former slaves from savagery toward civilization through an apprenticeship in republican virtue."[12] And there are strong reverberations, temporal, social, and political, between Saint Domingue and the Andean Civil War, as it is treated by Thomson. In both cases, visions of transformation inspired by the egalitarian rumors circulating at the end of the eighteenth century were transformed instead into racialized conflicts that redrew colonial divides.

Enlightenment-based visions and promises of national-democratic inclusion and equality, from the beginning of their implementation in Europe and Latin America, excluded peoples deemed uncivilized in the context of colonialism. The political mapping of peoples onto a historical continuum between barbarism and civilization, what Dipesh Chakrabarty has called the "not-yet" approach to the historical agency of colonized peoples, also made its way across Latin America in the nineteenth century as challenges to elite hegemony in the newly independent republics were met by the geographical and political remapping of racial boundaries.[13]

During the first half of the twentieth century, a new revolutionary opening combined with movements for decolonization to open a second window of opportunity for multiethnic and multiracial liberation. As María Josefina Saldaña-Portillo suggests in her work on revolutionary subjectivity and Sandinista agrarian reform, however, there was more than a passing resemblance between colonial capitalism's subjugation of "backward" peoples and narratives of socialist liberation and incorporation. In her analysis of Che Guevara's discourse of revolutionary transformation, for example, she notes the similarities between his vision of "leaving behind" an immature, prerevolutionary consciousness, and the development model's leaving behind of premodern practices and consciousness. "Both models invariably 'leave behind' the ethnic particularity of indigenous or peasant subjectivity," she writes, "while carrying forward a racialized and masculinist understanding of fully modern, revolutionary agency." In her discussion of the Sandinista agrarian reform, she notes the Sandinista belief that "land in the hands of land-poor peasants would lead to irrational production." Thus the modernizing state needed to oversee the education of those subaltern subjects not quite ready for revolutionary modernity.[14] We can, moreover, easily see the connection between Sandinista agrarian policy and the Sandinistas' initial confrontations with the indigenous peoples of the Atlantic Coast, where this same concern with educating revolutionary subjects helped bring that region to civil war.

The present moment in Latin American history, when seen in the context of these historical reflections, takes on additional layers of meaning. On one side, we can see how, at various points across the past two and a half centuries, recurring revolutionary openings have called up multiethnic and multiracial dreams of egalitarian community. At such moments, people could see beyond race as a naturalized phenomenon to a place where all could enjoy the equal benefits of citizenship. It was precisely the power of such a vision, of such a promise, that made it so dangerous.

Yet at the same time, the boundaries of class and race have not lined up neatly in Latin American history. The potentially egalitarian, multiethnic imaginings of an insurgent liberalism or socialism was dangerous not only for Creole or European elites, but also for the groups of more educated and prosperous indigenous mediators who, in their efforts to represent their communities, developed their own stake in the maintenance of power relations. As Thomson has argued elsewhere, a crisis of mediation in Aymara communities in the second half of the eighteenth century contributed mightily to the legitimacy of a leader like Tomás Katari, himself not of elite stock.[15] As Grandin has also shown for Quetzaltenango during the Guatemalan Spring of 1944–54, not all K'ich'e elites supported the more egalitarian project of Arévalo and Arbenz.[16] And from the other side of the class equation, as work on twentieth-century revolutionary moments in Latin American history has begun to make clear, popular organizations have not always taken indigenous or other racially distinct groups into equal account.[17]

In such a context, it might be useful to return to the essay by Hale in this volume. Focusing on the refusal of Chimaltenango's urban youth to be classified according to more recognizable categories of "Indian" and "ladino," he postulates the possibility of a "mestizaje from below" in contemporary Guatemala. While recognizing the persistence of color and cultural prejudice among intermediate social strata, Hale also points out the cultural creativity and basic rejection of more established racial labels contained in this new trend. He warns that, in the end, Maya cultural activists would do well to pay attention to this sector, lest it be wooed by the political right.

The work race does, then, is complicated, indeed. On the one hand, as the essays in this book have shown, racial categories and the mapping of racial hierarchies have proven to be extremely powerful weapons with which to deflect challenges to power and reestablish hierarchies and social control. On the other hand, as Thomson has suggested, racial categories and discourses of identity have also been important tools in the building of community, and in the unification of colonized peoples across lines of class and privilege. And even within the most powerful historical challenges to class power and colonialism, whether those challenges are insurgent liberalism or socialism, enduring teleologies of "progress," "education," and "modernity" have let racial hierarchies back in through the side door.

The present moment provides in some ways a unique opportunity to decolonize social relations by building yet another multiethnic coalition. The potential power of such a coalition, this time under the hegemony of indigenous and other colonized peoples, has been previewed over the past fifteen years in different incarnations, in situations as distinct from each other as those in Chiapas, Mexico, and Bolivia. A full excavation of Latin America's postcolonial palimpsest, however, also gives us pause. As earlier revolutionary experiments, as well as the contemporary case of Bolivia demonstrate, a multiethnic coalition, whether led by colonized people or not, carries within itself the memories, practices, and power relations of earlier constructions of race and power.

Notes

1. Skidmore 2002.

2. Andrade 1928 and, for an introduction to questions of Afro-Mexican history, see Andrews 2004.

3. Chomsky 2000.

4. Palacios 1918.

5. For a preview of some of these issues and arguments in relation to the Mapuche case, see Mallon 2009.

6. Early examples of this literature for Africa include Brass 1985 and Lonsdale 1977. Ann Laura Stoler has explored issues of race and colonial state-building in Stoler 1995 and 2002.

7. Earle 2007.

8. On Colombia, see Lasso 2007, Múnera 1998, Sanders 2004. On Cuba, see Ferrer 1999, Helg 1995. On Peru, see Mallon 1995, Thurner 1997. On Mexico, see Guardino 1996, Mallon 1995.

9. Gould and Lauria-Santiago 2008, Grandin 2004. Although Gould coauthored the book with Lauria-Santiago, I only cite Gould in reference to this idea because it comes from a part of the text for which he has main responsibility.

10. Grandin 2004; Mallon 2005 and 2009; Correa, Molina, and Yáñez 2005; Gotkowitz 2007; Becker 2008.

11. Arias 2001; Warren 1998a.

12. Colwill 1998, 214.

13. Chakrabarty 2000.

14. Saldaña-Portillo 2003. The citation about Guevara is on page 89; about the Sandinista agrarian reform, on page 147.

15. Thomson 2002.

16. Grandin 2000.

17. Hale 1994; Mallon 2003 and 2005.

BIBLIOGRAPHY

Abecia Baldivieso, Valentín. 1973. *Historiografía Boliviana*. La Paz: Editorial Juventud.
Abercrombie, Thomas. 1998. *Pathways of Memory and Power: Ethnography and History Among an Andean People*. Madison: University of Wisconsin Press.
Acuña, Víctor Hugo. 1995. "Autoritarismo y Democracia en Centroamérica: La Larga Duración (Siglos XIX y XX)." In *Nicaragua en busca de su identidad*, edited by Frances Kinloch Tijerino, 535–71. Managua: IHN-PNED.
Adams, David Wallace. 1995. *Education for Extinction: American Indians and the Boarding School Experience, 1875–1928*. Lawrence: University Press of Kansas.
Adams, Richard N. 1994. "Guatemalan Ladinization and History." *The Americas* 50, no. 4: 527–43.
———. 1992. "Las masacres de Patzicía en 1944: Una Reflexión." *Winak* 7, nos. 1–4: 3–40.
———. 1990. "Ethnic Images and Strategies in 1944." In *Guatemalan Indians and the State, 1540 to 1988*. Austin: University of Texas Press.
———. 1956. "La ladinización en Guatemala." In *Integración social en Guatemala*. Vol. 3, 213–44. Guatemala: Seminario de Integración Social Guatemalteca.
Adelman, Jeremy. 2004. "Latin American Longue Durées." *Latin American Research Review* 39, no. 1: 223–37.
Adorno, Rolena. 1986. *Guaman Poma: Writing and Resistance in Colonial Peru*. Austin: University of Texas Press.
Agamben, Giorgio. 2000. "What is a People?" In *Means without End: Notes on Politics*, translated and edited by Vincenzo Binetti and Cesare Casarino, 29–35. Minneapolis: University of Minnesota Press.
Agenda Defensorial No. 13. 2009. *Observando el Racismo: Racismo y regionalismo en el proceso autonómico: Hacia una perspectiva de clase*. La Paz: Defensor del Pueblo y Universidad de la Cordillera.

Albarracín, Waldo, and Pamela Calla. 2008. "Investigar el racismo para combatirlo mejor." In *Observando el Racismo: Racismo y regionalismo en el proceso constituyente*, Observatorio del racismo en Bolivia, Área de Investigación. La Paz: Defensor del Pueblo y Universidad de la Cordillera.

Albarracín Millán, Juan. 1978. *El Gran Debate: Positivismo e irracionalismo en el estudio de la sociedad boliviana*. La Paz.

Albó, Xavier. 2008. "El perfil de los Constituyentes." *Tínkazos: Revista boliviana de ciencias sociales* 23 and 24 (March): 49–63.

———. 2006. "El Alto, La Vorágine de Una Ciudad Única." *Journal of Latin American Anthropology* 11, no. 2: 329–50.

———. 2002. *Pueblos Indios en la Política*. La Paz: Plural Editores/CIPCA.

———. 1991. "El retorno del indio." *Revista Andina* 9, no. 2: 299–345.

Alonso, Ana María. 2005. "Territorializing the Nation and Integrating the Indian: 'Mestizaje' in Mexican Official Discourses and Public Culture." In *Sovereign Bodies*, edited by Thomas Blom Hansen and Finn Stepputat. Princeton: Princeton University Press.

———. 2004. "Conforming Disconformity: 'Mestizaje,' Hybridity and the Aesthetics of Mexican Nationalism." *Cultural Anthropology* 19, no. 4: 459–90.

———. 1995. *Thread of Blood: Colonialism, Revolution, and Gender on Mexico's Northern Frontier*. Tucson: University of Arizona Press.

———. 1994. "The Politics of Space, Time and Substance: State Formation, Nationalism, and Ethnicity." *Annual Review of Anthropology* 23: 379–405.

Alvarez, Sonia, Evelina Dagnino, and Arturo Escobar. 1998. Introduction to *Cultures of Politics, Politics of Cultures: Re-visioning Latin American Social Movements*, edited by Sonia Alvarez, Evelina Dagnino, and Arturo Escobar, 1–29. Boulder, Colo.: Westview Press.

Amnesty International. 1986. *Mexico: Human Rights in Rural Areas: Exchange of Documents with the Mexican Government on Human Rights Violations in Oaxaca and Chiapas*. London: Amnesty International.

Anaya Muñoz, Alejandro. 2004. "Explaining the Politics of Recognition of Ethnic Diversity and Indigenous Peoples' Rights in Oaxaca, Mexico." *Bulletin of Latin America Research* 23, no. 4: 414–33.

Andean Information Network. "Conflict and Consensus: The Anti-racism and Discrimination Law in Bolivia Part I, Content and Justification of the Legislation," October 15, 2010, http://ain-bolivia.org.

———. "Conflict and Consensus Part II: Bolivian Anti-Racism and Discrimination Regulations Address Freedom of Press Concerns," written by Emma Banks, February 4, 2011, http://ain-bolivia.org.

Anderson, Benedict. 1983. *Imagined Communities: Reflections on the Origin and Spread of Nationalism*. London: Verso.

Anderson, Perry. 1979. *Lineages of the Absolutist State*. New York: Verso.

Andolina, Robert. 2003. "The Sovereign and Its Shadow: Constituent Assembly and Indigenous Movement in Ecuador." *Journal of Latin American Studies* 35: 721–50.

Andolina, Robert, Nina Laurie, and Sarah A. Radcliffe. 2009. *Indigenous Development in the Andes: Culture, Power, and Transnationalism.* Durham: Duke University Press.

——. 1999. "Colonial Legacies and Plurinational Imaginaries: Indigenous Movement Politics in Ecuador and Bolivia." Ph.D. diss., University of Minnesota.

Andrade, Oswald de. 1928. "Manifesto Antropófago." *Revista de Antropofagia* 1, no. 1 (May).

Andrews, George Reid. 2004. *Afro-Latin America, 1800–2000.* Oxford: Oxford University Press.

Angrand, Léonce. 1866. *Antiquités américaines.* Paris: Imprimerie de J. Clayes.

Anonymous. 1897. *Tiahuanaco; Datos para la defensa de la capital de la segunda sección de Pacajes.* La Paz: Taller Tipo-Litográfico.

Appadurai, Arjun. 1988. *The Social Life of Things: Commodities in Cultural Perspective.* New York: Cambridge University Press.

Appelbaum, Nancy. 2003. *Muddied Waters: Race, Region, and Local History in Colombia, 1846–1948.* Durham: Duke University Press.

Appelbaum, Nancy, Anne MacPherson, and Karin Rosemblatt, eds. 2003a. *Race and Nation in Modern Latin America.* Chapel Hill: University of North Carolina Press.

——. 2003b. Introduction to *Race and Nation in Modern Latin America.* Edited by Nancy Appelbaum, Anne MacPherson, and Karin Rosemblatt. Chapel Hill: University of North Carolina Press.

Arenas Bianchi, Clara, Charles R. Hale, and Gustavo Palma Murga. 1999. *Racismo en Guatemala? Abriendo el debate sobre un tema tabú.* Guatemala: Asociación para el Avance de las Ciencias Sociales en Guatemala.

Ares Queija, Berta. 2000. "Mestizos, mulatos y zambaigos (Virreinato del Perú, siglo XVI)." In *Negros, mulatos, zambaigos: Derroteros africanos en los mundos ibéricos.* Coordinated by Berta Ares Queija and Alessandro Stella, 75–88. Seville: Escuela de Estudios Hispano-americanos.

——. 1997. "El papel de mediadores y la construcción de un discurso sobre la identidad de los mestizos peruanos (siglo XVI)." In *Entre dos mundos: Fronteras culturales y agentes mediadores.* Coordinated by Berta Ares Queija and Serge Gruzinski. Seville: Escuela de Estudios Hispano-americanos.

Arguedas, Alcides. 1936. *Pueblo enfermo.* 1909.

Ari Chachaki, Waskar T. 2007a. "Historia y presente del factor raza en Bolivia." *Fe y Pueblo* 20 (January): 4–18.

——. 2007b. "Color Line Gets Tense in Bolivia." *Nebraska Report* (February): 4.

Arias, Arturo, ed. 2001. *The Rigoberta Menchú Controversy.* Minneapolis: University of Minnesota Press.

——. 1997. "Comments on Hale," "Consciousness, Violence, and the Politics of Memory in Guatemala." *Current Anthropology* 38, no. 5, 824–26.

Asad, Talal. 2000. "Muslims and European Identity: Can Europe Represent Islam?" In *Cultural Encounters: Representing Otherness*, edited by Elizabeth Hallam and Brian Street, 11–27. London: Routledge.

———. 1973. Introduction to *Anthropology and the Colonial Encounter*, edited by Talal Asad, 9–20. Atlantic Highlands, N.J.: Humanities Press.

Bakhtin, Mikhail M. 1981. *The Dialogic Imagination: Four Essays*. Austin: University of Texas Press.

Barabas, Alicia Mabel, Miguel Alberto Bartolomé, and Benjamín Maldonado, eds. 2004. *Los Pueblos Indígenas de Oaxaca: Atlas Etnográfico*. Mexico: Conaculta, INAH.

Barragán, Rossana. 2002. "El Estado Pactante, Gobierno y pueblos: La configuración del Estado boliviano y sus fronteras, 1825–1880." Ph.D. diss., École des Hautes Études en Sciences Sociales, Paris.

———. 1999. *Indios, mujeres y ciudadanos: Legislación y ejercicio de la ciudadanía en Bolivia (siglo XIX)*. La Paz: Diálogo.

———. 1996. "Españoles patricios y españoles europeos: Conflictos intra-elites e identidades en la ciudad de La Paz en vísperas de la independencia, 1770–1809." In *Entre la retórica y la insurgencia: Las ideas y los movimientos sociales en los Andes, Siglo XVIII*, edited by Charles Walker, 112–71. Cuzco: Centro Bartolomé de las Casas.

———. 1992. "Identidades indias y mestizas: una intervención al debate." *Autodeterminación* 10: 17-44.

———. 1990. *Espacio urbano y dinámica étnica: La Paz en el siglo XIX*. La Paz: HISBOL.

Barstow, Jean. 1979. "An Aymara Class Structure: Town and Community in Carabuco." Ph.D. diss., University of Chicago.

Basave Benítez, Agustín. 1992. *México Mestizo: Análisis del nacionalismo Mexicano en torno a la mestizofilia de Andrés Molina Enríquez*. Mexico, D.F.: Fondo de Cultura Ecónomica.

Becker, Marc. 2008. *Indians and Leftists in the Making of Ecuador's Modern Indigenous Movements*. Durham: Duke University Press.

Benavides, Margarita. 2001. "Esta mesa nadie la instala." Interview with Martín Paredes. *Quehacer* 132, 102–6.

Bennett, Herman L. 2003. *Africans in Colonial Mexico: Absolutism, Christianity, and Afro Creole Consciousness, 1570–1640*. Bloomington and Indianapolis: Indiana University Press.

Bernal, Ignacio. 1990. *Museo Nacional de Antropología de México*. 1967. Mexico, D.F.: Aguilar.

Berry, Charles. 1981. *The Reform in Oaxaca*. Lincoln: University of Nebraska Press.

Bertonio, Ludovico. 1984. *Vocabulario de la lengua aimara*. 1612. Vol. 1 and 2. La Paz: CERES and MUSEF.

Bigenho, Michelle. 2006. "Embodied Matters: *Bolivian Fantasy* and Indigenismo." *Journal of Latin American Anthropology* 11, no. 2: 267–93.

Blanco, José J. 1977. *Se Llamaba Vasconcelos*. Mexico, D.F.: Fondo de Cultura Económica.

Bonfil Batalla, Guillermo, ed. 1993. *Simbiosis de culturas: Los inmigrantes y su cultura en México*. Mexico, D.F.: Fondo de Cultura Económica.

Bonifaz, Miguel. 1953. *Legislación agrario-indígena*. Cochabamba: Universidad Mayor de San Simón.

Bourdieu, Pierre. 2000. *Poder, Derecho y Clases Sociales*. Bilbao: Editorial Desclée de Brouwer, S.A.

———. 1990. *Sociología y Cultura*. Mexico: Consejo Nacional para la Cultura y las Artes/Editorial Grijalbo.

Bouysse-Cassagne, Thérèse, and Thierry Saignes. 1992. "El cholo: Actor olvidado de la historia." In *Etnicidad, economía y simbolismo en los Andes*, edited by Silvia Arze, Rossana Barragán, Laura Escobari, and Ximena Medinaceli, 129–41. La Paz: HISBOL/IFEA/SBH-ASUR.

Bowser, Frederick P. 1974. *The African Slave in Colonial Peru, 1524–1650*. Stanford: Stanford University Press.

Brading, David. 1991. *The First America: The Spanish Monarchy, Creole Patriots, and the Liberal State, 1450–1867*. Cambridge: Cambridge University Press.

———. 1988. "Manuel Gamio and the Official Indigenismo in Mexico." *Bulletin of Latin American Research* 7, no. 1: 75–89.

Brass, Paul, ed. 1985. *Ethnic Groups and the State*. London: Croom Helm.

Brattain, Michelle. 2007. "Race, Racism, and Antiracism: UNESCO and the Politics of Presenting Science to the Postwar Public." *American Historical Review* 112, no. 5 (December): 1386–1413.

Britton, John, ed. 1994. *Molding the Hearts and Minds: Education, Communications, and Social Change in Latin America*. Wilmington, Del.: Scholarly Books.

Bronfman, Alejandra. 2004. *Measures of Equality: Social Science, Citizenship, and Race in Cuba, 1902–1940*. Chapel Hill: University of North Carolina Press.

Brown, Jonathan. 1993. "Foreign and Native-Born Workers in Porfirian Mexico." *American Historical Review* 98, no. 3 (June): 786–818.

Brown, Lawrence A., Jorge A. Brea, and Andrew R. Goetz. 1988. "Policy Aspects of Development and Individual Mobility: Migration and Circulation from Ecuador's Rural Sierra." *Economic Geography* 64, no. 2: 147–70.

Brubacher, Rogers. 2002. "Ethnicity without Groups." *Archives européenes de sociologie* 43, no. 2: 163–89.

Brubacher, Rogers, and Frederick Cooper. 2000. "Beyond 'Identity.'" *Theory and Society* 29, no. 1: 1–47.

Brysk, Alison. 2000. *From Tribal Village to Global Village: Indian Rights and International Relations in Latin America*. Stanford: Stanford University Press.

———. 1996. "Turning Weakness into Strength: The Internationalization of Indian Rights." *Latin American Perspectives* 23, no. 2: 38–57.

Buck, Federico. 1933. "Conservemos los pocos monumentos que aún nos hablan de la grandeza de Tiahuanacu." Rotary Club, 1931, reproduced in *El Diario*, "A propó-sito de la traslación del monolito Bennet a La Paz" (May 2).

Burga, Manuel. 1988. *El nacimiento de una utopía: Muerte y resurección de los incas.* Lima: Instituto de Apoyo Agrario.

Burns, Kathryn. 1998. "Gender and the Politics of Mestizaje." *Hispanic American Historical Review* 78, no. 1 (February): 5–44.

Bustos, Santiago, et al. 2007. *Racismo y discriminación por razones étnicas: Una mirada desde Bolivia, Perú y Guatemala.* La Paz: Diakonía.

Cahill, David. 1994. "Colour by Numbers: Racial and Ethnic Categories in the Vice-royalty of Peru, 1532–1824." *Journal of Latin American Studies* 26, no. 2 (May): 325–46.

Cajigas Langner, Alberto. 1954. "El Vestido y el ornato zapotecas, origen y evolución del vestido tehuano." In *Monografía de Tehuantepec*, by Alberto Cajigas Langner, 73–90. Mexico, D.F.: Manuel Leon Sánchez.

Calderón Jemio, Raúl. 1994. "La 'deuda social' de los liberales de principios de siglo: Una aproximación a la educación elemental entre 1900 y 1910." *Data: Revista del Instituto de Estudios Andinos y Amazónicos* 5: 53–83.

Calla, Pamela. 2008. Introduction to *Observando el Racismo: Racismo y regionalismo en el proceso constituyente.* Observatorio del racismo en Bolivia, Área de Inves-tigación. La Paz: Defensor del Pueblo y Universidad de la Cordillera.

Camacho, José. 1920. "Tiahuanacu." *Boletín de la Sociedad Geográfica de La Paz* 49 and 50: 29–30.

Camp, Roderic A. 1985. *Intellectuals and the State in Twentieth-Century Mexico.* Austin: University of Texas Press.

Canessa, Andrew. 2006. "Todos somos indígenas: Towards a New Language of Na-tional Political Identity." *Bulletin of Latin American Research* 25, no. 2: 241–63.

——, ed. 2005. *Natives Making Nation: Gender, Indigeneity and the State in the Andes.* Tucson: University of Arizona Press.

Cañizares Esguerra, Jorge. 2001. *How to Write the History of the New World: Histories, Epistemologies, and Identities in the Eighteenth-Century Atlantic World.* Stanford: Stanford University Press.

——. 1999. "New World, New Stars: Patriotic Astrology and the Invention of Indian and Creole Bodies in Colonial Spanish America, 1600–1650." *American Historical Review* 104, no. 1: 33–68.

Capítulo de Derechos Humanos de Bolivia. June 2008. "Estado de situación de la legis-lación y proyectos en Bolivia sobre Racismo." Unpublished report. La Paz, Bolivia.

Carnoy, Martin, and Joel Samoff. 1990. *Education and Social Transition in the Third World.* Princeton: Princeton University Press.

Carrasco Alurralde, Inés Valeria, and Xavier Albó. 2008. "Cronología de la Asam-blea Constituyente." *T'inkazos: Revista boliviana de ciencias sociales* 23 and 24 (March): 101–24.

Carrera, Magali M. 2003. *Imagining Identity in New Spain: Race, Lineage, and the*

Colonial Body in Portraiture and Casta Paintings. Austin: University of Texas Press.

Carrera, Rafael. 1858. *Mensaje dirigido por el Exmo. Señor Presidente de la República de Guatemala, Capitán, General Rafael Carrera a la Cámara de Representantes en la apertura de sus terceras sesiones del segundo período constitucional, el día 25 de noviembre de 1858.* Guatemala.

Carriedo, Juan B. 1847. *Estudios Historicos y Estadísticos del Departamento de Oaxaca.* Oaxaca: printed by author.

Casaús Arzú, Marta Elena. 1991. *Linaje y racismo.* San José: FLACSO.

Cassidy, Thomas J. 1986–90. "Las haciendas oaxaquenas en el siglo XIX." In *Lecturas históricas del estado de Oaxaca,* edited by A. Romero Frizzi and Marcus Winter. Mexico, D.F.: Instituto Nacional de Antropología e Historia.

Castañeda, Jorge. 1993. "The Intellectual and the State in Latin America." *World Policy Journal* 10, no. 3: 89–95.

Castellanos Guerrero, Alicia. 2001. "Racismo, multietnicidad y democracia en América Latina." In *Visiones de fin de siglo: Bolivia y América Latina en el siglo XX,* edited by Dora Cajías et al. La Paz: IFEA, Coordinadora de Historia, Embajada de España en Bolivia.

Caulfield, Sueann. 2000. *In Defense of Honor: Sexual Morality, Modernity, and Nation in Early Twentieth-Century Brazil.* Durham: Duke University Press.

Cervone, Emma, and Freddy Rivera, eds. 1999. *Ecuador Racista: Imágenes e Identidades.* Quito: FLACSO.

Chakrabarty, Dipesh. 2000. *Provincializing Europe: Postcolonial Thought and Historical Difference.* Princeton: Princeton University Press.

Chambers, Sarah. 2003. "Little Middle Ground: The Instability of a Mestizo Identity in the Andes, Eighteenth and Nineteenth Centuries." In *Race and Nation in Modern Latin America,* edited by Appelbaum et al., 32–55. Chapel Hill: University of North Carolina Press.

Chance, John. 1978. *Race and Class in Colonial Oaxaca.* Stanford: Stanford University Press.

Chassen-López, Francie R. 2004. *From Liberal to Revolutionary Oaxaca: The View from the South, Mexico 1867–1911.* University Park: Pennsylvania State University Press.

Chasteen, John Charles. 1996. Introduction to *The Lettered City,* by Angel Rama, edited and translated by John Charles Chasteen, vii–xiv. Durham: Duke University Press.

Chavez, Leo Ralph. 1982. "Commercial Weaving and the Entrepreneurial Ethic: Otavalo Indian Views of Self and the World." Ph.D. diss., Stanford University.

Chervin, Arthur. 1908. *Anthropologie bolivienne.* 3 vols. Paris: Imp. Nacionale.

Chiaramonte, José Carlos. 1997. *Ciudades, Provincias, Estados: Orígenes de la Nación Argentina (1800–1846).* Argentina: Espasa Calpe.

Chin, Rita, and Heide Fehrenbach. 2009. Introduction to *After the Nazi Racial State:*

Difference and Democracy in Germany and Europe, edited by Rita Chin and Barbara Fehrenbach, 1–29. Ann Arbor: University of Michigan Press.

Chomsky, Aviva. 2000. "'Barbados or Canada?' Race, Immigration and Nation in Early Twentieth-Century Cuba." *Hispanic American Historical Review* 80, no. 3 (August): 415–62.

Choque Canqui, Roberto. 1994. "La problemática de la educación indigenal." *Data: Revista del Instituto de Estudios Andinos y Amazónicos* 5.

———. 1986. *La masacre de Jesús de Machaca*. La Paz: Chitakolla.

Choque, Roberto, and Esteban Ticona Alejo. 1996. *Jesús de Machaqa: La marka rebelde 2: Sublevación y masacre de 1921*. La Paz: CEDOIN/CIPCA.

Choque, Roberto, et al., eds. 1992. *Educación indígena: ¿Ciudadanía o colonización?* La Paz: Ediciones Aruwiyiri, Taller de Historia Oral Andina.

Cieza de León, Pedro. 1947. *Crónica de Perú*. Madrid: Biblioteca de Autores Españoles. 1553.

Clark, A. Kim. 1998. "Race, 'Culture,' and Mestizaje: The Statistical Construction of the Ecuadorian Nation, 1930–1950." *Journal of Historical Sociology* 11, no. 2: 185–211.

———. 1997. "Globalization Seen From the Margins: Indigenous Ecuadorians and the Politics of Place." *Anthropologica* 39: 17–26.

Claure, Karen. 1989. *Las escuelas indigenales: Otra forma de resistencia comunaria*. La Paz: HISBOL.

Cobo, Father Bernabé. 1983. *History of the Inca Empire*. 1653. Translated by Roland Hamilton. Austin: University of Texas Press.

———. 1956. *Obras del P. Bernabé Cobo*. Vol. 91. 1653. Biblioteca de Autores Españoles, tomos 91–92. Madrid: Ed. Atlas.

Colloredo-Mansfeld, Rudi. 1999. *The Native Leisure Class: Consumption and Cultural Creativity in the Andes*. Chicago: University of Chicago Press.

———. 1998. "'Dirty Indians,' Radical *Indígenas*, and the Political Economy of Social Difference in Modern Ecuador." *Bulletin of Latin American Research* 17, no. 2: 185–205.

Colwill, Elizabeth. 1998. "Sex, Savagery and Slavery in the Shaping of the French Body Politic." In *From the Royal to the Republican Body: Incorporating the Political in Seventeenth- and Eighteenth-Century France*, edited by Sara E. Melzer and Kathryn Norberg, 198–223. Berkeley: University of California Press.

Comisión Civil Internacional de Observación por los Derechos Humanos. 2008. *Informe de la situación de los derechos humanos en Chiapas, Oaxaca y Atenco*. VI Vista 2008. Mexico: UNAM.

Comisión de la Verdad y Reconciliación. 2003. *Informe Final*. Lima: CVR.

Compilación de las Leyes del Procedimiento Civil Boliviano. 1890. Edición particular. Sucre: Bolívar.

Comte de Castelnau, Francis. 1850–61. *Expédition dans les parties centrales de l'Amérique du Sud*. Paris.

Condarco Morales, Ramiro. 1983. *Zárate el "temible" willka: Historia de la rebelión indígena de 1899.* 2nd ed. La Paz: "Renovación."

Condori Chura, Leandro, and Esteban Ticona Alejo. 1992. *El esribano de los caciques apoderados: Kasikinakan purirarunakan qillqiripa.* La Paz: HISBOL/THOA.

Connolly, William. 1996. "Pluralism, Multiculturalism and the Nation-State: Rethinking the Connections." *Journal of Political Ideologies* 1, no. 1 (Winter): 53–73.

Consejo de Desarrollo de las Nacionalidades y Pueblos del Ecuador. 2000. *Propuestas de las nacionalidades y pueblos indigenas para el nuevo milenio.* Quito: Organizacion Internacional del Trabajo (http://oitandinaorg.pe).

Cope, R. Douglas. 1994. *The Limits of Racial Domination: Plebian Society in Colonial Mexico City, 1660–1720.* Madison: University of Wisconsin Press.

Cornblit, Oscar. 1995. *Power and Violence in the Colonial City: Oruro from the Mining Renaissance to the Rebellion of Túpac Amaru (1740–1782).* New York: Cambridge University Press.

Correa, Martín, Raúl Molina, and Nancy Yáñez. 2005. *La Reforma Agraria y las tierras mapuches: Chile 1962–1975.* Santiago: LOM Ediciones.

Cortés, José. 1861. *Ensayo sobre la historia en Bolivia.* Sucre: Beeche.

——. 1858. *Bosquejo de los progresos de Hispano América.* Valparaíso: Comercio.

Covarrubias Horozco, Sebastián de. 1989. *Tesoro de la lengua castellana o española* (1611). Edited by Martín de Riquer. Barcelona: Editorial Alta Fulla.

Crespo, Luis S. 1909–10. *Censo Municipal de la ciudad de La Paz (15 de Junio de 1909): Clasificaciones estadísticas precedidas de una reseña geográfica-descriptiva-histórica de la ciudad: Comisión Central del Censo.* La Paz: Taller Tip. Lit. José Miguel Gamarra.

Dalence, José María. 1975. *Bosquejo Estadístico de Bolivia.* 1848. La Paz: Editorial Universitaria.

Dalton, Margarita. 1997. *Oaxaca: Una historia compartida.* Oaxaca: Gobierno del Estado de Oaxaca.

——. 1987. "La historia de Oaxaca vista por los historiadores oaxaqueños." *Secuencia (Revista del Instituto Mora)* 9 (Mexico City): 23–41.

Davis, David Brion. 1984. *Slavery and Human Progress.* New York: Oxford University Press.

——. 1966. *The Problem of Slavery in Western Culture.* New York: Oxford University Press.

Dawson, Alexander S. 2004. *Indian and Nation in Revolutionary Mexico.* Tucson: University of Arizona Press.

——. 1998. "From Models for the Nation to Model Citizens: Indigenismo and the Revindication of the Mexican Indian, 1920–1940." *Journal of Latin American Studies* 30: 279–308.

De Acosta, José. 2002. *Natural and Moral History of the Indies,* edited by Jane E. Mangan. Durham: Duke University Press.

De Ballivián y Roxas, Manuel Vicente. 1977. *Archivo boliviano. Colección de docu-*

mentos relativos a la historia de Bolivia durante la época colonial. 1872. La Paz: Casa de la Cultura Franz Tamayo.

Dean, Carolyn, and Dana Leibsohn. 2003. "Hybridity and Its Discontents: Considering Visual Culture in Colonial Spanish America." *Colonial Latin American Review* 12, no. 1: 5–35.

Deere, Carmen Diana, and Magdalena Leon. 2001. "Institutional Reform of Agriculture under Neoliberalism: The Impact of the Women's and Indigenous Movement." *Latin American Research Review* 36, no. 2: 31–63.

Degregori, Carlos Iván. 2004. "Heridas abiertas, derechos esquivos: Reflexiones sobre la Comisión de la Verdad y Reconciliación." In *Memorias en conflicto: Aspectos de la violencia política contemporánea*, edited by Raynald Belay et al. Lima: Embajada de Francia, IEP, IFEA, Red para el Desarrollo de las Ciencias Sociales en el Perú.

——. 1998. "Ethnicity and Democratic Governability in Latin America: Reflections from Two Central Andean Countries." In *Fault Lines of Democracy in Post-Transition Latin America*, edited by Felipe Agüero and Jeffrey Stark, 203–34. Miami: North-South Center Press.

De la Cadena, Marisol. 2005. "Are 'Mestizos' Hybrids?: The Conceptual Politics of Andean Identities." *Journal of Latin American Studies* 37, no. 2: 259–84.

——. 2001. "Reconstructing Race: Racism, Culture, and Mestizaje in Latin America." NACLA 34, no. 6 (May/June): 16–23.

——. 2000. *Indigenous Mestizos: The Politics of Race and Culture in Cuzco, Peru, 1919–1991*. Durham: Duke University Press.

——. 1991. " 'Las mujeres son más indias': Etnicidad y género en una comunidad del Cusco." *Revista Andina* 9, no. 17 (July): 7–47.

De la Cruz, Rodrigo. 1995. "Los derechos indígenas." In *Los derechos de los pueblos indígenas: Situación jurídica y política de estado*, edited by Ramón G. Torres, 7–16. Quito: CONAIE, CEPLAES, Abya Yala.

De la Fuente, Alejandro. 2008. "The New Afro-Cuban Cultural Movement and the Debate on Race in Contemporary Cuba." *Journal of Latin American Studies* 40, no. 4 (November): 697–720.

——. 2001a. "The Resurgence of Racism in Cuba." NACLA 34, no. 6 (May/June): 29–34.

——. 2001b. *A Nation for All: Race, Inequality, and Politics in Twentieth-Century Cuba*. Chapel Hill: University of North Carolina.

De la Fuente Jeria, José. 2008. "Los alrededores de la Asamblea Constituyente." *T'inkazos: Revista boliviana de ciencias sociales*.

De la Peña, Guillermo. 1999. "Notas preliminares sobre la 'ciudadanía étnica' (El caso de México)." In *La sociedad civil: De la teoría a la realidad*. Mexico, D.F.: Colegio de México.

De la Torre Espinosa, Carlos. 2005. "Afro-Ecuadorian Responses to Racism: Between Citizenship and Corporatism." In *Neither Enemies or Friends: Latinos, Blacks, Afro-Latinos*, edited by Anani Dzidzienyo and Suzanne Oboler. New York: Palgrave Macmillan.

——. 2000. *Populist Seduction in Latin America: The Ecuadorian Experience*. Athens, Ohio: Ohio University Research in International Studies.

——. 1999. "Everyday Forms of Racism in Contemporary Ecuador: The Experiences of Middle Class Indians." *Ethnic and Racial Studies* 22, no. 1: 92–112.

——. 1996. *El racismo en Ecuador: Experiencias de los indios de la clase media*. Quito: Centro Andino de Acción Popular-CAAP.

Demélas, Marie-Daniele. 1981. "Darwinismo a la criolla: El Darwinismo social en Bolivia. 1880-1910." *Historia Boliviana* 1/2 (Cochabamba): 55–82.

Derby, Lauren. 1994. "Haitians, Magic and Money: Raza and Society in the Haitian-Dominican Borderlands, 1900–1937." *Comparative Studies in Society and History* 36, no. 3 (July): 488–526.

Díaz Rementería, Carlos. 1977. *El cacique en el Virreinato del Perú: Estudio histórico-jurídico*. Seville: Universidad de Sevilla.

Diccionario de la Lengua Castellana por la Academia Española. 1824. 7th edition. Paris-London.

D'Orbigny, Alcide. 1945. *Viaje a la América Meridional*. 4 vols. 1534–42. Buenos Aires: Futuro.

Duchet, Michel. 1975. *Antropología e Historia en el Siglo de las Luces*. Mexico: Editorial Siglo XXI.

Dulitzky, Ariel. 2005. "A Region in Denial: Racial Discrimination and Racism in Latin America." In *Neither Enemies nor Friends: Latinos, Blacks, Afro-Latinos*, edited by Anani Dzidzienyo and Suzanne Oboler. New York: Palgrave Macmillan.

Durán, Diego. 1994. *History of the Indies of New Spain*. Translated by Doris Heyden. Norman: University of Oklahoma Press.

Dzidzienyo, Anani, and Suzanne Oboler. 2005. *Neither Enemies nor Friends: Latinos, Blacks, Afro-Latinos*. New York: Palgrave Macmillan.

Earle, Rebecca. 2007. *The Return of the Native: Indians and Myth-Making in Spanish America, 1810–1930*. Durham: Duke University Press.

Edelman, Marc. 1999. *Peasants Against Globalization: Rural Social Movements in Costa Rica*. Stanford: Stanford University Press.

Elliott, J. H. 1963. *Imperial Spain, 1469–1716*. New York: St. Martin's Press.

Equipo Permanente de Reflexión Interdisciplinaria, conformado por María Teresa Zegada et al. 2007. "11 de Enero:¿Cochabamba a la deriva?" *Cuarto Intermedio*.

Erickson, Clark L. 1999. "Neo-environmental determinism and agrarian 'collapse' in Andean prehistory." *Antiquity* 73, no. 281 (September): 634–42.

Escobar, Arturo. 1995. *Encountering Development: The Making and Unmaking of the Third World*. Princeton: Princeton University Press.

Esparza, Manuel. 1988a. "Los proyectos de los liberales en Oaxaca." In *Historia de la cuestión agraria mexicana: Estado de Oaxaca*, edited by Leticia Reina. Mexico: Juan Pablos.

——, ed. 1988b. *Los Indios Oaxaqueños y sus Monumentos Arqueológicos*. Oaxaca de Juarez: Gobierno del Estado de Oaxaca.

Esparza Valdivia, Ricardo Cuauhtémoc. 2000. *El fenómeno magonista en México y en Estados Unidos (1905–1908)*. Zacatecas: Universidad Autónoma de Zacatecas.

Espósito Guevara, Carla. 2008. "El rumor para la construcción social del enemigo interno." In *Observando el Racismo: Racismo y regionalismo en el proceso constituyente*. Observatorio del racismo en Bolivia, Área de Investigación. La Paz: Defensor del Pueblo y Universidad de la Cordillera.

Estenssoro Fuchs, Juan Carlos. 2000. "Los colores de la plebe: Razón y mestizaje en el Perú colonial." In *Los cuadros de mestizaje del Virrey Amat: La representación etnográfica en el Perú colonial*, edited by Natalia Majluf, 67–107. Lima: Museo de Arte de Lima.

Esteva, Gustavo. 2007. "Oaxaca: The Path of Radical Democracy." *Socialism and Democracy* 21, no. 2 (July): 71–96.

Euraque, Darío A. 2004. *Conversaciones históricas con el mestizaje y su identidad nacional en Honduras*. San Pedro Sula, Honduras: Centro Editorial.

Euraque, Darío A., Jeffrey L. Gould, and Charles R. Hale, eds. 2005. *Memorias del mestizaje: Cultura política en Centroamérica de 1920 al presente*. Guatemala: CIRMA.

Fabian, Johannes. 1983. *Time and the Other: How Anthropology Makes Its Subject*. New York: Columbia University Press.

Farthing, Linda. 2007. "Everything Is Up for Discussion: A 40th Anniversary Conversation with Silvia Rivera Cusicanqui." *NACLA* 40, no. 4 (July/August): 4–9.

Favre, Henri. 1998. *Indigenismo*. Mexico: Fondo de Cultura Económica.

Fe y Pueblo. 2007. "Discriminación racial: Crítica de estructuras y manifestaciones de la exclusion étnica." 10 (January).

Ferrer, Ada. 1999. *Insurgent Cuba: Race, Nation, and Revolution, 1868–1898*. Chapel Hill: University of North Carolina Press.

FIDA (Fondo Internacional de Desarrollo Agricola). 1989. *Informe de la Misión Especial de Programación a la República del Ecuador*. Rome: FIDA.

Fields, Barbara J. 2003. "On Rogues and Geldings." *American Historical Review* 108, no. 5 (December): 1397–1406.

——. 2001. "Whiteness, Racism, and Identity." *International Labor and Working-Class History* 60 (fall): 48–56.

Findlay, Eileen. 1999. *Imposing Decency: The Politics of Sexuality and Race in Puerto Rico, 1870–1920*. Durham: Duke University Press.

Fischer, Brodwyn. 2004. "Quase pretos de tão pobres? Race and Social Discrimination in Rio de Janeiro's Twentieth-Century Criminal Courts." *Latin American Research Review* 39, no. 1 (February): 31–59.

Fisher, John. 2000. *El Perú borbónico, 1750–1824*. Perú: IEP.

Fletcher, Richard. 1992. *Moorish Spain*. Berkeley: University of California Press.

Flores Galindo, Alberto. 1987. *Buscando un inca: Identidad y utopía en los Andes*. Lima: Instituto de Apoyo Agrario.

Flores Moncayo, José. 1953. *Legislación boliviana del indio: Recopilación, 1825–1953*. La

Paz: Ministerio de Asuntos Campesinos, Departamento de Publicaciones del Instituto Indigenista Boliviano.

Floyd-Wilson, Mary. 2003. *English Ethnicity and Race in Early Modern Drama*. New York: Cambridge University Press.

Foley, Neil. 1997. *The White Scourge: Mexicans, Blacks, and Poor Whites in Texas Cotton Culture*. Berkeley: University of California Press.

Forbes, Jack. 1988. *Black Africans and Native Americans: Color, Race, and Caste in the Evolution of Red-Black Peoples*. Oxford: Basil Blackwell.

Forster, Cindy. 2001. *The Time of Freedom: Campesino Workers in Guatemala's October Revolution*. Pittsburgh: University of Pittsburgh Press.

Foucault, Michel. 1984. *The Foucault Reader*. New York: Panteón.

Francovich, Guillermo. 1985. *El pensamiento boliviano en el siglo XX*. 2nd ed. La Paz: Editorial Amigos del Libro.

———. 2002. *El pensamiento boliviano en el siglo XX*. 1956. Mexico City: Fondo de la Cultura.

Fredrickson, George. 2002. *Racism: A Short History*. Princeton: Princeton University Press.

Fuenzalida, Fernando. 1970. "Poder, raza y etnia en el Perú contemporáneo." In *El indio y el poder en el Perú*, edited by Fuenzalida et al. Lima: IEP.

Fuenzalida, Fernando, and Enrique Mayer. 1974. *El Perú de las tres razas*. New York: Instituto de las Naciones Unidas para la formación profesional e investigaciones.

Gamio, Manuel. 1966. *Consideraciones sobre el problema indígena*. 1942. Mexico, D.F.: Instituto Indigenista Interamericano.

———. 1922–23. "La Vida Mexicana Durante el Reinado de Moctezuma III." *Ethnos* 1, no. 1: 5–7.

———. 1916. *Forjando Patria*. Mexico, D.F.: Librería de Porrúa Hermanos, 1916.

García, María Elena. 2005. *Making Indigenous Citizens: Identities, Education, and Multicultural Development in Peru*. Stanford: Stanford University Press.

García, María Elena, and José Antonio Lucero. 2008. "Exceptional Others: Politicians, Rottweilers, and Alterity in the 2006 Peruvian Elections." *Latin American and Caribbean Ethnic Studies* 3, no. 3 (November): 253–70.

———. 2005. "Un país sin indígenas: Repensando los movimientos indígenas en el Perú." In *Las luchas para los derechos indígenas en América Latina*, edited by Nancy Grey Postero and León Zamosc. Quito: Abya-Yala.

———. 2004. "'Un País Sin Indígenas'? Re-thinking Indigenous Politics in Peru." In *The Struggle for Indian Rights in Latin America*, edited by Nancy Postero and León Zamosc, 158–88. Brighton: Sussex Academic Press.

García Canclini, Néstor. 1995. *Hybrid Cultures: Strategies for Entering and Leaving Modernity*. Minneapolis: University of Minnesota Press.

García Pabón, Leonardo. 1998. *La patria íntima: Alegorías nacionales en la literatura y el cine de Bolivia*. La Paz: Plural.

García Peláez, Francisco de Paula. 1943. *Memorias para la Historia del Antiguo Reino de Guatemala*. Vol. 3. Guatemala: Tipografía Nacional.

García Serrano, Fernando. 2002. "Política, estado y movimiento indígena: Nuevas estrategias de negociación en tiempos de la dolarización." Quito: Primer Encuentro de LASA sobre Estudios Ecuatorianos.

Garcilaso de la Vega, el Inca. 1991. *Comentarios Reales de los Incas*. Vol. 2. Edited by Carlos Araníbar. Lima: Fondo de Cultura Económica.

——. 1951. *The Florida of the Inca*. Translated by John and Jeannette Varner. Austin: University of Texas Press.

Garner, Paul. 1988. *La revolución en provincia: Soberanía estatal y caudillismo en las montañas de Oaxaca (1910–1920)*. Mexico, D.F.: Fondo de Cultura Económica.

Gay, Padre José Antonio. 1990. *Historia de Oaxaca*. 1881. Mexico: Porrúa.

Geertz, Clifford. 1973. *The Interpretation of Cultures*. New York: Basic Books.

Gelles, Paul. 2002. "Andean Culture, Indigenous Identity, and the State in Peru." In *The Politics of Ethnicity: Indigenous Peoples and Latin American States*, edited by David Maybury-Lewis, 239–66. Cambridge: Rockefeller Center Series on Latin American Studies, Harvard University.

——. 2000. *Water and Power in Highland Peru: The Cultural Politics of Irrigation and Development*. New Brunswick: Rutgers University Press.

Gerlach, Allen. 2003. *Indians, Oil, and Politics: A Recent History of Ecuador*. Wilmington, Del.: Scholarly Resources.

Gilroy, Paul. 2000. *Against Race: Imagining Political Culture Beyond the Color Line*. Cambridge, Mass.: Belknap.

——. 1987. *"There Ain't No Black in the Union Jack": The Cultural Politics of Race and Nation*. London: Hutchinson.

Giroux, Henry. 1992. *Border Crossings: Cultural Workers and the Politics of Education*. New York: Routledge.

Gobat, Michel. 2005. *Confronting the American Dream: Nicaragua under U.S. Imperial Rule*. Durham: Duke University Press.

Gómez, Laura E. 2007. *Manifest Destinies: The Making of the Mexican American Race*. New York: New York University Press.

Gonzales, Michael J. 1994. "United States Copper Companies, the State and Labour Conflict in Mexico, 1900–1910." *Journal of Latin American Studies* 26, no. 3 (October): 651–83.

González Echevarría, Roberto. 1999. "La metamorfosis del racismo en la élite de poder en Guatemala." In *Racismo en Guatemala? Abriendo el debate sobre un tema tabú*, edited by Clara Arenas Bianchi, Charles R. Hale, and Gustavo Palma Murga. Guatemala: Asociación para el Avance de las Ciencias Sociales en Guatemala.

——. 1990. *Myth and Archive: A Theory of Latin American Narrative*. Cambridge: Cambridge University Press.

Gootenberg, Paul. 1991. "Population and Ethnicity in Early Republican Peru: Some Revisions." *Latin American Research Review* 26, no. 3: 109–57.

Gordillo, José. 2007. "Se comenta el libro de José M. Gordillo, Alberto Rivera Pizarro y Ana Sulcata, ¿Pitaq kaypi kamachiq? (¿Quién manda aquí?) Las estructuras de poder en Cochabamba, 1940–2006 (La Paz, PIEB, 2007)," *La Prensa* (La Paz, Bolivia).

Gordon, Linda. 1999. *The Great Arizona Orphan Abduction*. Cambridge: Harvard University Press.

Gotkowitz, Laura. 2007. *A Revolution for Our Rights: Indigenous Struggles for Land and Justice in Bolivia, 1880–1952*. Durham: Duke University Press.

———. 2003. "Trading Insults: Honor, Violence, and the Gendered Culture of Commerce in Cochabamba, Bolivia, 1870s–1950s." *Hispanic American Historical Review* 83, no. 1 (February): 83–118.

Gould, Jeffrey L. 2005. "Proyectos del Estado-nación y la supresión de la pluralidad cultural: perspectivas históricas." In *Memorias del mestizaje: Cultura política en Centroamérica de 1920 al presente*, edited by Darío A. Euraque, Jeffrey L. Gould, and Charles R. Hale. Guatemala: CIRMA.

———. 2001. "Revolutionary Nationalism and Local Memories in El Salvador." In *Reclaiming the Political in Latin American History*, edited by Gilbert M. Joseph. Durham: Duke University Press.

———. 1998. *To Die in This Way: Nicaraguan Indians and the Myth of Mestizaje, 1880–1965*. Durham: Duke University Press.

Gould, Jeffrey L., and Aldo Lauria-Santiago. 2008. *To Rise in Darkness: Revolution, Repression, and Memory in El Salvador, 1920–1932*. Durham: Duke University Press.

Gould, Jeffrey L., and Lowell Gudmundson. 1997. "Central American Historiography after the Violence." *Latin American Research Review* 32, no. 2: 244–56.

Gow, David D., and Joanne Rappaport. 2002. "The Indigenous Public Voice: The Multiple Idioms of Modernity in Native Cauca." In *Indigenous Movements, Self-Representation, and the State in Latin America*, edited by K. B. Warren and J. E. Jackson, 47–80. Austin: University of Texas Press.

Graham, Laura R. 2002. "How Should an Indian Speak? Brazilian Indians and the Symbolic Politics of Language Choice in the International Public Sphere." In *Indigenous Movements, Self-Representation, and the State in Latin America*, edited by Kay Warren and Jean Jackson, 181–228. Austin: University of Texas Press.

Graham, Richard, ed. 1990. *The Idea of Race in Latin America, 1870–1940*. Austin: University of Texas Press.

Grandin, Greg. 2005. "The Instruction of Great Catastrophe: Truth Commissions, State Formation, and National Identity in Argentina, Chile, and Guatemala," *American Historical Review* 110, no. 1 (February): 46–67.

———. 2004. *The Last Colonial Massacre: Latin America in the Cold War*. Chicago: University of Chicago Press.

———. 2003. "History, Motive, Law, Intent: Combining Historical and Legal Methods in Understanding Guatemala's 1981–1983 Genocide." In *The Specter of Genocide:*

Mass Murder in Historical Perspective, edited by Robert Gellately and Ben Kiernan. Cambridge: Cambridge University Press.

——. 2000. *The Blood of Guatemala: A History of Race and Nation*. Durham: Duke University Press.

Graubart, Karen. 2004. "Hybrid Thinking: Bringing Postcolonial Theory to Colonial Latin American Economic History." In *Postcolonialism Meets Economics*, edited by Einman O. Zein-Elabdin and S. Charusheela, 215–34. New York: Routledge.

Greene, Roland. 1999. *Unrequited Conquests: Love and Empire in the Colonial Americas*. Chicago: University of Chicago Press.

——. 1992. "'This Phrasis is Continuous': Love and Empire in 1590." *Journal of Hispanic Philology* 16, no. 2: 237–52.

Greene, Shane. 2006. "Getting Over the Andes: The Geo-Eco-Politics of Indigenous Movements in Peru's Twenty-First Century Inca Empire." *Journal of Latin American Studies* 38, no. 2: 1–28.

Grieshaber, Erwin. 1985. "Fluctuaciones en la definición del indio: Comparación de los censos de 1900 y 1950." *Historia Boliviana* 5, nos. 1 and 2: 45–65.

Grimson, Alejandro. 2005. "Ethnic (In)Visibility in Neoliberal Argentina." NACLA 38, no. 4 (January/February): 25–29.

——. 2001. "A Hard Road for Argentina's Bolivians." NACLA 35, no. 2 (September/October): 33–35.

Grueso, Libia, Carlos Rosero, and Arturo Escobar. 1998. "The Process of Black Community Organizing in the Southern Pacific Region of Colombia." In *Cultures of Politics, Politics of Cultures: Re-Visioning Latin American Social Movements*, edited by S. E. Alvarez, E. Dagnino, and A. Escobar, 196–219. Boulder, Colo.: Westview.

Guamán Poma de Ayala, Felipe. 1980. 3 vols. *El primer nueva corónica y buen gobierno*. 1613. Mexico: Siglo Veintiuno.

Guardino, Peter. 1996. *Peasants, Politics, and the Formation of Mexico's National State: Guerrero, 1800–1857*. Stanford: Stanford University Press.

Gudmundson, Lowell, and Francisco A. Scarano. 1998. "Conclusion: Imagining the Future of the Subaltern Past—Fragments of Race, Class, and Gender in Central America and the Hispanic Caribbean, 1850–1950." In *Identity and Struggle at the Margins of the Nation-State*, edited by Aviva Chomsky and Lauria-Santiago, Aldo, 335–64. Durham: Duke University Press.

Guha, Ranajit. 1999. *Elementary Aspects of Peasant Insurgency in Colonial India*. 1983. Durham: Duke University Press.

Guha-Thakurta, Tapati. 2004. *Monuments, Objects, Histories: Institutions of Art in Colonial and Postcolonial India*. New York: Columbia University Press.

Guillén Pinto, Alfredo. 1919. *La educación del Indio: Contribución de la pedagogía nacional*. La Paz: González y Medina.

Gustafson, Bret. 2006. "Spectacles of Autonomy and Crisis; or, What Bulls and Beauty Queens Have to Do with Regionalism in Eastern Bolivia." *Journal of Latin American Anthropology* 11, no. 2: 351–79.

——. 2002. "Paradoxes of Liberal Indigenism: Indigenous Movements, State Processes, and Intercultural Reform in Bolivia." In *The Politics of Ethnicity: Indigenous Peoples in Latin American States*, edited by David Maybury-Lewis, 267–308. Cambridge: David Rockefeller Center on Latin American Studies, Harvard University.

Gutiérrez, Natividad. 1999. *Nationalist Myths and Ethnic Identities: Indigenous Intellectuals and the Mexican State*. Lincoln: University of Nebraska Press.

Guzmán Bockler, Carlos, and Jean-Loup Herbert. 1971. *Guatemala: Una interpretación histórica social*. Mexico: Siglo XXI.

Haenke, Tadeo. 1901. *Descripción del Perú*. Lima: El Lucero.

Hale, Charles A. 1989. *The Transformation of Liberalism in Late Nineteenth-Century Mexico*. Princeton: Princeton University Press.

——. 1984. "Political and Social Ideas in Latin America, 1870–1930." In *The Cambridge History of Latin America*, 396–97. Vol. 4. Cambridge: Cambridge University Press.

Hale, Charles R. 2006. *Más que un indio: Racial Ambivalence and Neoliberal Multiculturalism in Guatemala*. Santa Fe: School of American Research Press.

——. 2005. "Neoliberal Multiculturalism: The Remaking of Cultural Rights and Racial Dominance in Central America." *PoLAR* 28, no. 1: 10–28.

——. 2004. "Rethinking Indigenous Politics in the Era of the 'Indio Permitido.'" *NACLA* 38, no. 2 (September/October).

——. 2002. "Does Multiculturalism Menace? Governance, Cultural Rights and the Politics of Identity in Guatemala." *Journal of Latin American Studies* 34: 485–524.

——. 1997a. "Consciousness, Violence, and the Politics of Memory in Guatemala." *Current Anthropology* 38, no. 5: 817–24.

——. 1997b. "Cultural Politics of Identity in Latin America." *Annual Review of Anthropology* 26: 567–90.

——. 1994. *Resistance and Contradiction: Miskitu Indians and the Nicaraguan State, 1894–1987*. Stanford: Stanford University Press.

Hall, Stuart. 2000. "Conclusion: the Multi-cultural Question." In *Un/Settled Multiculturalisms: Diasporas, Entanglements, "Transruptions,"* edited by Barnor Hesse. London: Zed Books.

——. 1996. "The Question of Cultural Identity." In *Modernity: An Introduction to Modern Societies*, edited by Stuart Hall et al., 596–632. Oxford: Blackwell.

——. 1980. "Race, Articulation and Societies Structured in Dominance." In *Sociological Theories: Race and Colonialism*. Paris: UNESCO.

Handy, Jim. 1994. *Revolution in the Countryside: Rural Conflict and Agrarian Reform in Guatemala, 1944–1954*. Chapel Hill: University of North Carolina Press.

Hannaford, Ivan. 1996. *Race: The History of an Idea in the West*. Baltimore: Johns Hopkins University Press.

Harvey, Neil. 1998. *The Chiapas Rebellion: The Struggle for Land and Democracy*. Durham: Duke University Press.

Hedrick, Tace. 2003. "Blood-Lines That Waver South: Hybridity, the 'South,' and American Bodies." *Southern Quarterly* 42, no. 1: 39–52.

Helg, Aline. 2004. *Liberty and Equality in Caribbean Colombia, 1770–1835*. Chapel Hill: University of North Carolina Press.

———. 1995. *Our Rightful Share: The Afro-Cuban Struggle for Equality, 1886–1912*. Chapel Hill: University of North Carolina Press.

———. 1990. "Race in Argentina and Cuba, 1880–1930: Theory, Policies, and Popular Reaction." In *The Idea of Race in Latin America, 1870–1940*, edited by Richard Graham, 37–70. Austin: University of Texas Press.

Hendricks, Margo, and Patricia Parker. 1994. Introduction to *Women, "Race," and Writing in the Early Modern Period*, edited by Margo Hendricks and Patricia Parker, 1–14. New York: Routledge.

Hernández Díaz, Jorge. 2001. *Reclamos de la Identidad: La Formación de Las Organizaciones Indígenas en Oaxaca*. México, D.F.: UABJO & Miguel Angel Porrúa.

Hernández Navarro, Luis. 1999. "Reaffirming Ethnic Identity and Reconstituting Politics in Oaxaca." In *Subnational Politics and Democratization in Mexico*, edited by Wayne A. Cornelius, Todd A. Eisenstadt, and Jane Hindley, 153–73. La Jolla, Calif.: UCSD Center for U.S.-Mexican Studies.

Hess, Andrew C. 1968. "The Moriscos: An Ottoman Fifth Column in XVI-Century Spain." *American Historical Review* 74: 1–25.

Hodes, Martha. 2006. "Fractions and Fictions in the United States Census of 1890." In *Haunted by Empire: Geographies of Intimacy in North American History*, edited by Ann Laura Stoler. Durham: Duke University Press.

———. 2003. "The Mercurial Nature and Abiding Power of Race: A Transnational Family Story." *American Historical Review* 108, no. 1 (February): 84–118.

———. 1997. *White Women, Black Men: Illicit Sex in the 19th-Century South*. New Haven: Yale University Press.

Holt, Thomas C. 2000. *The Problem of Race in the 21st Century*. Cambridge: Harvard University Press.

———. 1998. "Explaining Racism in American History." In *Imagined Histories: American Historians Interpret the Past*, edited by Anthony Molho and Gordon S. Wood. Princeton: Princeton University Press.

———. 1995. "Marking: Race, Race-making, and the Writing of History." *American Historical Review* 100, no. 1: 1–20.

Htun, Mala. 2005. "Racial Quotas for a 'Racial Democracy.'" *NACLA* 38, no. 4 (January/February).

———. 2004. "From 'Racial Democracy' to Affirmative Action: Changing State Policy on Race in Brazil." *Latin American Research Review* 39, no. 1 (February): 60–89.

Hudson, Nicholas. 1996. "From 'Nation' to 'Race': The Origin of Racial Classification in Eighteenth-Century Thought." *Eighteenth-Century Studies* 29, no. 3: 247–64.

Human Rights Watch. 1999. *Systemic Injustice: Torture, Disappearance, and Extrajudicial Execution in Mexico*. New York: Human Rights Watch.

——. 1997. *Implausible Deniability: State Responsibility for Rural Violence in Mexico*. New York: Human Rights Watch.

Hurtado, Javier. 1986. *Katarismo*. La Paz: HISBOL.

Hylton, Forrest, and Sinclair Thomson. 2007. *Revolutionary Horizons: Past and Present in Bolivian Politics*. London: Verso.

Informes del Director de la Oficina Nacional de Inmigración, Estadística y Propaganda Geográfica y del Presidente de la Sociedad Geográfica de La Paz, elevados al Ministerio de Fomento e Instrucción Pública sobre el movimiento de ambas oficinas en el año de 1901–1902. 1902. La Paz, Bolivia.

Irurozqui Victoriano, Marta. 2000. *"A Bala, Piedra y Palo": La construcción de la ciudadanía política en Bolivia, 1826–1952*. Seville: Diputación de Sevilla.

——. 1994. *La armonía de las desigualdades: Elites y conflictos de poder en Bolivia, 1880–1920*. Cuzco: Bartolomé de las Casas.

Jackson, Jean E. 1995. "Culture, Genuine and Spurious: The Politics of Indianness in the Vaupés, Colombia." *American Ethnologist* 22, no. 1: 3–27.

Jackson, Jean E., and Kay B. Warren. 2005. "Indigenous Movements in Latin America, 1992–2004: Controversies, Ironies, New Directions." *Annual Review of Anthropology* 34: 549–73.

Jacobson, Matthew Frye. 1998. *Whiteness of a Different Color: European Immigrants and the Alchemy of Race*. Cambridge: Harvard University Press.

Jaguaribe, Beatriz. 1999. "Modernist Ruins: National Narratives and Architectural Form." *Public Culture* 11, no. 1.

Jones, Ann Rosalind, and Peter Stallybrass. 1992. "Dismantling Irena: The Sexualizing of Ireland in Early Modern England." In *Nationalisms and Sexualities*, edited by Andrew Parker et al., 157–71. New York: Routledge.

Jordan, Winthrop. 1968. *White over Black: American Attitudes toward the Negro, 1550–1812*. Chapel Hill: University of North Carolina Press.

Juárros, Domingo Antonio. 1981. *Compendio de la Historia de la Ciudad de Guatemala (1500–1800)*. Guatemala: Piedra Santa.

Kaiser, David A. 1999. *Romanticism, Aesthetics, and Nationalism*. Cambridge: Cambridge University Press.

Katz, Friedrich. 1981. *The Secret War in Mexico: Europe, the United States, and the Mexican Revolution*. Chicago: University of Chicago Press.

Katzew, Ilona. 2004. *Casta Painting: Images of Race in Eighteenth-Century Mexico*. New Haven: Yale University Press.

Keck, Margaret, and Kathryn Sikkink. 1998. *Activists Beyond Borders*. Ithaca: Cornell University Press.

Keen, Benjamin. 1984. *La imagen azteca en el pensamiento universal*. Mexico: Fondo de Cultura Economica.

Klarén, Peter. 2000. *Peru: Society and Nationhood in the Andes*. Oxford: Oxford University Press.

Klein, Herbert. 1992. *Bolivia: The Evolution of a Multi-Ethnic Society*. New York: Oxford University Press.

——. 1969. *Politics and Political Change in Bolivia, 1880–1952*. Cambridge: Cambridge University Press.

Knight, Alan. 1990. "Racism, Revolution, and Indigenismo: Mexico, 1910–1940." In *The Idea of Race in Latin America, 1870–1940*, edited by Richard Graham, 71–114. Austin: University of Texas Press.

Kolata, Alan. 1993. *The Tiwanaku: Portrait of an Andean Civilization*. Cambridge: Blackwell.

Komisaruk, Catherine. 2010. "Becoming Free, Becoming Ladino: Slave Emancipation and Mestizaje in Colonial Guatemala." In *Between Race and Place: Blacks and Blackness in Central America*, edited by Lowell Gudmundson and Justin Wolfe. Durham: Duke University Press.

Konetzke, Richard. 1953. *Colección de documentos para la historia de la formación social de Hispanoamérica, 1493–1810*. Vol 1. Madrid: Consejo Superior de Investigaciones Científicas.

König, Hans-Joachim. 1984. "Símbolos nacionales y retórica política en la Independencia: El caso de la Nueva Granada." In *Problemas de la formación del estado y de la nación en Hispanoamérica*, edited by Inge Buisson et al., 389–405. Köln: Böhlau Verlag.

Korovkin, Tanya. 1997. "Indigenous Peasant Struggles and the Capitalist Modernization of Agriculture: Chimborazo, 1964–1991." *Latin American Perspectives* 24, no. 3: 25–49.

Kourí, Emilio. 2010. "Manuel Gamio y el Indigenismo de la Revolución Mexicana." In *Historia de los intelectuales en América Latina*, vol. 2, edited by Carlos Altamirano. Buenos Aires: Katz Editores.

Kramer, Pedro. 1899. *Historia de Bolivia*. La Paz: Tipo-Litográfico.

Kristal, Efraín. 1987. *The Andes Viewed from the City: Literary and Political Discourse on the Indian in Peru, 1848–1930*. New York: P. Lang.

Kubler, George. 1952. *The Indian Caste of Peru, 1795–1940*. Washington: Smithsonian.

Kuznesof, Elizabeth Anne. 1995. "Ethnic and Gender Influences on 'Spanish' Creole Society in Colonial Spanish America." *Colonial Latin American Review* 4, no. 1: 153–76.

Kyle, David. 2000. *Transnational Peasants: Migrations, Networks, and Ethnicity in Andean Ecuador*. Baltimore: Johns Hopkins University Press.

Lagos, María L., and Pamela Calla. 2007. Introduction to *Antropología del estado: Dominación y prácticas contestatarias en América Latina*, edited by María L. Lagos and Pamela Calla. La Paz: INDH/PNUD.

Lajo, Javier. 2005. "La Invisibilidad Indígena en el Perú y la Acción Disociadora del Antropologismo." Perulibre.blogspot.com/2005/06/la-invisibilidad-indigena-en-el-per.html.

Larson, Brooke. 2005. "Redeemed Indians, Barbarianized Cholos: Crafting an Exclusionary Political Culture in Bolivia, 1900–1910." In *Political Cultures of the Andes, 1750–1950*, edited by Nils Jacobsen and Cristóbal Aljovín de Losada. Durham: Duke University Press.

———. 2004. *Trials of Nation Making: Liberalism, Race, and Ethnicity in the Andes, 1810–1910*. Cambridge: Cambridge University Press.

———. 2003. "Capturing Indian Bodies, Hearths and Minds: 'El hogar campesino' and Rural School Reform in Bolivia, 1920s–1940s." In *Proclaiming Revolution: Bolivia in Comparative Perspective*, edited by Merilee S. Grindle and Pilar Domingo. Cambridge: DRCLAS, Harvard University and ILAS, University of London.

Las Casas, Bartolomé. 1989. *The Diario of Christopher Columbus's First Voyage to America 1492–1493*. Transcribed and translated by Oliver Dunn and James E. Kelley Jr. Norman: University of Oklahoma Press.

Las Siete Partidas del Sabio Rey D. Alfonso el Nono, copiadas (1250–1751) de la edición de Salamanca del año de 1555. 1851. Cotejadas con varios códices antiguos por la Real Academia de la Historia y glosadas por el Licenciado Gregorio López del Consejo Real de Indias de S.M. Paris. 4 volumes.

Lasso, Marixa. 2007. *Myths of Harmony: Race and Republicanism during the Age of Revolution, Colombia, 1795–1831*. Pittsburgh: University of Pittsburgh Press.

Lazar, Sian. 2008. *El Alto, Rebel City: Self and Citizenship in Andean Bolivia*. Durham: Duke University Press.

Lema, Ana María. 1994. *Bosquejo del estado en que se halla la riqueza nacional de Bolivia presentado al examen de la Nación por un Aldeano hijo de ella año de 1830*. La Paz: Plural.

León, Arnaldo. 1983. *They Called Them "Greasers": Anglo Attitudes Towards Mexicans in Texas, 1820–1900*. Austin: University of Texas Press.

Levinson, Bradley, et al., eds. 1996. *The Cultural Production of the Educated Person: Critical Ethnographies of Schooling and Local Practice*. Albany: State University of New York Press.

Lewin, Boleslao. 1967. *La rebelión de Tupac Amaru y los orígenes de la Independencia de Hispanoamérica*. 1943. Expanded 3rd ed. Buenos Aires: Hachette.

Lewin, Pedro, and Estela Guzmán. 2003. "La migración indígena." In *Los Pueblos Indígenas de Oaxaca: Atlas Etnográfico*, edited by Alicia Mabel Barabas, Miguel Alberto Bartolomé, and Benjamin Maldonado, 183–99. Mexico: Conaculta, INAH.

Lewis, Laura A. 2003. *Hall of Mirrors: Power, Witchcraft, and Caste in Colonial Mexico*. Durham: Duke University Press.

Lewis, Stephen E. 2006. "The Nation, Education, and the 'Indian Problem' in Mexico, 1920–1940." In *The Eagle and the Virgin: Nation and Cultural Revolution in Mexico, 1920–1940*, edited by Mary Kay Vaughan and Stephen E. Lewis, 176–95. Durham: Duke University Press.

Li, Tanya Murray. 2000. "Articulating Indigenous Identity in Indonesia: Resources, Politics, and the Tribal Slot." *Comparative Studies in Society and History* 42, no. 1: 149–79.

Lissón Chaves, Emilio, ed. 1944. *La Iglesia de España en el Perú*. Vol. 10. Sevilla.

Litwack, Leon. 1998. *Trouble in Mind: Black Southerners in the Age of Jim Crow*. New York: Knopf.

Lockhart, James. 1984. "Social Organization and Social Change in Colonial Spanish America." In *The Cambridge History of Latin America*, edited by Leslie Bethell. Cambridge: Cambridge University Press.

———. 1968. *Spanish Peru, 1532–1560: A Colonial Society*. Madison: University of Wisconsin Press.

Lokken, Paul. 2004. "Transforming Mulatto Identity in Colonial Guatemala and El Salvador." *Transforming Anthropology* 12, nos. 1 and 2: 9–20.

———. 2001. "Marriage as Slave Emancipation in Seventeenth-Century Rural Guatemala." *The Americas* 58, no. 2 (October): 175–200.

Lomnitz, Claudio. 2009a. "Once tesis acerca de Molina Enríquez." In *En busca de Molina Enríquez: Cien años de "Los grandes problemas nacionales,"* edited by Emilio Kourí, 65–78. Mexico, D.F.: El Colegio de México.

———. 2009b. "Chronotopes of a Dystopic Nation: The Birth of 'Dependency' in Late Porfirian Mexico." In *Clio/Anthropos: Exploring the Boundaries Between History and Anthropology*, edited by Andrew Willford and Eric Taggliatozzo, 102–38. Stanford: Stanford University Press.

———. 2006. "Final Reflections: What Was Mexico's Cultural Revolution?" In *The Eagle and the Virgin: Nation and Cultural Revolution in Mexico, 1920–1940*, edited by Mary Kay Vaughan and Stephen E. Lewis, 335–49. Durham: Duke University Press.

———. 2005. "Mexico's Race Problem: And the Real Story behind Fox's Faux Pas." *Boston Review* (November/December).

———. 2001a. *Deep Mexico, Silent Mexico: An Anthropology of Nationalism*. Minneapolis: University of Minnesota Press.

———. 2001b. "Bordering on Anthropology." In *Deep Mexico, Silent Mexico: An Anthropology of Nationalism*, by Claudio Lomnitz. Minneapolis: University of Minneapolis Press.

———. 1992. *Exits from the Labyrinth: Culture and Ideology in the Mexican National Space*. Berkeley: University of California Press.

Lonsdale, John. 1977. "When Did the Gusii (Or Any Other Group) Become a 'Tribe'?" *Kenya Historical Review* 5: 123–33.

López, Rick A. 2006. "The Noche Mexicana and the Exhibition of Popular Arts: Two Ways of Exalting Indianness." In *The Eagle and the Virgin: Nation and Cultural Revolution in Mexico, 1920–1940*, edited by Mary Kay Vaughan and Stephen E. Lewis, 23–42. Durham: Duke University Press.

López Martínez, Héctor. 1964. "Un motín de mestizos en el Perú (1567)." *Revista de Indias* 24: 367–81.

López Ruiz, Mariano. 1898. "Historia de la Nacion Mixteca." *Boletín de la Sociedad Científica Antonio Alzate*.

Loveman, Mara. 2009. "The Race to Progress: Census-Taking and Nation-Making in Brazil." *Hispanic American Historical Review* 89, no. 3: 435–70.

Lucero, José Antonio. 2008. *Struggles of Voice: The Politics of Indigenous Representation in the Andes*. Pittsburgh: University of Pittsburgh Press.

——. 2006. "Representing 'Real Indians': The Challenges of Indigenous Authenticity and Strategic Constructivism in Ecuador and Bolivia." *Latin American Research Review* 41, no. 2: 31–56.

——. 2002. "Arts of Unification: Political Representation and Indigenous Movements in Bolivia and Ecuador." Ph.D. diss., Princeton University.

——. 2001. "High Anxiety in the Andes: Crisis and Contention in Ecuador." *Journal of Democracy* 12, no. 2: 59–73.

Macas, Luis, Linda Belote, and Jim Belote. 2003. "Indigenous Destiny in Indigenous Hands." In *Millenial Ecuador: Critical Essays on Cultural Transformations and Social Dynamics*, edited by Norman Whitten Jr., 216–41. Iowa City: University of Iowa Press.

MacCormack, Sabine. 1999. "Ethnography in South America: The First Two Hundred Years." In *The Cambridge History of the Native Peoples of the Americas*. Vol. 3, pt.1, edited by Frank Salomon and Stuart Schwartz, 96–187. Cambridge: Cambridge University Press.

Mallon, Florencia. 2009. "El Siglo XX Mapuche: Esferas públicas, sueños de auto-determinación y articulaciones internacionales." In *Movimientos indígenas en Chiapas y Araucanía*, edited by Christian Martínez Neira and Marco Estrada Saavedra. Santiago: Catalonia.

——. 2005. *Courage Tastes of Blood: The Mapuche Community of Nicolás Ailío and the Chilean State, 1906–2001*. Durham: Duke University Press.

——. 2003. "Barbudos, Warriors, and Rotos: The MIR, Masculinity, and Power in the Chilean Agrarian Reform, 1965–1974." In *Changing Men and Masculinities in Latin America*, edited by Matthew C. Gutmann, 179–215. Durham: Duke University Press.

——. 1996. "Constructing Mestizaje in Latin America: Authenticity, Marginality, and Gender in the Claiming of Ethnic Identities." *Journal of Latin American Anthropology* 2, no. 1 (September): 170–81.

——. 1995. *Peasant and Nation: The Making of Postcolonial Mexico and Peru*. Berkeley: University of California Press.

———. 1992. "Indian Communities, Political Cultures, and the State in Latin America, 1780–1990." *Journal of Latin American Studies* 24: 35–53.

Mamani, Carlos. 1991. *Taraqu, 1866–1935: Masacre, guerra y "renovación" en la biografía de Eduardo L. Nina Qhispi*. La Paz: Aruwiyiri.

Mamani, Pablo. 2007. "Evo Morales entre revolución india o contra revolución india." *Revista Willka* 1, no. 1: 15–49

Mannarelli, María Emma. 1993. *Pecados públicos: La ilegitimidad en Lima, siglo XVII*. Lima: Ediciones Flora Tristán.

Manrique, Nelson. 2002. *El tiempo del miedo: La violencia política en el Perú, 1980–1996*. Lima: Fondo Editorial del Congreso del Perú.

———. 1998. "The War for the Central Sierra." In *Shining and Other Paths: War and Society in Peru, 1980–1995*, edited by Steve J. Stern, 193–223. Durham: Duke University Press.

———. 1996. "Racismo y violencia política en el Perú." *Pretextos* 8: 89–105.

———. 1995. "Political Violence, Ethnicity, and Racism in Peru in Time of War." *Journal of Latin American Cultural Studies* 4, no. 1: 5–18.

———. 1993. *Vinieron los Sarracenos: El universo mental de la conquista de América*. Lima: DESCO.

Mariaca, Juvenal, and A. Peñaranda. 1918. *Proyecto de organización de una escuela normal agrícola de indígenas, en el altiplano*. La Paz: Litografía Boliviana.

Marof, Tristan. 1934. *La tragedia del altiplano*. Buenos Aires: Claridad.

Martínez, Françoise. 1995. "La création des 'escuelas ambulantes' en Bolivie (1905)." *Cahiers de l' U.F.R. d'etudes iberique et latino-americaines* 10 and 11: 161–71.

Martínez, Juan Carlos. 2004. "El proceso de reforma constitucional en materia indígena y la posición del estado de Oaxaca: Una aproximación sociojurídica." In *El Estado y los indígenas en tiempos del PAN: Neoindigenismo, legalidad e identidad*, edited by Rosalva Aída Hernández, Sarela Paz, and María Teresa Sierra, 233–60. Mexico, D.F.: Cámara de Diputados, LIX Legislatura, Centro de Investigaciones y Estudios Superiores en Antropología Social, Miguel Angel Porrúa.

Martínez, María Elena. 2008. *Genealogical Fictions: Limpieza de sangre, Religion, and Gender in Colonial Mexico*. Stanford: Stanford University Press.

Martínez, Oscar. 2001. *Mexican Origin People in the United States: A Topical History*. Tucson: University of Arizona Press.

———. 1996. *U.S.-Mexico Borderlands: Historical and Contemporary Perspectives*. Wilmington, Del.: Scholarly Resources.

Martínez Echazabal, Lourdes. 1998. "Mestizaje and the Discourse of National/ Cultural Identity in Latin America, 1845–1959." *Latin American Perspectives* 100 (May): 21–42.

Martínez Gracida, Manuel. 1888. *El Rey Cosijoeza y su familia*. Mexico: Secretaría de Fomento.

Martínez Palaez, Severo. 1971. *La Patria del Criollo*. Guatemala: EDUCA.

Martínez Vásquez, Víctor Raúl, ed. 1993. *La Revolución en Oaxaca, 1900–1930*. Mexico, D.F.: CONACULTA.

Martz, Linda. 2003. *A Network of Converso Families in Early Modern Toledo*. Ann Arbor: University of Michigan Press.

Mayer, Enrique. 1970. "Mestizo e indio: el contexto de las relaciones interétnicas." In *El indio y el poder en el Perú*, edited by Fernando Fuendaliza. Lima: IEP.

Mazzotti, José Antonio. 1996. *Coros Mestizos del Inca Garcilaso: Resonancias Andinas*. Mexico City: Fondo de Cultura Económica.

McBride, George McCutchen. 1923. *The Land Systems of Mexico*. New York: American Geographical Society.

McCreery, David. 1994. *Rural Guatemala: 1760–1940*. Stanford: Stanford University Press.

———. 1989. "State Power, Indigenous Communities, and Land in Nineteenth Century Guatemala." In *Indian Communities and the State: Guatemala, 1540–1988*, edited by Carol Smith. Austin: University of Texas Press.

McNamara, Patrick J. 2007. *Sons of the Sierra: Juárez, Díaz, and the People of Ixtlán, Oaxaca, 1855–1920*. Chapel Hill: University of North Carolina Press.

Meisch, Lynn. 2002. *Andean Entrepreneurs: Otavalo Merchants and Musicians in the Global Arena*. Austin: University of Texas Press.

———. 1998. "The Reconquest of Otavalo Ecuador: Indigenous Economic Gains and New Power Relations." In *Research in Economic Anthropology*, vol. 19, edited by B. L. Isaac, 11–30. Stamford, Conn.: JAI Press.

Memoria del Ministerio de Relaciones Exteriores y Culto. 1837. La Paz, Bolivia.

Mendoza, Zoila. 2008. *Creating Our Own: Folklore, Performance, and Identity in Cuzco, Peru*. Durham: Duke University Press.

———. 2000. *Shaping Society through Dance: Mestizo Ritual Performance in the Peruvian Andes*. Chicago: University of Chicago Press.

Mendoza García, Edgar. 2004. "Las primeras misiones culturales ambulantes en Oaxaca, 1926–1932: ¿Éxito o fracaso?" *Cuadernos del Sur* 10, no. 20 (March): 71–86.

Menéndez, Baldomero. 1860. *Manual de Geografía y Estadística del Alto Perú por D. Baldomero Menéndez, Gobernador de provincia, cesante y ex catedrático de Geografía e Historia en el Seminario de Vergara*. Paris: Enciclopedia Popular.

Mignolo, Walter. 2003. *The Darker Side of the Renaissance: Literacy, Territoriality, and Colonization*. 2nd ed. Ann Arbor: University of Michigan Press.

———. 1996. *The Darker Side of the Renaissance: Literacy, Territoriality, and Colonization*. Ann Arbor: University of Michigan Press.

Miller, Nicola. 1999. *In the Shadow of the State: Intellectuals and the Quest for National Identity in Twentieth-Century Spanish America*. New York: Verso.

Milton, Cynthia E. 2007. "At the Edge of the Peruvian Truth Commission: Alternative Paths to Recounting the Past." *Radical History Review* 98 (spring): 3–26.

Mires, Fernando. 1991. *El discurso de la indianidad*. San José, Costa Rica: Editorial Departamento Ecuménico de Investigaciones.

Mitre, Bartolomé. 1954. *Las Ruinas de Tiahuanaco*. 1879. Buenos Aires: Libreria Hachette S.A.

Monasterios, Karin, et al. 2007. *Reinventando la nación en Bolivia*. La Paz: CLASCO/Plural Editores.

Monsalve Pozo, Luis. 1943. *El indio: Cuestiones de su vida y de su pasión*. Cuenca: Austral.

Montoya, Rodrigo. 1998. *Multiculturalidad y Política: Derechos Indígenas, Ciudadanos y Humanos*. Lima: SUR Casa de Estudios del Socialismo.

Mora, Raúl M. 1998. "Afirman pueblos indígenas: Rumiñahui, no se mueve del parque central." *La Verdad*.

Morales-Moreno, Luis Gerardo. 1994. "History and Patriotism in the National Museum of Mexico." In *Museums and the Making of "Ourselves": The Role of Objects in National Identity*, edited by Flora E. S. Kaplan, 171–91. London: Leicester University Press.

Mörner, Magnus. 1970. *La corona española y los foráneos en los pueblos de indios de América*. Stockholm: Instituto de Estudios Ibero-Americanos.

———. 1967. *Race Mixture in the History of Latin America*. Boston: Little, Brown.

Múnera, Alfonso. 1998. *El fracaso de la nación: Región, clase y raza en el Caribe colombiano (1717–1821)*. Bogotá: Banco de la República/El Áncora Editores.

Muñoz Enríquez, Susana. 2000. "Imágenes y Discursos de los Grupos Etnicos en el Museo Nacional de Antropología." B.A. thesis, Department of Anthropology, Universidad de las Américas-Puebla.

Muratorio, Blanca, ed. 1994. *Imágenes e imagineros: Representaciones de los indígenas ecuatorianos, siglos XIX y XX*. Quito: FLACSO.

NACLA, *Report on the Americas*. 2005. "The Paradoxes of Racial Politics: The Politics of Race and Globalization." Part II, 38, no. 4 (January/February): 19.

———. 2001a. "Crossing Borders: Race and Racism in the Americas." Part II, 35, no. 2 (September/October): 13.

———. 2001b. "The Social Origins of Race: Race and Racism in the Americas." Part 1, 34, no. 6 (May/June): 15.

———. 1999. "Argentina: Taking Aim at Illegal Immigrants." 32, no. 5 (March/April): 50–52.

Nahmad, Salomón. 2001. "Autonomia indígena y la soberanía nacional: El caso de la Ley Indigena de Oaxaca." In *Costumbres, leyes y movimiento indio en Oaxaca y Chiapas*, edited by Lourdes de León Pasquel. Mexico, D.F.: CIESAS & Miguel Angel Porrúa.

Ngai, Mae M. 1999. "The Architecture of Race in American Immigration Law: A Reexamination of the Immigration Act of 1924." *The Journal of American History* 86, no. 1 (June): 67–92.

Nirenberg, David. 2003. "Enmity and Assimilation: Jews, Christians, and Converts in Medieval Spain." *Common Knowledge* 9, no. 1: 137–55.

———. 2000. "El concepto de raza en el estudio del antijudaísmo ibérico medieval." *Edad Media* 3: 39–60.

Nobles, Melissa. 2000. *Shades of Citizenship: Race and the Census in Modern Politics.* Stanford: Stanford University Press.

Nuevo Diccionario de la Lengua Castellana. 1883. Paris-Mexico.

Núñez Reguerin, Bethel. 2008. "Relativismo cultural y mujeres transgresoras." In *Observando el Racismo: Racismo y regionalismo en el proceso constituyente.* Observatorio del racismo en Bolivia, Área de Investigación. La Paz: Defensor del Pueblo y Universidad de la Cordillera.

Nye, Robert. 1975. *The Origins of Crowd Psychology: Gustave LeBon and the Crisis of Mass Democracy in the Third Republic.* London: Sage.

Obras Completas de Ricardo Flores Magón. 2000. Correspondencia 1 (1899–1918). Compilación, prólogo y notas: Jacinto Herrera Bassols. Mexico: Consejo Nacional para la Cultura y las Artes.

Observatorio del racismo en Bolivia, Área de Investigación. 2008. *Observando el Racismo: Racismo y regionalismo en el proceso constituyente.* La Paz: Defensor del Pueblo y Universidad de la Cordillera.

Oficina Nacional de Inmigración, Estadística y Propaganda Geográfica. 1973. *Censo general de la población de la República de Bolivia según el empadronamiento de 1 de Septiembre de 1900, Tomo. 2.* Cochabamba: Editorial Canelas S.A.

———. 1900. *Reglamento de Estadísticas del 29 de Diciembre de 1899.* La Paz: Tipografía de El Telégrafo.

Oglesby, Elizabeth. 2007. "Educating Citizens in Postwar Guatemala: Historical Memory, Genocide, and the Culture of Peace." *Radical History Review* 97: 77–98.

Olsen, Patrice E. 1998. "Revolution in the Streets: Changing Nomenclature, Changing Form in Mexico City's Centro Histórico and the Revision of Public Memory." Paper prepared for the Latin American Studies Association meetings, Chicago, Ill.

———. 1997. "Issues of National Identity: Obregón, Calles, and Nationalist Architecture, 1920–1930." Paper delivered at the annual meeting of the Latin American Studies Association, Guadalajara, Mexico.

Omi, Michael, and Howard Winant. 1987. *Racial Formation in the United States.* New York: Routledge.

O'Phelan Godoy, Scarlett. 1995. *La gran rebelión en los Andes: De Túpac Amaru a Túpac Catari.* Cuzco: Centro Bartolomé de las Casas.

———. 1988. *Un siglo de rebeliones anticoloniales: Perú y Bolivia, 1700–1783.* Cuzco: Centro Bartolomé de Las Casas.

O'Toole, Rachel Sarah. 2001. "Inventing Difference: Africans, Indians, and the Antecedents of 'Race' in Colonial Peru (1580s–1720s)." Ph.D. diss., University of North Carolina, Chapel Hill.

Ovando Sanz, Jorge Alejandro. 1985. *El tributo indígena en las finanzas bolivianas del siglo XIX.* La Paz: Comité Ejecutivo de la Universidad Boliviana.

Ozouf, Mona. 1976. *Fête révolutionnaire, 1789–1799*. Paris: Gallimard.

Pacheco, Diego. 1992. *El indianismo y los indios contemporáneos en Bolivia*. La Paz: HISBOL.

Pacheco, José Emilio. 1976. "La Patria Perdida: Notas sobre Clavijero y la Cultura Nacional." In *En Torno a la cultura nacional*, edited by Héctor Aguilar Camín et al., 16–50. Mexico: CONACULTA & INI.

Pagden, Anthony. 1987. "Identity Formation in Spanish America." In *Colonial Identity in the Atlantic World, 1500–1800*, edited by Nicholas Canny and Anthony Pagden, 15–93. Princeton: Princeton University Press.

——, trans. and ed. 1986a. *Hernán Cortés: Letters from Mexico*. New Haven: Yale University Press.

——. 1986b. *The Fall of Natural Man: The American Indian and the Origins of Comparative Ethnology*. Cambridge: Cambridge University Press.

Palacios, Nicolás. 1918. *Raza chilena: Libro escrito por un chileno y para los chilenos*. 2 vols. 2nd ed. Santiago: Editorial Chilena/Imprenta Universitaria.

Pallares, Amalia. 2002. *From Peasant Struggles to Indian Resistance: The Ecuadorian Andes in the Late Twentieth Century*. Norman: University of Oklahoma Press.

Paredes, Manuel Rigoberto. 1979. *El Kollasuyu*. 1916. La Paz: Ediciones Isla.

——. 1965. *La Altiplanicie: Anotaciones etnográficas, geográficas y sociales de la comunidad Aymara*. 1914. La Paz: ISLA.

——. 1955. *Tiahuanacu y la provincia de Ingavi*. La Paz: Ediciones Isla.

——. 1923. "La altiplanicie: Rasgos psicológicos de sus moradores." *Revista boliviana de instrucción pública* 1.

——. 1911. *Política Parlamentaria de Bolivia*. 1907. 3rd ed. La Paz: Velarde.

——. 1906. *Provincia Inquisivi: Estudios geográficos, estadísticos y sociales*. La Paz: Gamarra.

——. 1898. "Monografía de la Provincia Muñecas." *Boletín de la Sociedad Geográfica de La Paz* Año 1, Tomo 1, No. 1.

Parrenin, Georges, and Jean-Pierre Lavaud. 1980. "Pour une approche de l'indigenisme en Bolivie, 1900–1932." *Document de travail* 14. Paris: ERSIPAL.

Pastor, Rodolfo. 1987. *Campesinos y reformas: Sociedad y economía en la Mixteca, 1750–1856*. Mexico: El Colegio de México.

Patzi, Felix. 1999. *Insurgencia y sumisión: Movimientos indigeno-campesinos, 1983–1998*. La Paz: Muela del Diablo.

Paz Gonzáles, Eduardo. 2008. "Anulando al antagonista político en las Comisiones de la Asamblea Constituyente." In *Observando el Racismo: Racismo y regionalismo en el proceso constituyente*. Observatorio del racismo en Bolivia, Área de Investigación. La Paz: Defensor del Pueblo y Universidad de la Cordillera.

Penry, Elizabeth. 1996. "Transformations in Indigenous Authority and Identity in Resettlement Towns of Colonial Charcas (Alto Perú)." Ph.D. diss., University of Miami.

Pentland, J. B. 1975. *Informe sobre Bolivia (1826)*. Vol. 8, No. General. Potosí: Colección Segunda, Autores del Siglo XIX.

Pérez Montfort, Ricardo. 2003. *Estampas de nacionalismo popular mexicano: Diez ensayos sobre la cultura popular y nacionalismo*. 2nd Edition. Mexico, D.F.: CIESAS; Cuernavaca: CIDHEM.

Pérez Velasco, Daniel. 1928. *La mentalidad chola en Bolivia*. La Paz: Ed. López.

Platt, Tristan. 1993. "Simón Bolívar, the Sun of Justice and the Amerindian Virgin: Andean Conceptions of the *Patria* in Nineteenth-Century Potosí." *Journal of Latin American Studies* 25: 159–85.

Ponce Sanjinés, Carlos. 1995. *Tiwanaku: 200 años de investigaciones arqueológicas*. La Paz: Producciones CIMA.

Poole, Deborah. Forthcoming. "Ambiguous Distinctions: Visual Memories and the Language of Diversity in Postrevolutionary Oaxaca." In *Popular Memory and Official History in Mexico*, edited by W. Beezley. Wilmington, Del.: Scholarly Resources Press.

——. 2009. "Affective Distinctions: Race and Place in Oaxaca." In *Contested Histories in Public Space: Memory, Race, and Nation*, edited by Lisa Knauer and Daniel Walkowitz. Durham: Duke University Press.

——. 2007. "Political Autonomy and Cultural Diversity in the Oaxaca Rebellion." *Anthropology Newsletter* (March): 10–11. Washington, D.C.: American Anthropological Association.

——. 2006. "Los usos de la costumbre: Hacia una antropología jurídica del Estado neoliberal." *Alteridades* 16, no. 31: 9–21.

——. 2004a. "Siempremuertas: El sacrificio femenino desde Zehotoba a Donají." *Acervos* (Oaxaca) 7, no. 27 (August): 46–52.

——. 2004b. "An Image of 'Our Indian': Type Photographs and Racial Sentiments in Oaxaca, 1920–1940." *Hispanic American Historical Review* 84, no. 1 (winter): 37–82.

——. 1997. *Vision, Race, and Modernity: A Visual Economy of the Andean Image World*. Princeton: Princeton University Press.

——. 1990. "Ciencia, peligrosidad y represión en la criminología indigenista peruana." In *Bandoleros, abiegos y montoneros: Criminalidad y violencia en el Perú, siglos XVIII-XX*, edited by Carlos Aguirre and Charles Walker. Lima: Instituto de Apoyo Agrario.

Poole, Deborah, and Gerardo Rénique. 1992. *Peru: Time of Fear*. London: Latin American Bureau.

Portal Ariosa, María Ana, and Xóchitl Ramírez. 1995. *Pensamiento Antropológico en México: Un Recorrido Histórico*. Mexico, D.F.: Universidad Autónoma Metropolitana.

Posnansky, Arthur. 1945. *Tihuanacu, the Cradle of American Man*. New York: J. J. Augustin.

———. 1943. *¿Las Américas son un nuevo mundo o un mundo mucho más antiguo que Europa y Asia? Pruebas incontrovertibles de que el hombre americano es originario de América.* La Paz: Editorial del Instituto Tihuanacu de Antropología, Etnografía y Prehistoria.

———. 1942. "Que es raza?" *Revista de Antropología de Bolivia* 1: 17–29.

———. 1937a. *Antropología y sociología de las razas interandinas y de las regiones adyacentes.* La Paz: Editorial Renacimiento.

———. 1937b. *Un parque nacional en Bolivia.* La Paz: Editorial Renacimiento.

———. 1911. *Tihuanacu y la civilización prehistórica en el altiplano andino.* La Paz: Imprenta Artística.

Preston, David A., Gerado A. Taveras, and Rosemary A. Preston. 1981. "Emigración rural y desarrollo agrícola en la sierra Ecuatoriana." *Revista Geográfica* 93 (January–June): 7–35.

Programa de Investigación Estratégica en Bolivia (PIEB). 2007. "El mestizaje en tiempos de indigenismo." *Temas de Debate* 4, no. 8 (April): 1–4.

Putnam, Lara. 2002. *The Company They Kept: Migrants and the Politics of Gender in Caribbean Costa Rica, 1870–1960.* Chapel Hill: University of North Carolina Press.

Qayum, Seemin. 2002a. "Nationalism, Internal Colonialism and the Spatial Imagination: The Geographic Society of La Paz in Turn-of-the-Century Bolivia." In *Studies in the Formation of the Nation-State in Latin America*, edited by James Dunkerley, 275–98. London: ILAS.

———. 2002b. "Creole Imaginings: Race, Space, and Gender in the Making of Republican Bolivia." Ph.D. diss., Goldsmiths College, University of London.

Qayum, Seemin, María Luisa Soux, and Rossana Barragán. 1997. *De terratenientes a amas de Casa: Mujeres de la élite de La Paz en la primera mitad del siglo XIX.* Serie Protagonistas de la Historia, Coordinadora de la Historia. La Paz: Ed. Ministerio de Desarrollo Humano, Secretaría de Género.

Quijano, Anibal. 2000. "Coloniality of Power, Eurocentrism, and Latin America." *Nepantla* 1, no. 3: 533–80.

———. 1980. *Dominación y cultura: Lo cholo y el conflicto cultural en el Perú.* Lima: Mosca Azul.

Raimondi, Antonio. 1874. *El Perú.* Lima: Imprenta del Estado.

Rama, Angel. 1996. *The Lettered City.* Edited and translated by John Charles Chasteen. Durham: Duke University Press.

Ramírez Vásquez, Pedro, et al. 1968. *The National Museum of Anthropology, Mexico: Art, Architecture, Archaeology, Ethnography.* New York: Harry N. Abrams/Helvetica Press.

Rancière, Jacques. 2001. "Ten Theses on Politics." *Theory and Event* 5, no. 3.

Rappaport, Joanne. 2005. *Intercultural Utopias: Public Intellectuals, Cultural Experimentation, and Ethnic Pluralism in Colombia.* Durham: Duke University Press.

Recondo, David. 2007. *La política del gatopardo: Multiculturalismo y democracia en Oaxaca.* Mexico: CIESAS Y CEMCA.

——. 2001. "Usos y costumbres, procesos electorales y autonomía indígena en Oaxaca." In *Costumbres, leyes y movimiento indio en Oaxaca y Chiapas*, edited by Lourdes de León Pasquel, 91–113. DF: CIESAS & Miguel Angel Porrúa.

Recopilación de Leyes de los Reinos de las Indias. 1774. 4 volumes. 3rd ed. Madrid.

Red Oaxaqueña de Derechos Humanos. 2006. *VI Informe: Situación de los derechos humanos en Oaxaca*. Oaxaca: Red Oaxaqueña de Derechos Humanos.

Reeves, René. 2006. *Ladinos with Ladinos, Indians with Indians: Land, Labor, and Regional Ethnic Conflict in the Making of Guatemala*. Stanford: Stanford University Press.

Remy, María Isabel. 1994. "The Indigenous Population and the Construction of Democracy in Peru." In *Indigenous Peoples and Democracy in Latin America*, edited by Donna Lee Van Cott, 107–30. New York: St. Martin's Press.

Rénique, Gerardo. 2007. "Subaltern Political Formation and the Struggle for Democracy in Oaxaca." *Socialism and Democracy* 21, no. 2 (July): 62–73.

——. 2003. "Race, Region, and Nation: Sonora's Anti-Chinese Racism and Mexico's Postrevolutionary Nationalism, 1920s–1930s." In Appelbaum et al., *Race and Nation in Modern Latin America*. Chapel Hill: University of North Carolina Press.

Restall, Matthew. 2005. "Introduction: Black Slaves, Red Paint." In *Beyond Black and Red: African-Native Relations in Colonial Latin America*, edited by Matthew Restall, 1–13. Albuquerque: University of New Mexico Press.

Rich, Adrienne. 1978. "Cartographies of Silence." In *The Dream of the Common Language*, by Adrienne Rich. New York: Norton.

Rico Mansard, Luisa F. F. 2000. "Los Museos de la Ciudad de México: Su Organización y Función Educativa (1790–1910)." Ph.D. diss., Universidad Nacional Autónoma de México.

Rivera Cusicanqui, Silvia. 1993. "La Raíz: Colonizadores y colonizados." In *Violencias encubiertas en Bolivia*, edited by Xavier Albó and Raul Barrios. La Paz: CIPCA.

——. 1984. *"Oprimidos pero no vencidos": Luchas del campesinado aymara y qhechwa, 1900–1980*. La Paz: UNRISD, HISBOL, CSUTCB.

Robins, Nicholas A. 2002. *Genocide and Millennialism in Upper Peru: The Great Rebellion of 1780–1782*. Westport, Conn.: Praeger.

Rodas Martínez, Hernán. 2001. "Globalización y transmigración." *Ecuador Debate* 54: 47–58.

Rogers, Mark. 1998a. "Spectacular Bodies: Folklorization and the Politics of Identity Formation in Ecuadorian Beauty Pageants." *Journal of Latin American Anthropology* 3, no. 2: 54–85.

——. 1998b. Introduction to "Performing Andean Identities." *Journal of Latin American Anthropology* 3, no. 2: 2–19.

Rojas, Isaías. 2003. *The Push for Zero Coca: Democratic Transition and Counternarcotics Policy in Peru*. Washington, D.C.: WOLA.

Rojas, Ricardo. 1909. *La restauración nacionalista*. Buenos Aires: Ministerio de Justicia é Instrucción Pública.

Roldán, Mary. 2002. *Blood and Fire: La Violencia in Antioquia, Colombia, 1946–1953.* Durham: Duke University Press.

Romero, Carlos. 1919. *Las taras de nuestra democracia.* La Paz: ARNO.

Romero, Victor H. 2007. "Periodismo: Medias verdades, desequilibrio y algunas reflexiones." In *Cochabamba 11 de Enero . . . Análisis y Reflexiones,* 3–18. Cochabamba: Editorial Verbo Divino.

Rose, Nikolas. 1999. "Advanced Liberalism." In *Powers of Freedom: Reframing Political Thought,* 137–66. Cambridge: Cambridge University Press.

Rosemblatt, Karin Alejandra. 2009. "Other Americas: Transnationalism, Scholarship, and the Culture of Poverty in Mexico and the United States." *Hispanic American Historical Review* 89, no. 4 (November): 603–41.

Ross, Kathleen. 1999. "Native Americans and Early Modern Concepts of Race." In *Empire and Others: British Encounters with Indigenous Peoples, 1600–1850,* edited by Martin Daunton and Rick Halpern, 79–100. Philadelphia: University of Pennsylvania Press.

Rouma, Georges. 1928. *Una página de la historia educacional boliviana.* Sucre: López.

———. 1911. *Las bases científicas de la educación.* Sucre: Bolívar de Pizarro.

Rowe, John. 1954. *Max Uhle, 1856–1944: A Memoir of the Father of Peruvian Archaeology.* Berkeley: University of California Press.

Rubin, Jeffrey. 1997. *Decentering the Regime: Ethnicity, Radicalism, and Democracy in Juchitán, Mexico.* Durham: Duke University Press.

Ruck, Ernesto. 1875. *Miscelánea Estadística de Bolivia.* Colección Ruck 535. Archivo Nacional de Bolivia/Biblioteca Nacional de Bolivia. Sucre, Bolivia.

Ruck, Ernesto, and Benedicto Medinaceli. 1874. *Archivo Estadístico. Órgano de la Comisión de Estadística Nacional de Bolivia.* Tomo 1. Sucre, 19 de Enero de 1874, No. 1.

Ruiz Cervantes, Francisco José. 1986. *La Revolución en Oaxaca: El movimiento de la Soberanía (1915–1920).* Mexico, D.F.: Fondo de Cultura Económica.

Russell-Wood, A. J. R. 1995. "Before Columbus: Portugal's African Prelude to the Middle Passage and Contribution to Discourse on Race and Slavery." In *Race, Discourse, and the Origin of the Americas: A New World View,* edited by Vera Lawrence Hyatt and Rex Nettleford, 134–68. Washington, D.C.: Smithsonian Institution Press.

Saavedra, Bautista. 1995. *El Ayllu.* 1913. La Paz: Librería Editorial Juventud.

———. 1987. *El ayllu: Estudios sociológicos.* 1903. La Paz: Juventud.

———. 1921. *La democracia en nuestra historia.* La Paz: Velasco y Medina.

Safford, Frank. 1991. "Race, Integration, and Progress: Elite Attitudes and the Indian in Colombia, 1750–1870." *Hispanic American Historical Review* 71, no. 1: 1–33.

Said, Edward. 1979. *Orientalism.* New York: Vintage Press.

Saldaña-Portillo, María Josefina. 2003. *The Revolutionary Imagination in the Americas.* Durham: Duke University Press.

Saldivar, Emiko. 2008. *Prácticas cotidianas de indigenismo: Una etnografía del estado*. Mexico: Universidad Iberoamericana.

Salmón, Josefa. 1997. *El espejo indígena: El discurso indigenista en Bolivia, 1900–1956*. La Paz: Plural Editores/UMSA.

Salomon, Frank, and George L. Urioste. 1991. *The Huarochirí Manuscript: A Testament of Ancient and Colonial Andean Religion*. Austin: University of Texas Press.

Sánchez Bustamante, Daniel. 1918. *Programa político*. La Paz.

———. 1903. *Principios de Sociología: Primera entrega*. La Paz: Artística.

Sanders, James E. 2004. *Contentious Republicans: Popular Politics, Race, and Class in Nineteenth-Century Colombia*. Durham: Duke University Press.

Sanford, Victoria. 2003. *Buried Secrets: Truth and Human Rights in Guatemala*. New York: Palgrave Macmillan.

Santa Cruz, Andrés. 1852. *Código de procederes, Santa-Cruz*. Nueva edición. La Paz: Paceña.

Sawyer, Suzana. 1997. "The 1992 Indian Mobilization in Lowland Ecuador." *Latin American Perspectives* 24, no. 3 (May): 65–82.

Schirmer, Jennifer. 1998. *The Guatemalan Military Project: A Violence Called Democracy*. Philadelphia: University of Pennsylvania Press.

Schwartz, Stuart. 1995. "Colonial Identities and the *Sociedad de Castas*." *Colonial Latin American Review* 4, no. 1: 185–201.

———, ed. 1994. *Implicit Understandings: Observing, Reporting, and Reflecting on the Encounters between Europeans and Other Peoples in the Early Modern Period*. Cambridge: Cambridge University Press.

Schwartz, Stuart B., and Frank Salomon. 1999. "New Peoples and New Kinds of People: Adaptation, Readjustment, and Ethnogenesis in South American Indigenous Societies (Colonial Era)." In *The Cambridge History of the Native Peoples of the Americas*, vol. 3, pt. 2, edited by Frank Salomon and Stuart B. Schwartz, 443–501. Cambridge: Cambridge University Press.

Seigel, Micol. 2009. *Uneven Encounters: Making Race and Nation in Brazil and the United States*. Durham: Duke University Press.

Selverston, Melina. 1994. "The Politics of Culture: Indigenous Peoples and the State in Ecuador." In *Indigenous Peoples and Democracy in Latin America*, edited by Donna Lee Van Cott, 131–52. New York: St. Martin's Press.

Sicroff, Albert A. 2000. "Spanish Anti-Judaism: A Case of Religious Racism." In *Encuentros and Desencuentros: Spanish Jewish Cultural Interaction Throughout History*, edited by Carlos Carrete Parrondo et al., 589–613. Tel Aviv: University Publishing Projects.

———. 1985. *Los estatutos de limpieza de sangre: Controversias entre los siglos XVI y XVII*. Madrid: Taurus Ediciones, S.A.

Sieder, Rachel. 2001. "Rethinking Citizenship: Reforming the Law in Postwar Guatemala." In *States of Imagination: Ethnographic Explorations of the Postcolonial*

State, edited by Thomas Blom Hansen and Finn Stepputat. Durham: Duke University Press.

Sierra, Aída. 2000. "La creación de un símbolo." *Artes de México* 49 (Special Issue on La Tehuana): 16–25.

Sierra, María Teresa. 1998. "Autonomía y pluralismo jurídico: el debate mexicano." *América Indígena* 58, nos. 1 and 2 (January–June): 19–48.

Silverblatt, Irene. 2004. *Modern Inquisitions: Peru and the Colonial Origins of the Civilized World*. Durham: Duke University Press.

——. 2000. "New Christians and New World Fears." *Comparative Studies in Society and History* 42, no. 3: 524–47.

Siñani de Willka, Tomasa. 1992. "Breve biografía del fundador de la 'escuela ayllu': Un testimonio escrito sobre Avelino Siñani." In *Educación indígena: Ciudadanía o colonización?* edited by Roberto Choque et al., 25–134. La Paz: Aruwiyiri.

Skidmore, Thomas E. 2002. "Raízes de Gilberto Freyre." *Journal of Latin American Studies* 34, no. 1: 1–20.

Smith, Carol A. 1997. "The Symbolics of Blood: Mestizaje in the Americas." *Identities* 3, no. 4: 495–521.

——. 1995. "Race-Class-Gender Ideology in Guatemala: Modern and Anti-Modern Forms." *Comparative Studies in Society and History* 37, no. 4: 723–49.

Smith, Richard Chase. 2002. "Los indígenas amazónicos suben al escenario internacional: Reflexiones sobre el accidentado camino recorrido." In *Lo Transnacional: Instrumento y desafío para los pueblos indígenas*, edited by Françoise Morin and Robert Santana, 203–41. Quito: Abya Yala.

——. 1983. "Search for Unity Within Diversity: Peasant Unions, Ethnic Federations, and Indianist Movements in the Andean Republics." Paper presented at the Cultural Survival Symposium, Cambridge, Mass.

Solórzano Pereira, Juan de. 1739. *Política Indiana*. 4 volumes. 1647. Madrid.

——. 1947. *Política Indiana. Antología*. Selección y Prólogo de Luis García Arias. 2 volumes. 1647. Madrid.

Speed, Shannon, and Jane Collier. 2000. "Limiting Indigenous Autonomy in Chiapas, Mexico: The State Government's Use of Human Rights." *Human Rights Quarterly* 22: 877–905.

Spivak, Gayatri Chakravorty. 1994. "Can the Subaltern Speak?" In *Colonial Discourse and Post-Colonial Theory: A Reader*, edited by P. Williams and L. Chrisman. New York: Columbia University Press.

Squier, Ephraim George. 1877. *Peru, Incidents of Travel and Exploration in the Land of the Incas*. New York: Harper and Bros.

Starn, Orin. 1999. *Nightwatch: The Politics of Protest in the Andes*. Durham: Duke University Press.

——. 1998. "Villagers at Arms: War and Counterrevolution in the Central-South Andes." In *Shining and Other Paths: War and Society in Peru, 1980–1995*, edited by Steve J. Stern, 224–57. Durham: Duke University Press.

Ste. Croix, G. E. M. de. 1981. *The Class Struggle in the Ancient Greek World: From the Archaic Age to the Arab Conquests*. Ithaca: Cornell University Press.

Stepan, Nancy. 1991. *The "Hour of Eugenics": Race, Gender, and Nation in Latin America*. Ithaca: Cornell University Press.

Stephen, Lynn. 2002. *Zapata Lives! Histories and Cultural Politics in Southern Mexico*. Berkeley: University of California Press.

Stern, Alexandra. 2009. "Eugenics and Racial Classification in Modern Mexican America." In *Race and Classification: The Case of Mexican America*, edited by Ilona Katzew and Susan Deans-Smith. Stanford: Stanford University Press.

———. 2004. "Nationalism on the Line: Masculinity, Race, and the Creation of the U.S. Border Patrol, 1910–1940." In *Continental Crossroads: Remapping U.S.–Mexico Borderlands History*, edited by Samuel Truett and Elliot Young, 299–323. Durham: Duke University Press.

———. 2003. "From Mestizophilia to Biotypology: Racialization and Science in Mexico, 1920–1960." In *Race and Nation in Modern Latin America*, edited by Nancy Appelbaum et al. Chapel Hill: University of North Carolina Press.

Stern, Steve J., ed. 1998. *Shining and Other Paths: War and Society in Peru, 1980–1995*. Durham: Duke University Press.

———. 1992. "Paradigms of Conquest: History, Historiography, and Politics." *Journal of Latin American Studies*, Quincentenary Supplement 24: 1–34.

———. 1987a. "The Age of Andean Insurrection, 1742–1782: A Reappraisal." In *Resistance, Rebellion, and Consciousness in the Andean Peasant World, 18th to 20th Centuries*, edited by Steve J. Stern, 33–93. Madison: University of Wisconsin Press.

———, ed. 1987b. *Resistance, Rebellion, and Consciousness in the Andean Peasant World, 18th to 20th Centuries*. Madison: University of Wisconsin Press.

Stewart, Susan. 1993. *On Longing*. Durham: Duke University Press.

Stolcke, Verena. 1994. "Invaded Women: Gender, Race, and Class in the Formation of Colonial Society." In *Women, "Race," and Writing in the Early Modern Period*, edited by Margo Hendricks and Patricia Parker, 272–86. New York: Routledge.

Stoler, Ann Laura. 2002. *Carnal Knowledge and Imperial Power: Race and the Intimate in Colonial Rule*. Berkeley: University of Calfornia Press.

———. 1997. "Racial Histories and Their Regimes of Truth." *Political Power and Social Theory* 11: 183–206.

———. 1995. *Race and the Education of Desire: Foucault's History of Sexuality and the Colonial Order of Things*. Durham: Duke University Press.

Suárez Arnez, Faustino. 1958. *Historia de la educación*. La Paz.

Svampa, Maristella, and Pablo Stefanoni. 2007. "Evo simboliza el quiebre de un imaginario restringido a la subalternidad de los indígenas: Entrevista con Álvaro García Linera, vicepresidente de Bolivia." In *Reinventando la nación en Bolivia*, edited by Karin Monasterios et al., 147–71. La Paz: CLASCO/Plural Editores.

Sweet, James. 1997. "The Iberian Roots of American Racist Thought." *William and Mary Quarterly* 54, no. 1: 143–66.

Szeminski, Jan. 1987. "Why Kill the Spaniard? New Perspectives on Andean Insurrectionary Ideology in the 18th Century." In *Resistance, Rebellion, and Consciousness in the Andean Peasant World, 18th to 20th Centuries*, edited by Steve J. Stern, 166–92. Madison: University of Wisconsin Press.

Taller de Historia Oral Andina. 1984. *El indio Santos Marka T'ula: Cacique principal de los ayllus de Qallapa y apoderado general de las comunidades originarias de la República*. La Paz: THOA.

Tamayo, Franz. 1988. *Creación de la pedagogía nacional*. 1910. La Paz: Juventud.

Tamayo Herrera, José. 1982. *Historia social e indigenismo en el altiplano*. Lima: Ediciones Trentaitrés.

Tapia, Luis. 2007. "El triple descentramiento. Igualdad y cogobierno en Bolivia." In *Reinventando la nación en Bolivia*, edited by Karin Monasterios et al. La Paz: CLASCO/Plural Editores.

Taracena Arriola, Arturo. 2005. "Guatemala: El debate historiográfico en torno al mestizaje, 1970–2000." In *Memorias del mestizaje: Cultura política en Centroamérica de 1920 al presente*, edited by Darío A. Euraque, Jeffrey L. Gould, and Charles R. Hale. Guatemala: CIRMA.

——. 2004. *Etnicidad, estado y nación en Guatemala, 1944–1985*. Vol. 2. Antigua: CIRMA (con la colaboración Enrique Gordillo Castillo, Tania Sagastume Paiz, et al.).

——. 2002. *Etnicidad, estado y nación en Guatemala, 1808–1944*. Vol. 1. Antigua: CIRMA (con la colaboración Gisela Gellert, Enrique Gordillo Castillo, Tania Sagastume Paiz, and Knut Walter).

Tenorio Trillo, Mauricio. 2009. "Del mestizaje a un siglo de Andrés Molina Enríquez." In *En busca de Molina Enríquez: Cien años de "Los grandes problemas nacionales*," edited by Emilio Kourí, 33–64. Mexico, D.F.: El Colegio de México.

Thomson, Sinclair. 2002. *We Alone Will Rule: Aymara Politics in the Age of Insurgency*. Madison: University of Wisconsin Press.

——. 1987. "Bolivia's Turn-of-the-Century Indian Problem: The Case of Manuel Rigoberto Paredes." M.A. thesis, University of Wisconsin.

Thorp, Rosemary, Corinne Caumartin, and George Gray-Molina. 2006. "Inequality, Ethnicity, Political Mobilisation and Political Violence in Latin America: The Cases of Bolivia, Guatemala and Peru." *Bulletin of Latin American Research* 25, no. 4: 453–80.

Thurner, Mark. 1997. *From Two Republics to One Divided: Contradictions of Postcolonial Nationmaking in Andean Peru*. Durham: Duke University Press.

Tinker Salas, Miguel. 1997. *In the Shadow of the Eagles: Sonora and the Transformation of the Border During the Porfiriato*. Berkeley: University of California Press.

Tocqueville, Alexis de. 1952. *L'ancien régime et la révolution*. 1856. Paris: Gallimard.

Todorov, Tzvetan. 1989. *Nous et les autres: La reflexión française sur la diversité humaine*. Paris: Editions du Seuil.

Tórrez, Yuri F. 2007. "El discurso del mestizaje hecho trizas." In *Cochabamba 11 de Enero . . . Análisis y Reflexiones*, 39–54. Cochabamba: Editorial Verbo Divino.

Torrico Zas, Martín Gabriel. 2008. "El mito que reactualizó el racismo y reavivó una guerra heredada." In *Observando el Racismo: Racismo y regionalismo en el proceso constituyente*. Observatorio del racismo en Bolivia, Área de Investigación. La Paz: Defensor del Pueblo y Universidad de la Cordillera.

Touraine, Alain. 1978. *La voix et la régard*. Paris: Editions du Seuil.

Traffano, Daniela. 2002. *Indios, curas y nación: La sociedad indígena frente a un proceso de secularización, Oaxaca, siglo XIX*. Mexico: CIESAS.

Truett, Samuel, and Elliott Young. 2004. "Making Transnational History: Nations, Regions, and Borderlands." In *Continental Crossroads: Remapping U.S.-Mexico Borderlands History*, edited by Samuel Truett and Elliott Young, 1–32. Durham: Duke University Press.

Turits, Richard. 2002. "A World Destroyed, A Nation Imposed: The 1937 Haitian Massacre in the Dominican Republic." *Hispanic American Historical Review* 82, no. 3 (August): 589–636.

Van Cott, Donna Lee. 2000. *The Friendly Liquidation of the Past: The Politics of Diversity in Latin America*. Pittsburgh: University of Pittsburgh Press.

Vanderwood, Paul J. 1998. *The Power of God against the Guns of Government: Religious Upheaval at the Turn of the Nineteenth Century*. Stanford: Stanford University Press.

Vasconcelos, José. 1997. *La raza cósmica*. 1925. Baltimore: Johns Hopkins University Press.

——. 1979. *La Raza Cósmica: Bilingual Edition*. Translated by Didier Tisdel Jaén. Los Angeles: Centro de Publicaciones, California State University.

——. 1926. "The Latin-American Basis of Mexican Civilization." In *Aspects of Mexican Civilization*, by José Vasconcelos and Manuel Gamio, 3–102. Chicago: University of Chicago Press.

Vaughan, Mary Kay. 1997. *Cultural Politics in Revolution: Teachers, Peasants, and Schools in Mexico, 1930–1940*. Tucson: University of Arizona Press.

Vaughan, Mary Kay, and Stephen E. Lewis. 2006a. *The Eagle and the Virgin: Nation and Cultural Revolution in Mexico, 1920–1940*. Durham: Duke University Press.

——. 2006b. Introduction to *The Eagle and the Virgin: Nation and Cultural Revolution in Mexico, 1920–1940*, edited by Mary Kay Vaughan and Stephen E. Lewis, 1–20. Durham: Duke University Press.

Velasco, Margarita, Mercedes Olivera de Vásquez, Guillermo Bonfil Batalla, Enrique Valencia, and Arturo Warman. 1970. *De Eso Que Llaman Antropolgía Mexicana*. Mexico, D.F: Editorial Nuestro Tiempo.

Velásquez, Cristina. 2000. *El Nombramiento: Las elecciones por usos y costumbres en Oaxaca*. Oaxaca: Instituto Estatal Electoral de Oaxaca.

Villoro, Luis. 1979. *Los Grandes Momentos del Indigenismo en México*. 1950. Mexico, D.F.: Fondo de Cultura Económica.

Von Tschudi, Johann Jakob. 1851. *Antigüedades peruanas*. Vienna: Impr. Imperial de la Corte y del Estado.

Wade, Peter. 2008. "Race in Latin America." In *A Companion to Latin American Anthropology*, edited by Deborah Poole, 177–92. Malden, Mass.: Blackwell.

——. 2005. "Rethinking *Mestizaje*: Ideology and Lived Experience." *Journal of Latin American Studies* 37: 239–57.

——. 2003. Afterword to *Race and Nation in Modern Latin America*, edited by Nancy Appelbaum et al. Chapel Hill: University of North Carolina Press.

——. 2000. *Raza y etnicidad en Latinoamérica*. Quito: Abya-Yala.

——. 1997. *Race and Ethnicity in Latin America*. London: Pluto Press.

——. 1993. " 'Race,' Nature, and Culture." *Man* 28, no. 1: 1–18.

Walker, Charles. 1999. *Smoldering Ashes: Cuzco and the Creation of Republican Peru, 1780–1840*. Durham: Duke University Press.

Walsh, Catherine E. 2001. "The Ecuadorian Political Eruption: Uprisings, Coups, Rebellions, and Democracy." *Nepantla* 2, no. 1: 173–204.

Warren, Kay B. 2002. "Voting against Indigenous Rights in Guatemala: Lessons from the 1999 Referendum." In *Indigenous Movements, Self-representation, and the State in Latin America*, edited by Kay B. Warren and Jean J. Jackson. Austin: University of Texas Press.

——. 1998a. *Indigenous Movements and Their Critics: Pan-Maya Activism in Guatemala*. Princeton: Princeton University Press.

——. 1998b. "Indigenous Movements as a Challenge to the Unified Social Movement Paradigm for Guatemala." In *Cultures of Politics, Politics of Cultures: Re-visioning Latin American Social Movements*, edited by Sonia Alvarez, Evelina Dagnino, and Arturo Escobar, 165–95. Boulder, Colo.: Westview Press.

Warren, Kay B., and Jean J. Jackson. 2002a. *Indigenous Movements, Self-representation, and the State in Latin America*. Austin: University of Texas Press.

——. 2002b. "Introduction: Studying Indigenous Activism in Latin America." In *Indigenous Movements, Self-Representation, and the State in Latin America*, edited by Kay Warren and Jean Jackson, 1–46. Austin: University of Texas Press.

Weiner, Charles. 1880. *Pérou et Bolivie. Récit du voyage*. Paris: Hachette & cie.

Weinstein, Barbara. 2003. "Racializing Regional Difference: Sao Paulo versus Brazil, 1932." In *Race and Nation in Modern Latin America*, edited by Nancy Appelbaum et al. Chapel Hill: University of North Carolina Press.

Weismantel, Mary. 2001. *Cholos and Pishtacos: Stories of Race and Sex in the Andes*. Chicago: University of Chicago Press.

——. 1988. *Food, Gender, and Poverty in the Ecuadorian Andes*. Philadelphia: University of Pennsylvania Press.

Weismantel, Mary, and Stephen F. Eisenman. 1998. "Race in the Andes: Global Movements and Popular Ontologies." *Bulletin of Latin American Research* 17, no. 2: 121–42.

Whitaker, Morris D., and Duty Greene. 1990. "Development Policy and Agriculture." In *Agriculture and Economic Survival: The Role of Agriculture in Ecuador's Development*, edited by Morris D. Whitaker and Dale Colyer, 21–42. Boulder, Colo.: Westview Press.

Whitten, Norman E., Jr. 2004. "Ecuador in the New Millennium: 25 Years of Democracy." *Journal of Latin American Anthropology* 9, no. 2: 439–60.

———. 2003. Introduction to *Millennial Ecuador*, edited by N. E. Whitten Jr., 1–45. Iowa City: University of Iowa Press.

Wieviorka, Michel. 2002. *El racismo: Una introducción*. La Paz: Plural Editores.

Wilk, Richard. 1995. "Learning to be Local in Belize: Global Systems of Common Difference." In *Worlds Apart: Modernity through the Prism of the Local*, edited by Daniel Miller, 110–33. London: Routledge.

Williams, Brackette. 1991. *Stains on My Name, War in My Veins: Guyana and the Politics of Cultural Struggle*. Durham: Duke University Press.

———. 1989. "A Class Act: Anthropology and the Race to Nation across Ethnic Terrain." *Annual Review of Anthropology* 18: 401–44.

Williams, Patricia J. 1998. *Seeing a Color-Blind Future: The Paradox of Race*. New York: Noonday Press.

Williams, Raymond. 1976. *Keywords: A Vocabulary of Culture and Society*. New York: Oxford University Press.

Winant, Howard. 2001. *The World is a Ghetto: Race and Democracy since World War II*. New York: Basic Books.

Yashar, Deborah. 1998. "Contesting Citizenship: Indigenous Movements and Democracy in Latin America." *Comparative Politics* 31, no. 1: 23–42.

Young, Elliott. 2004. *Catarino Garza's Revolution on the Texas-Mexico Border*. Durham: Duke University Press.

Young, Robert. 1995. *Colonial Desire: Hybridity in Theory, Culture and Race*. London: Routledge.

Yrigoyen, Raquel. 2002. "Peru: Pluralist Constitution, Monist Judiciary—A Post-Reform Assessment." In *Multiculturalism in Latin America: Indigenous Rights, Diversity, and Democracy*, edited by Rachel Sieder, 157–83. New York: Palgrave Macmillan.

Zamosc, León. 1994. "Agrarian Protest and the Indian Movement in the Ecuadorian Highlands." *Latin American Research Review* 29, no. 3: 37–68.

Zavaleta Mercado, René. 1983. "Las masas en noviembre." In *Bolivia, hoy*, edited by René Zavaleta Mercado. Mexico: Siglo XXI.

Zea, Leopoldo. 1963. *The Latin American Mind*. Norman: University of Oklahoma Press.

Zegada, María Teresa. 2007. "Formas y trasfondos del conflicto." In *Cochabamba 11 de Enero . . . Análisis y Reflexiones*, 80–81. Cochabamba: Editorial Verbo Divino.

Zegarra Siles, Karim. 2008. "La Asamblea Constituyente: Una trampa para enmudecer." In *Observando el Racismo: Racismo y regionalismo en el proceso constituyente*. Observatorio del racismo en Bolivia, Área de Investigación. La Paz: Defensor del Pueblo y Universidad de la Cordillera.

Zulawski, Ann. 2007. *Public Health and Political Change in Bolivia, 1900–1950*. Durham: Duke University Press.

———. 2000. "Hygiene and 'the Indian Problem': Ethnicity and Medicine in Bolivia, 1910–1920." *Latin American Research Review* 35, no. 2: 107–29.

Zuñiga, Neptali. 1940. *Fenómenos de la Realidad Ecuatoriana*. Quito: Talleres Gráficos de Educación.

ROSSANA BARRAGÁN, a professor of history at the Universidad Mayor de San Andrés (La Paz), was director of the Archive of La Paz until 2010 and since then she heads the Latin American section at the International Institute of Social History in Amsterdam. She is the author of numerous works on Bolivian history, including *Asambleas Constituyentes: Ciudadanía y elecciones, convenciones y debates (1825–1971)* and *Miradas a la Junta del 16 de Julio de 1809.*

KATHRYN BURNS is a professor of history at the University of North Carolina, Chapel Hill. She is the author of *Colonial Habits: Convents and the Spiritual Economy of Cuzco, Peru* and *Into the Archive: Writing and Power in Colonial Peru.*

ANDRÉS CALLA is a member of the research team of the Observatory on Racism of the University of the Cordillera in La Paz. He is currently completing a licenciatura degree in sociology at the Universidad Mayor de San Andrés (La Paz). His research focuses on forms of distinction used by elites in exclusive spaces of La Paz.

PAMELA CALLA, an anthropologist, is director of the Observatory on Racism of the University of the Cordillera in La Paz and a visiting scholar at the Center for Latin American and Caribbean Studies at New York University. She is the author of works on race, gender, ethnicity, and state formation in Bolivia and coeditor of *Antropología del Estado: Dominación y prácticas contestatarias en América Latina.*

RUDI COLLOREDO-MANSFELD is an associate professor of anthropology at the University of North Carolina, Chapel Hill. He is the author of *The Native Leisure Class: Consumption and Cultural Creativity in the Andes* and *Fighting Like a Community: Andean Civil Society in an Age of Indian Uprisings.*

MARÍA ELENA GARCÍA, an anthropologist, is an associate professor in the Comparative History of Ideas Program and the Jackson School of International Studies at the University of Washington. She is the author of *Making Indigenous Citizens: Identities, Development, and Multicultural Activism in Peru*.

LAURA GOTKOWITZ is an associate professor of history at the University of Iowa. She is the author of *A Revolution for Our Rights: Indigenous Struggles for Land and Justice in Bolivia, 1880–1952*, which received the 2008 John E. Fagg Prize of the American Historical Association.

CHARLES R. HALE is a professor of anthropology and director of the Teresa Lozano Long Institute of Latin American Studies at the University of Texas, Austin. He is the author of *Resistance and Contradiction: Miskitu Indians and the Nicaraguan State, 1894–1987* and *"Más que un Indio": Racial Ambivalence and Neoliberal Multiculturalism in Guatemala*.

BROOKE LARSON is a professor of history at SUNY, Stony Brook. She is the author and editor of numerous works on colonial and modern Bolivia and the Andes. Her most recent books are *Ethnicity, Markets, and Migration in the Andes: At the Crossroads of History and Anthropology* (as coeditor) and *Trials of Nation Making: Liberalism, Race, and Ethnicity in the Andes, 1810–1910*.

CLAUDIO LOMNITZ is Campbell Family Professor of Anthropology at Columbia University. He is the author of numerous works on culture and politics in Latin America, especially Mexico. His most recent books are *Deep Mexico, Silent Mexico: An Anthropology of Nationalism* and *Death and the Idea of Mexico*.

JOSÉ ANTONIO LUCERO is an associate professor of international studies and chair of Latin American and Caribbean Studies at the Henry M. Jackson School of International Studies at the University of Washington. He is the author of *Struggles of Voice: The Politics of Indigenous Representation in the Andes*.

FLORENCIA MALLON is Julieta Kirkwood Professor of History at the University of Wisconsin, Madison, and the author of numerous works on the Andes, Mexico, and Chile. Her most recent books are *When a Flower is Reborn: The Life and Times of a Mapuche Feminist* (as editor and translator) and *Courage Tastes of Blood: The Mapuche Community of Nicolás Ailío and the Chilean State, 1906–2001*, which received the 2005 Bolton-Johnson Prize of the Conference on Latin American History.

KHANTUTA MURUCHI is a member of the research team of the Observatory on Racism of the University of the Cordillera in La Paz. She received a licenciatura degree in sociology from the Universidad Mayor de San Andrés (La Paz). Her thesis is a case study of worker resistance in a furniture factory of El Alto.

DEBORAH POOLE is a professor of anthropology at Johns Hopkins University and the author of numerous works on Peru and Mexico. Her most recent books are

Vision, Race, and Modernity: A Visual Economy of the Andean Image World and *Anthropology in the Margins of the State*, which she coedited.

SEEMIN QAYUM is a historical anthropologist and consultant in issues of international environment, development, gender, and culture. She is the author and editor of several works on nationalism, elites, and gender in modern Bolivia and coauthor of *Cultures of Servitude: Modernity, Domesticity, and Class in India*.

ARTURO TARACENA ARRIOLA is a researcher at the Centro Peninsular en Humanidades y Ciencias de Sociales of the Universidad Nacional Autónoma de México (CEPCHIS- UNAM), Mérida, Mexico. He is the author of numerous works on colonial and modern Mesoamerica, including the two-volume *Etnicidad, estado y nación en Guatemala* and *De la nostalgia por la memoria a la memoria nostálgica. La prensa literaria y la construcción del regionalismo yucateco decimonónico*.

SINCLAIR THOMSON is an associate professor of history at New York University. He is the author of *We Alone Will Rule: Native Andean Politics in the Age of Insurgency* and coauthor of *Revolutionary Horizons: Past and Present in Bolivian Politics*.

ESTEBAN TICONA, a sociologist and an anthropologist, is a doctoral candidate in Latin American Cultural Studies at the Universidad Andina Simón Bolívar in Ecuador. He teaches anthropology at the Universidad Mayor de San Andrés in La Paz. His recent publications include *Saberes, conocimientos y prácticas anticoloniales del pueblo aymara-quechua* and *Lecturas para la descolonización: Taqpachani qhispiyasipxañani (Liberémonos todos)*.

Page numbers in italics indicate figures and maps.

anthropology and ethnology (*cont.*)
74; founding of, 206; Lajo's critique
of, 286–87; material culture described
in, 186–88; Mexican state policy
influenced by, 20–21; possibilities of
engaged and collaborative type of,
291, 298n30; race and ethnicity in,
89n6. *See also* archaeology
antiracist movements: agenda of, and
legislation passed, 311–16; earlier discourses of, 50–51n119; geopolitics of
knowledge in, 33–34; indigenous
mobilization in, 28–33; racialized discourse and confrontations in, 34–37;
racism intensified in context of, 28–
30; truth commissions' role in, 27–28.
See also authenticity and legitimacy;
Bolivian Constituent Assembly;
Chimaltenango; *cholos* (youth gang);
decolonization; indigenous movements; insurgencies; Nina Qhispi,
Eduardo Leandro
arawaks, 168–69
archaeology: genealogical truths in, 187–
88; interests and requests to conduct,
162–63; Oaxaca and Zapotec linked
via, 185; site conservation vs. removal
of artifacts debate, 170–71. *See also*
anthropology and ethnology; Bennett
Stela; Tiwanaku ruins
Argentina: migrants scapegoated in, 26–
27; public discourse on victims of
violence in, 51n129; public education
in, 136
Arguedas, Alcides, 145, 147, 149
Arguedas, José María, 19
artisans: census on, 127; gendered definition of, 133n68; migration of, 224–
25; organizations of, 222, 225, 229–31,
236–37, 243; Plaza de Ponchos conflict and, 230–31; political identity of,
236–38; status of, 122, 124, 236

assimilation: civilization as requirement
for, 96–98, 106–7, 242; colonial goals
of, 11, 59–60; indigenismo linked to,
20–21, 161; of indigenous authorities
and nobility, 15, 60, 106; institutions
for indigenous, 110–11; in national
project, 95; of non-Indians, 85–86;
Spanish language and, 17, 141–42, 143,
151, 243. *See also* mestizaje; neoliberal
multiculturalism; segregation
Association of Indigenous Painters and
Artisans of Tigua-Quiloa (earlier,
Association of Small Traders), 225
Atawalpa, Juan Santos, 79
authenticity and legitimacy: beauty pageant conflict and, 231–33; commentators' view of, 279; geopolitics of
knowledge in, 34; Guelaguetza committee on, 180, 192, 193; NGOs' perspective and decisions in context of,
289–90; of production for native use
vs. foreigners, 230–31; rethinking
ideas about, 290–93
ayllu, 84, 91n30. *See also* indigenous
communities
Aymara people: alleged decline of, 168–
69; characteristics assigned to, 149–
50; civilizing projects for, 136–37;
defense of, 138; identification as, 32;
language of, 176n12, 176n20; in
Morales government, 302; national
decline blamed on, 147; origin myths
of, 164; partisan motives in sending
teachers to, 143; purity and authenticity of, 148–49, 152–53, 168–69; Felipe Quispe's appeal to, 292; spatialization of Bolivia and, 163; studies of,
140–42, 145–46. *See also* Morales
Ayma, Evo; Nina Qhispi, Eduardo
Leandro; Tiwanaku ruins
Aztec past, 21–22, 185
Azuela, Mariano, 212

Brazil: affirmative action initiative in, 26; Canudos rebellion in, 211; expanded influence of, 204–5; term race in, 208, 324–25

Bucaram, Abdala, 232

Buffon, Comte du, 104, 121

caciques (colonials): in anticolonial insurrection of 1780–81, 77; conversion of, 60; elimination of, 119; school for sons of, 120; status of, 117–18, 131n18

caciques-apoderados (twentieth-century network): alliance of, with Bautista Saavedra, 175n11; meanings of multiethnic community and, 329–30; mobilization under, 150–51, 161, 328; Santos Marka T'ula and, 309n8

campesinos, 280, 289, 292, 294

Cárdenas, Victor Hugo, 173

Carrera, Rafael, 112n3

casta paintings, 69n31, 70–71n48

caste: system in Mexico, 75; use of term, 47n42, 67n3, 115–17. *See also* racial classification (categories)

caste wars, 208–9

Castilian language. *See* Spanish language

Catholic Church: conversion to, 11–13, 58–60, 68n8, 97; mestizos as priests in, 64–65; Porfirian reforms and, 183–84, 201n17, 209. *See also* Christianity; *conversos*

census and data collection: in Guatemala, 107–8; in Mexico, 206–7; motivations for, 16–17, 114–15; in U.S., 25. *See also* Bolivian census; racial classification (categories)

Centro Educativo de Aborígenes Bartolomé de las Casas, 248

Centro Educativo Kollasuyo (La Paz): activities of, 247–48, 250; documents on, 240; founding of, 246, 252n2; organizing base of, 243; plans to organize, 245. *See also* Sociedad República del Kollasuyo (La Paz)

Chaco War (1932), 248–49

Chávez, Hugo, 307

Chervin, Arthur, 141

Chicano movement, 325

Chile: Bolivian students sent to, 140; nationality in, 325; public discourse on victims of violence in, 51n129

Chimaltenango (Guatemala): *cholos* (youth gang) of, 31, 256–57, 264–66, 273; ethnic ideologies in, 257–62, 273–76, 331–32; intermediate groups' emergence in, 263–64, 267–73; mestizaje from below in, 33, 255, 273, 276

cholos (youth gang): identification with, 31, 264–66, 270, 273, 274, 276; mestizos as, 129; national decline blamed on, 147–48; questions about, 256–57, 334; Spanish identity claimed by, 78; use of term, 265

Choque, Roberto, 315

Choquehuanca, David, 302

Christianity: evangelization politics in, 61–66; missionaries' educational methods and, 140; purity of, 58–59, 68nn8–9; social organization of gangs vs. evangelical churches, 272–73. *See also* Catholic Church

Cieza de Léon, Pedro, 160, 163, 164

CISA (Indian Council of South America), 284

citizenship: eligibility and designations of, 116, 130n16; equality before law as basis for, 208–9; Indians excluded from, 98–103; work of race in, 325–30. *See also* assimilation; multiethnic egalitarianism; segregation

civil conflicts. *See* insurgencies and civil conflicts

civil institutions. *See* indigenous communities; *specific entities*

civilization: barbarism vs., 129–30; debates about race, property, and, 183–88; required for assimilation, 96–98, 106–7, 242

class system: caste interchangeable with, 116–17; Isthmus women and, 186; mestizos as middle class in, 122–24; q'aras (term) and, 84, 91n29; race functioning as, 6, 10, 15; transition from caste system to, 113–14. *See also* social order

Clavijero, Francisco, 182

clientelism, 37, 110, 142, 200–201n5

clothing and footwear: census count affected by, 126; of *cholos* (youth gang), 264; discrimination on basis of, 304, 305–7; ethnicity identified by, 258, 263, 269, 276; as evidence of "civilizing," 97, 106; of government officials, 128; in Guelaguetza festival, 193–94, 195, 196–97, 198; in *Homenaje Racial*, 189–91, 202–3n38; of Isthmus de Tehuantepec women, 185–86; social order and ethnic cross-dressing, 85–86, 323; varieties of, 186–88

Cobo, Bernabé, 74, 89n8, 91n20

Cochabamba (Bolivia): confrontations in, 1–2, 308n1

Cojtí, Demetrio, 267, 275

collective psychology concept, 147. *See also* identity, collective

Colombia: indigenous peoples in, 44–45n12

colonialism (c.1500–1820s): collective identities constructed in, 75–76; decrees on mestizas and mestizos, 64–65; *padrones* (censuses) in, 114; racism and discrimination embedded in, 3, 28, 84; reconstructions of, in work of race, 323–25; "two republics" fiction

of, 59–60, 78; writing, urbanism, and power linked in, 134–35. *See also* Spanish conquistadors; Spanish laws; Spanish people; *specific countries*

colonial terms for race: assimilation and conversion key to, 11, 59–60; blood and religious purity ideas in, 9, 45–46n27, 58–59, 65–66; categories in, 44n11, 60–64, 117–22; historicizing and denaturalizing of "race," 72–78; Indian self-understandings and, 84–86; Indians vs. Spaniards in, 78–80; overview of, 11–13; Spanish-morisco conflicts and, 57–58, 63, 64, 65, 70n35, 70n40; whiteness in, 80–81

colonos (resident workers): definition of, 16; education policy for, 108, 143, 144; Indians as, 16

Columbus, Christopher, 59, 68n13, 74

comerciantes (merchants), 127–28

community: political hegemony in, 85–86; terms for, 84, 91n30. *See also* indigenous communities

COMPA (Coordinadora Oaxaqueña Magonista Popular Antineoliberal), 179–81, 193

CONACAMI (National Coordinator of Communities Affected by Mining), 278–79, 282–83, 288, 294–95, 296

CONAMAQ (Consejo Nacional de Ayllus y Markas del Qullasuyu), 282–83, 289

CONAPA (Peruvian National Commission for Andean, Amazonian, and Afro-Peruvian Peoples), 279, 282, 295, 297n5

Condori Churi, Leandro, 240–42

Conejo, Mario, 232, 233, 235, 236–37

Confederación de Nacionalidades Indígenas de la Amazonía Ecuatoriana (CONFENAIE), 228

Confederación de Nacionalidades Indígenas del Ecuador (CONAIE): educa-

Federal War (Bolivia, 1899), 37, 52n169, 53n172, 138, 142, 161, 175–76n12, 322, 326, 331

festivals and commemorations: alternative to government festival, 181, 201n15; authenticity decisions in, 180, 192, 193; Colla Raymi, 230, 232; May 25, 1809, commemoration, 36, 311; Mixtec culture and, 197–98; revival of, 226; San Juan, 231. *See also* beauty pageants; Guelaguetza festival; *Homenaje Racial* (Racial Homage)

Flores Magón, Ricardo, 214–15

forced labor: in Bolivia, 118, 119, 120, 131n22; as exclusive duty of Indians under Spanish, 118, 131n22; in Guatemala, 15–16, 18, 48n60, 95, 97, 100, 101, 105–6, 108–10

Fox, Vicente, 179

France: national unity in, 206; racialization in, 207; revolution and empire in, 332–33; Tiwanaku artifacts taken to, 167

Freyre, Gilberto, 324

FRG (Republican Guatemalan Front), 275

Fujimori, Alberto, 281

Gamio, Manuel, 24, 215

gangs, 272–73. See also *cholos* (youth gang)

García, Alan, 296

García Peláez, Francisco de Paula, 105–6

Garcilaso de la Vega, el Inca, 61–64, 69n23, 69–70n33, 70n35

gender: artisan identity and, 133n68; discrimination based on, 314, 317n5; in Guelaguetza festival, 193–94, *195*, 196–97, 198; imbalances in, captured in census, 125–26; occupational structure and, 17; Zapotec civilization and, 185–86. *See also* beauty pageants; clothing and footwear; women

Geographical Society of La Paz: founding and members of, 124, 125, 163, 177n29; nation envisioned by, 159–60; race and civilization rhetoric of, 172; Tiwanaku and, 166, 167, 177n31

Gobineau, Arthur de, 146

Gran Cruzada Nacional Pro-indio (Grand National Crusade for Indians), 243

guampos, 91n27

Guatemala: census of, 107–8; civilization as requirement for assimilation in, 96–98, 106–7; constitution of (1879), 102; degeneration of Indians ideology in, 95, 103–8, 109, 326; independence of, 96; Indian forced labor in, 15–16, 18, 48n60, 95, 97, 100, 101, 105–6, 108–10; Indian-ladino bipolarity in, 15–16, 33, 97–98, 111, 254, 261–62, 268; indigenous movements in, 29, 30–31; judicial system in, 17–18; liberal reforms and racemaking in, 14–18, 100–103, 106–8; Maya majority in, 31; mestizo category in, 33; multiculturalism and "four peoples" in, 271, 274; national project of, 95–96, 108–11; October Revolution (1944) in, 37, 48n60, 110–11; Peace Accords of, 31, 272, 275; population statistics of, 3; segregation in, 15–16, 48n69, 98–103, 254, 262, 267–70, 274, 277n11; truth commission in, 28, 38; violence in, 27, 37, 38–39, 53n174, 270–71. *See also* Chimaltenango; Maya people; *mistados*

Guelaguetza festival (Oaxaca): Authenticity Committee of, 180, 192, 193; *Diosa Centeotl* contest of, 193–94, *195*, 196–97, 198; exclusions of, 22–23, 181, 192–93; predecessor to, 189, 191; protests against, 179–80

Guelaguetza Popular (Oaxaca), 181, 201n15
Guevara, Che, 333
Guzmán, Felipe, 153

Haenke, Tadeo, 116, 132n40, 132n42
hate crimes, 313, 317n3
Hispanic ancestry, rehabilitated, 104–5
Hispanism, 171–72, 178n46
history: reteaching of, 226; Tiwanaku in, 159, 163–65; truth commissions and, 38–39
Homenaje Racial (Racial Homage), 188–91, 202–3n38, 327. *See also* Guelaguetza festival (Oaxaca)
Huarochirí Manuscript, 44n11, 77
Humboldt, Alexander von, 206

identity: language as defining, 226; mestizaje endorsed as national, 181–83, 196–97, 261; work and trades linked to, 223. *See also* authenticity and legitimacy; ethnicity; work of race
identity, collective: in Iberian discourse, 74; of mestizas and mestizos, 81–82; modern identity vs., 73; "race" in context of, 75–78; self-understandings of Indians, 84–86; solidarities invoked in, 86–88; of Spaniards, 78–80
ideology: of barbarism vs. civilization, 129–30; of "degeneration" of Indians, 95, 103–8, 109, 326; Indian-ladino bipolarity in, 15–16, 33, 97–98, 107–8, 111, 254, 261–62, 268; of Indians as *miserables*, 118–19. *See also* class system; ethnic ideologies; indigenismo; liberal reforms; mestizaje; neoliberalism
Inca past, 22, 85–86, 160
Indian: use of term, 13, 44n11, 89–90n10
Indian Council of South America (CISA), 284

Indianist movements: different views on, 279, 291, 298n33; indigenismo vs., 161, 175n10; organizations in, 284, 285; stance of, 290–93
Indian statue (in Otavalo), 32, 233–35
indígenas: category of, 117–20; use of term, 113, 130n1
indigenismo: concept of, 19, 22, 160–61, 327–28; Indianist movements vs., 161, 175n10; in lived experience and performance, 23–24; mestizaje compared with, 19–21; national differences in, 175n8; racialized underside of, 21–23; Tiwanaku's symbolism for, 159–61, 171–72
indigenous communities: autonomy of, 99; commercial orientation of, 100; community councils of, 222, 224–26, 228–29; dispossessed lands of, 137, 143–44; elections via *usos y costumbres*, 181, 200–201n5; haciendas' seizures of lands, 241–42; Porfirian reforms and, 183–88; of rural vs. urban areas, 221–24; Tiwanaku site takeover by, 172–75. *See also caciques-apoderados*; indigenous movements
indigenous movements: academic models of, 289–90, 292, 293–95; complex dynamics of, 51–52n148; elite ambivalence in wake of, 31–32; emergence of, 28–29; in neoliberal multiculturalism context, 198–200; in opposition to national project and exclusion, 108–11; racist responses to, 29–30; in rural vs. urban areas, 32–33, 221–24; Tiwanaku and, 173, 174–75. *See also specific organizations*
indigenous peoples: Bolivia and Guatemala compared, 37–38; collective self-understandings of, 84–86; incorporated into Qolla solidarity, 87; Jews conflated with, 63–64, 70n36;

ilitación de mozos) in, 15, 48n60, 101–2, 112n6; educational system linked to, 146, 149–53, 326–27; peasant freedom from obligations in, 224; racialization and wage differences in, 210–11; segregation in, 14–16, 18. See also *colonos* (resident workers); forced labor; occupations and occupational structure; social order

La Calancha deaths (Sucre, 2007) and aftermath, 35–36

ladinization: debate on, 260–61, 262; process of, 98, 254–55. *See also* assimilation

ladinos: ambivalence of, about Maya political power, 31; assimilation of, 96–98, 106–7; on cholos (gang), 264, 266; denials of Indian ancestry by, 259–60; economic successes of, 100–102; failed uprisings of, 99; heterogeneity of, 276–77n1; identity boundaries of, 257–59, 264, 267–68; massacre of, 37, 53n174; mestizaje idea taken on by, 262; mestizos distinguished from, 255; military conscription of, 103; mistado group between indigenous peoples and, 254; use of term, 15–16

Lajo, Javier, 284, 285, 286–88, 289, 298n33

land and property system: appropriation of communal and uncultivated lands, 100–101, 241–42; debates about civilization, race, and, 183–88; hacienda expansion into Indian lands, 137, 143–44; Indian holdings in, diminished, 14, 47n53; redistribution of, to mestizos, proposed, 209; Sandinista agrarian reform and, 333–34. *See also* rural areas

land ownership, 97, 106, 126–27, 209

language: indigeneity defined in terms of, 226. *See also specific groups and languages*

La Paz (Bolivia): as Bolivian seat of government, 35, 52n169, 175–76n12; description of, 125; dissident indigenistas and literacy in, 148–50; education debates and work in, 136–37, 242–48, 251–52; full-capital issue and, 34–36, 300, 304, 305–6, 309n4, 312, 331; indigenous mobilization (1920s) in, 32–33; social mobilization in (2003), 308n1. *See also* Andean anticolonial insurrection; Bolivian census; Tiwanaku ruins

La Raza. See "Mexican race"; race (*raza*)

Las Casas, Bartolomé de, 59

Latin America: biological and cultural racism in, 6–10; constitutional changes and indigenous peoples in, 29, 50–51n119; indigenismo and mestizaje in, 18–25; key moments concerning race in, 11, 46–47n37; liberal reforms and racemaking in, 13–18; migration within and to other continents, 26–27; questions about race in, 321–22; recent revolutionary moments in, 330–35. *See also* colonialism (c.1500–1820s); *specific countries*

Le Bon, Gustave, 147

Legión Cívica, 249

Leguía, Augusto, 19

letrados concept, 134, 153n2

"lettered city": campo distinguished from, 152–53; concept of, 134–35, 152; Indians excluded from, 146, 149–53, 326–27; literacy ideal in, 135–36; modernization's impact on, 136–37. *See also* elites; Geographical Society of La Paz; liberal reforms

Levantamiento Indígena Nacional (Ecuador, 1990), 227

Leyes de Indias, 99

liberalism: decline of, 145–46; insurgent, 329–30, 332

liberal reforms: anxieties about culture and property underlying, 183–88; judicial system and, 17–18; land and labor systems and, 14–16, 137, 143–44; overview of, 13–14; partisan motives in, 142–45. *See also* Bolivian Liberal Party; educational policy; *specific topics*

Libertad del Indio, 110

libretas, 18, 48n69

literacy: as evidence of "civilizing," 97; "lettered city" ideal of, 135–36; Nina Qhispi's and, 245–48; partisan motives in fostering, 142–45; power and urbanism linked to, 134–35; as threat to elites, 144–45, 146, 148–53. *See also* educational policy; schools

llama: use of term, 40, *41*, 300

Lux de Cojtí, Otilia, 275

mandamiento, 100, 101, 112n4. *See also* labor system

Mariátegui, José Carlos, 19, 276

Marof, Tristan, 154n15

marriage, 59–60, 69n20, 257–59

Martínez Gracida, Manuel, 184, 185–88, 202n24

MAS (Movimiento al Socialismo), 40, *41*, 251–52, 299, 305, 306, 308

material culture, 186–88. *See also* clothing and footwear

Mayan past, 104–5

Maya people: elite of Quetzaltenango, 15; genocide of, 28; identification as mestiza and as, 263; intermediate identity groups as threat to, 255, 274–75; ladinos and, 31, 259, 262; as majority in Guatemala, 31; perceived "degeneration" of, 95, 103–8, 109, 326; political ascendancy of, 271–72; views on cholos (gang), 266

Mesoamerica: Andes region compared to, 3, 6, 14–17, 37–38; map of, *4*. *See also specific countries*

mestizaje: concept of, 18–19, 199–200; experience and performance, 23–24; factors promoting idea of, 208–14; "from below," 33, 255, 273, 276, 332, 334; ideal of equality and, 262; identities downplayed in, 271; indigenismo vs., 19–21, 161; indigenous sphere and government's discourse on, 129; national decline linked to, 146–47; neoliberal multiculturalism and, 50n95; political fragmentation and, 188–91, 327; racialized underside of, 21–23; Rumiñahui statue as project of, 233–35; state sanctioned identity of, 181–83, 196–97, 261; as whitening, 141. *See also* indigenismo

mestizas and mestizos: affirmation of cult of, 20–21; beauty pageant conflict and, 231–33; census and, 125–28; ethnic ideology possibilities and, 274, 275; identification as Maya and as, 263; increased identification as, 33; ladinos vs., 255; mistados vs., 257–58; as Others, 81–82; paradox of, 272; Qolla solidarity and, 87; Rumiñahui statue placed by, 233–35; separation from whites in census, 122–24, 129; Spanish decrees on, 64–65; Spanish identity claimed by, 78; Tiwanaku's symbolism for, 160–61; transformation into national race, 24–25, 209–10; urban indigenous movement and, 223–24; uses of term, 60–61, 62–64, 113, 182; women identified as, 17. See also *ladinos; mistados*

mestizophilia, 208, 215

"Mexican race": census classifications of, 206–7; discourses concerning, 214–15; emergence of idea, 24–25,

207–14; social and psychological implications of, 215–16; use of term, 207. *See also* U.S.-Mexico border

Mexican Revolution (1910), 24, 25, 188–91, 212, 214

Mexican Society of Geography and Statistics, 206–7

Mexico: agrarian reform laws, 209; Aztec ruins venerated in, 21–22; Brazil and Cuba in relation to, 324–25; caste in, 75; census and classification of peoples in, 206–7; cultural vs. economic policies in, 180–81; economic development and mestizaje in, 204–5, 209–10; Indians as citizens in, 99; indigenismo and mestizaje in, 19, 20–21, 22–24; indigenous rights law, 181, 201n6; mestizaje as sanctioned identity in, 181–83, 208–9; mestizo as national race of, 24–25; millenarian revolts in, 211–12; multiculturalism as context for indigenous claims in, 198–200; racialization and wage differences in, 210–11; slogan of, 214; statistics on population of, 3; U.S. relations with, 204–5, 212–13. *See also* "Mexican race"; Oaxaca; Porfiriato; U.S.-Mexico border

migrants and migration: attempts to increase, 115, 209; contradictions faced by, 224–25; mestizaje linked to, 210; political activism harmed by, 222; racism intensified due to, 26–27

mining areas, 209, 212, 213, 241–42, 296. *See also* National Coordinator of Communities Affected by Mining (CONACAMI)

mistados: identification of, 254; "mestizaje from below" and, 255, 273, 276, 334; mestizos vs., 257–58. See also *cholos* (youth gang)

Mitre, Bartolomé, 163, 170, 176n19

Mixtec people and culture, 182, 187, 191, 194, 196–99, 201n10, 210

modernization processes, 75–86, 136–37, 143–44, 227

Molina Enríquez, Andrés, 24, 204, 209, 215, 216n4

montañés: uses of term, 62–64, 69n30

Monte Albán site (Mexico), 182, 201n10

Montes, Ismael, 140, 143–44, 252n4

Morales Ayma, Evo: decolonization under, 251–52; election of, 44n3, 299, 301; La Calancha deaths and, 36; opposition to, 35, 40, *41*, 44n1, 309n7; polarization and racial violence during presidency of, 1–2, 6, 34–37, 308, 312; proindigenous stance of, 1, 29, 221, 302, 314; Felipe Quispe and, 292; Tiwanaku visit of, 174–75. *See also* Movimiento al Socialismo (MAS)

Moreno, Gabriel René, 146

moriscos, 58, 63–65, 70n35, 70n40

Movimiento al Socialismo (MAS), 40, *41*, 251–52, 299, 305, 306, 308

Movimiento Unificado de Lucha Triqui (Unified Movement of Triqui Struggle): protest by, 180

mozos (in debt peonage), 15, 48n60, 101–2, 112n6

mulattas and mulattos, 16, 60–61, 62, 91n24, 98

multiculturalism. *See* neoliberal multiculturalism

multiethnic egalitarianism: hopes for, 38, 274, 328–29; recognition of, 107–8; in twentieth century, 330–32, 333–35

multilingualism, 99

multiracialism, 145

Muslim people, 58–59, 68n11. See also *moriscos*

names and naming: function of, 113–14, 129–30; index of identity and, 257, 263; of violence, 313–14 nation (*nación*): Cobo's concept of, 89n8; indigenous movements as perceived threat to, 29, 30; race as overlapping with notion of, 75–76, 325–30. *See also* nationalism; nationalist mythologies; *specific countries*

National Autonomous University of Mexico, 215–16

National Coordinator of Communities Affected by Mining (CONACAMI), 278–79, 282–83, 288, 294–95, 296

National Indian Institutes (Guatemalan schools), 102–3

nationalism: education and, 136–45; examining unity and, 204–5; "lettered city" ideals of, 135–36; U.S. and French approach to, 205–6

nationalist mythologies: Bennett Stela and, 170–75; indigenismo vs. mestizaje in, 18–25; local politics linked to, 161–65; mestizaje as sanctioned identity in, 181–83; national race in, 207–8; political cosmology as, 168–70; Tiwanaku's symbolic potency in, 159–61. *See also* festivals and commemorations; indigenismo; mestizaje; "Mexican race"; neoliberal multiculturalism; Tiwanaku ruins

national pedagogy: concept of, 145, 155n33; Indians as manual laborers in, 146, 149–53, 326–27

"negro": emergence of term, 90n19

neoliberalism: dislodging of elite linked to, 302–4; economic crises and, 204–5; protests against, 179–81. *See also* neoliberal multiculturalism

neoliberal multiculturalism: exclusions of, 22–23; indigenous claims and, 198–200; intermediate groups ignored in, 255; in Oaxaca, 181–83; shift from assimilationist mestizaje to, 50n95. *See also* Guelaguetza festival (Oaxaca); neoliberalism

neoracism. *See* cultural racism

Nicaragua: indigenismo in, 22

Nina Qhispi, Eduardo Leandro: background of, 240–42; Chaco War and imprisonment of, 248–49; decolonization of Bolivia and, 251–52; ethical and methodological principles of, 245–48; on "renovation" of Bolivia, 240, 249–51; social and political context of, 32–33, 250, 328; views of, on education and literacy, 242–45, 251–52

North America: anti-imperialist assumptions about, 291; census-taking in, 16; racism in, 8, 10. *See also* Oxfam-America; *specific countries*

Nueva Izquierda Oaxaca (New Left Oaxaca), 180

Oaxaca (Mexico): civilization, property, and race in, 183–88; excess and presence in, 191–98; homage to mestizo city of, 188–91, 327; human rights situation in, 181, 201n6; multiculturalism as context for indigenous claims in, 198–200; neoliberal cultural policies of, 22–23; protests in, 179–81. *See also* Guelaguetza festival

occupations and occupational structure: census counts on, 126–30; race embedded in, 17. *See also* labor system; social order

operationalization of race, 46n32. *See also* work of race

Otavalo (Ecuador): activism and politics of place in, 222–24; beauty pageant conflict in, 230, 231–33; indigenous organizations in, 229–30; mayoral race in, 236–38; monuments and central plaza conflict in, 233–35; plaza and marketplace conflict in, 230–31

Oxfam-America: broader perspective on, 290–91; critiques of, 287, 288–89; perspective and decisions of, 281, 285, 289–90; Peruvian organizations and, 282, 283, 285; use of term, 297n18

Pacari, Nina, 228
Pachakuti: use of term, 174, 178n51
Paniagua, Valentín, 282
Paraguay: Chaco War with Bolivia, 248–49
Paredes, Manuel Rigoberto: on Aymara farmers, 149; on Bennett Stela, 171; on D'Orbigny, 176–77n22; on Kollasuyu, 176n18; on mestizos, 124; on national decline, 145–46, 147–48; on Tiwanaku, 163–66, 170
Partido Revolucionario Institucional (PRI), 180–81, 200–201n5
Party of National Advancement (PAN), 275
Pauw, Cornelius de, 104
Pérez, Elizardo, 251
Permanent Conference of the Indigenous Peoples of Peru. *See* COPPIP-Coordinadora
Peru: absence of indigenous movement in, 278–83, 293, 294; Amazonian organizations in, 280, 283; authenticity and legitimacy debates in, 34; indigenismo and mestizaje in, 19, 22, 23, 161; indigenous influence on politics of, 296; indigenous organizations in, 278–79, 280–84, 287–89; labor market issues in, 2; pro-mining president of, 296; racial formation and identity in, 280, 297n13; statistics on population of, 3; violence and civil war in, 27, 279, 296, 298n34. *See also* Cuzco
Peruvian National Commission for Andean, Amazonian, and Afro-

Peruvian Peoples (CONAPA), 279, 282, 295, 297n5
Peruvian Truth and Reconciliation Commission (Comisión de la Verdad y Reconciliación), 27–28, 39, 279, 281
pinturas de casta, 69n31, 70–71n48
piquetero movement, 27
Plan Puebla-Panama, proposed, 179, 200n1
plurinational state, 227–28, 234, 274
pobres de solemnidad, 119–20, 131n35
PODEMOS (Poder Democrático y Social), 299, 305, 308n2
Ponce Sanjinés, Carlos, 166, 169, 173
Popular Participation Law (Bolivia, 1994), 174
Porfiriato (Mexico, 1876–1911): civilization, property, and race in, 183–88; intellectuals and images abroad in, 21; migration policy in, 209; racism of, 23
Portillo, Alfonso, 275
Posnansky, Arturo: Bennett Stela and, 170–72; Nina Qhispi's relationship with, 249; Tiwanaku promoted by, 166–70, 175n11, 177–78n42
postcolonialism: persistent power of, 330–32; work of race in, 325–30
PRI (Partido Revolucionario Institucional), 180–81, 200–201n5
pueblo: use of term, 181, 190, 194
pukakunga (red neck), 66–67, 83, 84
purity/impurity associations, 47n48. *See also* blood purity; race: purity of

q'aras (term), 83, 84, 91n27
Qollas, 85–88, 168, 169, 323
Quechua language, 27, 82–84, 176n20. *See also* Kichwa
Quechua people, 32, 140–42, 145–46, 280
Quiloa community council (Cotopaxi), 221, 222, 225–26

Quimbo, José Manuel, 232, 233, 235, 236, 237

Quispe, Felipe (*El Mallku*), 289, 291–92

race (*raza*): alternative meanings of, 10, 324, 327; approach to, 2–3, 6, 11; blackness legible only as, 193; caste and, 117; caste distinguished from, 47n42; debates about civilization, property, and, 183–88; elite and subaltern uses of, 12–13, 38, 76–78; genealogical discourses on, 57–58, 187–88, 193–98, 259; historicizing (unfixing) of term, 57–67, 72–78, 208; historiography of, 72–75, 95, 103–8, 109, 323; pedagogy of, 145–53; persistence of term, 88; in precolonial societies, 89n; purity of, 148–49, 152–53, 168–69; questions about, 321–22; scare quotes for, 57–58; use of term, 208. *See also* blood purity; colonial terms for race; "Mexican race"; nationalist mythologies; racial classification; racialization; work of race

racemaking (production of race): approach to, 3, 6; colonial period and, 11–13; liberal reforms and, 13–18;. *See also* racialization and the state (long 19th cen.); work of race

racial classification (categories): census use of, 16–17, 115–22; ethnicity and, 113; hierarchy of, 121–22, 260; of Linnaeus, 90–91n20; local, historical contexts and terms for, 57–67; motivations underlying, 114–15; physical characteristics in (phenotypes), 74–75, 91n20, 258–62, 305; power relations mapped in, 327; psychological, physiological, and anthropometric studies of, 140–42, 145–46; social content of, 125–28; Spanish terms for, 11–12; spatial and temporal hier-

archies marked in, 172. *See also* Bolivian census; caste; census and data collection

racialization: concept of, 11, 46n35, 113–14, 305; examples of, 207–8; of Mexican as product of U.S.-Mexico border, 210–14. *See also* antiracist movements; colonial terms for race; nationalist mythologies; racial classification (categories); racialization and the state (long 19th cen.); racial stereotypes

racialization and the state (long 19th cen.): in census categories and census-taking, 16–17, 115–22; in judicial systems, 17–18; in land and labor systems, 14–16; motivations underlying data collection and, 114–15; overview of, 13–14; pedagogy of race and, 145–53; social order and, 113–14. *See also* Bolivian census; educational policy; schools

racial profiling, 66

racial stereotypes: historical context in understanding, 66–67; indigenous struggles and, 235–36; official discourse and, 107–8; rural (indigenous) vs. urban (mestizo), 32, 221, 222, 226–27, 331. *See also specific terms*

racism: antiracist politics and, 26–38; approach to, 1–3, 6, 11; biological and cultural, 7–10; denials of, 2, 44n10; notions of illegitimacy and, 66, 70n45; persistence of, 269, 274–75; "pliant," 139; political and economic interests and, 95–96; sources of idea, 74–75; specificity of, 10, 48–49n70; structural and silent vs. open and violent, 34, 37–38, 300–301, 303–8; studying "race" as evasion of, 67n1. *See also* antiracist movements; assimilation; colonial terms for race; cultural racism; discrimination; nationalist mythologies; scientific racism; segregation

Raynal, Guillaume-Thomas, 104

religion, 9, 13. *See also* Catholic Church; Christianity; *conversos*; Jewish people; Muslim people

religious racism, 58

Renan, Ernest, 121

Republican Guatemalan Front (FRG), 275

republicanism, 146–47

Reyes Villa, Manfred, 44n1

rituals, 80, 90n18, 171, 174, 221, 244. *See also* festivals and commemorations

Rojas, Ricardo, 155n33

Rouma, Georges, 140–42, 148, 150, 151

Ruck, Ernesto O., 114–15, 130n7

Rufino Barrios, Justo, 107

Rumiñahui ("Indian General"), 233–35

rural areas: appropriation of communal and uncultivated lands, 100–101; clothing and, 304; effects of plundering in, 146–47; elite interests in, 137; hacienda expansion into Indian lands, 137, 143–44; Indian authenticity and authority linked to, 32, 221, 222, 226–27, 331; Indian holdings in, diminished, 14, 47n53; Indians relegated to, 146, 149–53, 326–27; indigenous movements and, 221–29; Kichwa politics in, 229–31; "lettered city" vs., 152–53. *See also* land and property system; schools, rural

Saavedra, Bautista, 138, 145, 175n11, 177n29

Salamanca, Daniel, 170, 171, 248–50

Sánchez Bustamante, Daniel, 138–39, 140, 144–45

Sánchez de Lozada, Gonzalo, 309n6

Sandinista agrarian reform, 333–34

Sandino, Augusto, 20

Santa Cruz, Andrés, 165

Saracho, Juan, 139, 140, 143, 144, 148

Sara Ñusta (Corn Princess) pageant, 230, 232, 233

schools: *castellanización* and curricula in, 141–42, 143, 151; for children of Spanish nobility, 120; as "disciplinary regimes," 154n8; inspections of, 139–40; intercultural relations in, 263–64; Nina Qhispi's work in, 244; segregation of, 17, 137–38; shift from ladino to Indian majority in, 257–58, 263. *See also* educational policy; literacy; schools, rural; students

schools, rural: failure of, 102–3; partisan motives and, 142–45; refocused on manual labor, 146, 149–53, 326–27

science: census-taking and, 16–17; Tiwanaku and, 162–65. *See also* anthropology and ethnology; archaeology; scientific racism

scientific racism: assumptions about, 75; debates on race in context of, 6–10, 57; emergence of, 73–74; persistence of, 46n29; Posnansky's views in context of, 168–70; socioeconomic criteria intertwined with, 113–14. *See also* cultural racism; racism

Second World War, 9, 45n18, 46n29, 321

segregation: colonial use of, 60–61; in educational policy and schools, 17, 102–3, 108, 137–38; in Guatemala, 15–16, 48n69, 98–103, 262; in labor system, 14–16, 18; in national project, 95. *See also* "separate and unequal"

Sendero Luminoso (Shining Path), 27, 279, 332

"separate and unequal": in Bolivia, 153; in Guatemala, 254, 262, 267–70, 274, 277n11. *See also* segregation

Sierra, Justo, 215

Siles, Hernando, 244–45

Siñani, Avelino, 143, 251

skin color: race distinguished from (in sixteenth century), 67n4; racial categorization based on, 258, 269, 305; racial violence due to, 305–6

slavery, 13, 206, 332–33

Smith, Richard Chase, 283, 284, 287, 289–92, 294

social Darwinism, 107, 125

socialism: liberation and empowerment projects of, 19, 333, 334–35; rise of, 38, 146, 329, 330

social order: census as state-driven image of, 17, 128–30; Indians vs. Africans in, 13; pedagogy of race and, 145–53; racialization of, 113–14. *See also* caste; class system; occupations and occupational structure; race

Sociedad de Amigos del País (Society of Friends of the Country), 96

Sociedad República del Kollasuyo (La Paz): educational projects of, 240–41, 251; founding of, 245, 246, 248; organizing base of, 243, 250–51; political focus of, 252n2. *See also* Centro Educativo Kollasuyo (La Paz)

Solidarity with Youth and Children (SNJ), 272–73

South America: Brazil's status in, 204–5; Tiwanaku as cradle of civilization in, 162–63, 167–68. *See also specific countries*

Spain: blood purity statute in, 68n8; Christian conversion as task of, 59–60; collective identity and otherness discussed by writers from, 74; conflicts with *moriscos* in, 63, 64, 65, 70n35, 70n40; New and Old Christians in, 58–59; racialization in, 207. *See also* colonialism; colonial terms for race

Spanish conquistadors: mental baggage of, 59, 68n13, 74; quincentennial anniversary of conquest, 173. *See also* colonialism

Spanish Inquisition, 58, 59, 68n6

Spanish language: blood purity concept and, 60–64; as "companion of empire," 134; as evidence of "civilizing," 97, 108; genealogy of "race" in, 57–58; indigenous appropriation of, 134–35; "race" in, 57–58, 67n4; racial terms from, 61–64, 90n19; training in (*castellanización*), 17, 141–42, 143, 151, 243

Spanish laws: cacique vs. Indian in, 117–18, 131n18; (forced) labor for the common good, 118, 131n22; writing, urbanism, and power linked in, 134–35

Spanish people: as census category, 120; distinctions among, 78–79, 120; identification as, 78, 90n13; native categories for, 82–84; in Paredes's spatialization of Bolivia, 163; targeted in Andean insurgency, 78–80, 90n18; "whites" (term) and, 81, 87–88, 117. *See also blancos* (whites); Spanish conquistadors

students: ethnic identities of, 256, 257–59; full-capital plan supported by, 300; on intercultural relations, 263–64. *See also cholos* (youth gang)

subaltern uses of race, 12–13, 38, 76–78. *See also* postcolonialism

Sucre (Bolivia): full-capital issue in, 34–36, 175–76n12, 300, 304, 305–6, 309n4, 312, 331; racialization in, 305–7; teacher training institute in, 140, 141; violence in (2008), 35–37, 40, 41–43, 311–14. *See also* Bolivian Constituent Assembly

Sucre, Antonio José de, 165

whiteness: in Linnaeus's classifications, 90–91n20; local uses of term, 80–81; meanings of, 107; Spaniards linked to, 87–88. See also *blancos* (whites)

Willka, Zárate, 161, 175n11

women: as artisans, landowners, and storekeepers, 126–28; in *Diosa Centeotl* contest, 193–94, *195*, 196–97, 198; discrimination and racism against, 314, 317n5; in *Homenaje Racial*, 189–91, 202n37; indigenous community council growth detrimental to, 229; pageants as identity performances of, 233; Zapotec civilization and clothing of, 185–86. *See also* beauty pageants; gender

work of race: biology, culture, and, 6–10; for class, 6, 10, 15; colonial roots and reconstructions in, 323–25; complexities of, 332–35; concept of, 10, 322; in indigenous movement, 32; Latin American specifics in, 321–22; postcolonialism and, 330–32; in state-making and exclusionary citizenship, 325–30. *See also* racemaking (production of race)

World Bank, 282, 288

World War II, 9, 45n18, 46n29, 321

writing as cultural symbol, 135–36

xenophobia, 26–27

xumos: use of term, 275

Yamor beauty pageant, 230, 231–33

yokallas, 171, 178n44

youth culture, 33, 272–73. See also *cholos* (youth gang); students

zambo: use of term, 60–61, 79

Zapotec people and culture, 180, 182, 185–88, 191, 196, 201n10

Laura Gotkowitz is an associate professor in the
Department of History at the University of Iowa.
She is author of *A Revolution for Our Rights:
Indigenous Struggles for Land and Justice in Bolivia,
1880–1952*, also published by Duke University Press.

✳

Library of Congress Cataloging-in-Publication Data
Histories of race and racism : the Andes and Mesoamerica
from colonial times to the present / Laura Gotkowitz, ed.
p. cm.
Includes bibliographical references and index.
ISBN 978-0-8223-5026-2 (cloth : alk. paper)
ISBN 978-0-8223-5043-9 (pbk. : alk. paper)
1. Racism—Latin America—History. 2. Latin America—Race
relations—History. 3. Race—History. I. Gotkowitz, Laura.
F1419.A1H57   2012
305.80098—dc23
2011021944